THE STEPHEN BECHTEL FUND

IMPRINT IN ECOLOGY AND THE ENVIRONMENT

The Stephen Bechtel Fund has

established this imprint to promote

understanding and conservation of

our natural environment.

The publisher gratefully acknowledges the
generous contribution to this book provided
by the Stephen Bechtel Fund.

The Atlas of Global Conservation

The Atlas of Global

UNIVERSITY OF CALIFORNIA PRESS BERKELEY LOS ANGELES LONDON

THE NATURE CONSERVANCY

Conservation

CHANGES, CHALLENGES, AND OPPORTUNITIES TO MAKE A DIFFERENCE

**JONATHAN M. HOEKSTRA, JENNIFER L. MOLNAR,
MICHAEL JENNINGS, CARMEN REVENGA, MARK D. SPALDING,
TIMOTHY M. BOUCHER, JAMES C. ROBERTSON, AND
THOMAS J. HEIBEL, WITH KATHERINE ELLISON**

EDITED BY JENNIFER L. MOLNAR

Jennifer Molnar

To future generations, and the planet they will inherit,
and in recognition of the generous support and vision of
Bill Barclay and Ofelia Miramontes

Citation: Hoekstra, J. M., J. L. Molnar, M. Jennings, C. Revenga, M. D. Spalding, T. M. Boucher, J. C. Robertson, T. J. Heibel, with K. Ellison. 2010. *The Atlas of Global Conservation: Changes, Challenges, and Opportunities to Make a Difference.* Ed. J. L. Molnar. Berkeley: University of California Press.

University of California Press, one of the most distinguished university presses in the United States, enriches lives around the world by advancing scholarship in the humanities, social sciences, and natural sciences. Its activities are supported by the UC Press Foundation and by philanthropic contributions from individuals and institutions. For more information, visit www.ucpress.edu.

University of California Press
Berkeley and Los Angeles, California

University of California Press, Ltd.
London, England

The mission of The Nature Conservancy is to preserve the plants, animals and natural communities that represent the diversity of life on Earth by protecting the lands and waters they need to survive.

Library of Congress Cataloging-in-Publication Data

The atlas of global conservation : changes, challenges and opportunities to make a difference / Jonathan M. Hoekstra [et al.] ; edited by Jennifer L. Molnar.
    p. cm.
Includes bibliographical references and index.
ISBN 978-0-520-26256-0 (cloth : alk. paper)
1. Conservation of natural resources. 2. Environmental protection. 3. Globalization. I. Hoekstra, Jonathan M.
II. Molnar, Jennifer L.
S936.A75 2010
333.95'16--dc22

                                                                                    2009023617

Project Management: Michael Bass Associates
Cartography: Paula Robbins, XNR Productions
Design and Composition: Nicole Hayward Design
Text: Adobe Garamond Pro
Display: Berthold Akzidenz Grotesk
Prepress, Printing, and Binding: FourColour Imports, Ltd.
Title page photo: Ami Vitale

Manufactured in China

18 17 16 15 14 13 12 11 10
10 9 8 7 6 5 4 3 2

This book has been printed on FSC Paper to be environmentally conscientious. The paper used in this publication meets the minimum requirements of ANSI/NISO Z39.48-1992 (R 1997) (*Permanence of Paper*). ∞

nature.org/atlas

Contents

4. A WORLD OF CHANGE

5. TAKING ACTION

6. CONCLUSION OUR FUTURE, OUR CHOICES

Mark D. Spalding

Acknowledgments

THIS BOOK BEGAN as a project to bring global science to the development of conservation strategies and priorities within The Nature Conservancy. To assemble the global maps included in this book, the authors have collaborated with many institutions and individuals. The maps represent the work of hundreds of scientists. We would like to extend our gratitude to our partners who have generously shared data and/or worked with us to develop these maps (see appendix B). We also want to recognize the support of invaluable individuals who were advisers, leaders, marketers and designers, reviewers, and philanthropic supporters.

Institutional Partners

African Mammal Databank

Alliance for Zero Extinction (AZE)

American Rivers

Australian Commonwealth Scientific and Research Organization (CSIRO)

Australian Government, Department of Environment, Water, Heritage, and the Arts

Australian Institute of Marine Science

Biogeography of Chemosynthetic Ecosystems (ChEss) Project, University of Southampton

BirdLife International

Bureau of Land Management (BLM)—Wild and Scenic Rivers

Center for Aquatic Conservation, University of Notre Dame

Center for Environmental Systems Research, University of Kassel

Center for International Earth Science Information Network (CIESIN), Columbia University

Chesapeake Bay Program (CBP)

College of Engineering, University of Washington

Conservation Biology Institute (CBI)

Conservation International—Center for Applied Biological Science (CI-CABS)

Council for Scientific and Industrial Research (CSIR)

Department of Geography, University of Idaho

ESRI

European Commission—Joint Research Centre (JRC)

Food and Agriculture Organization of the United Nations (FAO)—Fisheries Department

Forest Stewardship Council (FSC)

German Federal Institute for Geosciences and Natural Resources (BGR)

Global Amphibian Assessment

Global Land Cover Facility, University of Maryland

Global Water Analysis Group, University of New Hampshire

Intergovernmental Panel on Climate Change (IPCC)

International Center for Tropical Agriculture (CIAT)

International Food Policy Research Institute (IFPRI)

International Society for Mangrove Ecosystems (ISME)

International Union for the Conservation of Nature (IUCN)

IUCN European Mammal Assessment

IUCN Global Invasive Species Programme (GISP)

IUCN Species Programme

IUCN Species Survival Commission, Chiroptera Specialist Group

IUCN Species Survival Commission, Crocodile Specialist Group

IUCN Species Survival Commission, Otter Specialist Group

IUCN Species Survival Commission, Rodent Specialist Group

IUCN World Commission on Protected Areas (WCPA)

Landscape Ecology Department, University of Umea

Marine Stewardship Council (MSC)

Millennium Ecosystem Assessment (MA)

Museum of Vertebrate Zoology, University of California, Berkeley

National Aeronautics and Space Administration (NASA)—Jet Propulsion Laboratory (JPL)

National Center for Ecological Analysis and Synthesis (NCEAS), University of California, Santa Barbara

National Center for Atmospheric Research (NCAR)

National Oceanic and Atmospheric Administration (NOAA)—National Geophysical Data Center

National Snow and Ice Data Center

NatureServe

Ramsar Convention Secretariat

Savannah River Ecology Laboratory, University of Georgia

Scripps Institution of Oceanography

Sea Around Us Project (SAUP), University of British Colombia

U.S. Department of the Interior—National Atlas of the United States

U.S. Geological Survey (USGS)

United Nations Educational, Scientific and Cultural Organization (UNESCO)

United Nations Environment Programme (UNEP)

UNEP World Conservation Monitoring Centre (UNEP-WCMC)

UNEP Global Environment Monitoring System (GEMS), GEMS Water

United Nations Population Division (UNPD)

University of Erlangen-Nürnberg

University of New South Wales

Wildlife Conservation Society (WCS)

World Fish Centre—Reefbase

World Resources Institute (WRI)

WRI—Global Forest Watch

World Wide Fund for Nature (WWF International)

World Wildlife Fund (WWF-US)

Zoological Society of London (ZSL)

Individual Collaborators: Robin Abell, Brad Ack, Jennifer C. Adam, Paul Adam, Thomas S. B. Akre, Jackie Alder, Giovanni Amori, Colin Apse, Angela Arthington, Lisa Bailey, Andrew Balmford, Harry Biggs, Stuart Blanch, Hunter Borcello, Meredith Brown, Robert Brumbaugh, Mark Bryer, Kurt A. Buhlmann, Jason Burke, Ian Campbell, Genevieve Carr, Marco Castro, Janice Chanson, Lorna Collins, Jim Conroy, Will Darwall, Mary Davis, Eric Dinerstein, Brian Dyer, Andrew Fahlund, Dan Faith, Zach Ferdana, Lucy Fish, Helen Fox, Andre Freiwald, Karen Frenken, Wendy Fulkes, Rebecca Gamboa, Michael Garrity, Deniz Gerçek, Patrick Gonzalez, Richard Grainger, Alexander Gritsinin, Qiaoyu Guo, Lynne Hale, Maurice Hall, Ben Halpern, Ian Harrison, Craig Hilton-Taylor, Mike Hoffman, Jenny Hoffner, Michele Hofmeyr, Jeanette K. Howard, Jon Hutton, Ethan Inlander, Tom Iseman, John Iverson, John Jorgensen, Deno Karapatakis, Gerold Kier, Jan Konigsberg, Carmen Lacambra, Andrew D. Lacatell, Bernhard Lehner, Dennis P. Lettenmaier, Colby Loucks, Kim Lutz, John Morrison, Jeanne Nel, Rebecca Ng, Ron Nielsson, Christer Nilsson, Jamie Oliver, Sally Palmer, Daniel Pauly, Paulo Petry, Jamie Pittock, Eva Ramirez Llodra, John Randall, Corinna Ravillous, Cathy Reidy-Liermann, Paul Racey, Elisabeth Renders, Andrea Richts, Taylor Ricketts, Ana Rodrigues, Fernando Rosas, Dirk Roux, Curtis Runyan, Eric Sanderson, Juan Jacobo Schmitter Soto, Lucy Scott, Wes Seachrest, John Seebach, Ayn Shlisky, Nikolai Sindorf, Paul Skelton, Michael E. Slay, Melanie Stiassny, Karen Stocks, Jim Stritholt, Wilhelm Struckmeier, Simon N. Stuart, Peter Sullivan, Xiaoming Sun, James Syvitski, Helen Temple, Matt Terry, Michele Thieme, J.E.N. (Charlie) Veron, Charles

Vorosmarty, Andrew Warner, Reg Watson, Will Wilhollim, Louisa Wood, Ugur Zeydanli, Shuang Zhang, Matt Ziegler, Sylvia Ziller

Advisory Committee: Peter Kareiva, Mary Ruckelshaus, Bill Waldman, Jolie Siebert, Michael Looker, Mark Burget, Andrew Deutz, Jim Petterson

Executive Support: Mark Tercek, Steve McCormick, Stephanie Meeks, M. Sanjayan, Bill Murdoch, Fran James, Joel Cohen

Marketing and Design Support: Elizabeth Ward, Teresa Duran, Andrew Simpson, Mark Godfrey, Bridget Lowell, Cara Byington, Lauren Stockbower, Paula Robbins and XNR Productions

Reviewers: Mike Beck, Dee Boersma, Mark Bryer, Teresa Duran, Zach Ferdana, Rebecca Goldman, Mary Harkness, Peter Kareiva, Bridget Lowell, Serene Marshall, Rob McDonald, Mary Anne Molnar, Kent Redford, Brian Richter, M. Sanjayan, Andrew Simpson, David Skelly, Mark P. Smith, Elizabeth Ward, David Wilcove

Philanthropic Support: Bill Barclay and Ofelia Miramontes, John Morgridge

A New View of Our Home

MARK TERCEK

I WAS ON A BOAT with some Nature Conservancy partners and donors off the coast of British Columbia when scientists first showed me an early mock-up of this book. We were accompanying science staff as they installed remote cameras to track and record the movements of predators, like grizzlies and wolves, within the Great Bear Rainforest.

Our guests' reactions to the atlas maps were consistent with mine. Bears and wolves faded into the background for a while as we all clamored to see where our homes or other places important to us were on the maps. What is the status of the habitat in which I live, the landscape where I was born, the places I recreate with my family?

That experience renewed some familiar notions. First, people connect with place. We care about places that nurture us physically and spiritually. We are intrigued to learn how we fit into the whole of our natural world. We want to understand how our world has changed, and we are concerned about what the future portends.

As a businessman, what attracted me to The Nature Conservancy is similar to what prompted these donors to invest in the work of the organization: its pragmatic approach; its focus on measurable, lasting results; and, of course, its science base. Those things go hand in hand: you need reliable science on which to base pragmatic conservation decisions that will yield tangible results.

But what if the science is incomplete or the data are scattered around countless locations and disparate formats? How do you make a practical conservation decision about one spot on the map without understanding the whole in which that spot exists and the natural forces that influence it, whether local, regional, or global? And how can you take quick and nimble action, when the very act of finding and consolidating the scientific knowledge is slow and laborious?

This atlas is a breakthrough in many regards. It is the first time that such comprehensive data on the status of our planet have been collected and integrated in one place with graphic representation for the benefit of conservation practitioners and the conservation-concerned public.

Collecting and integrating these data was not a small feat. Although The Nature Conservancy was a catalyst for this project, it is actually the collaborative product of some seventy institutions around the world and the work—sometimes the life work—of hundreds of scientists, some crunching numbers in offices and many others collecting on-the-ground data in the far reaches of our planet. This book is testament to those institutions and the people who have been collecting these data for decades.

I cannot overstate what a revolution this atlas represents. Conservation scientists, by necessity, are usually very focused specialists, and they often operate in isolation and obscurity. Collecting and consolidating such specialized data was a combination of investigative sleuthing and cat herding, and I commend The Nature Conservancy's science team for their dedication and tenacity to see this project through over a four-year period.

And while this book itself is a landmark accomplishment, it is the data behind the publication's maps that truly have the power to transform. These data are now being made available to all to use in making better-informed decisions about conservation, land and water use, resource allocation, and a wealth of other planning and activities that impact our natural world.

Undoubtedly, some significant bad news is contained in these pages—diminished habitats, declining species, and overdeveloped landscapes that threaten not only our planet's rich web of life but ultimately our own well-being. It is sobering to examine the maps here and realize that there is not a habitat on Earth that has not been affected by our single species.

Fishing in the mangroves of Micronesia. Conservation has impacted the lives and livelihoods of people around the world

It is not all doom and gloom, however—there is hope. This publication graphically documents the significant efforts under way to prevent degradation, stem loss, and mount recovery. Furthermore, the maps on which this book is based have tremendous prescriptive value. They have the power to jump-start conservation blueprints of a scope and scale unimagined before.

I am reminded of a story I heard from Bill Raynor, one of The Nature Conservancy's conservation pioneers who lives on a tiny dot in the Pacific Ocean—the Micronesian island of Pohnpei. In his early days there, he faced the daunting task of convincing fellow islanders of the need to establish a

watershed reserve to protect the island's dwindling interior forests. He was met with significant opposition.

Bill's solution was to acquire aerial photographs of the island at that time and from twenty years earlier. The diminishing forest was shockingly apparent. He then took these two images, printed side by side on a poster, and distributed them to all the little roadside kiosks that encircle the island and where local people buy basic household staples.

By offering Pohnpeians a view of their island home that they had never seen, he tapped into their innate love of place and helped them understand their impact on

that place. Opposition to the reserve evaporated, and conservation action accelerated.

In many ways, that's what we hope this atlas will accomplish on a much grander scale—in fact, on a global scale. Here is a multifaceted view of *our* island home—one we have never before been able to see in such complexity and with such clarity. May it inform us, inspire us, prod us, and unite us to make the choices that will secure the landscapes seascapes, flora and fauna, natural resources, and processes on which we all depend.

MARK TERCEK IS THE PRESIDENT AND CEO OF THE NATURE CONSERVANCY.

Conservation Connections

PAUL R. EHRLICH

TODAY'S MOST CRITICAL human enterprise must be preserving the biodiversity that is essential to maintaining services that nature provides to people—the very future of humanity depends on it.

This atlas provides a global view of the challenge before us and a starting point for seeing the many different interacting forces and drivers that threaten to undermine nature's ability to support humanity. What is not easily portrayed in maps is the complexity of the problem, the interactions among local and global pressures, and the fact that our world is a nonlinear living and dynamic system. Maybe someday we will have the technology to display this; instead of flat maps we might envision pulsating, fluid, flowing, shifting, colorful surfaces depicting the dynamics of biodiversity, consumption, population growth, perverse incentives, and so on. Recent advances in the understanding of complicated dynamic systems indicate that complex systems are vulnerable to catastrophic collapse—and that collapse can follow gradual, seemingly incremental changes. The gradual trends depicted in this atlas could foreshadow feedbacks and degradations that will measurably impact the quality of our children's lives. This is not about extrapolating trends toward some distant doom-and-gloom scenario. This is about a complicated system of interacting species, changing climates, altered biogeochemical processes, and rapidly evolving human cultures shifting toward an entirely different global reality. And this complicated system is being driven by our individual choices about reproduction and consumption.

The collective results of each person operating in his or her perceived self-interest are felt broadly. For example, individual choices in consumption and transportation contribute to climate change, which is now producing regional alterations of temperature, precipitation, and storm frequency and severity. These are now starting to feed back on Earth's biota, altering the geographic distribution and abundance of many organisms, and creating major challenges for conservation. The globalization of our activities means that threats now travel rapidly to once-isolated areas of the planet (e.g., pesticide pollution in the far Arctic, chlorofluorocarbons in the Antarctic stratosphere), and the entire system lacks the modularity that tended to isolate past ecological collapses. It is now widely accepted that our species could be entraining an extinction event as severe as the one sixty-five million years ago that wiped out all of the dinosaurs except for the birds.

When reading the wonderful essays in this atlas and exploring its diverse maps, keep in mind the interconnected nature of the global system and three related connections.

The first connection is that virtually every major human activity creates threats to biodiversity, and all these threats are intertwined. Humanity's impacts and their connections to each other are described in the **I** = **PAT** equation. The negative **I**mpact of society on biodiversity is the product of **P**opulation size, per capita consumption (**A**ffluence), and the use of environmentally malign **T**echnologies and socioeconomic systems to service that consumption. As human populations grow, each added individual, all else equal, demands a larger share of Earth's resources than did the previous person. Each new consumer must on average be fed from inferior farmland; be supplied with metals from lower-grade ores; use petroleum, natural gas, and water from wells drilled deeper; burn fuels and drink water transported farther. After all, people are smart and have already picked the low-hanging resource fruit. They used the richest and most accessible sources of supply first: copper is no longer lying on Earth's surface in almost pure form and new natural seeps of petroleum are not going to supply our SUVs.

Second, in depleting biodiversity, *Homo sapiens* is risking its own future. Biodiversity is an irreplaceable element of humanity's natural capital, capital that supplies society with a flow of essential services. These include such things as ameliorating the climate, regulating flows of freshwater, creating and maintaining soils, controlling pests that attack crops or carry disease to people, pollinating crops, recycling nutrients essential to agriculture and forestry, and supplying fish from the sea. Human survival is thus linked to biodiversity. So is the well-being of numerous people who receive cultural services—recreational benefits, aesthetic pleasure, and spiritual support—from nature.

The third connection, especially important in the context of an atlas, is that although there is great heterogeneity in the distribution of both biodiversity and threats to biodiversity, the maps show collectively that the negative human impact on biodiversity is essentially universal. They display the intertwining of the threats.

Some generalities should be remembered about what menaces biodiversity. For instance, many if not most of Earth's increasing conservation problems trace to the human agricultural system. Though the current system is vast, it still leaves at least six hundred million people hungry and over a billion malnourished. The problem looks even more serious when one considers that by 2050, there will be an additional 2.5 billion people to feed, requiring the expansion and intensification of agricultural activities. This will put additional pressure on biodiversity and the services it provides people, and push more rural poor people into cities. With changing climates altering precipitation patterns, thereby making some irrigation systems obsolete, there will be further pressure on natural populations as new dams and canals are built and new land brought under cultivation. On top of this is the push to increase biofuel production, which has already accelerated enormously in recent years. While biofuels are represented as a renewable resource to replace petroleum products that are in dwindling supply, they are anything *but* green. Their net energy yield is often overestimated, as are their contributions to reducing CO_2 flow into that atmosphere—which in some circumstances can be higher than that involved with petroleum use. Biofuels are becoming a major engine of extinction by promoting the destruction of natural habitats from the lowland forests of Southeast Asia (for oil palms) to the Amazon basin (soybean oil for biodiesel, sugar cane for ethanol).

Another major global threat to biodiversity is the toxification of Earth, which is tied tightly to levels of population and consumption, and involves the use of malign technologies. But it receives too little attention from the conservation community. Toxification has already caused extensive extinctions of avian populations (e.g., raptors falling victim to DDT, vultures to veterinary drugs) and may be threatening organisms as diverse as frogs, polar bears, and even people. Tens of thousands of potentially toxic human-made chemical compounds are being released into the environment. Conservation biologists need to work with toxicologists to determine which are potentially the most toxic to natural systems and people, investigate the multitudinous possible interactions among the toxins, and then map likely hotspots of contamination. Biologists need to cooperate with economists to evaluate the costs and benefits of the releases by weighing the costs of testing for effects on human health and other organisms (and through them on ecosystem services) against the benefits to society (or individual firms) from the use of each chemical released (an especially difficult area for research because of proprietary rights). As a starter, we badly need a test case of what procedures might be used, perhaps based on a sample of compounds

stratified by those that are released as final products for direct human use that often escape into ecosystems (e.g., deodorants, pharmaceuticals, plastic bottles), those used for human benefit in ecosystems (pesticides, cloud-seeding chemicals), and those that are intermediate products of manufacturing processes (solvents). The overall task is gigantic, but considering the global spread of thousands of such compounds, the fact that many of them are toxic, carcinogenic, or mimic human hormones, and given our total ignorance of interactions, thresholds, and lag times, it is high time both conservation biologists and ecological economists paid more attention.

I am delighted that this atlas shows the geographic distribution of consumption, population growth, and water stress. Overconsumption, a major driver of biodiversity loss is geographically concentrated in the richest nations, although some developing nations (or segments within developing nations) are striving to catch up. But the impact of poverty on preserving biodiversity is also substantial. For example, in many less developed countries, fuelwood is a vital resource that is increasingly overexploited by people who must be able to cook their food in order to eat it, but who cannot afford to buy kerosene. Similarly, in many such nations, growing human populations threaten animals with extinction by harvesting them for "bush meat," pets, or, especially in Asia, folk medicines. Some of the animals most threatened by this trend are our closest relatives: chimpanzees, bonobos, and gorillas. The differential ability of nations to protect their biodiversity has led to the concept of political endemism, the restriction of a species to a single nation. A species restricted to a very poor country may be much more endangered than one whose distribution straddles the border of two nations—if one nation has an effective conservation program, even if the total area it occupies is much smaller than that of the politically endemic species. The problems

of conservation thus are closely connected to the population-poverty-equity nexus.

Finally, I hope this atlas will help to remind us that in spite of ever-popular tendencies to want to establish global priorities for conservation, the global problem demands that we work everywhere to protect populations, species, and ecosystems. If we end up with a fortress mentality, in which we simply try to collect a few representatives of each species, our conservation success will simply look like freckles on the global maps in this atlas. Without the diversity of species and habitats across the globe that provide food and other services to humanity, our species would quickly die out. Humanity needs to blanket the globe with strong actions to protect the diversity of populations and species. It must institute sociopolitical and economic change to accomplish this daunting task. And it must recognize the threat of utter collapse in the global human-environment system in the event of failure. This atlas can serve as an important tool in planning how to avoid such a catastrophe.

PAUL R. EHRLICH IS PRESIDENT OF THE CENTER FOR CONSERVATION BIOLOGY, STANFORD UNIVERSITY.

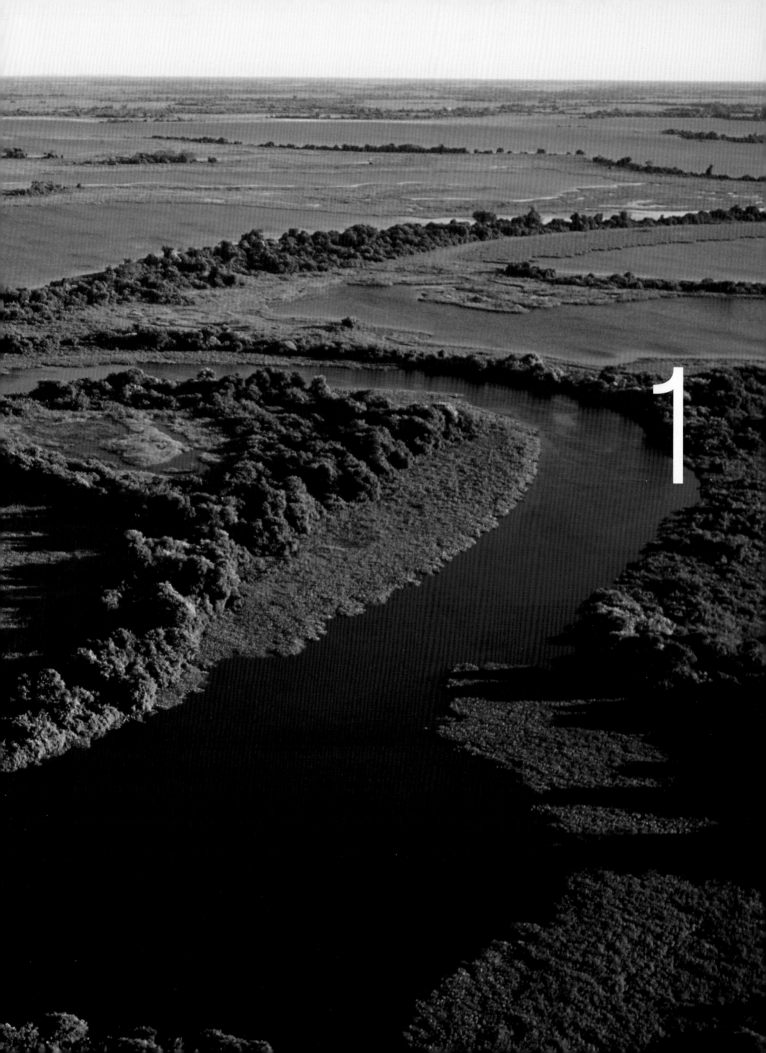

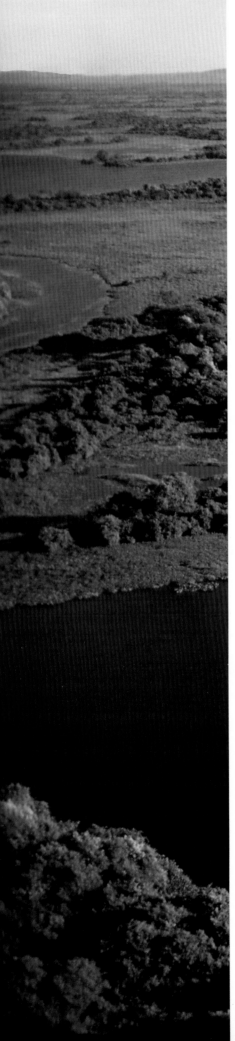

Introduction

Before I flew I was already aware of how small and vulnerable our planet is; but only when I saw it from space, in all its ineffable beauty and fragility, did I realize that human kind's most urgent task is to cherish and preserve it for future generations.
—SIGMUND JÄHN, GERMAN, SOVIET COSMONAUT, 1978

OURS IS THE FIRST generation in human history with the capacity to look beyond our horizons, to use technology to see and understand the entire planet, all at once. Satellites scan the Earth's surface constantly, and expert interpretation of their images enables us to map the patchwork of habitats that pattern our planet.

Even without making the trip to space, many of us now have a planetary perspective. We have almost unfettered access to information, goods, and services from around the globe. News from almost anywhere is available instantly. Planes, trains, and boats carrying people and cargo crisscross the globe, while our individual reach extends across continents with each visit to the supermarket, where foods from every nation line the shelves.

Yet today, our reach often extends further than we realize. The tiny choices we make every day reverberate around the world in ways we can scarcely imagine. The planet is changing, and *we* are changing it. This atlas attempts to bring a global perspective to illuminate the extent of our reach—collectively and individually—and to understand the impacts of our choices.

This book illustrates, at a global level, some of the key stories of life on Earth and the changes that are now underway. Central to the atlas are the maps. The book invites readers to make their own assessments, whether comparing between regions on a single map or evaluating changes in patterns across maps of natural systems, human pressures, and conservation actions.

Making connections is critical to driving meaningful responses. Think for a minute about the changes you have witnessed in your own hometown or the region in which you live. Perhaps a woodland has become a new housing development or shopping mall. How does your perspective change

Image courtesy of the Image Science & Analysis Laboratory, NASA Johnson Space Center

when you learn that forests are under siege worldwide, with over 40 percent lost since the 1700s, and those that remain are subject to rampant deforestation, degradation, and conversion to agricultural fields and urban areas? Many changes are occurring in the natural world, but we may see only a narrow piece of them, whether there are fewer songbirds arriving in the spring or different types of fish being caught from a favorite dock. With a broader perspective on our world, we are better able to recognize changes and react with actions at the scale necessary.

This atlas represents a unique achievement. Never before has it been possible to see, under one cover and in a standard format, such a broad array of information describing the natural world, the challenges it faces, and the actions that can protect it.

Chapter 2 focuses on the habitats that occupy our planet. We take a tour from forests and deserts, through rivers and lakes, down into coastal waters, coral reefs, and the deep ocean. In chapter 3, a second wave of maps populates these places with species—showing the great centers of abundance around the tropics but also the subtle shifts in these patterns as we turn the pages and move from plants to fish to birds and mammals.

These maps show clearly places of greatest diversity of particular habitats or species. But viewed page after page, they show that almost every part of our planet has unique, rich, and irreplaceable nature. Humans have a place here, too, and the vast benefits we derive from nature are considered.

Chapter 4 takes us beyond nature to the effects of people on the natural systems on which we rely. It starts by considering three of the greatest drivers of change: population growth, overconsumption, and the growing imprint of climate change. A complex web of change is described, from pollution to invasive species. Critically, chapter 5 points to solutions. Although the challenges are immense, we know and understand them, and there is a growing movement to confront them. And increasingly we have the tools for action.

Every map in this book tells its own story. On every page readers can seek out places they know or that they dream of. They can orient those places to a wider world. And from page to page a story unfolds. Whether reading cover to cover or making their own path through the maps, readers can draw connections and conclusions, coming away with a fuller appreciation for our world and the place each of us occupies in it.

Patterns of Life

Imagine stepping into an expansive plain of grass. Dry and flat, it stretches to the horizons with small shrubs and trees dotting the landscape. In the distance large animals are grazing as a hawk glides overhead looking for prey.

Without looking closer, this could be any grassland on Earth.

Then there is a rustling in the grass nearby. Is it a bison, indicating we are in the prairies of North America? Or a zebra evading a lion on the savannas of Africa? Or a graceful Mongolian gazelle? The wind changes, the grass moves, and a kangaroo bounds into view: we are in Australia.

Life is not distributed randomly around the globe, nor are plants and animals the same everywhere. Habitats like grasslands are found on every continent, but closer inspection reveals enormous variation from place to place. Species of plants, mammals, and birds, even fungi and bacteria, make each region distinct.

Understanding such variation is critical in a changing world. Natural systems are complex, with each species playing a role to support a functioning whole. Changes that impact one part of the system can have far-reaching consequences. Revealing patterns in these habitats and the human influences on them can help us to target conservation to where we can make a difference as well as to broaden our efforts to ensure that the broad diversity of nature is captured in our conservation efforts.

For these reasons, maps in this book use the natural patterns of life, rather than political boundaries, to tell the story of our world. The following sections provide a guide to broad patterns that help define what is found where.

Common Links around the Globe

Majestic forests of evergreen trees. Arid expanses with water-storing plants. The humid world beneath the lush rain forest canopy. Frozen tundra covered with scattered heath and sedge.

Each of these habitats is distinct from the others, yet each can be found in many places around the world. Plants and animals adapt to local conditions such as temperature, rainfall, and seasons, but when comparable conditions are found in different places, remarkably similar forms of life evolve.

On land, these major types of habitat are called *biomes* and are often defined by the plants that dominate them, such as forests or grasslands. Plants and animals develop similar strategies to thrive under the conditions found in the biome.

Take deserts, for example. With little rain and intense sun, deserts are difficult places in which to live. Only hardy plants and animals can survive, and different species have found surprisingly similar ways to conserve water and deal with the harsh conditions.

In the Sonoran Desert of southwestern North America, for example, the giant saguaro cactus gathers water during rare rains, with its surface swelling until up to 90 percent of its trunk is made up of water. In dry periods its skin comes to resemble corduroy as it draws on its large store of water. Half a world away, the African baobab tree has similar strategies. Native to drylands in southern Africa, it stores water in its enormous trunk. During droughts, the baobab relies on the stored water, but it takes advantage of infrequent rains to sprout large numbers of green leaves from its branches.

Just as plants and animals around the world develop similar adaptations, humans, too, adapt to the places they live. It's not surprising, then, that far-flung examples of biomes can have the same vulnerabilities to human pressure. For example, the flat fertile soils of grasslands have been used for grazing and farming for millennia. When these activities are intensified or expanded, they threaten native plants and animals. Conservationists can use parallel strategies to address these human impacts and protect these habitats.

Worlds Apart

Some of the most striking variations can be seen when moving between continents or oceans. Whether on continents separated by oceans or in oceans separated by continents, plants and animals and their habitats have evolved in isolation.

The most famous example of this type of divide is Wallace's Line, which runs from the Indian Ocean through Indonesia to the Philippine Sea. In traveling by boat through the region in the mid-nineteenth century, the British naturalist Alfred Russell Wallace noticed dramatic changes in animals and plants from one island to the next. To the west, islands were populated by rhinoceros, tigers, monkeys, and apes. To the east, separated in places by just a short stretch of water, were cockatoos and kangaroos, birds of paradise, and mammals that lay eggs. It was as if there were invisible boundaries that were separating quite different worlds of plants and animals. Over a century later, scientists found that Wallace's Line runs close to the boundary of two tectonic plates. So while land bridges could have connected islands on either side of the line, allowing animals to mix, they would not have linked islands across it, leaving them to evolve in isolation.

At a broad scale, *realms* are defined as wide areas of ocean or continent separated by divides like Wallace's Line where evolution has run its course in relative isolation for millions of years. While similar habitats may be found in different realms, they are often populated by very distinct creatures.

Another dramatic example of these differences can be observed by comparing coral reefs on either side of the Isthmus of Panama. While superficially similar, these reefs have no species in common due to the long separation of the Pacific Ocean from the Caribbean Sea.

Natural Neighborhoods

Despite similarities to other habitats nearby or in other parts of the world, each place on Earth has a unique mix of plants and animals, adapted to particular conditions.

Relatively large areas of land or water that contain distinct communities of plants and animals are called *ecoregions.*

On land, ecoregions are unique pockets within the same biome. For example, southwestern North America has a vast expanse of desert, but it is not all the same. This is even evident from the window of a Greyhound bus on a long drive through the region. Starting in southern Arizona, the Sonoran Desert is full of large saguaro and other cacti that get slightly more moisture than neighboring regions during two short rainy seasons. Driving northwest into California, the Joshua tree dominates the drier Mohave Desert. Heading northeast, the road climbs to higher elevations approaching the Great Basin of Nevada and the Colorado Steppe, where there are few if any cacti but lots of low-growing pines and shrubs that can survive winter snows.

The boundaries of many marine ecoregions are hidden below the surface, marked by shifts in currents, temperatures, or even the diffusing spread of freshwaters and nutrients from a major river, but in a few places they also trace changes on the shore. For example, the channels and fjords of the Southern Chile ecoregion are marked by a complex array of deep fjords sheltering kelp forests, rocky shores, and small estuaries, with offshore waters plunging rapidly to deep ocean. The adjacent Patagonian Shelf has a much simpler coastline, still with estuaries and kelp forests, but giving way to a wide and highly productive continental shelf.

Each freshwater ecoregion contains lakes and rivers that are home to a unique mix of fish and other aquatic species adapted to local conditions such as water flow, climate, topography, and geology. Even within the same river basin, there can be a diversity of shapes and forms of freshwater that support different communities of species. All the water within the massive Amazon River basin is interconnected, but it flows toward the mouth of the river through diverse landscapes and climates that define ecoregions. Upstream ecoregions have fish species adapted to cool, fast-flowing waters, while the slow-moving, deep waters of the main stem of the Amazon are full of sediment and support a completely different set of species.

In This Atlas

The maps in this atlas have been designed with these broad natural patterns in mind. By using ecoregions, biomes, and realms—instead of countries or other political units—the maps not only provide local context for a particular habitat but also allow comparisons between similar habitats, whether nearby or somewhere else in the world.

Why Ecoregions?

TAYLOR RICKETTS

I GREW UP OUTSIDE SEATTLE, Washington, which made me a resident of the Puget lowland forests ecoregion. Only after an internship at World Wildlife Fund (WWF), working to delineate the terrestrial ecoregions of North America, did I realize how important that residency was. Turns out, I share more natural heritage with my fellow ecoregional inhabitants in Oregon and even Canada than I do with Washingtonians in other parts of the state. Douglas fir, old man's beard lichens, salmon, the rain—these natural elements define our ecoregion and those of us living in it.

Look at the maps on these pages. To which ecoregion do you belong? What is unique and interesting about your native ecoregion, relative to the hundreds of others on Earth? Decades of scientific and conservation work, much of it summarized in this book, has made it a snap to answer these questions.

In the past ten years, ecoregions have become the common language of conservationists, changing the way we conserve global biodiversity. The world's three largest conservation organizations—Conservation International, The Nature Conservancy, and WWF—now define their global priorities in an ecoregional framework. The United Nations' recent Millennium Ecosystem Assessment—a five-year, thousand-scientist effort to evaluate the state of the world's ecosystems—uses ecoregions as its global classification scheme. The list goes on.

Why is that? Why ecoregions?

The simplest answer is that biodiversity doesn't respect political boundaries. National borders bisect natural systems all over the world. Wildebeest migrate between Kenya and Tanzania each year, and the rain forests of the Amazon basin span no fewer than five countries. For conservationists working to save wildebeests or rain forests—or any species or habitat—ecoregions provide the appropriate, biologically relevant frame to evaluate urgency, to track our gains and

losses, and to allocate scarce conservation resources for greatest effect. Conserving wildebeest in Tanzania alone won't work if the habitat they rely on in Kenya is destroyed. Conversely, investing significant effort to save a rare habitat within one country when it is common in the country next door is simply inefficient.

Ecoregions encourage conservationists to think big. An ecoregion is knit together not only by shared species and habitats but also by ecological processes that operate at large scales, like wildfires and floods. Such periodic ecological disturbances are actually engines of life, fostering renewal and diversity, and species that have evolved in the presence of such disturbances often rely on them for survival. Tallgrass prairies, for instance, require regular fires to burn dead and woody plants and renew the soil to maintain an abundance of grazers, birds, and grasses. These and other disturbances typically affect areas much larger than an individual protected area. If the goal is to conserve the diversity and functioning of the entire ecoregion, then it becomes clear that a myopic focus on a given park or plant population won't cut it.

Thinking "ecoregionally" has remarkable power to motivate conservation at a new scale. A good example is the Congo Basin (which actually comprises several terrestrial and freshwater ecoregions). In 2000, scores of local scientists, government representatives, and conservationists worked together to articulate a clear, compelling, and gigantic vision for conserving the ecoregions of the basin. In response, the heads of ten nations committed to protecting it, nine nongovernmental organizations signed on to help out, and the U.S. government provided $45 million in support. Since then, five million new hectares of protected areas have been declared, three million hectares of additional forests are more sustainably managed, and over $200 million in additional funding has been committed to the effort. Thinking big, and setting out to conserve entire ecoregions in all their splendor, inspired this remarkable level of action.

Ecoregions have also advanced the scientific foundations of conservation. They

categorize the natural world, helping us ensure that our conservation efforts represent the full diversity of life on Earth. At the 1992 World Parks Congress, for example, participants called on nations to set aside 10 percent of Earth's surface as protected areas. Now, over twenty years later, we are at roughly 14 percent worldwide. Success, right? Perhaps not. This 14 percent is spread unevenly across the world. Some ecoregions, like temperate conifer forests, enjoy an average of over 25 percent protection, while others, including Mediterranean systems worldwide, average less than 5 percent protection, and some have none at all. Global ecoregion classifications allow us to identify these gaps and prioritize our efforts to fill them.

One of the most intriguing realizations about ecoregions (at least terrestrial ones) is that they seem to escape one of the few real laws in ecology: as the size of a place increases, so does the number of species found within it. This law holds almost no matter where you are in the world or what taxon you consider; and at these scales, it is because larger areas tend to have more diverse habitats, so they provide homes to more species. With terrestrial ecoregions, though, this pattern vanishes; statistically, the species richness of large ecoregions doesn't tend to be any greater than that of smaller ones. What this means is that ecoregion delineations are sensitive to the patterns of habitat diversity, just as they should be. In areas of rapid turnover, where different habitats are packed in tightly, ecoregions tend to be smaller, reflecting the heterogeneity of that part of the world. (For examples, check out the Andes Mountains in Colombia and Ecuador, and the coastal and mountain regions of California.) Conversely, in areas where habitats are similar over thousands of kilometers (like the boreal forests of Canada), ecoregions are accordingly large. In short, ecoregions extend until there is enough change to warrant a line. When changes come quickly, ecoregions are small; when changes are slow, ecoregions are big. The result? A set of global units that capture roughly equivalent amounts of habitat

Montane grasslands of the Northern Andean páramo ecoregion in Ecuador

diversity and therefore species richness, even though their sizes vary dramatically. Frankly, I'm still thinking through all the implications here, but at the very least it confirms that ecoregions reflect real patterns of diversity on the ground.

It is important to understand that the ecoregion boundaries on these maps are not precise lines across which—wham!— everything changes from one system to another. Instead, they represent "ecotones," zones of transition. Walking across one, you'd notice over the course of perhaps ten kilometers— or even one hundred—that things were getting drier, grasslands were giving way to woodlands, or the dominant tree species were yielding to others. To expect precise

lines is to misunderstand both what ecoregions denote and how nature works.

Just as biology ignores political borders, political processes typically ignore biological boundaries. This sets up an interesting tension. Ecoregions are a wonderful tool for assessing biological diversity and threats facing it, but policies to address those threats ultimately must be shaped within political units such as countries, states, provinces, and so forth. Translating from one type of unit to the other is messy at times but well worth the cost if it helps leaders understand that their ecological futures are shared so tightly with their neighbors.

So back to the beginning: To which ecoregion do you belong? To which ones will your travels take you next, and what's

unique about them? Keep this book and its Web sites handy. Some people even maintain a "life list" of ecoregions they've visited, like a bird-watcher recording birds seen. Even if you don't go that far, whether you are a student, teacher, researcher, conservationist, or closet naturalist, you'll learn a lot about how our natural world is put together.

TAYLOR RICKETTS IS THE DIRECTOR OF CONSERVATION SCIENCE, WORLD WILDLIFE FUND.

Terrestrial Ecoregions, Realms, and Biomes

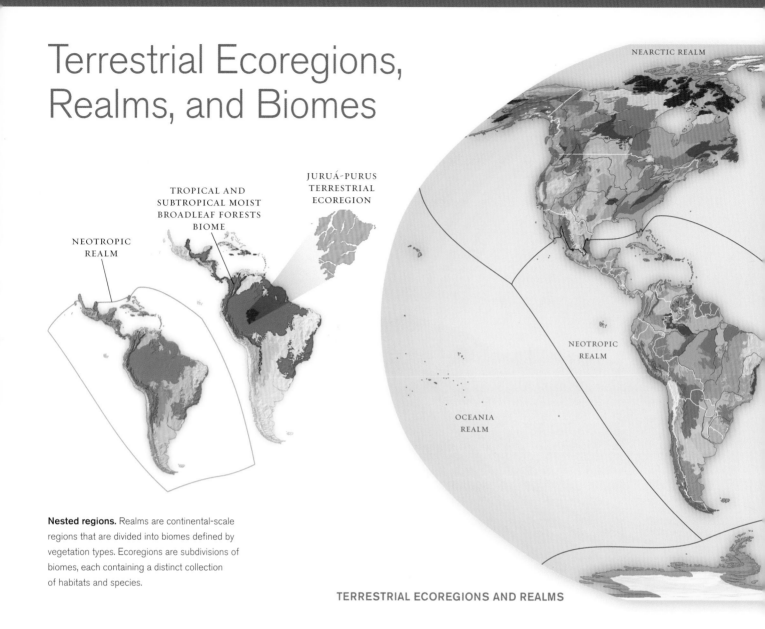

NEARCTIC REALM

JURUÁ-PURUS TERRESTRIAL ECOREGION

TROPICAL AND SUBTROPICAL MOIST BROADLEAF FORESTS BIOME

NEOTROPIC REALM

NEOTROPIC REALM

OCEANIA REALM

Nested regions. Realms are continental-scale regions that are divided into biomes defined by vegetation types. Ecoregions are subdivisions of biomes, each containing a distinct collection of habitats and species.

TERRESTRIAL ECOREGIONS AND REALMS

ECOREGIONS divide the world into regions of similar habitat. Terrestrial ecoregions draw boundaries that approximate where one set of similar habitats blends with another. Each of the world's 825 terrestrial ecoregions bounds a natural area in which a unique collection of ecosystems, natural communities, and species is found.

REALMS group ecoregions that have related flora and fauna. Ecoregions can be grouped into "realms" according to the evolutionary similarities of their flora and fauna. The terrestrial realms are eight continent-sized regions of the world, separated by oceans, deserts, or high mountains,

which have limited the exchange of species, so that plants and animals have evolved in relative isolation. The most familiar example is the Australasian realm, where unique species such as kangaroos and koalas, found nowhere else, evolved.

BIOMES group ecoregions that have similar vegetation. Although each ecoregion has its distinctive features, ecoregions can be grouped into larger units based on their similar climate and habitat structure and ecological similarity. Examples of biomes include temperate grasslands, tropical moist forests, and deserts. There are fourteen terrestrial biomes.

Terrestrial Biomes

- Tropical and subtropical moist broadleaf forests
- Tropical and subtropical dry broadleaf forests
- Tropical and subtropical coniferous forests
- Temperate broadleaf and mixed forests
- Temperate conifer forests
- Boreal forest/taiga
- Tropical and subtropical grasslands, savannas, and shrublands
- Temperate grasslands, savannas, and shrublands
- Flooded grasslands and savannas
- Montane grasslands and shrublands
- Mediterranean forests, woodlands, and scrub
- Deserts and xeric shrublands
- Tundra
- Mangroves
- Rock and ice

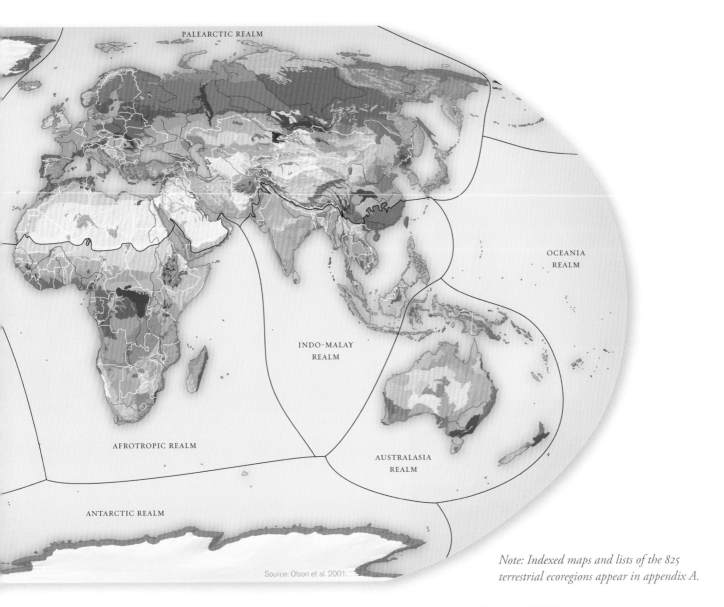

PALEARCTIC REALM

OCEANIA
REALM

INDO-MALAY
REALM

AUSTRALASIA
REALM

AFROTROPIC REALM

ANTARCTIC REALM

Source: Olson et al. 2001.

Note: Indexed maps and lists of the 825 terrestrial ecoregions appear in appendix A.

TERRESTRIAL BIOMES

Source: Olson et al. 2001.

Freshwater Ecoregions and Basins

Pantanal wetlands of the Paraguay ecoregion

Distinctive flowing habitats. Freshwater ecoregions are defined by the types of fish that live within them. Different forms of freshwater harbor distinct communities of species, whether fast flowing coastal rivers or wide expanses of wetland.

White Salmon River of the Columbia Glaciated ecoregion

FRESHWATER ECOREGIONS

FRESHWATER ECOREGIONS divide the world into regions that contain similar freshwater species. Each of the world's 426 freshwater ecoregions contains a distinctive suite of fish species, other aquatic species, and freshwater habitats.

RIVER BASINS indicate hydrologic divisions of freshwater habitats. The rivers, lakes, and wetlands within a basin are interconnected; therefore they share both species and human threats such as pollution. Water management decisions are often made at the scale of river basins.

Managing water to meet resource needs and sustain natural ecosystems across a large and complicated river basin is challenging because of variability in habitats, threats, and water usage. How much water can be withdrawn from a river while sustaining river habitat for fish species? How will decisions about using water in the headwaters affect fisheries and habitats downstream? Answering these sorts of questions requires broad knowledge about the different species and freshwater habitats found in different parts of large river basins. However, such information is often limited to only a few lakes, wetlands, or small basins. Freshwater ecoregions help inform management and conservation planning decisions by providing a tool for mapping freshwater biodiversity and habitat changes across entire basins.

Source: Abell et al. 2008.

Note: Indexed maps and lists of the 426 freshwater ecoregion names are included in appendix A.

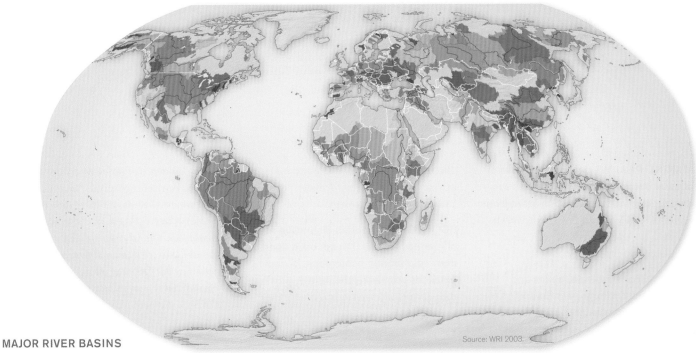

MAJOR RIVER BASINS

Source: WRI 2003.

Marine Ecoregions, Provinces, and Realms

Kelp in the Puget Trough/Georgia Basin ecoregion

Drawing salty lines. Marine ecoregions contain unique assortments of coastal habitats and species. Each is distinguished by physical characteristics like flow patterns and shoreline type, as well as dominant habitats like coral reefs or kelp forests.

Coral reefs of the Bismarck Sea ecoregion

MARINE ECOREGIONS

MARINE REALMS define wide areas of coastal ocean where evolution has run its course in relative isolation for millions of years. While similar ecosystems may be found in different realms, they are often populated by very different creatures.

PROVINCES subdivide realms and reflect similar, though less dramatic, patterns of evolutionary separation.

This difference can be seen, for example, in marine life between the Mediterranean Sea and nearby Atlantic coasts.

ECOREGIONS contain distinctive mixes of marine habitats that set each apart from neighboring ecoregions. Within provinces, ecoregions are distinguished by their ecological characteristics, since they are rarely isolated enough to evolve their own species. Ecoregions may also be characterized

by the influence of different ocean currents or a major river such as the Amazon.

Marine ecoregions describe only coastal and shelf waters. These are the places where marine life is most concentrated and where the influence of human activities is most pronounced. Ongoing efforts will eventually extend this system to map biogeography of the high seas and deep ocean floor.

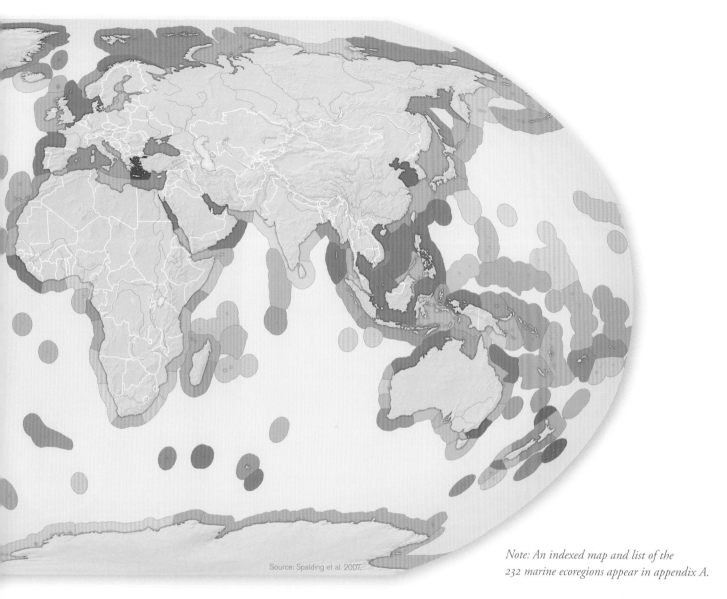

Source: Spalding et al. 2007.

*Note: An indexed map and list of the
232 marine ecoregions appear in appendix A.*

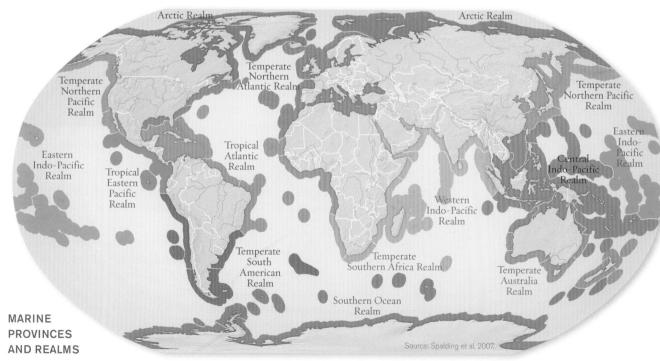

Arctic Realm

Arctic Realm

Temperate
Northern
Atlantic Realm

Temperate
Northern
Pacific
Realm

Temperate
Northern Pacific
Realm

Eastern
Indo-Pacific
Realm

Eastern
Indo-
Pacific
Realm

Tropical
Atlantic
Realm

Tropical
Eastern
Pacific
Realm

Central
Indo-Pacific
Realm

Western
Indo-Pacific
Realm

Temperate
South
American
Realm

Temperate
Southern Africa Realm

Temperate
Australia
Realm

Southern Ocean
Realm

MARINE
PROVINCES
AND REALMS

Source: Spalding et al. 2007.

The Stories That Maps Tell

JON CHRISTENSEN

C'est le grand avantage des méthodes graphiques appliquées aux différents objets de la philosophie naturelle, de porter dans l'esprit cette conviction intime qui accompagne toujours les notions, que nous recevons immédiatement par les sens.*

—*Alexander von Humboldt*

Humboldt's World

I have been asked to tell you a story about the stories that maps tell. For me, this story begins with Alexander von Humboldt, because this is a story about using ecological maps to think and act, globally and locally. And Humboldt was one of the first to do so, nearly two hundred years ago.

We no longer live in Humboldt's world, and we can't go back there. But we live in a world of maps he imagined. This atlas has aspirations worthy of Humboldt's wildest dreams about the ways in which maps, images, graphs, charts, and stories can help us know and feel connected to our world. Both were important to Humboldt: knowing and feeling. He believed in science and sentiment, information and experience, objectivity and subjectivity.

As a young man, Humboldt may have run away from home—and the stifling bourgeois expectations of late eighteenth-century Germany—to avoid knowing and feeling some things about himself. Who among us has not at some point? So off he went, to find the fabled passage between the Orinoco and Amazon rivers; to climb Mount Chimborazo in the Andes, at the time believed to be the highest peak in the world; to map the volcanoes along the spine of the Americas. Humboldt had a reckless, nearly fatal attraction to nature, and he found what he was looking for. "In the New

World," he wrote, "man and his productions almost disappear amidst the stupendous display of wild and gigantic nature."

But Humboldt wasn't just running away. He had a plan to bring something back—and it was big: nothing less than "to study the great harmonies of nature" and to "recognize the general connections that link organic beings." The night before he left Europe, Humboldt wrote to a friend, "My eyes will always be directed to the combination of forces, to the influence of inanimate creation on the animate world of animals and plants, to this harmony." He was after the "unity in the diversity" of nature. But to get there, he first had to measure and map everything he could. Humboldtian science became the new thing in science in the early nineteenth century. And its creed, writes historian Susan Faye Cannon, was "measurement and the promotion of accurate worldwide observations."

But observations alone were "not really interesting except when we can dispose of their results in such a way as to lead to general ideas," Humboldt wrote. And Humboldtians ever since have prized maps and graphs that convey analysis and synthesis of a variety of data. Humboldt showed how this could be done with his famous map of the vegetation zones he found as he gained elevation climbing Mount Chimborazo, then even more so as he linked those changes to patterns of vegetation across wider latitudinal and continental scales, and especially as he mapped isolines of temperature and climate variation around the globe. Humboldt connected patterns of physical geography, climate, and biology to connect the processes of life on Earth.

"The ties which unite these phenomena," he wrote, "the relations which exist between the varied forms of organized beings, are discovered only when we have acquired the habit of viewing the globe as a great whole."

Humboldt's view was a global view, built up from facts on the ground, through a network of travels, correspondence, and wide reading. This was the unity in diversity that he sought, one world made out of many. It is in seeking this view that the mapmakers

Examining a map in the Adelbert Mountains, Papua New Guinea

in this atlas inhabit our world with the Humboldtian spirit.

Reading the Stories That Maps Tell

We bring such stories to maps, but maps also have their own stories to tell, their own arguments to make.

Maps are powerful. They make persuasive arguments about spatial relationships—what can be found where and its relationships

---

* "The great advantage of applying graphic methods to the different objects of natural history is that graphics convey in spirit that intimate conviction that always accompanies notions that we receive directly through our senses."

with other things in the same space. By the same token, atlases make arguments about the relationships between maps. This atlas invokes the myth that all atlases implicitly invoke: that we, like Atlas, carry the world on our shoulders. And that is the overarching story that this atlas tells.

Thus, one could begin to understand this atlas first by understanding that it is a myth. That might seem odd, since this atlas

is firmly rooted in an empirical tradition. The maps in this atlas represent an unfailing faith in facts. These maps are built from the best available data. Every shape and color in this atlas has a database behind it. But even the most empirical maps are fantasies or fictions.

How so? First, these maps show the globe whole, an impossible view in fact. And maps like these give us the illusion that we are

seeing something we can at least wrap our heads around, if not put our arms around, and perhaps in this way even control—even if we really can't control what is actually happening on the ground or in the water that these maps portray.

You will get the most out of these maps, like all maps, if you read them critically. They may look pretty. They are. And the message may seem obvious. But you should

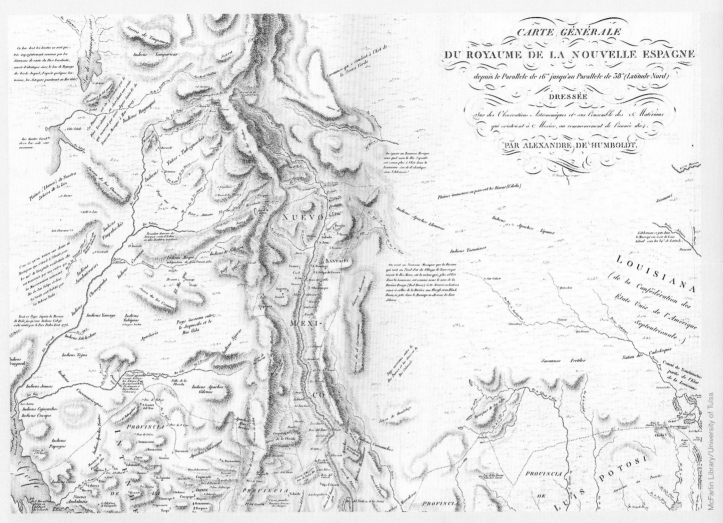

Eighteenth-century map by the first biogeographer, Alexander von Humboldt

not stop at the surface. Probe. Ask questions. Argue with these maps.

Start with scale. Scale is an essential element in maps. Most of these maps are at one scale: a global scale. All of us live at multiple scales. Life on Earth exists at multiple scales. Processes happen at multiple scales. To make truly useful stories out of these maps, you will want to think about these scales.

While these maps are nearly all at one global scale, they have regions mapped on them. On some maps, national boundaries appear prominent, but in most maps ecoregions are used. When data are shown, for example, by marine ecoregion, national boundaries fade in importance. Yet, nations have strong determining interests in what happens in the oceans—legally up to two hundred miles from shore and practically far beyond that.

Does this global view give us an accurate picture of what is happening on the ground in any particular place on these maps? Hardly. And the mapmakers know this. So texts and photographs sometimes bring a sharper focus on particular places. But can the places they highlight really stand in for other places, as these cartographic collages suggest? Is Three Gorges Dam a synecdoche for our hydrologically altered world? Are the British Columbian coastal forests a metaphor for what once was?

In a world in flux, thematic maps such as these are arguments about invisible phenomena, interactions, and change. These maps use symbols and colors to communicate these themes. What do the symbols and colors convey? What is included? What might be left out? How do text and images and other graphs work with the maps to tell a story? What is the story? Are there other possible stories that could be told?

Remember: The map is not the territory. It may not even represent the territory that well. But what it invariably does quite well is represent ideas about the territory.

Maps can inspire and inform. They can also limit and deceive. The more maps try to tell us, the more questions we should ask. If these maps do not start some arguments, they will have failed. These arguments matter. Many of them are about priorities and actions. They are about life and death on Earth.

It's a Humboldtian World after All

A number of arguments are being made in this atlas that put it squarely in the Humboldtian tradition, in which maps and graphs interact to make arguments and tell stories about our world. The first is an argument about scale: this is an atlas of global environmental and ecological processes. The second is an argument about content: this is an atlas in which people and nature matter and their relationships matter. And third is an argument about process: this is an atlas of a world in flux. We do not live in a world where things are fixed, as they are on maps in atlases. And that is why, although these maps are not dynamic, they represent dynamic processes.

Finally, an implicit argument is being made in this atlas that maps are not just documentation of discoveries already made. Maps are tools for new discoveries. If maps are arguments, maps can and must change. And the act of reading the story a map tells can itself change the map and be the beginning of a new map to a new world. This was Humboldt's vision.

"Humboldt recognized that cartography offered powers beyond description," writes geographer Denis Cosgrove. "The mapped image could itself test an experimental hypothesis, revealing aspects of the world invisible to the eye." Climatic zones, for example, cannot be seen unless they are represented on a map.

Humboldt experimented with a new language—a graphic, analytical, spatial language—that has now become much more commonplace, among scientists, to be sure, and increasingly at large in the world. This is a language for making arguments through maps and graphs and images that combine specialist forms of knowledge in what we might now call a "mash-up," a hybrid that allows understanding and knowledge and debate to flow across the map— and out into the world. As Cosgrove writes, "the map, like the scientific laboratory, could generate as well as illustrate new knowledge, creating a world that could then be explored empirically."

In a letter written before he embarked on his own global pilgrimage and life's work, Humboldt outlined "the objects which seem worthy of attention," a number of which this atlas is still pursuing: the description of the extension of plants on Earth's surface, the habitability of different places, the migration of plants and animals and people, and the species that have followed people, some of which we now call invasives. On one level, Humboldt's goal was utilitarian: "a more enlightened employment of the products and forces of nature." But he was also interested in "the diverse expressions of joy and melancholy that the world of plants evokes" in people.

Humboldt connected climate to biology, biology to geology, and geology to history, all within the ample embrace of geography. And with history, he included the political, moral, and material history of people; their need for sustenance; and the relationship between nature and the human spirit and intellect. So it is fitting that we are still trying to find our way in the world using Humboldtian maps. For, as Humboldt wrote, "It is through this research that we open the way to intellectual delight, to a moral liberty which fortifies us against the blows of destiny and which no exterior power can undermine."

JON CHRISTENSEN IS THE ASSOCIATE DIRECTOR OF THE SPATIAL HISTORY PROJECT IN THE BILL LANE CENTER FOR THE AMERICAN WEST AT STANFORD UNIVERSITY.

2

Habitats

FOR CHEETAHS, it is African savannas like the Serengeti. For heelsplitter mussels, it is the muddy side channels of the Mississippi River. For the bizarre parasite *Symbion pandora*, it is the lips of Norwegian lobsters.

Habitats are homes where species find their niches. They can be placid lakes, snowy mountaintops, arid deserts, or deep ocean trenches—anywhere on Earth where species can find food, shelter, and opportunities to reproduce.

As a global species, humans depend on many different habitats far beyond the towns and cities where most of us spend our lives. We rely on the oceans for fish, grasslands for farmland and pastures, and lakes and rivers for water. Forests provide wood and other natural resources, and they also help moderate changes in climate. Even if we rarely visit these habitats in person, we cannot live without them.

Some habitats, like coral reefs and grasslands, are named after the dominant species found there, but all habitats—and the vast variety of lives that they sustain—are ultimately shaped by the physical environment.

On land, climate gradients create different habitats from warm, wet tropical forests with their mind-boggling diversity of trees, orchids, birds, and insects to cold, dry tundra where only the hardiest heath plants, grouse, and caribou wait out

the frigid and dark winters to revel in the midnight sun of arctic summer. In between these extremes, different combinations of temperature and precipitation sustain grasslands, evergreen and deciduous forests, and deserts.

Lake and river habitats are molded by topography, geology, and climate, and they in turn can shape their environment. Steep mountains are pocked with cold, glacial lakes and cut by fast, cascading streams that provide homes for aquatic insects and trout. In lowlands, wide plains let rivers meander and fill shallow lakes and wetlands that provide habitat for larger fish and other species adapted to slower waters.

In the sea, habitats are shaped by currents and temperature, and change with water depth. Along the coasts, bays and estuaries are carved by waves, rivers, tides, and currents. Coral reefs and kelp forests grow in sunlit shallow waters. As the water deepens and darkens offshore, scallops and cod make their homes across the continental shelf, while myriad strange life-forms live in the ocean's depths.

In an ever-changing world, the distribution of habitats can change with the climate and currents. But the pace of human-driven changes in land use, water management, and ocean exploitation is so great that there is a mounting risk that habitats and the species that depend on them may not be able to adjust quickly enough.

This section of the atlas explores the global variety and current distribution of major kinds of habitat. Each page highlights the uniqueness of these habitats, the benefits they provide, the dangers faced from human development, and some ways that people can act to protect them.

Shaped by, and shaping, topography. Lake and river habitats are molded by topography, geology, and climate. Mountains are pocked with cold, glacial lakes and cut by fast, cascading streams. Lowland plains let rivers meander and fill shallow lakes and wetlands.

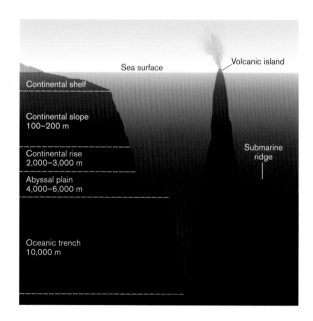

Varied with ocean depth. Marine habitats change with water depth, temperature, and currents. Coral reefs grow in sunlit shallow waters, while deeper, darker waters are home to varied species, from tuna plying remote oceans to luminescent fish living at extreme depths.

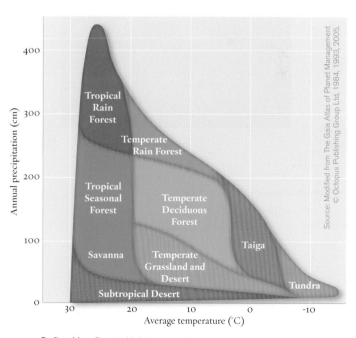

Source: Modified from The Gaia Atlas of Planet Management
© Octopus Publishing Group Ltd, 1984, 1993, 2005.

Defined by climate. Habitats on land are shaped by the combination of temperature and precipitation that they experience. Warm, wet conditions support tropical rain forests, while cold, dry conditions support tundra.

Forests and Woodlands
Giving Trees

Sergio Pucci / TNC

Scott Warren

Natural complexities.
Wild forests (above)
have complex structures,
providing valuable
habitat unmatched by
plantations of trees (left)
grown and harvested
as a crop.

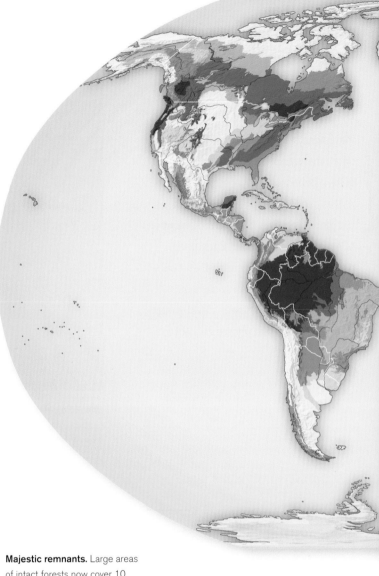

Stephen Alvarez

Majestic remnants. Large areas
of intact forests now cover 10
percent of Earth's land surface,
but they once spread over almost
half of it.

FROM THE AMAZON JUNGLES to California's
oak groves, forests and woodlands are always
much more than collections of trees. Rather,
they are communities of interdependent
plants, animals, fungi, and bacteria, which,
together, support human survival as well.
Woodlands differ from forests only in that
they have more space between the trees,
allowing a more open canopy.

Forests and woodlands produce much
of the oxygen that people breathe and help
stabilize the climate by absorbing carbon
dioxide, a leading greenhouse gas. They also
help filter rain and melting snow entering
streams, and offer shade that keeps the water
cool for fish and frogs. Natural forests additionally provide millions of sustainable jobs,
especially in the developing world where
many rural people still live off the land,
whether by tapping latex from wild rubber
trees; gathering medicines, food, spices, and
fuelwood; or, increasingly, working as stewards or guides in protected wild places.

Forests—especially tropical forests—are
some of the most diverse habitats on Earth.
Nearly 1,500 species of amphibians, birds,
mammals, and reptiles have been found
in the southwestern Amazon rain forest—
about five times the number of those species
documented in forests in the eastern United
States. Elsewhere, forests harbor remnants of
ancient history. China's temperate broadleaf
forests include plants closely related to those
in the southeastern United States, echoing a
time before the continents drifted apart. The
evergreen "monkey puzzle" forests of South
America evolved in Gondwana—the

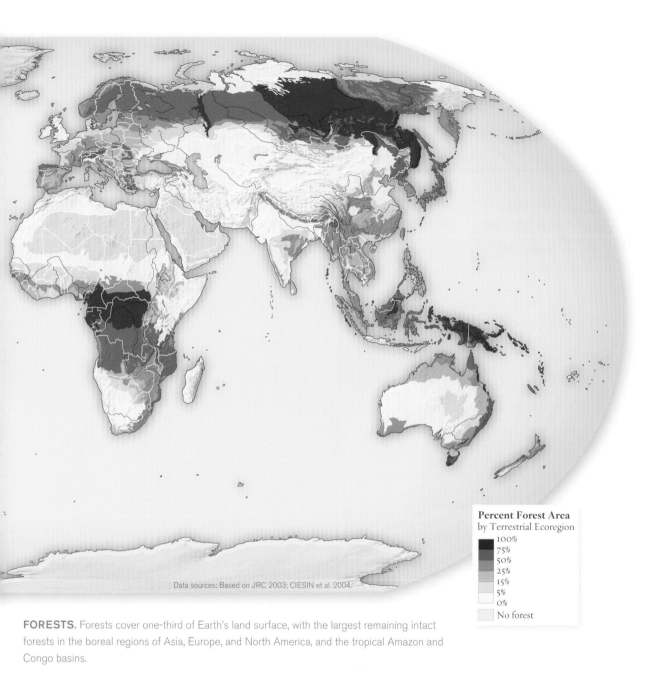

Percent Forest Area
by Terrestrial Ecoregion

100%
75%
50%
25%
15%
5%
0%
No forest

Data sources: Based on JRC 2003; CIESIN et al. 2004.

FORESTS. Forests cover one-third of Earth's land surface, with the largest remaining intact forests in the boreal regions of Asia, Europe, and North America, and the tropical Amazon and Congo basins.

supercontinent that contained most of Earth's land mass millions of years ago. Many types of trees can live for centuries, creating old-growth forest habitats essential for the survival of many animal and plant species that have adapted there over time, such as the great apes of Indonesia and marbled murrelets, seabirds that nest only in ancient forests along the northwest coast of North America.

About 42 percent of Earth's original forests have been lost worldwide since the early 1700s—converted to human settlements and agriculture as well as timber plantations, which resemble forests yet do not provide the same range of benefits or support as many species. The modern rate of loss is accelerating, as is the degradation of what remains, due to mining, logging, road building, and clearing for cropland.

As people become more aware of the contributions of intact forests—gifts becoming ever more conspicuous in their absence—increasing efforts are being made to preserve what is left. With growing appreciation of forests' contributions to climate stability, for instance, more forests are being managed to store carbon. One of these is the Noel Kempff Mercado National Park in Bolivia, an area twice the size of New York's Long Island, which is being managed with the goal of preventing the release of 5.8 million tons of carbon to the atmosphere while conserving habitat and preserving traditional forest jobs.

Grasslands

Where the Buffalo Roamed

Drama on the plains. Herds, like these wildebeests in the African savanna, migrate great distances across grasslands.

Life-sustaining fire. Fire is a recurring event in most grasslands, maintaining habitats that many grassland plants and animals depend on.

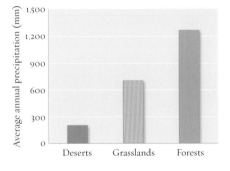

Not too wet or too dry. Grasslands occur where it is too dry to support forests yet too wet for deserts.

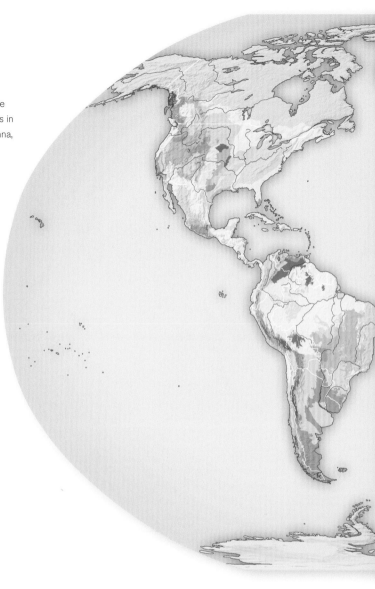

GRASSLANDS THROUGHOUT HISTORY have been open-air theaters of violent drama, as migrating, meat-eating predators have stalked their migrating, grass-eating prey. On the hot, rolling African savannas—grasslands dotted by acacia trees—lions and hyenas today still chase herds of wildebeest, zebras, and antelopes. Such scenes of pursuit and flight were once also common on the prairies of North America, where wolves and grizzlies chased bison and elk over land now covered with farms, cities, and towns.

Grasslands occur in climates too dry to sustain forests but too wet for deserts. They are found on every continent except Antarctica. In the heart of South America, savannas occupy an area about one-fourth the size of Canada, offering homes for the large capybara rodent and marsh deer. On the remote high plains of the Tibetan Plateau, grasslands cover an area almost as large as the U.S. state of Montana.

Many different animals have evolved to make the most of life in these wide open spaces. Creatures native to grasslands tend to have long legs or large wings, which help them travel great distances. Grasslands similarly have played a role in human evolution: transitioning from a four-footed life in the jungles, humans learned to walk and run and scan the horizon for prey.

The grassland drama of carnivore and herbivore is mirrored in the struggles between

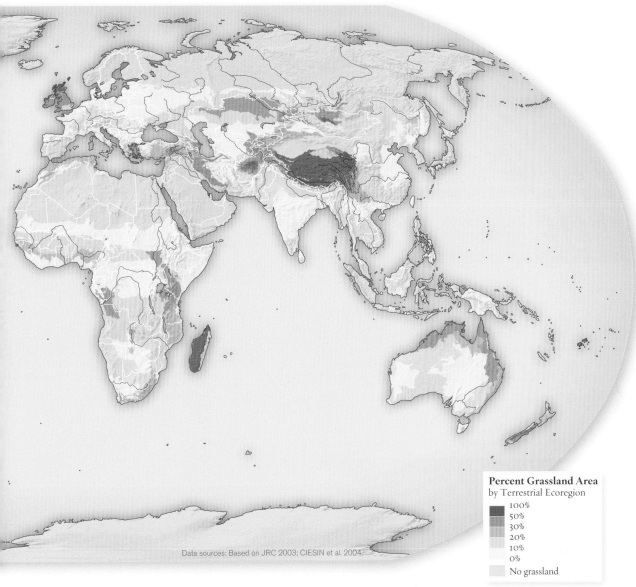

Percent Grassland Area
by Terrestrial Ecoregion

- 100%
- 50%
- 30%
- 20%
- 10%
- 0%
- No grassland

Data sources: Based on JRC 2003; CIESIN et al. 2004.

GRASSLANDS. Many grasslands have been plowed under or converted to pasture for livestock, yet vast intact grasslands still remain in eastern Africa, central Asia, and northern South America.

herbivore and plant. Grassland flora is specialized for survival, whether with long roots that can reach a deep water table, thick bark to resist the frequent fires, or thorns to ward off hungry animals.

Yet despite their adaptive arsenal, grasslands and the life they support are succumbing rapidly to human development. The features that make them most hospitable to life—their flatness and fertility—put them most at risk. Ideally suited for ranching and agriculture, in many regions they have been overgrazed and overfarmed. A more indirect danger is that increased human settlements have led to suppression of the fires on which some grasses rely to release seeds from their tough husks. By the early twenty-first century, up to one-half of the world's original grasslands had vanished, with most remnants sliced up by roads.

The ancient dramas of grassland life might seem to be in their final season, were it not for new conservation efforts by scientists, activists, and governments. Over the past fifteen years, conservationists have shown that managing grazing and fires can help restore native communities of grassland plants and even support the reintroduction of large mammals, such as the American bison.

In Mongolia, private and government groups have helped conserve twenty-eight thousand square kilometers of the world's largest intact temperate grassland, an area threatened by nearby development of roads, mines, and oilfields yet still home to migrating nomads with their yaks.

Deserts and Aridlands

Hardy Life under Harsh Conditions

Man-made deserts. While natural deserts can be vibrant and full of life, vast regions are being converted from dry grasslands to barren deserts. This human-induced *desertification*—the loss of vegetation and the degradation and drying of the soil—is a product of deforestation, overgrazing, and wasteful irrigation practices, aggravated by climate change. Desertification threatens the survival of more than 250 million people, like this Tanzanian herder, who depend on drylands for crops and grazing of livestock.

Quenched by fog and dew. In the Namib Desert, *Welwitschia mirabilis*, also known as "tumboa," absorbs moisture through its leaves. The tumboa grows very slowly and can live for over a thousand years.

LOW, UNPREDICTABLE RAINFALL, high evaporation rates, and, in most cases, an abundance of paradoxes are common denominators of the world's aridlands, which cover about 40 percent of the world's total land surface. While deserts seem empty, they are usually full of life.

Look closer at the seemingly bare landscapes beyond the scraggly foliage of the world's driest places. It turns out many are not really bare but are covered by algae and lichens called *cryptogams*. Combined with bacteria and fungi, cryptogams form a living crust that holds scarce water in place and keeps soil from blowing away. But cryptogamic crusts can crumble under the weight of just a footstep, making deserts some of Earth's most fragile landscapes.

Resident animals are characterized by extraordinary adaptations that allow them to survive in these all but inhospitable terrains. The endangered Arabian oryx, which resembles a long-horned antelope, has thick, bright white fur that reflects the sun's rays in summer but absorbs the warmth in winter. Gila monsters store water in their tails. The Namibian tumboa plant absorbs fog and dew through its leaves. Australia's Eyrean grasswren, a small bird, has such efficient kidneys that it does not need to drink water—it gets all the moisture it needs from the seeds and insects it eats. Plants have similarly evolved to fit their habitat: many of them grow, flower, make seeds, and die in just the few days of rain during the year.

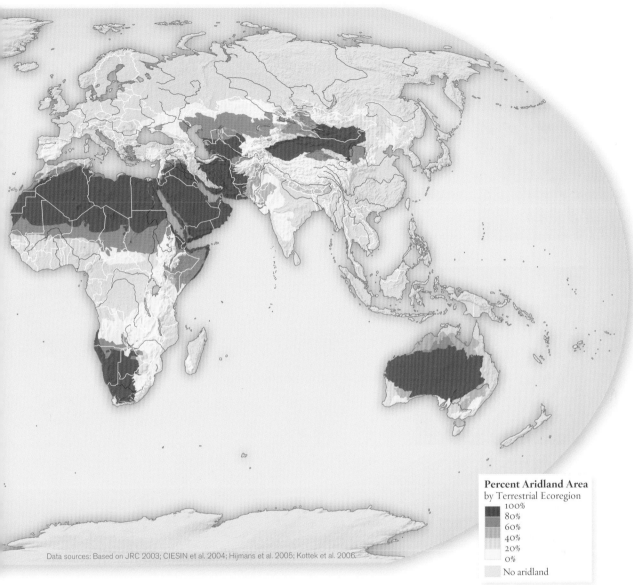

Data sources: Based on JRC 2003; CIESIN et al. 2004; Hijmans et al. 2005; Kottek et al. 2006.

Percent Aridland Area
by Terrestrial Ecoregion
- 100%
- 80%
- 60%
- 40%
- 20%
- 0%
- No aridland

DESERTS AND ARIDLANDS. The world's major deserts include the Sahara, Arabian, Gobi, and Great Basin in western North America.

Apparently timeless and unchanging, deserts are increasingly being transformed by human activities. Eight percent of the world's human population live in deserts and the aridlands on their margins, eking out incomes from livestock, mining, and minimal farming. Desert and aridland habitats throughout the world have also been lost to irrigated farming and urbanization, while the introduction of invasive plant species and the suppression of fires have transformed immense expanses of these habitats.

Throughout the ages, travelers in search of solitude and inspiration have also been drawn to desert wilderness. These incursions have damaged the fragile environments. Cryptogamic crusts and other fragile flora have been destroyed by off-road vehicles and other means.

Many opportunities do remain to protect desert habitats with improved fire management, careful grazing practices, and control of invasive plants. Invasive yellow star thistle

and cheatgrass, for example, have taken over and devastated huge areas of North America's Great Basin Desert. However, in at least one area, Hells Canyon of Idaho, conservation groups and state agencies have been tracking the plants' progress by flying over the area in small planes and helicopters, returning by land to remove the invasives, whether with fire or grazing animals, or by pulling the plants out by hand.

Rivers and Wetlands
The Planet's Lifeblood

Brian Richter/TNC

Life-giving floods.
The annual rainy season brings essential water and nutrients to the Okavango Delta. Hundreds of species, from Cape buffaloes and lechwe antelope to tiny invertebrates, could not survive without this seasonal flooding.

Richard Du Toit/Minden Pictures

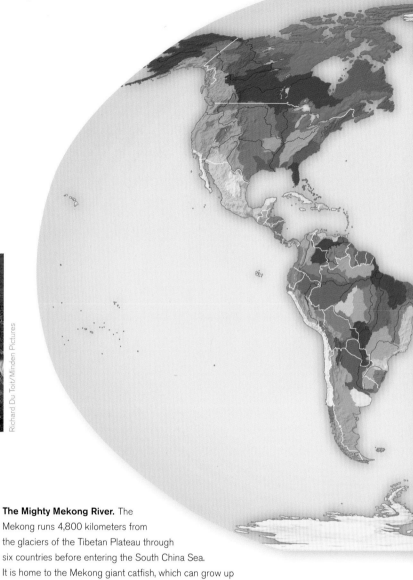

Zeb Hogan

The Mighty Mekong River. The Mekong runs 4,800 kilometers from the glaciers of the Tibetan Plateau through six countries before entering the South China Sea. It is home to the Mekong giant catfish, which can grow up to three meters in length and weigh three hundred kilograms and is now close to extinction because of overfishing and habitat loss. The lower Mekong Basin waters contain the world's most productive inland fisheries, providing protein and incomes to forty million rural dwellers.

RIVERS HAVE ALWAYS BEEN POTENT symbols of time and change, shifting shape as they travel from the mountains to the sea. Fast-flowing streams dominate their upper reaches, growing larger and slower as they descend toward wetlands and the coast.

No two rivers are exactly alike. Climate, geology, the chemistry of the water, and the contours of the land all determine a river's characteristics and the varieties of life that it supports. As a rule, large fish such as the Mekong giant catfish can be found in the

deep, slow-moving waters of main river channels. Smaller species, such as Australia's climbing galaxids, which got their name for their ability to wriggle up waterfalls, inhabit the shallower headwater streams. Other species, native to arid regions, have adapted to periods when rivers run dry or are reduced to a few standing pools until the next rainy season. The Australian salamanderfish, for example, clings to life during the annual dry period by burrowing in the mud and covering itself with a thick layer of mucus.

Floodplains and wetlands typically harbor the greatest number of species. Renewed each year with river-borne nutrients, these habitats are sprawling nurseries for aquatic plants, insects, worms, and other invertebrates, which in turn attract large numbers of fish, mammals, and birds to feed and breed. One of the world's most magnificent wetlands is Africa's Okavango Delta in the margins of the Kalahari Desert, an alluvial fan of fifteen thousand square kilometers that floods every rainy season as the

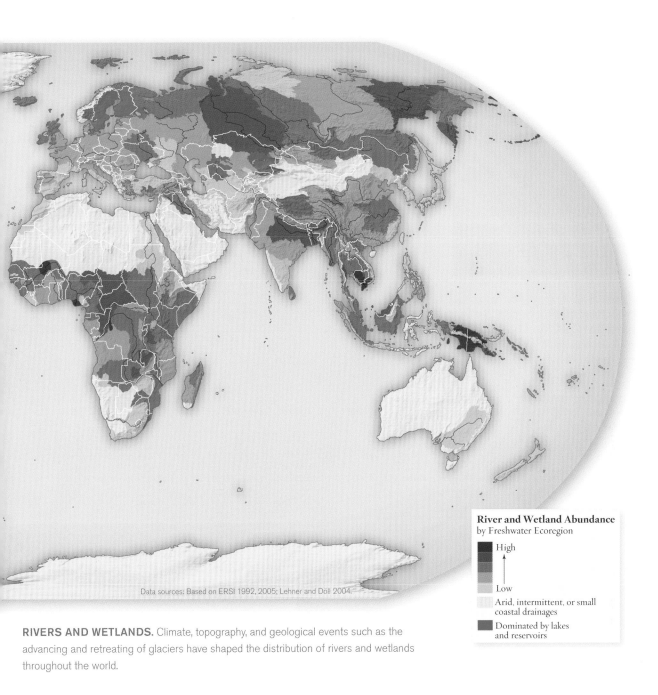

River and Wetland Abundance
by Freshwater Ecoregion

- High
↑
- Low
- Arid, intermittent, or small coastal drainages
- Dominated by lakes and reservoirs

Data sources: Based on ERSI 1992, 2005; Lehner and Döll 2004.

RIVERS AND WETLANDS. Climate, topography, and geological events such as the advancing and retreating of glaciers have shaped the distribution of rivers and wetlands throughout the world.

Okavango River flows down from the highlands of Angola. The Okavango offers habitat for a large array of plants and animals that would otherwise succumb to the desert heat. It also provides food for more than a hundred thousand indigenous people, and spectacular views for visitors supporting Botswana's lucrative tourism industry.

Throughout the world, rivers and wetlands play similarly vital roles in people's lives, providing shipping routes, hydropower, recreation, jobs, and food and drinking water.

Indeed, river and wetland fisheries often provide the only source of animal protein for people in much of the developing world, particularly the rural poor who turn to fishing when they cannot find other jobs. In Laos, over 70 percent of farmers are also involved, at least part-time, in fishing activities to augment their family food supplies and incomes.

Over time, we have heavily altered waterways to fit our needs by building dams, levees, and canals. Other harmful practices, which today are unfortunately widespread,

include draining wetlands, withdrawing too much water for agriculture, polluting rivers with fertilizer, dumping waste, over-harvesting fish, and introducing non-native species. All these threats pose major challenges to conservationists, who nonetheless are making progress. A case in point in the United States is the Connecticut River and its tributaries, which are reviving today after forty years of efforts to protect land, restore shoreline vegetation, improve sewage treatment, and manage fish and recreation.

Lakes
Fragile Pools of Life

Broudy/Donohue Photography/Corbis

Saving Himalaya's lakes. Lake Gokyo was one of the four glacial lakes protected by Nepal in 2007 under the Convention on Wetlands. This system of lakes near Mount Everest is a vital water source for local communities and is home to threatened species, including the reclusive snow leopard.

Konrad Wothe/Minden Pictures

The unique freshwater seal of Baikal. The nerpa, found only in Lake Baikal, is the world's only strictly freshwater seal. It can live over fifty years and stay underwater for up to forty-three minutes.

World's largest lake. Lake Baikal holds one-fifth of the world's freshwater. More than 330 streams flow into the lake, but only the Angara River flows out toward the sea.

Konstantin Mikhailov/ Foto Natura/Minden Pictures

FROM THE VAST Great Lakes of North America to tiny Gokyo Lake, nestled high in the Himalayas, lakes in their many different forms sustain a wide variety of natural life. Much like islands, they provide habitats in which freshwater plants and animals can evolve in isolation.

Lakes are formed after glaciers, volcanoes, or earthquakes leave craters that fill with water. Next, species from surrounding waters, as well as seeds carried by wind and wildlife,

colonize these new environments and gradually adapt to their conditions.

Lake Baikal in southern Siberia is the world's oldest and deepest freshwater lake. Formed by a deep crack in Earth's crust more than twenty-five million years ago, it holds nearly one-fifth of all the world's freshwater, roughly equal to the volume of all the North American Great Lakes combined. And just as outstanding as its size is the quantity and variety of plants and animals that it sustains: in all, 2,630 species, three-quarters of which are found nowhere

else on Earth. In comparison with Lake Baikal, most other lakes in the world are relatively young, having formed within the last ten to twenty thousand years. Younger lakes generally have many fewer species, but these species continue evolving today.

Reservoirs look like lakes and are often mistaken for them. Yet they are different in important ways. Reservoirs are artificial environments, formed by a dam that interrupts a river's flow and floods the land behind it. Reservoirs transform flowing river

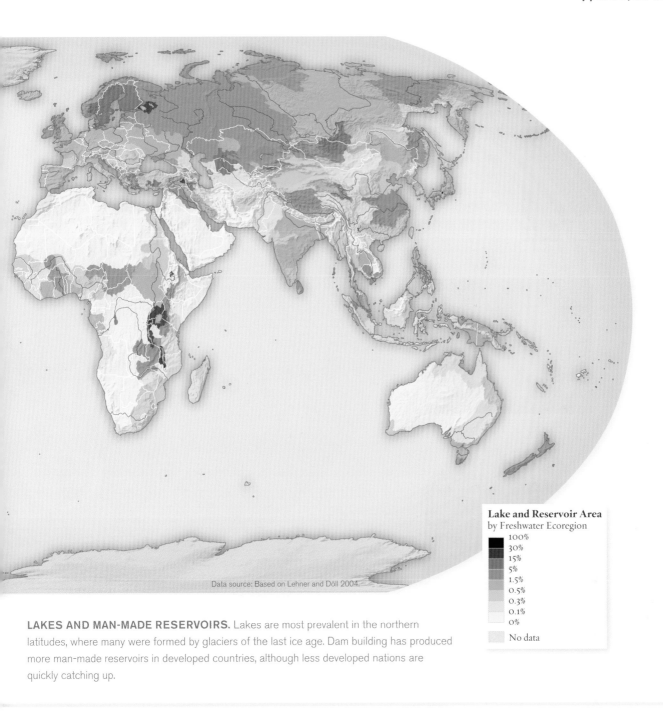

Data source: Based on Lehner and Döll 2004.

Lake and Reservoir Area
by Freshwater Ecoregion

100%
30%
15%
5%
1.5%
0.5%
0.3%
0.1%
0%

No data

LAKES AND MAN-MADE RESERVOIRS. Lakes are most prevalent in the northern latitudes, where many were formed by glaciers of the last ice age. Dam building has produced more man-made reservoirs in developed countries, although less developed nations are quickly catching up.

water into standing water, with the result that native river fauna often cannot adapt and survive. Many reservoirs are also intentionally stocked with non-native fish species, such as trout or bass, which can end up competing with native species. While there are still many more lakes than reservoirs, there are now reservoirs on nearly every river system on Earth.

People use lakes and reservoirs in all sorts of ways—they are fish tanks, sources of irrigation water, and fields for Jet Skis. And as with other elements of nature, we often love our lakes to death. The most prevalent threats to lakes today are pollution from sewage, industrial effluents, and fertilizers running off farmland. Nutrients in sewage and fertilizer end up feeding algae and plant life that then rob the water of its oxygen as they die and decay. This process—called *eutrophication*—results in the suffocation of fish and other species. Other pressures on lakes include overharvesting of fish, the proliferation of invasive species, and the lowering of water levels from excessive water use.

Some of these threats can be abated through sound management and conservation. Back in the 1960s, Lake Washington in the U.S. Pacific Northwest was dominated by toxic algae and unfondly called "Lake Stinko" by locals, as a result of many years of dumping of raw sewage from Seattle and surrounding areas. The lake has since recovered, however, as managers have built sewage treatment plants, and is now a popular place for recreation and home to nearly thirty species of fish.

Caves and Karst

Troves of Subterranean Species

Henry Watkins &
Yibran Aragon/Reuters/Corbis

An underground blue world. The Quintana Roo province in Mexico contains more than 685 kilometers of underground rivers, including the Ox Bel Ha, the world's longest surveyed underwater cave system.

Rare and out of sight. The endangered Benton Cave crayfish is found in just four sites within the Ozark karst system of the U.S. state of Arkansas, with only forty individuals known to exist.

Stephen Alvarez

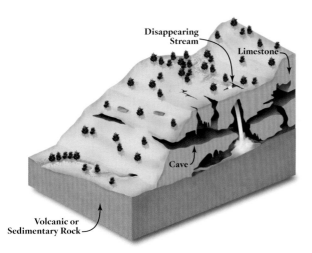

Disappearing Stream

Limestone

Cave

Volcanic or Sedimentary Rock

Interconnected landscapes. Karst caves contain their own ecosystems, and their freshwaters often nourish aboveground rivers and streams.

HIDDEN AWAY BELOW OUR FEET, some of the world's rarest and weirdest creatures dwell in underground caverns, tunnels, and caves. These mysterious abodes have been created in various ways: from cooled tubes of lava, the force of waves battering rocky coasts, or, most often, from the formation of karst. Karst caves form when water percolates through soluble portions of Earth's crust, dissolving rocks such as limestone and dolomite. Small spaces over time become vast subterranean tunnels and grottoes, often traversed by streams, rivers, and lakes.

The darkest reaches of this cavernous world are home to a class of specially adapted creatures: troglobites, which, having evolved without light, rely on highly developed other senses, including smell, taste, and vibration detection. Usually these species have little or no pigmentation and either rudimentary eyes or no eyes at all. Troglobites also tend to have remarkably slow metabolisms, allowing them to thrive in environments with little food to spare.

Cave habitats are usually so isolated from one another that they are high in endemism, with many troglobite species unique to a single location. The endangered Benton Cave crayfish—a blind, transparent crustacean that can live as long as a human—is found only in a handful of sites within the U.S. state of Arkansas's Ozarks karst system. Other, more common species come and go as they please. Bats may roost within caves, leaving them to feed and, in the process, routinely importing nutrients back home. Other animals, such as frogs and bobcats, spend most of their time aboveground but use caves for water and shelter during droughts or cold spells.

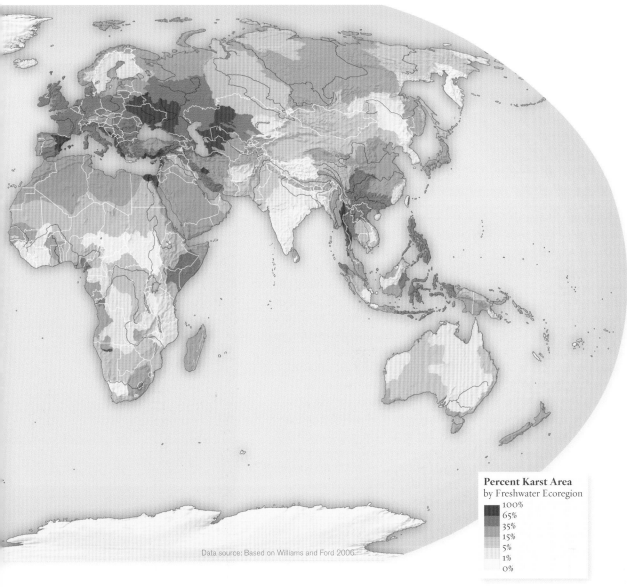

Percent Karst Area
by Freshwater Ecoregion
- 100%
- 65%
- 35%
- 15%
- 5%
- 1%
- 0%

Data source: Based on Williams and Ford 2006.

KARST TERRAIN. Many caves remain unexplored or even still undiscovered, but karst terrain—limestone or other soluble rock formations—illustrates where karst caves, and thusly cave species, are likely to exist.

Scientists estimate that karst terrain occupies nearly 15 percent of Earth's surface—a vast area that nonetheless remains largely unexplored, with many still-unknown species. Once documented, these permanent cave dwellers are ideal indicators of the health of a given environment, since they are extraordinarily sensitive to changes in the quantity and quality of the water seeping in from above. Unfortunately, many of them are not faring well.

As increasing human populations aboveground use water for irrigation and drinking, and pollute water with pesticides and fertilizers, sensitive cave species suffer. The blind Aigamas Cave catfish found only in the Aigamas Cave in Namibia, has arrived at the brink of extinction as karst water supplies have dwindled. Similarly, water pollution and diversion to reservoirs has damaged Central Europe's vast Dinaric karst, threatening such unique species as the "human fish" salamander.

Yet together with the new threats to cave species has come new interest in understanding and preserving them. Between 1980 and 2005, the rate of discovery of new subterranean fish species quadrupled in comparison with findings from the preceding sixty years. And recently, an ad hoc coalition of conservationists, landowners, and public officials has worked to protect sensitive habitats in the Ozark karst system by improving groundwater quality, regulating disposal of hazardous materials, conducting volunteer cleanups and restricting access to important cave sites. Other countries such as Brazil, Australia, Mexico, and Croatia have recently taken measures to protect cave habitats as well.

Hope in Habitats

STEVEN J. McCORMICK

I FIRST BECAME ENRAPTURED with the natural world in the late 1950s, playing with a band of friends in the woods—or, should I say, "the jungle." For that was the name we gave to the mixed oak woodland (not a phrase that was in the lexicon of eight-year-old boys) behind our neighborhood in Northern California.

Many weekends we'd march off to the jungle for a long day of climbing the burly, gnarled limbs of coast live oaks and exploring the dark, spicy interiors of dense bay forests. Those boyhood experiences, pursued solely for the sheer joy of unconstrained, unstructured adventure, profoundly influenced and shaped my growth to adulthood.

We didn't think of the jungle as a "habitat type," but we did appreciate the forest as more than just a bunch of trees. The creeks were full of "water skeeters" and other bugs; salamanders were abundant in early spring; gopher snakes prowled the open areas; quail erupted from underbrush; deer were almost always browsing early in the morning.

I can't say that my experiences in the jungle launched a career in conservation, but they were certainly a powerful influence on my life. When I first started working for The Nature Conservancy in 1977, I was convinced that we should focus more on conserving "natural communities" (a synonym for "habitat types") than on individual species, because—as I knew from my days in the jungle—not only was the whole system more than the sum of the parts, but the parts required the whole system (a pretty sophisticated ecological awareness for someone trained as a lawyer).

When I became president of The Nature Conservancy in 2001, I wanted to make this the guiding principle for the whole organization. And, inasmuch as the mission of the Conservancy compels a global vision ("to preserve the … diversity of life *on Earth*"—my emphasis), I was committed to undertaking a global assessment of all habitat types to determine conservation priorities based on considerations such as threat, and the extent to which habitat types are currently protected in different regions of the world.

This atlas is a culmination of that commitment. And what a wonderful, insightful resource it is! While no major habitat types are sufficiently conserved on a global scale, what this atlas reveals is that some are alarmingly overlooked. Temperate grasslands, for example, do not have the glamour or drama, say, of an African savanna or the abundance of species of a so-called tropical rain forest hotspot, but as an element of biological diversity, these grasslands are no less significant. Yet less than 5 percent of the world's temperate grasslands are represented in protected areas, and most are heavily altered by a long history of human agricultural use.

Focus on habitats also requires us to think in terms of what it will take to assure conservation of functioning natural systems, and to go beyond the convention of thinking of protected areas as the only approach for conservation. At the enormous scale required to assure meaningful conservation, we'll need to act with a commitment to assuring legitimate human needs and desires. Those of us who've had the luxury of coming to a conservation ethic in a prosperous nation must understand that the terminology we use—*protect*, *preserve*, *save*, *set aside*—is taken as arrogant at best, and confiscatory at worst, to those struggling for survival. The term *habitat* should be appreciated for its imperative for human well-being, not just for the preservation of the other species that reside there. After all, we humans also live in virtually every habitat on the planet. This realization suggests a whole new precept: conservation of habitats *for* people; not protection of nature *from* people. We also need to collaborate with many partners to develop creative solutions. It is clear that no one approach or one group can single-handedly reverse the current extinction crisis, tackle climate change, or prevent ecosystem degradation.

Last year I returned to live in Northern California. The jungle is still there, intact.

Mediterranean woodlands, California, United States

It's smaller and less exotic than I recall it. But the forest, redolent of bay and tanbark oak—what I now know is Mediterranean, a habitat type that has been heavily impacted by people here and elsewhere around the world—not only brought back powerful, and immediate, memories of a wondrous boyhood but also kindled a profound sense

of hope for the future. This small but enduring habitat, surrounded by development,
was alive with small children, doing exactly
what I did at their age.

STEVEN J. MCCORMICK IS PRESIDENT OF THE
GORDON AND BETTY MOORE FOUNDATION.

Coasts and Shelves

The Sea's Sunlit Margins

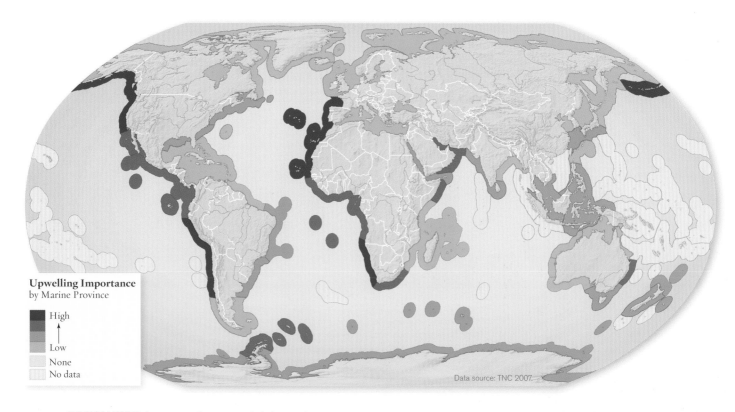

Upwelling Importance
by Marine Province

High

Low

None

No data

Data source: TNC 2007.

UPWELLINGS. In many regions, currents bring cool, nutrient-rich waters from the deep sea onto the continental shelf, feeding diverse forms of life. Upwellings off Peru and Chile are the richest, supporting over 15 percent of the world's marine fish catch.

Above the tides. Though scoured by wind and doused by sea spray, marine turtles and seabirds like the red-footed booby shown here find coastlines inviting places to rest, nest, and rear their young.

Mark D. Spalding

WHEREVER LAND TILTS into the sea there is a complex transition of worlds. First comes the intertidal zone, a place of constant motion, swept by currents, waves, and tides, yet sustaining myriad creatures and plants. Below the tides' play, shallow sunlit waters teem with life. The seafloor slopes gently away from the land, and as the waters deepen, the flow of nutrients from land diminishes, sunlight is filtered, and the seabed becomes more sparsely populated.

The intertidal zone is a strand of sometimes-water, sometimes-land that harbors communities of life that vary according to the nature of the seabed and the force of the waves. Salt marshes and mangroves grow in fine silt or mud where waters are calm. Below these, mudflats often stretch out in wide expanses, providing habitat for bacteria, algae, and burrowing animals such as razor clams, which in turn attract masses of wading birds, foraging fish, and crabs.

Different types of coastlines are home to distinct assortments of life. Rocky shores host a suite of flora and fauna that includes seaweeds (macroalgae), mollusks, anemones, crustaceans, and tiny bryozoans, which cling to the rocks, competing for space where sunlight and oxygen are plentiful. Sandy shores, by contrast, are not so densely populated but provide resting areas for turtles and seals. Estuaries and deltas are more complex places, forming the nexus of land, freshwater wetlands, and the ocean. Here, insect larvae and crustaceans scurry together, and schools of fish congregate to spawn, leaving billions of eggs and fish larvae. Mud crabs filter the sediment, while, in the tropics, large crocodiles hide in ambush.

The continental shelf is a shallow coastal region stretching as far as hundreds of

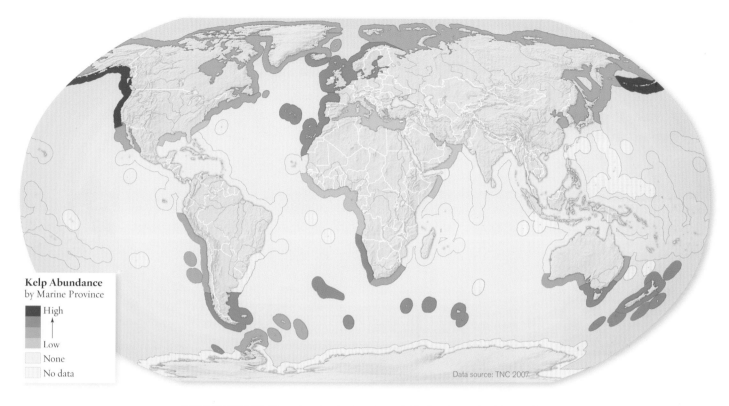

Kelp Abundance
by Marine Province

- High
- ↑
- Low
- None
- No data

Data source: TNC 2007.

KELP FORESTS. Though not a dominant coastal feature in much of the world, kelp forests are abundant and diverse in the temperate waters of the northern Pacific Ocean.

Jennifer Molnar

Intertidal. Salt marshes, mangroves, and shellfish reefs thrive in dynamic zones that are covered and uncovered by the tides.

Richard Herrmann

Beyond the waves. The continental shelf is home to plants, invertebrates, and in some regions even underwater forests of kelp that form three-dimensional habitats.

kilometers from the coast, dominated by sand and mud. Scientific convention holds that the continental shelf stops when it reaches a depth of about two hundred meters, after which there is often a steep drop to the inky depths of the deep sea, a place still rarely visited and poorly understood. Areas reached by sunlight may be colonized by plants, including seagrasses and algae, and by invertebrates such as worms, mollusks, and starfish. Rocks rising from the seabed support larger life-forms, including corals, sponges, sea fans, and large seaweeds known as kelp. Found throughout the

world's oceans, kelp are most widespread in cooler, nutrient-rich waters, such as the Pacific Ocean coast of Canada and the United States. There, rich kelp forests grow up from the seafloor to heights of twenty meters or more.

Living reefs are another common feature of the continental shelf. Best known, and home to the greatest diversity of species, are the coral reefs found in tropical zones. But other large reefs formed from the skeletons of animals and plants, including worms, mollusks, and even a red-colored algae, called *maerl*, are found in cooler waters,

providing homes to many species of fish and crustaceans.

Marine life is most varied and abundant in coastal waters—and human activities such as fishing and boating are also most intense here. In addition, human development along the coasts has had a tremendous and mounting impact on adjacent waters. In contrast to efforts on land, however, conservation efforts in coastal waters have been much more limited, with fewer areas protected and fewer regulations to prevent pollution or over-exploitation.

Coral Reefs
Crown Jewels of the Ocean

Steve Allen/Getty Images

Tiny builders, big results. Tiny coral animals form colonies that provide shelter for fish and the raw materials that have built great coral reefs and even islands, such as here in the Cook Islands.

Providing crucial resources. The rich resources of coral reefs are widely utilized, not only by birds, but by millions of fishers in over one hundred countries.

Mark D. Spalding

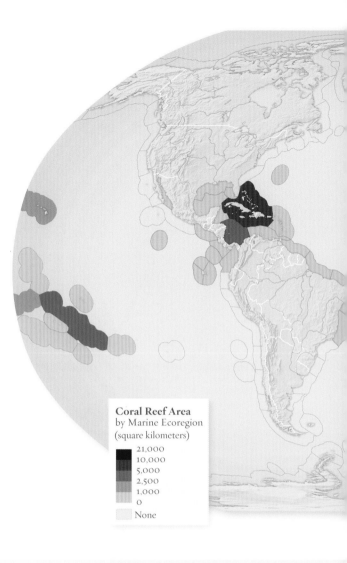

Coral Reef Area
by Marine Ecoregion
(square kilometers)

21,000
10,000
5,000
2,500
1,000
0
None

CORAL REEFS are undersea monuments, built up over thousands of years by billions of stony coral polyps. The polyps are tiny creatures, each consisting of little more than stinging tentacles, a mouth, and a stomach. They live in close-packed colonies, and as they die, they leave behind limestone skeletons to which new polyps attach. Over time, the skeletons become reefs, which can extend for hundreds of kilometers, growing up toward the surface of the sea. The still-living polyps are what give the reefs their jewel-like colors. The Great Barrier Reef, the largest geological structure ever built by living things, stretches almost two thousand kilometers along the northern coast of Australia, covering an area the size of Finland.

Coral reefs have long been famous for the diversity of life that they support, vying even with tropical rain forests in that regard. Yet even reef experts were surprised after one

marine biologist identified 284 different fish species during a single dive along the reefs of the Raja Ampat Islands, Indonesia. In subsequent expeditions, scientists have tallied a total of 1,149 different fish, 537 different coral species, and more than 700 mollusks from these islands, which lie in the Coral Triangle, home to the richest variety of all marine life.

Coral reef scientists recognize two major regions of coral reefs in the world. The vast Indo-Pacific region, stretching from East Africa and the Red Sea to the central Pacific Ocean, has the greatest extent of reefs and highest diversity of species. By contrast, the Atlantic coral reefs, most abundant around the Caribbean and the Bahamas Archipelago, have lower diversity, but their corals and fish are unique to this region, having evolved in isolation for hundreds of thousands of years.

People living on tropical islands depend on the reefs for their diets and incomes. Inhabitants of tiny atolls, such as the Maldives and Marshall Islands, actually live on land made of coral and sand, piled up by storms, or sometimes uplifted by ancient earthquakes. In many countries, reefs are a lucrative tourist attraction, since visitors will travel far to snorkel and scuba dive among healthy, diverse coral gardens. Reefs also reduce the impacts of waves, providing protection from storms.

Despite this immense value, many coral reefs are in decline. They are highly vulnerable to overfishing; in parts of Southeast Asia, they are being destroyed by fishers who use explosives to guarantee a maximum catch. Pollution and silt from inland agriculture and coastal development are also degrading the reefs. The greatest long-term threat may be the warming of the oceans due to climate

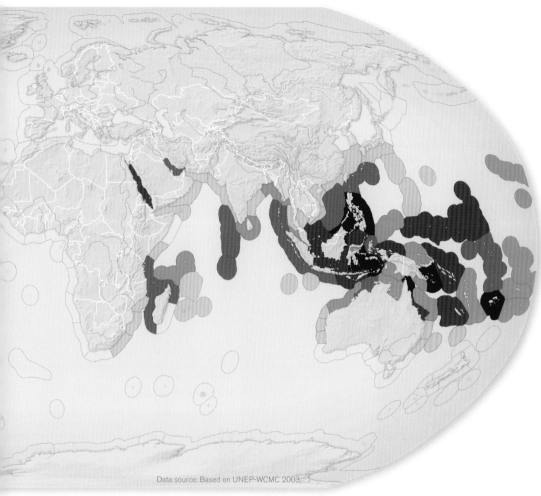

CORAL REEFS. Coral reefs are abundant throughout the Indo-Pacific ocean region, from East Africa and the Red Sea to the central Pacific Ocean, where many of the islands are built entirely by coral reefs. Reefs are also abundant through the Caribbean.

change. Corals are highly sensitive to fluctuations in sea temperature, and since the mid-1990s, warm summers in the Caribbean, the Western Indian Ocean, and the Great Barrier Reef have caused widespread coral death.

Hope rests in a combination of science, common sense, and concerted efforts. Scientists have realized that small areas of reef often survive the more widespread coral death that has occurred in recent warm summers, and that reef recovery more generally is enhanced where reefs are free from other human impacts such as overfishing. Working with expert knowledge of both scientists and local fishers, conservationists have created a plan for the communities around Kimbe Bay, Papua New Guinea, to safeguard these resilient coral reefs and to foster rapid recovery from future impacts, using traditional management approaches but ensuring that critical areas are safeguarded for the future.

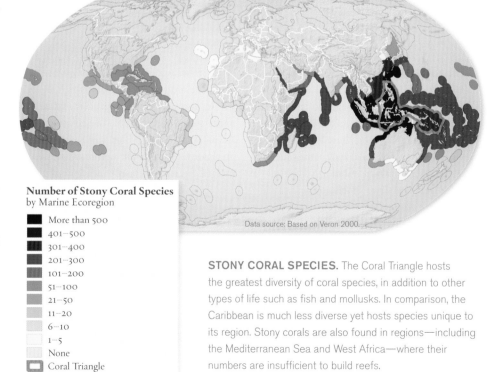

Number of Stony Coral Species
by Marine Ecoregion

- More than 500
- 401–500
- 301–400
- 201–300
- 101–200
- 51–100
- 21–50
- 11–20
- 6–10
- 1–5
- None
- Coral Triangle

STONY CORAL SPECIES. The Coral Triangle hosts the greatest diversity of coral species, in addition to other types of life such as fish and mollusks. In comparison, the Caribbean is much less diverse yet hosts species unique to its region. Stony corals are also found in regions—including the Mediterranean Sea and West Africa—where their numbers are insufficient to build reefs.

Mangrove Forests
Bridging Land and Sea

Courtesy of AsiaExplorers/www.asiaexplorers.com

A tended forest provides. The Matang forest of Malaysia is likely the longest continuously harvested tropical forest in the world. Beginning in 1902, Matang's stewards have carefully tended the four hundred square kilometer forest and have been richly rewarded. Today, some 2,200 people are employed in timber extraction and processing, while the associated fishing industries provide livelihoods for over 10,000 people.

A rare sight. Found only on the island of Borneo, the proboscis monkey dines on mangrove leaves and unlike other monkeys it is an excellent swimmer.

Thomas Marent/Minden Pictures

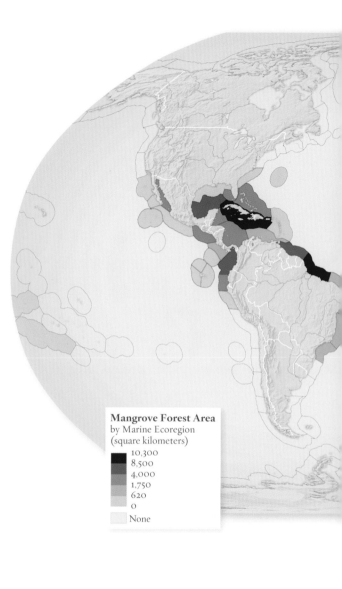

Mangrove Forest Area
by Marine Ecoregion
(square kilometers)

- 10,300
- 8,500
- 4,000
- 1,750
- 620
- 0
- None

MANGROVES TREES inhabit a world midway between land and sea. They thrive in swamps, their roots sometimes inundated by the rising tide. Scientists have catalogued some sixty-five species of these trees, all uniquely adapted to survive in the intertidal zone, sometimes in salty water, always in waterlogged earth. Mangroves' most distinctive features are their strange, adaptive root structures, all exposed to air at least part of the day so as to sip precious oxygen from an otherwise anaerobic terrain. These include pneumatophores, root extensions growing upright from the mud; "prop roots," looping from branches and trunks; and "knee roots," resembling strange knobby knees that poke up through the mud from the web of roots below.

In and among the great forests formed by these trees dwells an equally distinct mix of animals. Hordes of fiddler crabs march across the mud as the tide falls, the males waving a specialized giant pincer—attracting mates and deterring rivals. Mudskippers, an amphibious fish, climb up tree roots to graze on algae in the open air. Archerfish stay submerged but squirt jets of water from their mouths to dislodge insects from the leaves above. In the vast Sundarbans mangrove of Bangladesh and India, tigers stalk their prey. Hippos rest in the mangroves of West Africa, while the extraordinary, long-nosed proboscis monkey, which feasts on mangrove leaves, is found only on the island of Borneo.

Mangroves also support millions of people by providing timber, fuelwood, and food. The mud crabs and oysters, prawns and finfish nurtured among their roots add protein to the diets of nearby villages and provide income as valuable exports. They are an important nursery for many coral reef and seagrass fish. Even far offshore, species such as the prawns taken in northern Australia's massive prawn capture fishery rely on mangroves for part of their lives.

In many parts of the world, mangrove forests are living sea walls. They baffle waves, prevent erosion, and protect coastal settlements from devastation by storms. News reports in the wake of the 2004 Indian Ocean tsunami said mangroves helped shield some villages from the worst ravages of that disaster. Their complex roots and meandering channels also filter water and help consolidate the shore by capturing sediment carried by rivers or swept along the coast.

Mangrove forests are disappearing faster than any other forest type. Between 1980

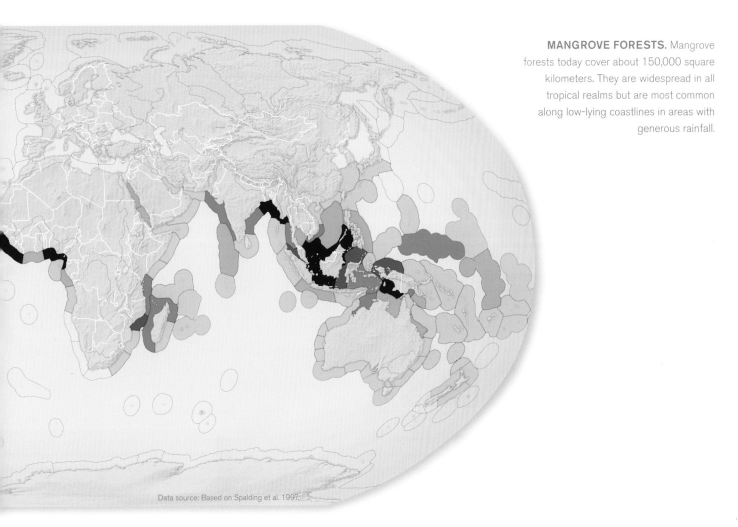

Data source: Based on Spalding et al. 1997.

MANGROVE FORESTS. Mangrove forests today cover about 150,000 square kilometers. They are widespread in all tropical realms but are most common along low-lying coastlines in areas with generous rainfall.

and 2005, they lost thirty-five thousand square kilometers, almost one-fifth of their total extent. This was mostly through overharvesting of wood or to make way for aquaculture ponds, agricultural land, and urban or tourist resort development. And now, as their gifts are being recognized, many mangrove forests are receiving increasing levels of protection, while others are being managed sustainably for forestry and fisheries. Countries such as Cuba, Bangladesh, Vietnam, and the Philippines have each planted hundreds of square kilometers of mangroves to replace lost forests and to safeguard coastlines and fish stocks.

Data source:
Based on Spalding et al. (forthcoming).

Number of Mangrove Species
by Marine Ecoregion

- 33–39
- 22–32
- 12–21
- 6–11
- 1–5
- None

MANGROVE SPECIES. The vast majority of the world's sixty five mangrove tree species are found in the Central Indo-Pacific, which is also a center of diversity for corals and seagrasses. Far fewer species are in the Atlantic and the Tropical Eastern Pacific.

Seagrass Beds

Marine Meadows

In cold waters. Unlike corals and mangroves, sea-grasses grow in temperate and even polar waters. Here a giant Pacific octopus is foraging the waters off British Columbia, Canada.

Gentle giant. The dugong is a marine mammal that feeds on seagrasses, here in Vanuatu, Pacific Ocean.

Protecting the young. Seagrasses can form dense beds over sands and silts and provide important shelter for juvenile fish.

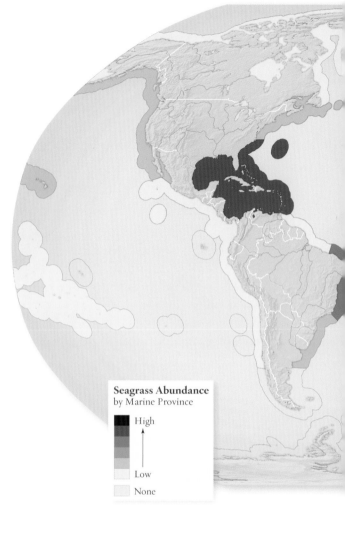

Seagrass Abundance by Marine Province

High

↑

Low

None

PICTURE A MEADOW where turtles and manatees graze. The ebb and flow of water ruffles the foliage like a breeze, while millions of crustaceans, mollusks, and starfish stand in for scurrying insects and rodents.

This underwater field is made of seagrasses, the world's only fully submerged plants with roots in marine and tidal zones. Scientists to date have identified some sixty of these strange and highly specialized plants, originating from a variety of different plant families. None are in fact true grasses, but many have grasslike blades. Given sufficient bright sunlight and a soft bed for their roots, they will spread over vast expanses of the shallow seafloor.

At first glance, these uniform underwater meadows might not seem capable of supporting rich and diverse species. Yet just like grassy fields on land, they are fast growing and highly productive, while the complex network of roots and leaves creates a three-dimensional habitat. Algae and small invertebrates settle and grow on the seagrasses themselves, accompanied by hundreds of species of fish and large invertebrates such as shrimps and crabs. A study of seagrass bed inhabitants in just one bay in temperate Australia found 631 invertebrate species, while in the U.S. state of Florida 113 different kinds of algae were found growing on and among the plants.

Hidden just beyond our crowded shores, seagrass beds are an often-undervalued part of nature. Yet they do much to support other life, including humans. The great range of biodiversity they sustain includes important fishery species, among them crustaceans, mollusks, and fish such as snappers and seahorses. The conch and lobster fisheries from undamaged seagrass areas in countries such as Belize and the Bahamas are worth many millions of dollars in exports every year.

Seagrass beds also improve water quality, by filtering out nutrients and contaminants and trapping sediments. The complex networks formed by their roots help stabilize the seafloor and soften the impacts of waves, preventing erosion not only underwater but also on adjacent shores, and reducing property damage from storms.

With all these benefits largely unknown or ignored, seagrasses around the world are diminishing. Pollution has spurred increased growth of algae and phytoplankton that block vital sunlight from the seabed; coastal development has smothered wide areas with sand and rubble; and in many areas, these

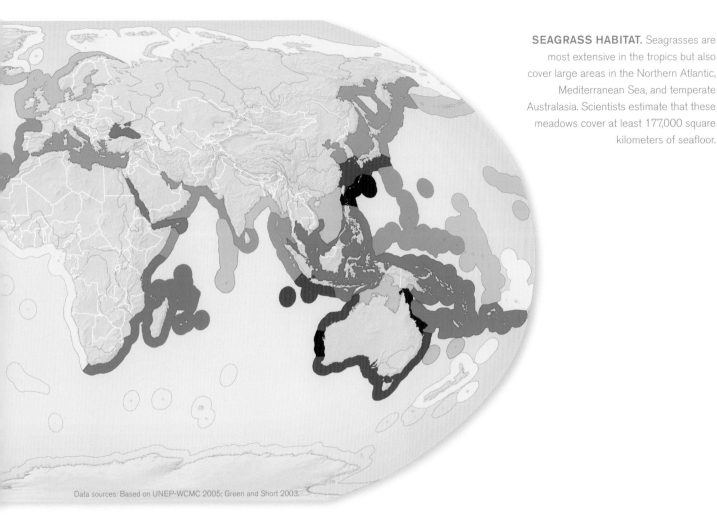

SEAGRASS HABITAT. Seagrasses are most extensive in the tropics but also cover large areas in the Northern Atlantic, Mediterranean Sea, and temperate Australasia. Scientists estimate that these meadows cover at least 177,000 square kilometers of seafloor.

underwater meadows are being plowed under by trawling and dredging. While there are no accurate measures for the overall loss, one conservative estimate suggested that some twelve thousand square kilometers of seagrasses vanished from the mid-1980s to the mid-1990s.

The extraordinary-looking giant dugong, typically weighing in at one-quarter of a metric ton, seems an unlikely savior for the seagrasses, but in Had Chao Mai, Thailand, the appearance of these rare creatures led to a mass media campaign, with local conservation organizations persuading villagers to stop using fishing methods that were damaging the dugong's seagrass food, and to use fish traps instead. Since then the seagrasses have expanded, and, to the delight of the fishers, the recovering environment also led to higher and more profitable fish catches.

Number of Seagrass Species
by Marine Ecoregion

- 14–17
- 12–13
- 8–11
- 2–7
- 1
- None

SEAGRASS SPECIES. As with coral reefs and mangrove forests, the major center of seagrass diversity is in the Central Indo-Pacific Ocean. However, seagrasses have other centers of diversity in the warm temperate waters of southwestern Australia, and in the northwestern Pacific Ocean.

Salt Marshes

Living Filters along Our Coasts

Mark D. Spalding

Remaining European wilderness. Salt marshes are among the only truly natural remaining habitats around the North Sea. One hundred thousand waterfowl overwinter on the north Norfolk coast every year.

James Randklev/Getty Images

Filtering and sheltering. The complex array of tidal creeks and salt marshes (here in Georgia, United States) filters pollutants and provides safe haven for many species.

Barry Truitt/TNC

A smorgasbord for birds and fish. Salt marshes provide rich feeding grounds for wading birds (here whimbrels in Virginia, United States) and fish.

NORTHERN EUROPE has some of Earth's most altered landscapes. Its few remaining forest patches have been managed since record keeping began, while the vast, low-lying wetlands of the Netherlands and eastern England were drained several centuries ago. Even so, you can still see traces of a natural wilderness fringing the edges of these lands: dense pastures of grasses, herbs, and shrubs fringing the sea. These are salt marshes: muddy expanses where land plants have put down their roots. They occur along

the world's calmest coastlines, behind barrier islands or in the sheltering arms of estuaries, protected from waves that would otherwise stir the sediments. With each rising tide, parts of these marshlands are inundated with saltwater that the plants have adapted to withstand. Then the receding waters drain into convoluted networks of channels carving deep into the mud, twisting and turning on their way out to sea.

Salt marshes can be found throughout the world, from the poles to the tropics. Able to tolerate dry and saline settings, they

thrive in desert regions such as the edges of the Arabian Peninsula, Mexico, and parts of northern and western Australia. In contrast with coral reefs, mangroves, and seagrasses, however, they are most abundant in the world's more temperate realms, and it is in the North Atlantic region that they are most diverse in terms of species.

Coastal salt marshes are among the planet's most productive natural factories of food for a great web of life. Birds gather in vast numbers as permanent residents or as

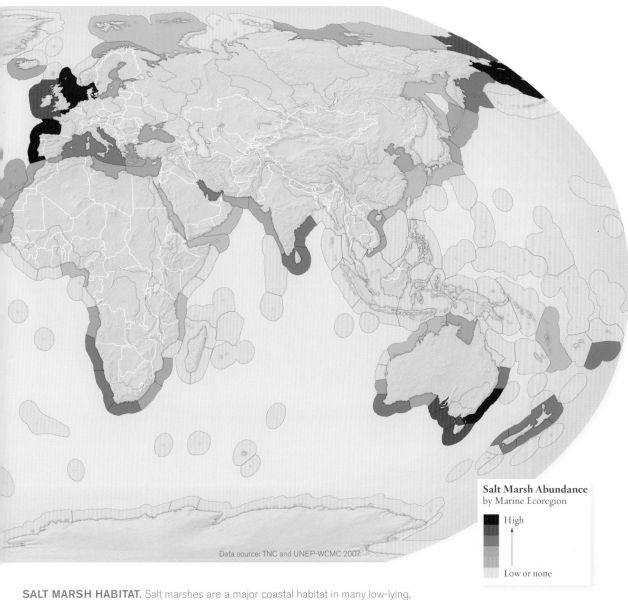

Salt Marsh Abundance
by Marine Ecoregion

High
↑
Low or none

Data source: TNC and UNEP-WCMC 2007.

SALT MARSH HABITAT. Salt marshes are a major coastal habitat in many low-lying, sheltered areas in temperate and northern polar regions. In the tropics, they often mingle with mangroves, but they can also survive in harsher conditions.

seasonal migrants. Some species, such as geese, graze directly on the salt marsh plants, while others feast on the numerous invertebrates found in their muddy pastures. Crustaceans and juvenile fish shelter in the complex maze of channels.

Humans greatly benefit from this abundance, from the wealth of fish, mollusks, and invertebrates that we capture in their vicinity. In addition, wetland plants serve as filters, holding back nutrients and toxic pollutants that would otherwise enter the ocean from coastal settlements. Their leaves,

stems, and roots also help capture drifting sand and silt and hold it together, reducing erosion and often helping build out new land into the sea and lessen the impacts of storms by buffering waves. Yet like wetlands all over the world, salt marshes are highly threatened, and vast areas have already been damaged by marine pollution or converted to agricultural land and urban or industrial development.

But on the Blackwater Estuary in southern England, an alternative future is being tested. Here, since the mid-1990s, the sea

has been allowed back into several former marshes. Seawalls protecting agricultural land have been breached, and salt marshes have returned. The now-regular flow of tides has deposited new sediments, raising the elevation of the newly flooded land. Such "managed realignment" of coastlines offers a much cheaper alternative to maintaining sea defenses. It offers a better future for salt marshes and for the people who live nearby, particularly in an era where sea levels are starting to rise.

High Seas and Deep Oceans

Earth's Uncharted "Inner Space"

Seamounts, Vents, and Seeps
- Vents and seeps
- Seamount

	0 m
	200 m
	3,000 m
	6,500 m
	11,034 m

Data sources:
Kitchingman and Lai 2004; Ramirez-Llodra and Baker 2006.

SEAMOUNTS, VENTS, AND SEEPS. By interrupting the flow of currents, seamounts receive a rich food supply and offer safe harbor to plants and animals—many of which are found only at one or a few adjacent seamounts. Large fishing vessels have begun to exploit the life seamounts nurture and are destroying these isolated communities. On the seafloor, superheated and mineral-rich waters of hydrothermal vents and the methane and sulfide-rich waters that leak out as cold seeps support life as well.

Dr. Bob Embley, NOAA PMEL

Nourishing flows. In deep dark waters, far from the life-giving rays of the sun, the rich mineral nutrients of vents and seeps nourish great densities of bacteria. These in turn feed expansive colonies of clams, worms, and mussels.

OF ALL OF EARTH'S HABITATS, the largest is liquid—the vast open space of the oceans and seas. Oceans cover two-thirds of the planet, yet they remain mostly foreign to humanity. Many more people have journeyed to outer space than have visited even the average depths of the world's oceans, a distance of some 3,800 meters.

Facing recent evidence suggesting that some 40 percent of oceans have been strongly affected by human activities, scientists have joined in a race to understand the open seas—the pelagic ocean—and the seabed before they are irrevocably changed.

Staying still is never an option in the open sea. Throughout its depths, hunters and hunted play their parts in constant motion, shifting with the winds and currents. At the bottom of the food chain are microscopic algae and phytoplankton, which convert solar energy to sugars and nutrients, the stuff of life. They in turn provide meals for plankton, such as crustaceans and jellyfish, which subsequently feed ocean-faring hunters, including tuna, billfish, sharks, whales, and even giant squid, as well as large ocean-roving seabirds such as the albatross.

Scientists continue to identify new ocean species. A few smaller whales are known from just a handful of sightings or from skulls washed onto remote shores. But even as species are still being discovered, they are facing mounting dangers from human development. Fishing vessels have scoured the high seas for centuries, first targeting the great whales, but now tuna, billfish, sharks, and even tiny krill. Whale stocks have collapsed,

COLD-WATER CORAL REEFS. Less famous than their closely related tropical cousins, cold-water reefs harbor extraordinary communities of life. Most have been found in the North Atlantic, where research has concentrated. The largest, Rost Reef, covers one hundred square kilometers off the coast of Norway. Trawl fishing is a major and increasing threat to these reefs.

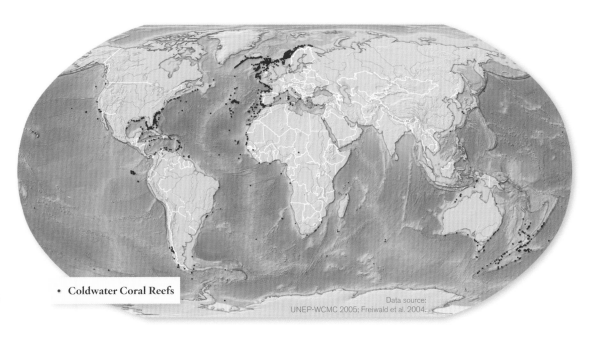

• **Coldwater Coral Reefs**

Data source:
UNEP-WCMC 2005; Freiwald et al. 2004.

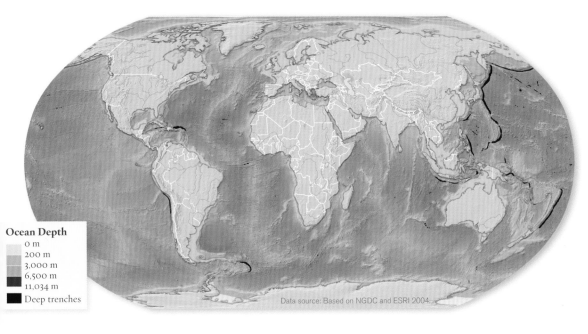

Ocean Depth

	0 m
	200 m
	3,000 m
	6,500 m
	11,034 m
	Deep trenches

Data source: Based on NGDC and ESRI 2004.

DEEP-OCEAN TRENCHES. Two kilometers deeper than Mount Everest is tall, the Mariana Trench is the world's deepest known point. Such exceptionally deep trenches occupy less than 1 percent of the ocean floor, mostly in long narrow channels where one continental plate is being subducted under another. They are exotic worlds dominated by sea cucumbers, mollusks, crustaceans, and worms.

tuna are being overexploited, and many shark species are threatened with extinction.

Spreading over twice the area of all the continents combined, the deep seabed is dark, cold, and crushed by immense water pressure. Until the late nineteenth century, scientists assumed these conditions could not possibly sustain life. But then small samples of the seabed were hauled up, containing previously unknown sea cucumbers, worms, and crustaceans. Modern evidence has revealed there could be as many as ten million still-unidentified types of animals living in

the ocean's muddy depths, primarily concentrated on the undersea mountains known as seamounts and in the communities around hot volcanic vents and cold seeps.

Reports of the declining state of the oceans have prompted efforts to manage them better. There are regulations controlling fishing in deep waters adjacent to many countries, but the "high seas," outside any national jurisdiction, are by nature a much greater challenge. Making up half the total area of Earth, it will take concerted international

collaboration to protect their biodiversity. At this writing, there was not a single protected area in all their expanse. But there have been some victories. A 1986 moratorium on commercial whaling saved a number of whale species from extinction, while bans by several nations in the early 1990s curbed the use of large-scale drift nets in the high seas. The nets—dubbed "walls of death" by some environmentalists—were up to fifty kilometers long. Aimed at tuna and billfish, they caught everything in their path, including dolphins, turtles, and seabirds.

3

Jeff Yanover

Species

IF YOU THINK OF THE SHEER NUMBER of kinds of life on Earth, we humans are simply a twig on a bountiful tree. From tiny ants to towering redwoods, drab fungus to brilliant tropical fish, the species all around us come in a staggering array of sizes, shapes, and colors. Biologists have already described more than 1.5 million unique species, with thousands more discovered every year. There may be as many as fourteen million in all.

Each species evolves to adapt to its home, no matter how harsh the conditions. Emperor penguins brood their single egg through the dark and frigid Antarctic winter. "Extremophile" bacteria thrive in the boiling hot springs of Yellowstone National Park. Saber-toothed viperfish patrol the deepest ocean trenches miles below the water's surface. Throughout the world, species have adapted to every conceivable niche on land and in the water where they can compete for resources to eat and reproduce. Plants root for water and reach for the sun. Herbivores—from seaweed-eating snails to elephants—roam in search of their favorite plants, even as predators hone their hunting skills in search of prey.

These adaptations testify to life's resilience but belie its fragility. Species depend on one another in myriad ways. If one species disappears, the web of life is torn, and other species may suffer. When sea otters along the Pacific coast of North America were decimated by fur hunters, their sea urchin prey overgrazed the kelp, depriving fish, crabs and abalones of their sea

forest homes. Now, as sea otter populations recover, so, too, do the kelp forests and the diversity of life they sustain.

Despite species' natural resilience and adaptability, thousands are at increased risk of extinction because of widespread habitat loss and overexploitation of natural resources. Even once-abundant species such as salmon and migratory birds are becoming rare as we deplete fisheries and change land use. Part of the solution to this threat is to recognize the many ways that humans depend on the world's diversity of species for everything from food, wood, and fiber to medicine. Every day, modern "bioprospectors" discover new benefits from diverse species such as disease-resistant genes from the wild relatives of food crops and cancer-fighting drugs from sea squirts.

To organize our understanding of the world's species, biologists group closely related species into a genus. Related genera (the plural of genus) are further grouped into a hierarchy of families,

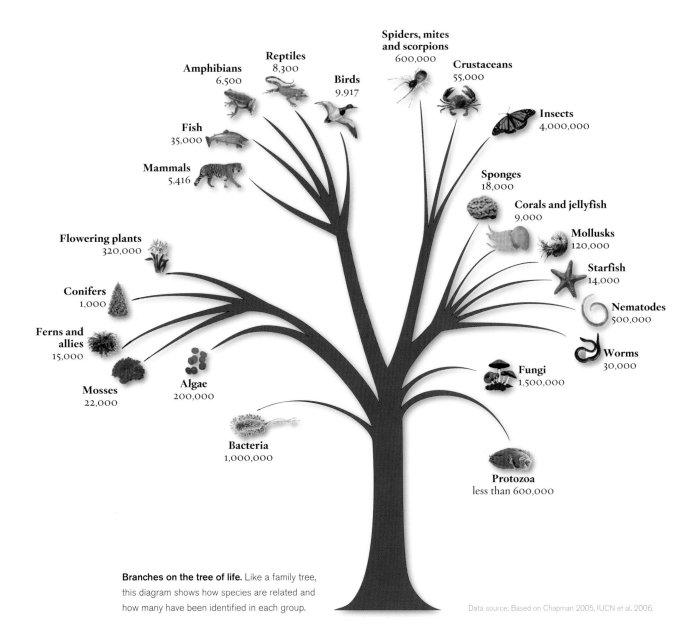

Spiders, mites and scorpions
600,000

Reptiles
8,300

Amphibians
6,500

Birds
9,917

Crustaceans
55,000

Insects
4,000,000

Fish
35,000

Mammals
5,416

Sponges
18,000

Corals and jellyfish
9,000

Mollusks
120,000

Flowering plants
320,000

Starfish
14,000

Conifers
1,000

Nematodes
500,000

Ferns and allies
15,000

Worms
30,000

Mosses
22,000

Algae
200,000

Fungi
1,500,000

Bacteria
1,000,000

Protozoa
less than 600,000

Branches on the tree of life. Like a family tree, this diagram shows how species are related and how many have been identified in each group.

Data source: Based on Chapman 2005, IUCN et al. 2006.

orders, classes, phyla, and kingdoms. The five kingdoms encompass plants, animals, fungi, bacteria, and organisms called archaeons, and they are subdivided into phyla that describe fundamental body plans. For example, the animal kingdom comprises phyla such as vertebrates (like us), arthropods (e.g., insects, spiders, and crabs), and mollusks (e.g., snails and clams). This hierarchical organization of species is often described as the "tree of life."

This section of the atlas features maps that show the diversity of several familiar groups of species—plants, fish, amphibians, reptiles, birds, and mammals. Each page highlights some of the important roles that these species play in nature and the benefits they provide to people. These pages also illustrate some of the factors that make species vulnerable and what people can do to protect them. The maps show global data about where species occur, portraying a picture of life on Earth

that was not possible only a few years ago. Patterns of endemic species (those found in only one ecoregion) and evolutionary distinction are also presented in this section. At the same time, the current lack of maps for other groups of species—such as the insects and most marine species—is a reminder that exciting new discoveries are still to be made and that opportunities abound to improve our understanding about the natural world.

Plants

A Vital Variety

Karen Foerstel/TNC

Green lungs. The green leaves of plants absorb carbon dioxide along with moisture and sunlight, in turn releasing oxygen that we and other animals need to survive.

Unique landscape. The Eastern Cape region of South Africa is home to over 6,200 unique plants, like the "red hot poker" flower, that are found nowhere else.

Jennifer Molnar

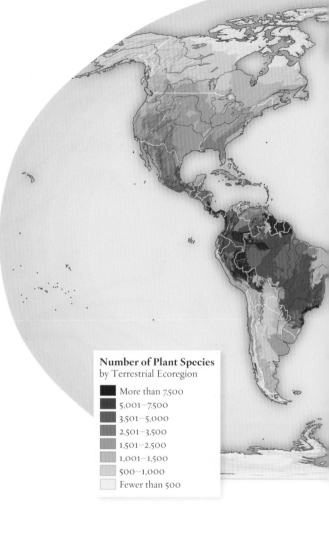

Number of Plant Species
by Terrestrial Ecoregion

- More than 7,500
- 5,001–7,500
- 3,501–5,000
- 2,501–3,500
- 1,501–2,500
- 1,001–1,500
- 500–1,000
- Fewer than 500

PLANTS ARE OUR LIFE PARTNERS, sustaining humans and animals by converting sunlight, water, and carbon dioxide into food and oxygen. Scientists estimate that there are up to 420,000 species of the so-called higher plants—trees, vines, grasses, and crops such as vegetables, fruits, and legumes—which, unlike algae and moss, have veins that transport water and sap. They are found everywhere on land except for the surface of glaciers and the driest deserts, with new species discovered every year.

People rely on plant variety in many ways. Aspirin, morphine, and quinine are just a few important medicines directly derived from some of the millions of different chemical compounds found in plants. Taxol,

a compound discovered in the bark of the Pacific yew tree in 1967, is now used to treat various kinds of cancer.

Plant variety is also important in agriculture, where a broad array of genetic material ensures against the risk that a single pest or pathogen could wipe out an entire crop. Wild relatives of crops such as corn, rice, potatoes, and wheat can provide genes that improve yield, nutritional value, and disease resistance. When the southern corn blight attacked North American farms in 1970, scientists found genes in wild plants that, when bred into corn, made them immune to the blight.

From a global perspective, conservationists are interested in areas of the world where plant species not only are numerous but also

are most unusual. Throughout the world, endemic plant species (those found in only one area and nowhere else) have evolved in isolation, adapting to local conditions that can include extreme temperatures and sustained droughts. The small geographic ranges of endemic plants put them at special risk, since a change in their habitat could drive them to extinction.

Endemic plants are often found on islands, such as Hawaii and Ecuador's Galápagos Islands, although the Cape Region of South Africa and much of California also stand out for the number of unique species they host.

Land conversion is the single biggest threat to plant biodiversity today, raising

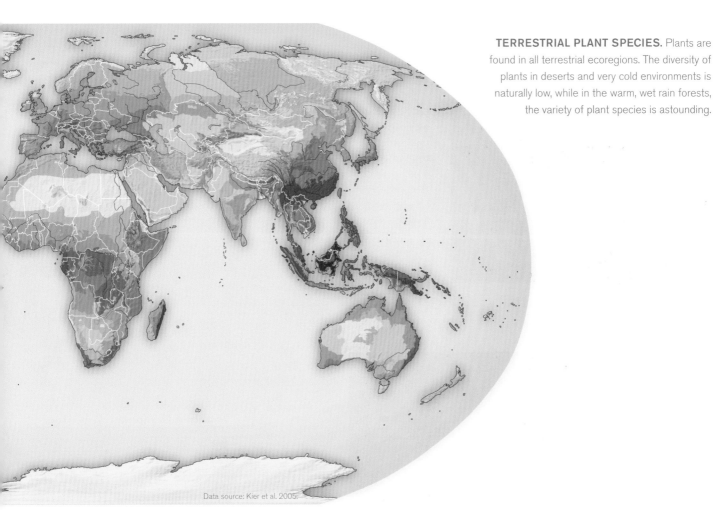

TERRESTRIAL PLANT SPECIES. Plants are found in all terrestrial ecoregions. The diversity of plants in deserts and very cold environments is naturally low, while in the warm, wet rain forests, the variety of plant species is astounding.

Data source: Kier et al. 2005.

the stakes for private groups and government agencies working to protect large areas of underdeveloped land for many reasons. These include aesthetic values. Charles Darwin, in 1859, wrote, "It is interesting to contemplate an entangled bank, clothed with many plants of many kinds….There is grandeur in this view of life."

More recently, there is interest in the ecosystem services, such as water filtration and carbon sequestration, that are delivered by untrammeled natural vegetation. As scientists build their case for the critical importance of the diversity of plants on Earth, this value, too, has begun to guide decisions as to where to invest in conservation.

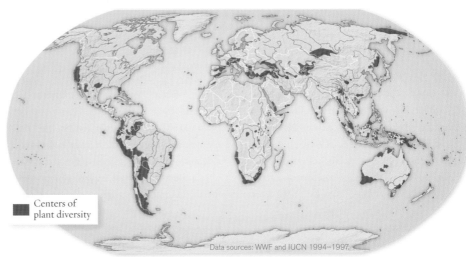

Centers of plant diversity

Data sources: WWF and IUCN 1994–1997.

CENTERS OF PLANT DIVERSITY. These centers are places that have high concentrations of species unique to a region or simply very high numbers of species.

Freshwater Fish

A Diverse Cast

Flip Nicklin/Minden Pictures

Belly-up but still breathing. The tiny blotched upside-down catfish, found in Africa's Congo River, swims belly-up to feed on insect larvae floating on the water's surface.

Expensive tastes place relics in peril. The world's increasing hunger for caviar, the sturgeon's eggs, drives legal and illegal markets that threaten all seven species in the Caspian Sea with extinction.

Bridget Besaw

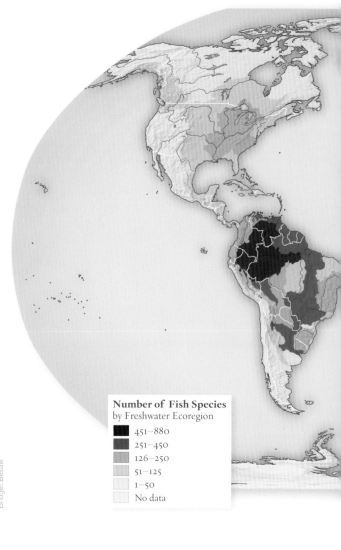

Number of Fish Species
by Freshwater Ecoregion

- 451–880
- 251–450
- 126–250
- 51–125
- 1–50
- No data

THE UPSIDE-DOWN CATFISH swims belly-up to gobble floating insect larvae. Tiny piranhas have been known to chomp on human swimmers with their sharp teeth, though their fame as vicious hunters of people is allegedly only a myth. The beluga sturgeon grows up to six meters long, weighing 1,200 kilograms, making it one of the world's biggest vertebrates.

These are just a few stars of a cast of more than fourteen thousand species of freshwater fish, accounting for roughly one-quarter of all the world's vertebrate species. Most fish can be found in the world's largest rivers, including the Amazon (home to the piranha), Mekong, and Congo. Many others reside in just one river or lake. Africa's Rift Valley Lakes, for instance, host hundreds of unique species found nowhere else in the world.

Some fish are long-distance migrants that undertake freshwater journeys of more than a hundred kilometers (some, like the renowned sockeye salmon, even swim over a thousand kilometers), returning to spawn after a life at sea. These travelers help feed life throughout an entire river basin as they spawn and die. Terrestrial animals, including bears, raccoons, and eagles, feed on eggs and salmon carcasses, after which their excrement helps fertilize local plants.

Humans throughout the world depend on fish for protein. The global wild catch of freshwater fish measured in 2004 was 9.2 million metric tons—90 percent of which was caught in Asia and Africa. Hundreds of millions of impoverished residents of these two continents depend on such fish for protein.

Yet like so many other living species, freshwater fish now face serious threats from overharvesting, loss of habitat, pollution, and competition from invasive species. Human activities, like fishing, farming, and dam building, contribute to these dangers. For the beluga and six other sturgeon species native to the Volga River and Caspian Sea, it is the growing worldwide demand for caviar—these fishes' eggs. These "living fossils," which have remained practically unchanged for the last two hundred million years, are now threatened with extinction due to this booming luxury market and new dams blocking their annual spawning journeys. In the 1960s, some twenty-six thousand Belugas were entering the Volga each year to spawn; by 2002, this number had dropped to fewer than three thousand. Similarly, the legal sturgeon catch in the North Caspian Sea shrank from more than twenty-three

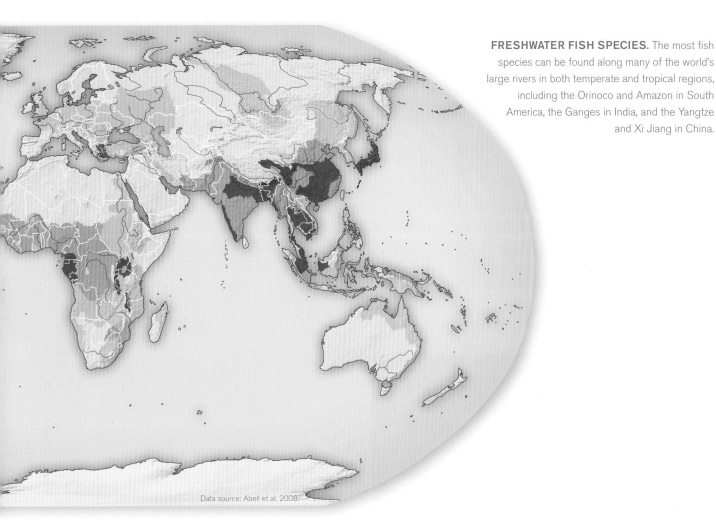

FRESHWATER FISH SPECIES. The most fish species can be found along many of the world's large rivers in both temperate and tropical regions, including the Orinoco and Amazon in South America, the Ganges in India, and the Yangtze and Xi Jiang in China.

thousand metric tons per year in 1975 to less than five hundred metric tons twenty-nine years later. The annual illegal trade in Russia alone in 2001 was estimated at $400 million.

The pressures on freshwater fish are so complex and intense that very few species have managed to recover. A dramatic exception is the revival of the shortnose sturgeon population in New York City's Hudson River, which has more than quadrupled since the 1970s. This hopeful fish tale owes much of its success to the U.S. Endangered Species Act of 1973, which has required persistent collaborative efforts by government agencies to conserve habitat, ban harvests, reduce bycatch, and clean up the river.

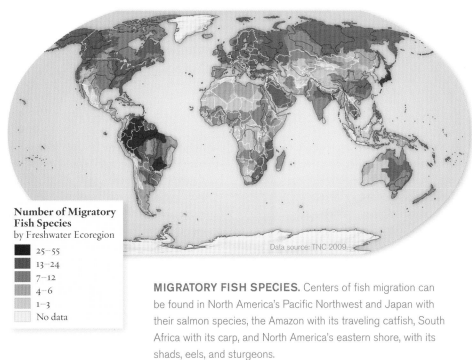

Number of Migratory Fish Species
by Freshwater Ecoregion

- 25–55
- 13–24
- 7–12
- 4–6
- 1–3
- No data

MIGRATORY FISH SPECIES. Centers of fish migration can be found in North America's Pacific Northwest and Japan with their salmon species, the Amazon with its traveling catfish, South Africa with its carp, and North America's eastern shore, with its shads, eels, and sturgeons.

Amphibians
Fragile Markers of the Planet's Health

J. M. Storey/www.carleton.ca/~kbstorey

Frogsicle. The wood frog's body freezes in cold winter months, before thawing in the spring. It is one of the few amphibian species that can live in cold climates.

Removing invaders. Yellow-legged frogs in the mountains of California, United States, rebounded after introduced trout were removed from lakes, giving hope for larger-scale restoration.

Ellen Schafhauser/Phase.com/thepalebluedot

Number of Amphibian Species by Freshwater Ecoregion

- More than 201
- 121–200
- 81–120
- 56–80
- 31–55
- 16–30
- 6–15
- 1–5
- None

THE WORD *amphibian* comes from the Greek and means "double life." It refers to the watery larval adolescence and terrestrial adulthood shared by most of the world's 6,453 described amphibian species—including, most commonly, frogs and toads, plus more than 578 different types of newts and salamanders and 176 legless, earthworm-like caecilians. Even so, more than 1,700 amphibian species live their lives entirely on land. Some live only in trees, while others have adapted in even more unusual ways to their environments.

Wood frogs have one of the most remarkable survival strategies. They endure winters above the Arctic Circle by freezing—their breathing and heart actually stop. Come spring, they thaw out, to feed and reproduce before the winter returns.

Adult amphibians feed on insects, an important means of pest control. They also provide food for many other animals, including birds, mammals, fish, reptiles, and even spiders.

Yet neither amphibians' creative survival tactics nor their important ecological niche has helped them skirt disaster in recent decades. In 2004, a consortium of conservation groups released the first global survey of amphibians, revealing that nearly one in three species had suffered drastic population declines, while as many as 159 may have gone extinct—even from seemingly pristine parts of the world, such as protected rain forests in Costa Rica and Australia. Their precipitous decline in modern years is a clear sign that something serious is going wrong in their environment—and ours.

The problem is that there are so many possible suspects to blame, separately and together, for the species' collapse. Habitat loss, climate change, and various types of pollution are just a few of the candidates that have left amphibians more vulnerable to the infectious diseases that deliver the coup de grâce—including a newly discovered disease caused by the Chytrid fungus. That is why efforts with any hope of helping amphibians survive must include a variety of

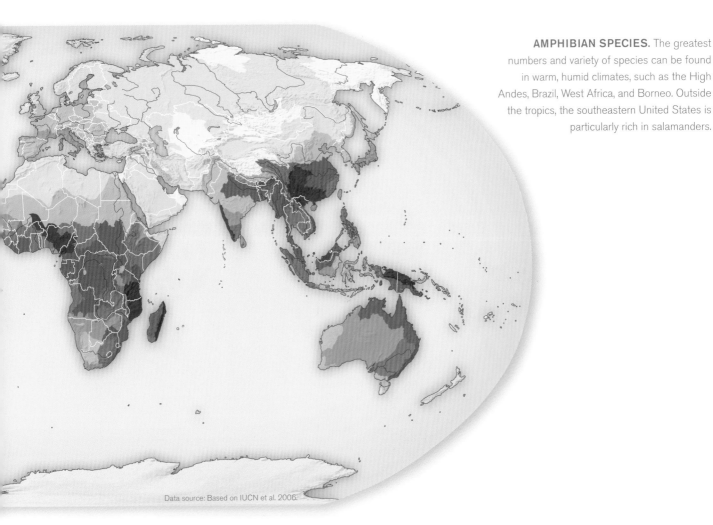

Data source: Based on IUCN et al. 2006.

AMPHIBIAN SPECIES. The greatest numbers and variety of species can be found in warm, humid climates, such as the High Andes, Brazil, West Africa, and Borneo. Outside the tropics, the southeastern United States is particularly rich in salamanders.

Data source: Stuart et al. 2004.

approaches, ranging from habitat conservation to captive breeding of species.

Down at the newt's eye level, one proven strategy helping species rebound is the removal of invasive species. Researchers from the University of California employed this tactic beginning in the mid-1990s to determine whether they could help the mountain yellow-legged frog revive in the pools and lakes of California's Sierra Nevada Mountains. Trout that had been introduced in the region since the mid-1880s had been eating the frogs and had nearly wiped out all traces of them. But soon after the trout were removed from a few lakes, the frogs returned, sending an encouraging sign for potentially broader future efforts.

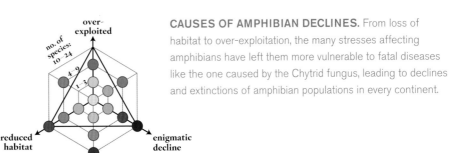

no. of species:
10–24
4–9
1–3

over-exploited

reduced habitat

enigmatic decline

CAUSES OF AMPHIBIAN DECLINES. From loss of habitat to over-exploitation, the many stresses affecting amphibians have left them more vulnerable to fatal diseases like the one caused by the Chytrid fungus, leading to declines and extinctions of amphibian populations in every continent.

Reptiles

Prehistoric Survivors

Number of Lizard and Snake Species
by Terrestrial Ecoregion

- More than 300
- 201–300
- 151–200
- 101–150
- 51–100
- 25–50
- Fewer than 25
- None

Data source: WWF WildFinder 2006.

LIZARD AND SNAKE SPECIES. While the greatest numbers of terrestrial reptile species occur in tropical rain forests, many have also adapted to hotter, drier climates of deserts and grasslands, and two species can even survive in the Arctic Circle.

Andy Drumm/TNC

Instilling fear. Indonesia's Komodo dragon, the world's largest reptile, can quickly ambush its prey—a deer, goat, or other large animal—as it reaches speeds of twenty kilometers per hour in short bursts.

REPTILES HAVE ENDURED since before the age of their giant, less fortunate distant cousins, the dinosaurs, and are now found on every continent except Antarctica. A clue to their survival can be found in some of the remarkable ways they have adapted to their various homes. Indonesia's giant Komodo dragon can smell prey from miles away and patiently wait in ambush to bring down deer, goats and even large water buffalo, while the tiny gecko is able to climb upside down on tree limbs and ceilings to pursue its prey, due to a kind of static electricity emanating from hundreds of thousands of tiny, flat-tipped hairs sticking out from its toes. A desert tortoise survives droughts by means of its large bladder, which holds enough water and, separately, liquid waste, to allow it to survive several months without a drink.

Nearly eight thousand species of reptiles have been identified, the vast majority of them scaly, egg-laying lizards, snakes, and amphisbaenids, or "worm-lizards," plus about three hundred species of turtles and tortoises, and two dozen species of crocodiles, gharials, and caimans.

Reptiles play an important role in their habitat. Many are predators, such as rodent-hunting snakes that help control pest populations. Other reptiles—especially those that live in freshwater—tidy up their habitat by scavenging on dead animals.

As with so many other creatures, however, reptiles today are vulnerable to a broad array of threats stemming from human development: from pollution to habitat loss to the escalating wildlife trade. People historically have coveted exotic lizards, snakes, and turtles as pets, while their skins are prized

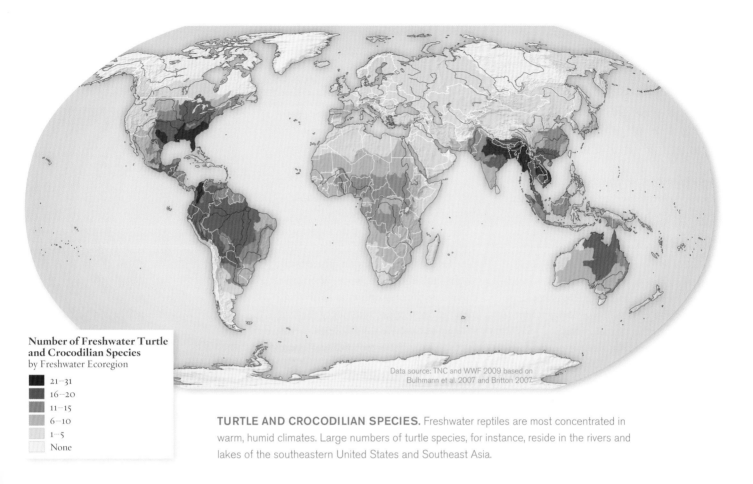

Number of Freshwater Turtle and Crocodilian Species
by Freshwater Ecoregion

- ■ 21–31
- ■ 16–20
- ■ 11–15
- ■ 6–10
- ■ 1–5
- □ None

Data source: TNC and WWF 2009 based on Bulhmann et al. 2007 and Britton 2007.

TURTLE AND CROCODILIAN SPECIES. Freshwater reptiles are most concentrated in warm, humid climates. Large numbers of turtle species, for instance, reside in the rivers and lakes of the southeastern United States and Southeast Asia.

Nigel J Dennis

Susceptible to subtle shifts. With sexes determined by differences in egg temperature, South African Nile crocodiles are threatened by an invasive plant shading nests, causing more female births.

Andrea Seale/SuperStock

Pitching in to save sea turtles. In Brazil, local residents and fishermen help out a sea turtle "hatch and release" program, while former turtle hunters are paid to monitor their coastal habitats.

in leather products. Particularly in Asia, turtles are a frequent ingredient in meals and traditional medicine. By the first decade of the twenty-first century, half of the world's crocodile species and 40 percent of freshwater turtles were threatened with extinction.

Climate change is a particularly insidious danger for reptiles, as many are sensitive to seemingly subtle changes in temperature and rainfall. For example, the gender of many species is determined by the temperature of their eggs during incubation, meaning that seemingly subtle changes could upset the balance between males and females.

Given the multitude of threats facing reptiles, effective conservation needs to include broad action on many fronts, including habitat protection and control of poaching. To save some of the most threatened species, some environmental groups have supported "hatch and release" programs, in which young reptiles are bred in captivity and released to supplement wild populations. Six of the world's seven sea turtle species are on the brink of extinction. In Brazil, coastal residents' traditional diet of sea turtle meat and eggs had threatened the five local

species. But beginning in 1980, the Tamar Project, run by the federal government, has worked to protect these species and educate local communities about their plight. Local residents, including fishermen, have come to account for 90 percent of Tamar's workers. Former turtle hunters are being paid to monitor spawning and feeding areas on one thousand kilometers of coastline and bring eggs collected from beach nests to hatcheries for protection. By 2003, six hundred thousand baby turtles were being released every year.

Migrations

MARTIN WIKELSKI
DAVID S. WILCOVE

EVERYTHING IS IN FLOW, everything moves. *Panta rei,* as the Greek philosopher Heraclitus rightly stated in approximately 500 BC, implying that movement is the essence of life. Indeed, there is no organism on Earth that does not move during some part of its life cycle, whether as pollen, seed, larva, juvenile, or adult. The distances range from a meter or less (in the case of a fruit that drops from a tree and takes root) to thousands of miles (in the case of wandering albatrosses and leatherback turtles). Most of these movements represent dispersal or migration events, and humans have been fascinated by and dependent on such events from their very own beginnings. In North America, Native American tribes developed cultures centered around migrating bison and salmon, while some Eskimo cultures depended on whales caught during their seasonal migrations into Arctic waters.

There is no all-encompassing definition for migration, nor is the distinction between migration and dispersal always clear. In general, we think of migration in the context of round-trip, seasonal journeys, such as those of songbirds, whales, and wildebeest. And we think of dispersal as involving unidirectional travel, typically when an animal leaves its natal home to find a territory or home range of its own.

But think about monarch butterflies: The adult monarchs that leave their wintering sites in central Mexico in March generally make it as far as the southeastern United States, where they lay their eggs and die. Their progeny continue the journey northward, also laying eggs and dying, and the process may continue for additional generations, until the butterflies have repopulated eastern North America. The last generation to be born in the summer then reverses course and heads back to Mexico, to the same mountaintops last inhabited by their great-grandparents. This sort of intergenerational migration may be typical of other

insects as well, including some crickets and grasshoppers in Africa, America, or Australia, as well as continental European aphids that invade England every year by using winds from the south to lift themselves over the English Channel, parachuting down onto fields and farms.

The fact that so many species migrate and that so many migratory species are abundant suggests that migration is beneficial for the individuals that move. Alternatively, it could be the only option an individual has—better to migrate in misery than stay in one place and die a rapid death. To answer questions about the costs and benefits of a life on the move, we must know a great deal about what individual animals do when they migrate and how they decide whether to stay or go. Unfortunately, scientists are still largely ignorant about the trade-offs involved in a migratory versus sedentary life history.

Indeed, it is disturbing how little we know about what individual animals do during migration, particularly about the key questions of when they decide to go, where they go, where they chose to stop en route, and, most important, where and when they eventually die. An ornithologist may bargain with an African kid to get all the bird bands the boy wears as jewelry on a chain around his neck. Assuming that those birds died locally, the scientist can then connect dots, plotting the location where the bird was first banded and the area where it subsequently died. If the ornithologist is exceptionally lucky, the bird in question may have been seen or recaptured in between at a stopover site, providing additional data on the migratory pathway of the animal. But all of this leaves us still ignorant about the question of whether this bird represents a typical member of its species or an unlucky individual that died because it was sick or was blown off course by a freakish storm en route to some other place. How much more informative it would be to follow the individual migrants throughout their journeys, whether they be birds, mammals, insects, or fish.

Fortunately, technology has advanced sufficiently on so many fronts that we will soon

Sandhill crane migration, Nebraska, United States

be able to piece together the movements of individuals of many species on a global scale. Sophisticated pattern analysis allows whale researchers to semiautomatically scan through hundreds of digital photographs taken of whales around the world. By identifying unique markings on the flukes and backs of these animals, these computer programs enable researchers to piece together the movements of individual whales with a

speed and accuracy that was unimaginable just a few years ago.

Satellite tracking devices are now small enough to include solar chargers, enabling Swedish researchers to track juvenile ospreys well into their adulthood and even to their deaths. Satellite tags weighing less than 10 grams were used recently to track the flight of 340-gram bar-tailed godwits as they flew across the Pacific from Alaska to New Zealand in one go. Many seabirds, sea

mammals, and fish make similar voyages, as evidenced by the tracking of tuna across the Atlantic or white sharks across the Pacific. At the same time, miniaturization now allows us to track larger insects such as dragonflies during their migratory flights. What we learn from these migrations is that the world is much more connected than we ever assumed. And again, we are just scratching the surface of what we could know—and will know—in the not-too-distant future.

It is quite possible that further studies will profoundly change our perception of just how dangerous and difficult migration really is. It is true that of the twenty billion or more songbirds that migrate every year, only every second or third one makes it back the next year. But do they vanish because of the difficulties associated with migration or because of factors unrelated to migration?

At least for some species, evidence is accumulating that migration, even long-distance

Monarch butterflies, the world's best-known migratory insect

migration, can be surprisingly safe. Jeff Hoover has shown that up to 80 percent of the adult prothonotary warblers that nest in southern Illinois and migrate to somewhere in Mexico or Central America for the winter will return to their original breeding sites the next spring, suggesting a total life span way beyond eight years. Their survival odds are probably much better than those of most of the songbird species that stay in southern Illinois year-round. Thus, at least for those prothonotary warblers, migration is not as-sociated with a markedly shorter life span.

Ironically, all of these technological breakthroughs and scientific discoveries are coming at precisely the time when some of the most dramatic migrations in the ani-mal kingdom are disappearing as a result of human meddling. Habitat destruction, overhunting, the creation of obstacles and barriers, and global climate change have taken a toll on many migratory species and threaten many more. North Americans will never again experience skies blackened by migrating passenger pigeons or Eskimo curlews. In other cases the species remain, but the spectacle is gone. South Africa still has plenty of springbok, but South Africans will never again witness hundreds of thou-sands or millions of them blanketing the arid Karoo grasslands. In North America, the bison is no longer in danger of extinc-tion, but the vast herds that sustained tens of thousands of Native Americans and astounded the first white settlers are a thing of the past. Declining populations of songbirds in Europe and North America;

salmon in the Pacific Northwest; wildebeests, elephants, and zebras in parts of East Africa; and bighorn sheep and pronghorn in North America are evidence that the phenomenon of migration is in trouble.

To preserve the remaining migrations, we will clearly need additional scientific research. For example, we need to fill the gaps in our knowledge about the behavior and physiology of individual migrants. How stressful is migration for them? What types of rest and refueling places do they need? How do changes in land use affect their mi-gratory behavior?

At the same time, we will need to change our approach to conservation in two fun-damental ways. First, migratory species are oblivious to the borders and boundaries that mean so much to us. Conserving migrants often requires an unprecedented degree of coordination at all levels—local, national, and international. This is easier said than done, given the intensity of turf battles between agencies, between states, and between nations. Second, to maintain the abundance of migratory species (which is, after all, what makes migration such an awe-inspiring phenomenon), we must be proactive with respect to conservation measures. If we wait until migratory species are endangered before attempting to secure their habitats or limit their harvest, we will lose the glory of migration. This, too, runs afoul of our customary approach to conservation, which tends to be highly reactive.

That said, there are promising signs of both greater cooperation and earlier intervention. Partners in Flight, a coalition of U.S. federal agencies, state agencies, nonprofit conservation organizations, corporate landowners, and academic scientists, was created in 1990 to develop a coordinated, proactive strategy for conserving North America's nongame birds. In February 2007, the U.S. Western Governors' Association approved a policy resolution calling for the protection of "wildlife migration corridors." Responding to losses of migratory routes for elk, bighorn sheep, mule deer, and other animals due to energy development and sprawl, the governors pledged to work together to protect those routes.

On the international front, the Convention on the Conservation of Migratory Species of Wild Animals, also known as the Bonn Convention, was created as far back as 1979.

Over one hundred nations are signatories to the treaty. Although noble in scope and ambition, the Bonn Convention has been something of a disappointment. It has no enforcement mechanism, relying instead on voluntary agreements between nations to achieve its goals. To date, it has come to the aid of relatively few migratory species, but this may change as public awareness of the problems facing migratory species grows.

In the long run, if we are successful at saving the great migrations, we will have created a network of interconnected reserves around the world, we will have curtailed the excessive harvest (for sport, commerce, or sustenance) of many species, and we will have come to grips with the crisis of climate change. In short, we will have gone a long way toward protecting much of Earth's imperiled biodiversity, migratory or not. And we will have given future generations the chance to marvel at the greatest show on Earth, the mass movements of wildlife through the land, air, and water. *Panta rei.*

MARTIN WIKELSKI IS THE DIRECTOR OF THE DEPARTMENT OF MIGRATION AND IMMUNO-ECOLOGY, MAX PLANCK INSTITUTE FOR ORNITHOLOGY, AND A PROFESSOR AND THE CHAIR OF ORNITHOLOGY AT KONSTANZ UNIVERSITY, GERMANY.

DAVID S. WILCOVE IS A PROFESSOR IN THE WOODROW WILSON SCHOOL AND THE DEPARTMENT OF ECOLOGY AND EVOLUTIONARY BIOLOGY, PRINCETON UNIVERSITY.

Birds

Everyday, Everywhere Wildlife

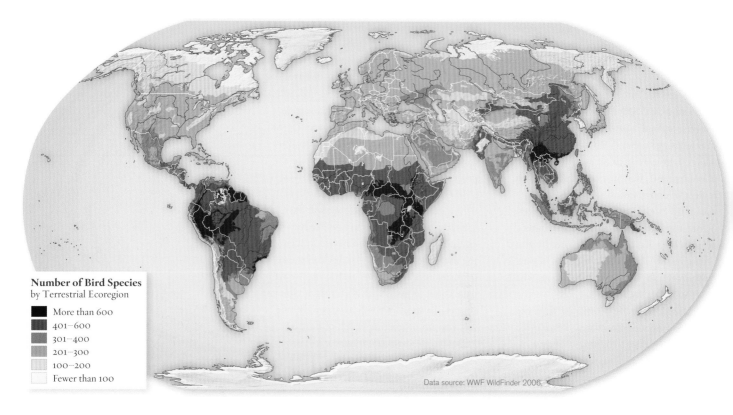

Number of Bird Species
by Terrestrial Ecoregion

- More than 600
- 401–600
- 301–400
- 201–300
- 100–200
- Fewer than 100

Data source: WWF WildFinder 2006.

TERRESTRIAL BIRD SPECIES. While birds live in all ecoregions on Earth, more than one-third of all documented bird species have been found in Central and South America—3,751 species in all.

Pigeon of the Southern Ocean. The Cape petrel, also known as the Cape pigeon, lives much of its life at sea feeding mostly on crustaceans by pecking at the sea surface, hence its nickname.

Timothy Boucher

Whale of a bill. The shoebill, or whale-headed stork, has a massive bill that allows it to capture lungfish, amphibians, turtles, and even young crocodiles in dense swamps in eastern Africa.

Timothy Boucher

THERE ARE PLENTY of reasons why birds, out of all of Earth's creatures, have attracted such a passionate human following. From the iridescent green and red flowing plumage of the resplendent quetzal to the drab brown thrasher, which has more than two thousand songs in its repertoire, birds catch the eye and ear alike.

Birds' behavior also captures imaginations. They have inspired generations of poets simply by taking flight, and astounded scientists with migrations between summer breeding and winter feeding grounds covering as many as 11,500 kilometers—that being the epic annual journey of the bar-tailed godwit, from Alaska to New Zealand, in eight days of nonstop flying.

For most people, birds are the most visible form of wildlife. Even some city dwellers can see a dozen or more different species in a single day. Others—devoted aficionados—travel the world in the hopes of spotting many of the almost ten thousand species described to date. Bird-watching is a lucrative industry throughout much of the world, with an estimated forty-two million U.S. bird-watchers spending more than $20 billion annually on travel, binoculars, feed, and even high-tech gizmos such as TV "nest cams." The economic benefits extend around the world, with bird fairs, guiding, and lodging catering to birders and boosting local economies as remote as Ecuador's tiny town of Mindo, where savvy local entrepreneurs have mastered the art of attracting elusive antpittas for delighted observers.

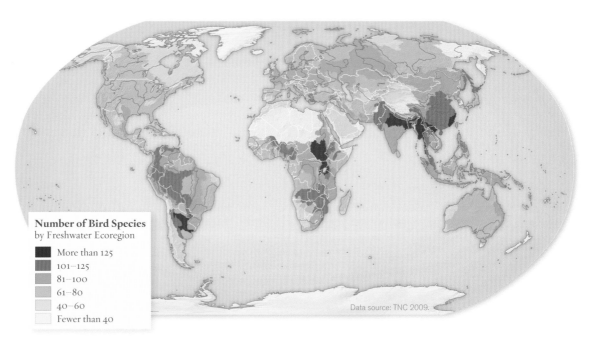

FRESHWATER BIRD SPECIES. More than eight hundred species of birds require the fragile, specialized habitat that rivers and wetlands provide. The East African wetlands have the highest diversity of freshwater birds, numbering more than 150 species.

Number of Bird Species
by Freshwater Ecoregion

- More than 125
- 101–125
- 81–100
- 61–80
- 40–60
- Fewer than 40

Data source: TNC 2009.

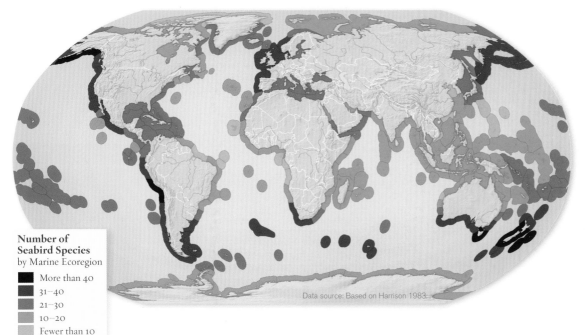

Number of Seabird Species
by Marine Ecoregion

- More than 40
- 31–40
- 21–30
- 10–20
- Fewer than 10

Data source: Based on Harrison 1983.

SEABIRD SPECIES. The greatest diversity of the world's seabirds can be found in the seas off the southern islands of New Zealand. There, the cold Southern Ocean offers particularly abundant resources of krill, fish, and other marine life on which to feed.

At the same time, birds, like all wildlife, are functioning parts of their ecosystems. Hummingbirds, sunbirds, and other nectar-loving species pollinate flowering plants, while fruit-eating birds like toucans and hornbills efficiently disperse seeds. Scavengers such as vultures clean the landscape, checking the spread of disease, by eating carrion, while predatory birds control rats and insects, including grasshoppers, caterpillars, and mosquitoes.

Despite all their benefits, however, the toll on birds is mounting. Researchers estimate that as many as 12 percent of all bird species may be extinct by 2100, and many more may be "functionally extinct." The principal causes involve habitat loss. Deforestation, conversion of grasslands, and the draining of wetlands is eliminating food sources, shelter, and breeding territory. Less visible but no less harmful are illegal trade, disease, and even long-line fishing, which drowns seabirds as they dive to eat the bait in the hooks.

Several bird species have responded well to conservation efforts, however. The bald eagle, the U.S. national icon, has become a symbol of this potential. In the wake of conservation measures that included the banning of the pesticide DDT, the eagle, which had been on the verge of extinction in the continental United States, has rebounded, and now it can even be seen soaring around Washington, DC.

Mammals

Shared Destiny with Our Closest Kin

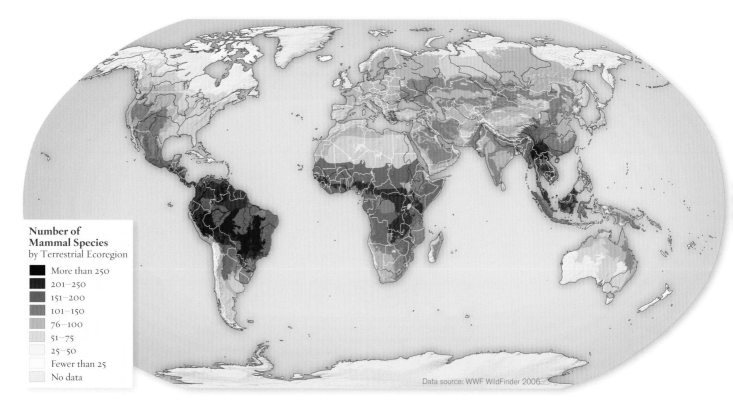

Number of Mammal Species
by Terrestrial Ecoregion

- More than 250
- 201–250
- 151–200
- 101–150
- 76–100
- 51–75
- 25–50
- Fewer than 25
- No data

Data source: WWF WildFinder 2006.

TERRESTRIAL MAMMAL SPECIES. While large numbers are found in warm climates, many mammal species are able to thrive in Earth's coldest regions with adaptations that include furry bodies and warm blood.

Slip sliding away. Up to six feet long, the endangered South American giant river otter or "river wolf" has been hunted extensively and only a few thousand remain in the wild.

Steffen Reichle

Making a recovery. Elephants are rebounding in parts of southern Africa due to conservation efforts and a ban on the trade of ivory.

Kenneth K. Coe

ABOUT 210 MILLION years ago, a small shrew, *Morganucodon oehleri*, known colloquially as "Morgie," lived among dinosaurs in Europe and Asia. Measuring only ten centimeters long, this earliest-known mammal scurried unobtrusively beneath the lumbering forms of the giant reptiles. Yet when the dinosaurs went extinct, descendants of the small shrew survived. And today, it is believed that every one of the planet's more than five thousand species of mammals—including humans— carry some of Morgie's DNA.

From this simple beginning, mammals have evolved into a dazzling array. Tigers, lions, and orcas reign at the top of their food chains, keeping the numbers of lower-level species in check by dining on them. Grazers, such as antelope, caribou, and whales, migrate long distances, seeking food and breeding grounds according to the seasons. Some mammals are ecological engineers, the most famous of these being beavers, which dam rivers to form ponds, creating habitat for birds and other species.

The great majority of mammals, from rodents to manatees to humans, carry their young in the womb until fully developed. But some 250 species of marsupials, such as kangaroos and opossums, give birth to young that keep developing while in their mother's pouch. And three species of mammals—the duck-billed platypus and two spiny anteaters—lay eggs.

Humans since ancient times have had a special relationship with many mammals, lavishing affection on pet dogs and cats,

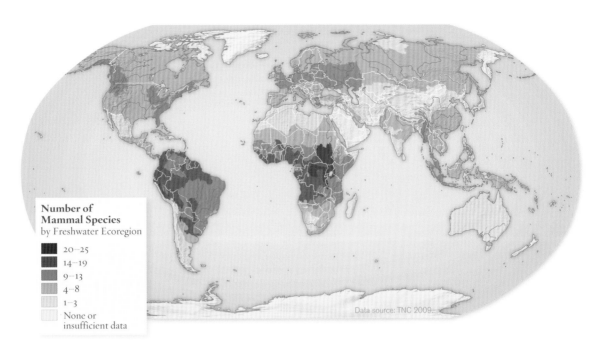

FRESHWATER MAMMAL SPECIES. Although mammals that feed and spend most of their time in and around freshwater are found in many parts of the world, the highest concentrations of species are in regions with tropical forests and lots of flowing water.

Number of Mammal Species
by Freshwater Ecoregion

- 20–25
- 14–19
- 9–13
- 4–8
- 1–3
- None or insufficient data

Data source: TNC 2009

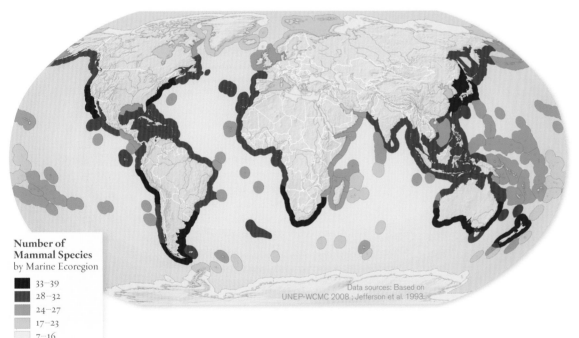

MARINE MAMMAL SPECIES. The most species are found in temperate regions, where upwelling zones provide water rich in nutrients. Some marine mammals live mostly in the open ocean, often migrating great distances between continents.

Number of Mammal Species
by Marine Ecoregion

- 33–39
- 28–32
- 24–27
- 17–23
- 7–16

Data sources: Based on UNEP-WCMC 2008 ; Jefferson et al. 1993.

relying on oxen and horses for labor, and drawing on the most "charismatic" mammals, such as polar bears and giant pandas, in advertising for soft drinks and conservation alike. Images of large, furry creatures such as deer and fur seals can often stir compassion in the hearts of children and adults alike.

Despite these close connections with the animal kingdom, however, the course of human development—in particular, land conversion and hunting—have caused a drastic decline in the numbers of many of Earth's large mammal species. The caribou and grizzly bear have lost much of their traditional territory due to human development. More recently, the African elephant was threatened with extinction when an increase in demand for ivory from elephant tusks led to an explosion of poaching in the 1970s and 1980s. Between 1976 and 1989, the number of elephants in Africa fell from 1,300,000 to just 610,000.

Humans and other mammals share not only a common origin but, quite likely, ultimately a common fate. And as the animals' plight has grown more desperate, people have worked harder to help them survive. In 1990, the Convention on International Trade in Endangered Species (CITES) banned the trade of ivory, a move that, combined with more aggressive conservation, helped lead to a rebound in elephant numbers in regions of Southern Africa.

Endemic Species

In the Narrowest Niches

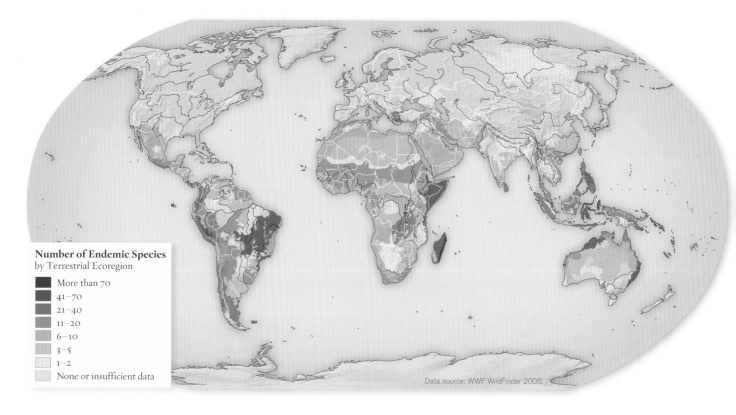

Number of Endemic Species
by Terrestrial Ecoregion

- More than 70
- 41–70
- 21–40
- 11–20
- 6–10
- 3–5
- 1–2
- None or insufficient data

Data source: WWF WildFinder 2006.

TERRESTRIAL ENDEMIC SPECIES. These species of birds, mammals, and reptiles are found in one place on Earth. They have often evolved in isolated habitats such as islands.

Death of the dodo. The flightless bird, found only on Mauritius, was too slow and land-bound to avoid threats that arrived with the European settlers in the 1600s.

Bristol City Museum/npl/Minden Pictures

THE PLUMP, FLIGHTLESS DODO once lived exclusively on the Indian Ocean island of Mauritius.

Today it lives nowhere at all.

The bird, related to modern pigeons found in Southeast Asia, gradually evolved to fit in with its new surroundings: an idyllic island environment with no natural predators. Over thousands of generations, it lost its ability to fly, in favor of leisurely waddling through the forest to nest on the ground. But around 1600, Europeans arrived on the island, bringing with them other new animals, such as dogs, cats, and rats. The animals raided the dodo nests, while the humans leveled the bird's forest homes. The rest is history.

The dodo's fate is a cautionary tale about the vulnerability of endemic species, which are found in just one habitat on Earth. Throughout the world, many such species have evolved to fit a particular environmental niche, with any abrupt changes in their surroundings posing a serious threat to their survival.

Such is the case with more than 1,400 species of small fish, known as cichlids,

that likely descended from a single fish species that colonized the lakes of East Africa's Rift Valley. Over millions of years, separate populations of these fish evolved in isolation, each taking advantage of small niches in the lakes, offering unique food sources, and varying temperatures and patterns of light. Some preyed on smaller fish; others ate only the scales of larger fish, while still others evolved with lips especially suited to suck insect larvae from the crevices between submerged rocks. Eventually they became entirely new species, some endemic to

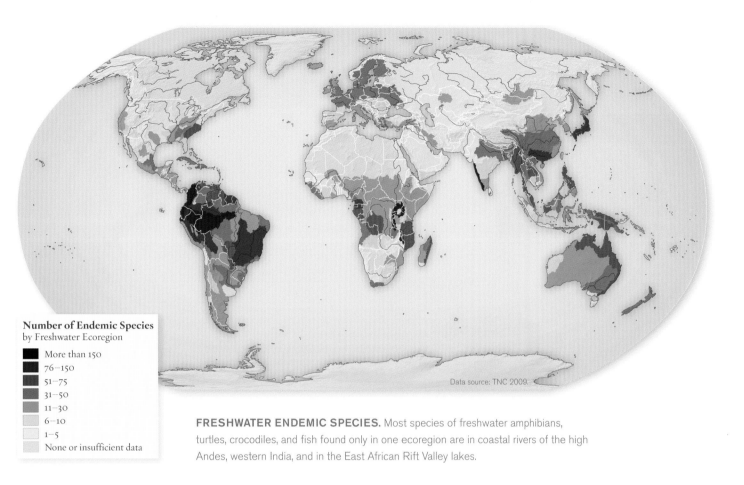

Number of Endemic Species
by Freshwater Ecoregion

- More than 150
- 76–150
- 51–75
- 31–50
- 11–30
- 6–10
- 1–5
- None or insufficient data

Data source: TNC 2009.

FRESHWATER ENDEMIC SPECIES. Most species of freshwater amphibians, turtles, crocodiles, and fish found only in one ecoregion are in coastal rivers of the high Andes, western India, and in the East African Rift Valley lakes.

Back from the brink. The lucky Mauritian kestrel, which nearly shared the dodo's fate, was saved from extinction through captive breeding and conservation efforts.

Nick Garbutt/npl/Minden Pictures

Diversely unique. The lakes of East Africa's Rift Valley are home to more than 1,400 species of cichlid fish, many of which are found nowhere else on Earth.

Flip Nicklin/Minden Pictures

just one lake, and together forming a uniquely remarkable, and remarkably vulnerable assemblage.

In 2008, cichlids ranked among the world's most endangered groups of vertebrates, with 208 species listed as threatened. Along with most other endemic species, their special adaptations, low numbers, and narrow ranges have made them especially sensitive to any change in their environments.

Their very fragility has made endemic species a special focus of the Alliance for Zero Extinction, a coalition that in 2009 encompassed sixty-eight conservation organizations

in eighteen countries. The organization works to save the world's most threatened endemic species—those endangered species found in only one place on Earth—chiefly through efforts to restore habitat.

Some species have already been pulled back from the brink of extinction. One such rescue involved the endemic Mauritian kestrel, which for millennia shared the island with the dodo and only narrowly escaped its fate. After surviving the European colonists' arrival, this bird's numbers plummeted in the mid-1900s, due to a combination of

DDT contamination and habitat loss. By 1974, there were only four kestrels known to be surviving in the wild. Some thirty years later, however, thanks to the establishment of a wildlife sanctuary and a captive-breeding program by the Durrell Wildlife Conservation Trust, The Peregrine Fund, and the Mauritius government, the population had rebounded to more than one thousand.

Evolutionary Distinction

Branches on the Tree of Life

A long branch on the tree of life. Although the aardvark is not in danger of extinction, if it were to become extinct, an entire order of the mammal class would die out.

A rare twig. The rainfrog is considered vulnerable to extinction because of its small geographic range but it has many more close relatives than the aardvark does.

Phylogenetic Diversity of Vertebrate Species by Terrestrial Ecoregion

High

Low

THE ORGANIZATION OF LIFE

GROUP:	EXAMPLE:
Kingdom	Animals
Phylum	Animals with backbones
Class	Birds
Order	Ducks, geese, swans
Family	All swans
Genus	Cygnus swans
Species	Black-necked swan

OF ALL THE WORLD'S vertebrate species, the aardvark is unique. Although it looks something like a pig and something like an anteater, it is not closely related to either. In fact, it is not really closely related to any other mammal at all. Instead, it is the only living representative of the obscure mammalian order Tubulidentata (meaning "tube-tooth," because their teeth are clusters of thin tubes). That means it carries many genes found in no other species.

In contrast, the rainfrog has plenty of close relations: it is directly related to 626 other frog species that share its genus, *Eleutherodactylus* (meaning "free toed" because their toes are free, not webbed), and it cannot claim a lot of unique genetic material.

The study of how organisms are related through evolution is known as *phylogenetics* (*phylo* being Greek for "related"). In recent years, as conservationists have become more scientifically savvy, this field of knowledge has become more relevant in guiding investments in habitat preservation.

Awareness of the comparative uniqueness of some species has made it seem all that more important to save them. Phylogenetic diversity—how closely related a group of species is—can be calculated for the assortment of species occurring in a particular region or a single nature preserve.

Phylogenetics breaks down all the world's living things into five kingdoms: animals, plants, fungi, bacteria, and archaea—single-celled microorganisms other than

bacteria—and afterward into progressively smaller groups.

As the classifications grow smaller, the organisms within each group are more closely related—an idea often illustrated by an image of a tree, with the larger groups shown as branches and the smaller ones as twigs. This image is called a "tree of life" or, in a more scientific term, a *cladogram*.

A crude way to account for the level of biodiversity at a location would be simply to count the species. But just the number of species at a location cannot tell you whether the place has evolutionarily unique species like the aardvark or species that are not so unique, such as the rainfrog.

The EDGE of Existence program uses phylogenetics to help conserve species that

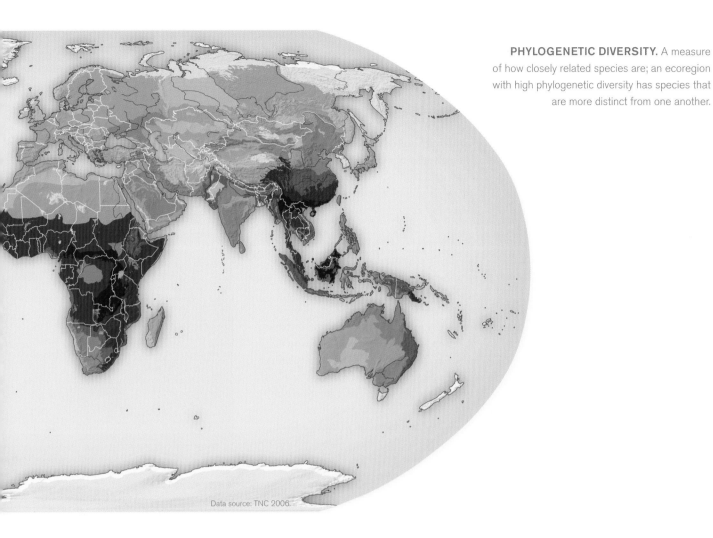

Data source: TNC 2006.

PHYLOGENETIC DIVERSITY. A measure of how closely related species are; an ecoregion with high phylogenetic diversity has species that are more distinct from one another.

are both *e*volutionarily *d*istinct and *g*lob-ally *e*ndangered ("EDGE"). A species of particular concern is the Hispaniolan sole-nodon *(Solenodon paradoxus)*, one of only two mammal species in the Solenodontidae family (the other solenodon species lives in Cuba and is also endangered). Just bigger than a guinea pig with a long snout, the Hispaniolan solenodon preys mostly on insects and amphibians (and occasionally a chicken) by injecting them with venom. It was one of the top predators on the island of Hispaniola before the European conquest but today is on the verge of extinction due to habitat loss and attacks by dogs and cats. Park rangers in the Dominican Republic are now working to protect this species in two parks.

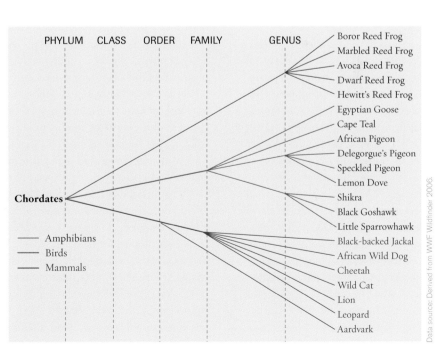

Data source: Derived from WWF Wildfinder 2006.

The tree of life. These branches show the relationship between African species. Some, like the reed frogs, are closely related on short twigs, while the aardvark is alone on its own branch.

Promoting Livelihoods, Saving Nature

GREG MOCK

IN GUATEMALA'S REMOTE Maya Biosphere Reserve, forest livelihoods are at the front lines of conservation. The government has granted thirteen communities the right to sustainably harvest forest tracts in the reserve's "multiple use zone" surrounding the core protected area. Within the boundaries of these community forestry operations, illegal logging, wildfires, and unplanned settlements—previously the biggest threats to the region's lush forests—have all dropped dramatically. As the value of the forests to their livelihoods became clear, the communities ratcheted up their enforcement of forest entry rules; fires and forest incursions are lower here now than in some nearby national parks. At the same time, studies show that forest structure has been maintained and biodiversity levels remain high in the locally managed forests. The community investment in good forest management has paid off at a household level: forest operations now make up 40 to 70 percent of the household income for community members—a significant boost in an area where poverty is high and job opportunities few.

The success of community forest management in Guatemala is just one example of how rural development and conservation can mix. And mix they must if most of the world's ecosystems and the communities that are dependent on them are to survive. It's nearly a truism today to assert that ecosystems are the world's green infrastructure, bound tightly into the economy of human well-being. We know that we depend on nature's services to feed and clothe us, provide employment, keep us healthy, relax and entertain us as tourists, and orient our spiritual compass. For those of us in urban areas, we mostly acknowledge this concept abstractly or understand it by conscious choice when we venture into nature for recreation. But for a large percentage of the world's rural population, particularly those in developing nations, dependence on nature is not an abstraction but an everyday reality. For these families, nature is a crucial source of livelihoods: a direct source of food, building materials, and medicines for daily subsistence and a source of cash when they sell their farm goods, livestock, fish, firewood, or other ecosystem goods at market.

The sheer dependence on ecosystems for livelihoods is impressive at every scale—global, national, and the household level. Globally, some 1.6 billion people depend on forests in some way for income or subsistence; this includes some 60 million indigenous peoples who are wholly dependent on forests. A 2004 World Bank study of the importance of forest income in seventeen countries on three continents found that forest products provided an average of 22 percent of total income to families living in or near forests. For the most part, this income was derived not from high-value timber, which local people often do not control, but from nontimber products like wild foods, fodder, thatch grass, medicines, and fuelwood. Wood fuels alone provide about a third of all forest income and are used by more than a third of the world population.

A similar story can be told for other major ecosystem types. Agroecosystems are the biggest source of environment-related livelihoods. While agribusiness generates much of global agricultural production, small-scale farmers—those with five hectares or less—still make up the bulk of the world's agricultural workforce. Small-scale agriculture accounts for 90 percent of Africa's agricultural production even today. Fisheries are nearly as crucial. Some 250 million people in developing countries are directly dependent on small-scale fisheries for food and income. In a study of coastal villages in Mozambique, fishing generated a third or more of villagers' cash income, not including the fish directly consumed. In the Lower Mekong River Basin, an estimated forty million rural farmers engage in seasonal fishing to augment their incomes and food supplies.

Susan Ellis/TNC

Harvesting coffee beans in the Guatemalan highlands

Add these figures together and it becomes clear that income derived from nature accounts for a large share of the rural economy in nearly all developing nations. Household survey data show that nature-based income, or *environmental income*, often contributes from one half to two-thirds of the total income stream of rural families, particularly those that are poor. Although both rich and poor rural families make use of nature's bounty, environmental income generally makes up a bigger share of the budget of poor families. Moreover, their livelihood dependence on ecosystems is more critical, since they have fewer employment alternatives. Making a living from nature is often the employment of last resort, but the investment it requires to become a fisher, farmer, pastoralist, or collector of medicinal plants is usually small and the training requirements minimal.

Such dependence is dangerous in an era when ecosystems are under pressure on every side. The rural poor suffer first and most when ecosystems decline and their productivity can no longer be relied on. A recent study in the Lacandona region of Mexico, where poor families depend heavily on the collection and sale of the leaves of the wild xate palm for use in flower arrangements, estimated that the severity of poverty in the area would increase 18 percent if the xate market were to disappear. For these and millions of nature-dependent households, sustainable management of ecosystems is a matter of immediate economic survival.

Fortunately, thousands of communities like those surrounding the Maya Biosphere Reserve in Guatemala have shown that, when given a chance, they can be good ecosystem stewards—often much better than the government. And this stewardship can form the basis of a new approach to rural development, one that recognizes that conservation and development can reinforce each other for greater effect. In this model, sustainable use of biodiversity becomes an engine of rural growth, and the demand for conservation springs from the support it provides for local livelihoods.

In northern Bangladesh, the promise of this approach is on display in the Hail Haor wetlands. Under state management, the wetlands—once renowned for their fish and waterfowl—had fallen on hard times from overuse, and local fishing communities were struggling to survive. In an innovative arrangement, the government granted 110 villages ten-year leases with exclusive rights to fish and manage the wetlands. With help from the government, environmentalists, and development experts, the villages formed local resource management committees and user groups that imposed conservation measures to restore the wetland and its depleted fisheries. They established no-fishing sanctuaries, reduced fishing pressure, replanted wetland trees, restocked the wetland with native fish, and successfully reintroduced ten threatened fish species. The

rationale for these measures was not conservation per se but restoration of their fishing-based economy, which had dwindled as the fishery declined. The results were gratifying: sustainable fish production more than doubled, raising household incomes 30 percent and increasing local food security. Villagers reaped social benefits as well, including a common purpose, a heightened sense of ownership of the resource base, experience with democratically formed management committees, and new technical skills for fishery management. These forms of local empowerment increase the likelihood that the villagers' success can be sustained over time.

The key to catalyzing this kind of conservation-based development is providing local communities a true stake in the restoration and sustainable use of the ecosystems they depend on. That means granting them real resource rights—the legal right to manage these ecosystems and reap the benefits of good stewardship. In the case of Hail Haor, this took the form of exclusive ten-year leases. Such rights provide the economic incentive that communities need to invest in the long-term productivity of ecosystems rather than rely on short-term exploitation.

Experience confirms the benefits of this approach for biodiversity conservation. Bringing local communities into the resource management loop tends to improve the success of conservation strategies by increasing the level of resource monitoring and enforcement. One recent study found that the vegetation density of community-managed forests, where local groups crafted the rules for forest use, was on a par with that in legally designated protected areas. Community-led management is effective conservation because it delivers clear benefits to those in the best position to protect the resource—the users themselves.

But making this approach work is not simple. It requires a concerted effort on the part of governments, conservation groups, and development organizations to provide

enabling conditions at the local level. For example, governments must provide local communities guidance and security in their management efforts, spelling out their ecosystem rights in legally binding language, and specifying the state's responsibilities for oversight and financial support. Conservation organizations, local community groups, and other nongovernmental organizations can help communities build their technical skills to monitor and manage their resources. They can also help communities configure their resource management committees so that they reflect the views of all members of the community—not just the elites—and distribute benefits equitably. Development groups can help provide business training and connect communities to sources of financing, so that they can be successful not only in managing their resources but in creating profitable nature-related businesses.

With this kind of support, local communities can begin to turn their ecosystem assets into sustainable livelihoods, using conservation to enhance their asset base and increase their "net worth." This is good for communities and good for the environment. It acknowledges that effective conservation is conservation that local communities support—conservation they have a stake in. This kind of conservation opens opportunities, builds human skills and capacities, and strengthens the communities that undertake it. It is a recipe for greater ecosystem and human resilience in an age of increasing peril.

GREG MOCK IS THE FORMER EDITOR-IN-CHIEF OF THE *WORLD RESOURCES REPORT*, WORLD RESOURCES INSTITUTE, AND CURRENTLY WRITES ON THE INTERSECTION OF DEVELOPMENT, POVERTY, AND THE ENVIRONMENT.

4

A World of Change

NATURE IS ALWAYS IN FLUX. Plants bloom and die; seasons change; rivers flow; glaciers advance and retreat. And all the while, evolution creeps forward as generations of humans and animals adapt, gene by gene, to our surroundings.

Change is the only constant, as it is said. Yet today, the natural world is changing faster and on a larger scale than at any previous time. The drivers are human population growth and consumption, as people raise families; clear land; cultivate crops; build homes, roads, and cities; and burn fossil fuels at an unprecedented and accelerating rate. And now climate change is driving more changes itself.

Each year, an area of forest the size of Germany is cleared. One-half of the water that annually flows through rivers and lakes is diverted to human uses or captured behind dams before it can reach the sea. Eighty percent of the world's fisheries are being fully or over-exploited; further expansion will be unsustainable. Species are going extinct faster than at any time since the fall of the dinosaurs, sixty-five million years ago. Ice caps are melting, seas are rising, and global temperatures are warming at twice the rate observed just fifty years ago.

Two hundred years ago, at the dawn of the Industrial Revolution, just one billion people lived in a world rich in natural resources. The human population has exceeded 6.7 billion, with an expected net of 80 million people being added to the planet in 2009 alone. Currently, we consume more than 40 percent of what nature can produce each year. Analysts project that human numbers will level off at nine billion by 2050, but that consumption of natural resources will more than double.

Humanity's ever-growing impacts on the planet have spurred questions about just how many people Earth can support. The World Wide Fund for Nature's Living Planet Report estimates that we are already overshooting Earth's natural productive capacity by almost 25 percent. Indeed, if all 6.7 billion people consumed as many natural resources as the average American, we would need four extra Earths to support ourselves.

The extent of our current impacts can be seen in the "human footprint"—a map of the world's land surface compiled by researchers from the Wildlife Conservation Society and Columbia University—that reveals where human population and activities such as farming, logging, and mining have left their indelible marks. Similar work on human impacts in the ocean, undertaken by an international team led from the University of California, Santa Barbara,

Data sources: Sanderson et al. 2002; Halpern et al. 2008.

Terrestrial Human Footprint

High

Low

Marine Human Impact

High

Low

THE HUMAN IMPACT. Few places on land or even at sea remain untouched by humans as we seek to meet our needs for food, water, and other natural resources. The map shows the geographic extent and intensity of human impacts, including those from population density, cities and towns, agriculture, transportation on land and water, overfishing, mines and petroleum extraction, and coastal pollution.

shows an equally broad swath of influence. Relatively pristine nature may still be found only in some of the most remote parts of the world—places like Antarctica, the middle of the Pacific Ocean, northern Canada's boreal forests, and the heart of the Amazon jungle.

For the first time in human history, we have the means to detect and begin to understand our impacts at a global scale. This section of the atlas features maps that show how human activity has changed the natural world. Each page examines the consequences of these changes for habitats and species, as well as for the future well-being of people, and considers ways that we might meet human needs without sacrificing nature.

Human Population

Outnumbering Nature

Scott Warren

Growing cities.
In Brazil, São Paulo has gained over 2 million people in the last decade and is expected to exceed 20 million by 2015.

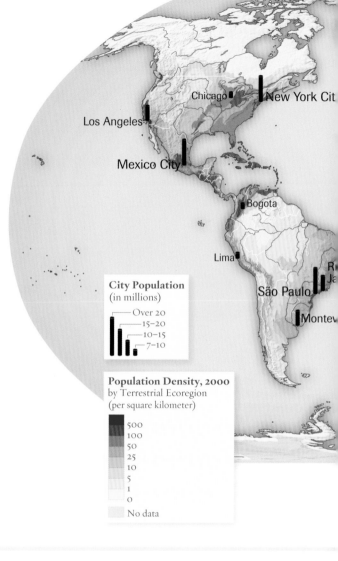

City Population
(in millions)
- Over 20
- 15–20
- 10–15
- 7–10

Population Density, 2000
by Terrestrial Ecoregion
(per square kilometer)
- 500
- 100
- 50
- 25
- 10
- 5
- 1
- 0
- No data

World human population from 1900 to 2050. After exponential growth through the twentieth century, the rate of growth has slowed, but there is still likely to be nine billion people by 2050.

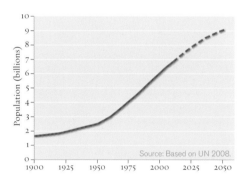

Source: Based on UN 2008.

AT THE BEGINNING of the twentieth century, the Earth held 1.5 billion people: the product of several million years of human history. Just one hundred years later, that number had ballooned to 6 billion, and counting. Estimates are that by 2050, the human population may reach close to nine billion—a number with potentially dire implications for the rest of the planet.

It is not just sheer numbers that determine human impact, but location, longevity, and income levels.

Throughout all but the last thin slice of history, the vast majority of people have survived by eating what they could raise from the land or catch in the water. But in 2008, for the first time, more people were living in cities than in rural areas, with estimates that by 2050, more than two-thirds of the population would be urbanites. China currently

needs to build the equivalent of more than six Manhattans a year just to keep up with the urban influx from the countryside.

While population growth rates have slowed and even fallen in much of the developed world, they remain significant in most developing nations. A notable contributor to humankind's ability to grow has been the relatively recent development of medical advances that have reduced infant mortality and helped people live considerably longer in most parts of the world.

Rich and poor, rural and urban populations all have varying influences on surrounding nature, leaving only the certainty that these impacts are starting to surpass Earth's capacity to withstand them. Wealthy city dwellers use much more electricity, often generated by fossil fuels, which add to the

threat of climate change. They also consume and subsequently discard many more natural resources in many forms, from cars to toys to frozen pizzas. Poor rural inhabitants, in contrast, depend heavily and directly on their surrounding natural environment for subsistence. Growing numbers of people with few livelihood alternatives have no choice but to turn to surrounding landscapes to cut trees for fuel, clear land for farming, pollute sources of water, and degrade the soil with misguided agriculture practices. In turn, this environmental degradation simply accelerates a downward spiral of increasing poverty and decreased human well-being.

The connections between population and the environment are clear but also fiercely controversial, raising issues of religion, culture, human rights, and personal beliefs. But in 1994, leaders from 179 nations reached

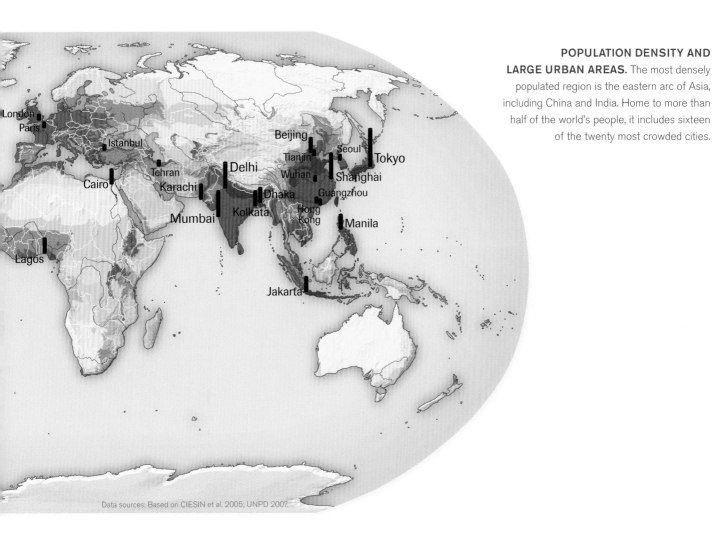

POPULATION DENSITY AND LARGE URBAN AREAS. The most densely populated region is the eastern arc of Asia, including China and India. Home to more than half of the world's people, it includes sixteen of the twenty most crowded cities.

the unprecedented consensus that individuals' needs and rights, rather than specific demographic targets, had to be addressed directly for the sake of sustainable development. Convening in Cairo, Egypt, at the International Conference on Population and Development (ICPD), nations signed a twenty-year plan of action known as the "Cairo Consensus," pledging to work toward goals such as universal access to education and reproductive health services, including family planning. Special emphasis was placed on the empowerment of women and reducing the education gap between boys and girls, as advancing gender equality, eliminating violence against women, and ensuring women's ability to control their own fertility are proven policies that reduce infant and maternal mortality, increase human well-being and further development.

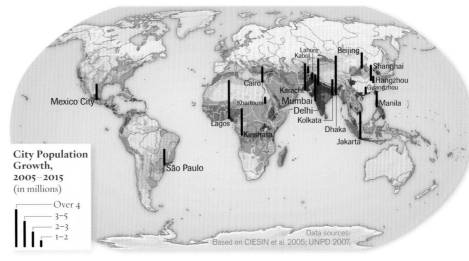

City Population Growth, 2005–2015 (in millions)

- Over 4
- 3–5
- 2–3
- 1–2

Population Growth, 2000–2015 by Terrestrial Ecoregion

- 100%
- 5.0%
- 2.5%
- 1.0%
- 0.25%
- 0.1%
- 0%
- Stable or declining
- No data

PROJECTED GROWTH IN POPULATION AND IN CITIES. Most projected growth is expected in less developed nations, due to both high birthrates and rural immigration. Growth has slowed or stopped in parts of Europe, North America, and Japan.

Consuming Nature
Running Out of Planet?

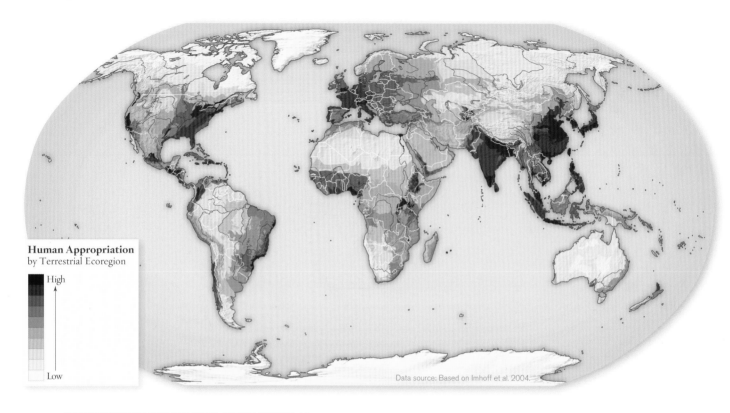

Human Appropriation
by Terrestrial Ecoregion

High

Low

CONSUMPTION RELATIVE TO PRODUCTION. Human appropriation of resources is estimated here as the amount of plants (crops, timber) grown in an area relative to the amount of plants consumed by humans each year. People in regions with higher consumption must import resources.

Ecological footprint. The ecological footprint measures humanity's total demand on the biosphere by estimating the area required to provide the resources we use and to absorb our waste.

Built-up land
Carbon uptake land
Fishing ground
Forest
Grazing land
Cropland

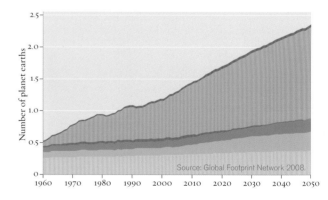

Number of planet earths

IN 2009, more than one in five people on Earth lacked access to clean drinking water. Fish stocks were collapsing around the world. The price of oil and even coal was rising steadily as more people with greater buying power pushed up demand for fossil fuel energy. Humans were using up the planet's raw materials about 20 percent faster than they were being replenished. And

it was estimated that total natural resource consumption would double or even quintuple by midcentury.

Resource consumption is the root of the world's largest environmental problems, from climate change, fueled by the burning of fossil fuels for energy, to habitat loss due to construction and farming, to species extinction from overexploitation. Compounding the problem is what happens *after* resources

are consumed—the mounting threats posed by toxic wastes and landfills packed to capacity. As human populations continue to grow, the rates of consumption and waste are increasing much more quickly, due to rising incomes and buying power.

To be sure, neither incomes nor consumption are growing at similar rates throughout the world. Developed countries consume about thirty-two times the

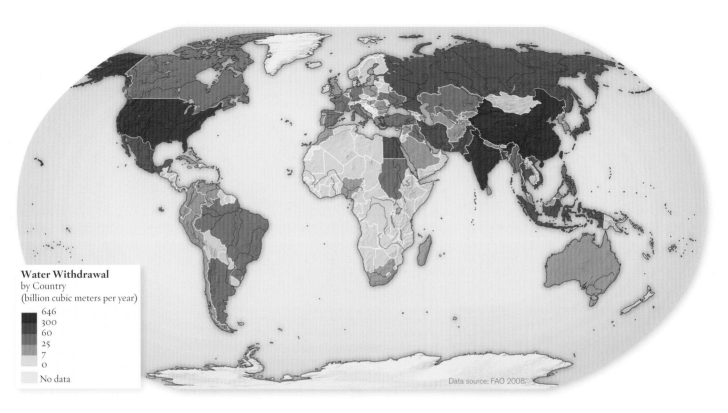

Water Withdrawal
by Country
(billion cubic meters per year)

- 646
- 300
- 60
- 25
- 7
- 0
- No data

Data source: FAO 2008.

WATER WITHDRAWAL. Because water actually *is* the space in which aquatic plants and animals exist, the water that humans take out of rivers and lakes leads uniquely to a direct consumption of habitat.

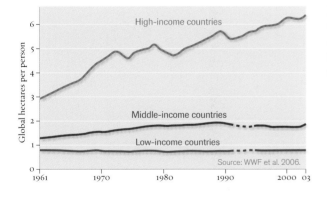

Bigger footprints. Most of the increasing consumption of natural resources has been in industrialized high-income countries.

resources per person than developing nations. And the impact of an average North American is double that of a European. Consider that the average American baby uses up 3,796 diapers before being potty-trained—diapers that can take hundreds of years to biodegrade.

Although there is no single solution, individuals can do many things to limit their consumption of natural resources. Smart

consumers can reduce the use of new materials by buying products without excess packaging and investing in longer lasting, non-disposable products. The reuse and recycling of materials can decrease the use of new resources. As environmental problems grow more serious—and natural limits have emerged ever more starkly—people throughout the world have been forced to focus more attention on consumption and

waste, and moving beyond individual action. One result, since the 1970s, has been a massive global adoption of recycling, of paper, glass, plastic, and aluminum. By 2003, in the United States, more than 8,800 curbside collection programs served about 140 million people, or nearly half the population.

Climate Change

The Planetary Emergency

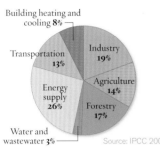

Greenhouse gas generators. Emissions result from a variety of human activities (forestry includes deforestation).

Building heating and cooling **8%**
Transportation **13%**
Energy supply **26%**
Water and wastewater **3%**
Industry **19%**
Agriculture **14%**
Forestry **17%**

Source: IPCC 2007.

DLILLC/Corbis

Weather extremes. Changes in temperature and precipitation patterns will increase the severity and duration of droughts in some regions, while more intense storms will bring floods to others.

David Frazier/Corbis

THE WORLD'S CLIMATE is changing. Over the past hundred years, average global temperature has increased 0.74°C. And it is getting hotter faster. Temperatures are expected to increase between 0.4° and 1°C in just the next two decades.

Human activities are the dominant contributing factor to these changes: cars that run on gasoline, homes and factories powered by coal and oil, and the burning or cutting down of forests. All of these actions emit so-called greenhouse gases—primarily carbon dioxide—that capture the sun's warmth like glass over a greenhouse. Carbon dioxide concentrations in the atmosphere have increased from preindustrial levels of 270 parts per million (ppm) to about 385 ppm in 2008, and they continue to rise by about 2 ppm every year.

These may seem like small changes, but just as a mild fever can still make you feel sick, the natural world feels them. Polar bears are feeling the heat but have nowhere cooler to go. Conifer forests in the western United States and Canada are being devastated by outbreaks of bark beetles that are surviving warmer winters. Coral reefs are bleaching because of warmer ocean temperatures. The oceans are also becoming more acidic as carbon dioxide dissolves, and they could become chemically inhospitable for corals, shellfish, or any other species that build calcium carbonate skeletons.

The real impacts of climate change will be felt by people, especially the poor. Extreme heat waves like the one that killed more than thirty thousand people in Europe in 2003

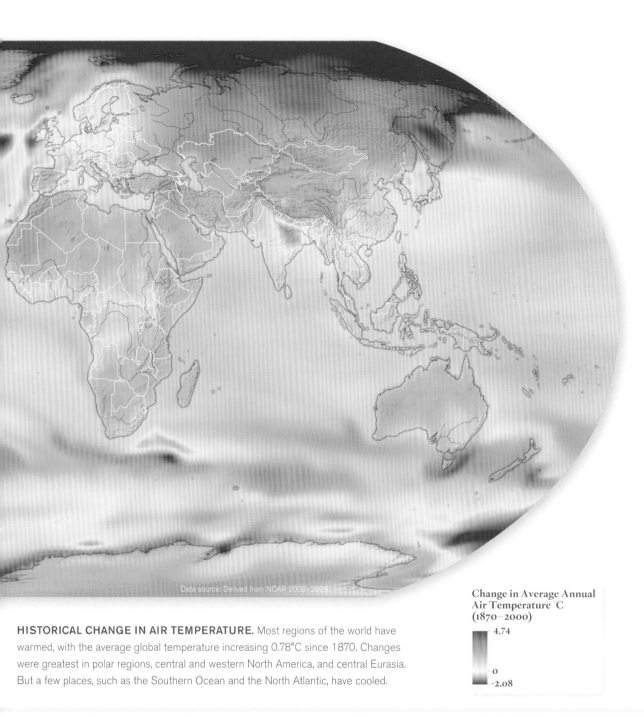

Data source: Derived from NCAR 2008-2009.

Change in Average Annual Air Temperature °C (1870–2000)

4.74

0
-2.08

HISTORICAL CHANGE IN AIR TEMPERATURE. Most regions of the world have warmed, with the average global temperature increasing 0.78°C since 1870. Changes were greatest in polar regions, central and western North America, and central Eurasia. But a few places, such as the Southern Ocean and the North Atlantic, have cooled.

could become common within thirty years. Water supplies for millions of people are drying up as glaciers and mountain snow-pack melt away. Deadly infectious diseases like malaria and dengue fever are spread-ing as warmer temperatures let mosquitoes spread into temperate areas. More intense droughts, especially in Africa and Australia, will likely reduce crop productivity and undermine food security. Rising sea levels—already up by 7.5 centimeters in the past fifty years—could drive as many as twenty-five million people to flee their homes in

Bangladesh alone. These impacts are likely to worsen without swift global action to signifi-cantly reduce emissions of greenhouse gases.

Every year, deforestation releases more greenhouse gases into the atmosphere than all the planes, trains, and automobiles in the world. By protecting intact forests and apply-ing sustainable forest management practices to keep them healthy, up to seven billion tons of greenhouse gas emissions could be avoided every year. Even more savings could be pos-sible if cut-over places like the Atlantic Forest

in Brazil or the Lower Mississippi Valley in the United States were reforested.

Conservation can also help address some of the unavoidable impacts of climate change. For instance, maintaining coastal habitats like mangroves and salt marshes can protect nearby communities from storm damage and rising seas while supporting local fisher-ies; and restoring natural floodplains can help contain floodwaters while improving river health. Such ecosystem-based strate-gies offer practical climate solutions that are good for people and good for nature.

Ultimate Agents of Global Change

JOEL E. COHEN

CONSERVATION FACES one crisis after another. Those who do conservation on the ground are frequently responding to immediate threats such as imminent deforestation or development. When conservationists protect habitats and species under siege, it is too easy to forget the long-term, chronic drivers of global change that lead to continual crises. Among those drivers are demographic, economic, environmental, and cultural forces. These drivers influence regional conservation threats, as well as what types of solutions might work to protect biodiversity.

A Senegalese Example

The waters off the coast of West Africa have been famous for centuries as rich fishing grounds. Upwelling waters of the North Atlantic nourish the food of large, commercially valuable fish, Senegal's foremost export commodity. Senegal's fishers used to operate wooden canoes called *pirogues*, often brightly painted in blues, yellows, and reds. Now they operate small motorized boats, still called pirogues.

Even with motorized boats, Senegalese fishers cannot keep up with the increasing numbers of large, freezer-equipped industrialized fishing boats that have come to Senegal's coastal waters in the past decade from France, Italy, Japan, China, and South Korea, as prime fisheries in the Mediterranean and elsewhere have collapsed. Some of these boats are legally licensed to fish in Senegal's waters through international agreements, and some were not. With the surge in foreign competition and advanced technology from abroad, the stocks of the large fish off West Africa have been rapidly depleted. The catches and profits of Senegalese fishers have fallen. One Senegalese nongovernmental organization devoted to the marine environment estimated that one pirogue now takes a month to catch the same amount of fish it used to catch in four days.

While Senegal's offshore stock of commercial fish has declined, its population of poor, unemployed youths has increased. By estimates made in 2001, the overall unemployment rate was 48 percent, and 54 percent of the population lived below the poverty line. In 2007, Senegal had about 12.5 million people, roughly as many as metropolitan Los Angeles. Unlike the people of Los Angeles, the people of Senegal had average incomes equivalent (by purchasing-power parity) to about $5 per day, or $1,800 per year. The population of Senegal was estimated to be growing at well over twice the global population growth rate, with 42 percent of the Senegalese under the age of fifteen and a median age of less than nineteen years.

In recent years, energy prices have also increased. In 2006, an energy crisis caused widespread blackouts in Senegal. As the price of fuel for the fishing boats rose and the yields from fishing fell, more and more fishers sought other ways to earn income from their capital assets and their expertise on the seas. They discovered a more valuable cargo than fish: people.

Many young men were willing to pay fishers to transport them 1,500 kilometers across dangerous seas from Senegal to the Canary Islands, colonies of Spain. Ferrying migrants to the Spanish islands required only enough gasoline to get to the islands and back and two working engines. If the fisher survived, the work was highly profitable.

Canary Island authorities were swamped by more than nine thousand illegal immigrants in the first five months of 2006, versus a total of ten thousand for the entire year of 2002. Immigrants without identification papers could not be repatriated and were flown to Spain from the Canary Islands at no cost to them. In 2006, the Spanish authorities sent an envoy to West Africa to discuss how Spain could give the West African countries economic help to keep people at home.

By August 2007, some dramatic changes were under way. The abrupt rise in sub-Saharan migration to the Canary Islands prompted Spain to patrol its shores more aggressively and take a tougher stance on immigration. At the same time, the Spanish and Senegalese governments launched a plan to stem the tide of immigration by giving hundreds of Senegalese workers one-year visas and jobs in Spain and bringing them to Spain legitimately—but not if they had migrated to Spain illegally. That same summer, Spain's labor minister signed agreements with the Gambia, Mali, and Mauritania to invest Spanish funds in training citizens of those countries who could be recruited for jobs in Spain.

Such programs for African workers are driven as much by demand from Spain as by desperation for decent jobs on the part of Africans. Spain did not have enough young workers to support its rapid economic growth, and it needed to hire thousands of migrants each year to work in agricultural fields, serve in restaurants, and build buildings. Spain's population was older and growing at only about one-tenth of the global rate. Only 14 percent of the population was under the age of fifteen, and the median age of the population exceeded forty years.

Whether the topic is fish stocks, migration, or rural livelihoods, local challenges and changes are no longer isolated; they are linked to and driven by regional and global trends. The world's fish stocks don't stop at the Mediterranean. The drivers of Senegal's climate don't stop at Senegal's national borders.

The Key Ingredients

The fabric of this story is woven of four threads: population, the environment, economics, and culture. These are the ultimate agents of global change. Let us focus on these threads, one at a time, and on their interactions.

POPULATION. From now to 2050, several billion more people will be added to the populations of developing countries, while the population sizes of most rich countries will stagnate or decline. Population growth will slow everywhere (first in the rich countries, later in the poor). Virtually all population increase

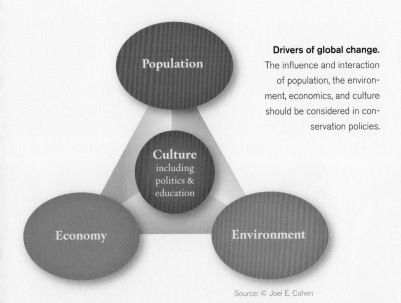

Drivers of global change.
The influence and interaction of population, the environment, economics, and culture should be considered in conservation policies.

Source: © Joel E. Cohen

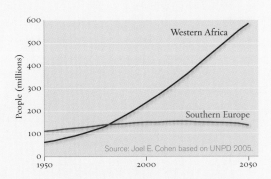

Different trajectories.
Populations grow dramatically in western Africa as they begin to decline in southern Europe.

Source: Joel E. Cohen based on UNPD 2005.

will be in cities, not rural areas. The fraction and number of aged people will increase at unprecedented rates to unprecedented levels (again, first in the rich countries, later in the poor). While the population of West Africa, including Senegal, is predicted to skyrocket, notwithstanding the expected declines in the population growth rate, the population of southern Europe, including Spain and Italy, is expected to rise only slightly, level off, and begin to decline in the next half century (see figure above).

Rural people of West African countries, including Senegal, have flocked to cities, especially coastal cities like Dakar. Such rural-urban migrants were pushed by poverty and environmental problems at home, and pulled by the prospects of a better life in cities. Senegal's environmental problems include coastal overfishing, wildlife poaching, deforestation, overgrazing, soil erosion, and desertification, and these challenges affect poor rural people the most because poor rural people depend more directly on the environment for their incomes than do urban people.

Migrants have always been principally young adults. With the rapid population growth of recent decades in poor countries, the proportion of young adults available to migrate in West African populations is very

high. Those migrants fuel demand for food and for jobs.

THE ENVIRONMENT. In Senegal and elsewhere in West Africa, high variability in rainfall from year to year and from decade to decade results in extended droughts, which make it difficult for rural farmers to survive, let alone produce a surplus for sale, in the absence of adequate investments. According to studies in central Senegal, poor health, inadequate village infrastructure, and rural unemployment undermine small farmers' capacity to adapt to climate change. Along with economic and institutional limitations, uncertain environmental resources in the interior push the poor to the coastal cities.

Meanwhile, a decline in the abundance and size of coastal fishes pushes people back to the interior or on to Europe. The large, commercially most valuable fish species reproduce at later ages and recover from a dip in population more slowly than do small fish species. The natural environment, through irregular rainfall and the slow population recovery times of large fish species, constrains human options.

ECONOMICS. Economics drive human activities in many ways. The estimated gross domestic product per person (after adjusting

for purchasing-power parity) of Spain in 2006 was $27,400, compared to Senegal's $1,800—a gap typical of that between the West African region and southern Europe. This inequality is an obvious incentive for fishers to transform fishing boats to vehicles of migration, and for unemployed young men to risk their lives to get to the Canary Islands.

Growing wealth outside West Africa also contributes to the demand for Senegal's fishes. In 2001, the United Nation's Food and Agricultural Organisation reportedly estimated that demand for fish had grown at twice the rate of human population growth over the forty preceding years. World fishery production at the beginning of the twenty-first century was more than six times that in the middle of the twentieth century, in part because of growing demand from elsewhere, in part because the technology of fishing evolved. Industrial fishing trawlers may stay at sea for months with built-in facilities for freezing and packing fish. The growing wealth, the changes in technology, and the arrivals of industrialized fishing boats from around the world are signs and symptoms of globalization: the movement of technologies, people, services, credit, capital, and markets wherever opportunities beckon. Globalization permits any industrial country

Senegalese with pirogues, their traditional fishing boats

Hervé Collart/Sygma/Corbis

to focus its fishing fleet wherever the fishing remains good, even if the local stock will be rapidly depleted and the local fishers will be rapidly displaced as a result.

Economic "rationality" drives this process. To simplify, if the global rate of interest is 4 percent, and if the rate of increase of a large fish population is 3 percent, then the economically "rational" thing to do for anyone with access to the fish population is to harvest as much of it as possible immediately and convert the fish into money, which can grow at a higher rate than the fish. In general, whenever the economic interest rate exceeds the population growth rate of a biological resource, the rational decision is to convert the biological resource to faster-growing money. As the BBC's Tim Judah reported in 2001, "West Africa has to choose between short-term cash and long-term fish....[T]he fish-rich West African countries face agonising choices, not dissimilar from those facing central African countries rich in timber. They need the money now, but once the fish and trees are gone, they are gone."

CULTURE. The links of politics to the collapse of the fisheries off Senegal are surprising. Environmentalists assert that, to allay the political dissatisfaction of Basque separatists in Spain, the European Union (EU) subsidized fishing fleets, including boats that employ thousands of fishermen from Basque country. As a result, the European Union created an overcapacity in its fishing fleets. As the waters legally accessible to the European Union were depleted of fish, the European Commission looked elsewhere for fish. West Africa's waters were the nearest target.

Africa also has internal politics. In 1975, Morocco occupied the territory of Western Sahara and controlled the rich waters off the coast. In 1995, Morocco began a lucrative four-year agreement with the European Union to allow EU fishing boats in Western Sahara waters. When the agreement lapsed at the end of November 1999, EU fishing boats were no longer able to fish off Western Sahara, and 4,300 Spanish and Portuguese fishers lost their jobs. Some of these fishers looked to waters farther south, off the shores of Senegal and its neighbors, to continue to make a living at sea. The struggles between and within Europe and Africa for power and money have a strong effect on how many and whose boats fish the waters.

Culture goes beyond politics. A usually unstated source of tension in the relations between Senegal and Spain is that Senegalese look different from Spaniards. While it was difficult for Spain initially to accept immigrant workers from Eastern Europe, it has proved even more difficult to accept immigrant workers, so different in appearance, from West Africa, including Senegal. The latest contracts of Senegalese workers in Spain offer single-year visas, renewable at the will of the Spanish side.

Moral of the Story

The four threads of population, the environment, economics, and culture are essential ingredients driving every complex global change. It is not enough for conservation policies to be based just on information about the environment. To be successful, they must also take account of the interacting influences of population, economics, and culture.

JOEL E. COHEN IS A PROFESSOR OF POPULATIONS AT ROCKEFELLER AND COLUMBIA UNIVERSITIES.

Habitat Loss on Land

Going, Going,...

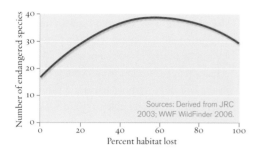

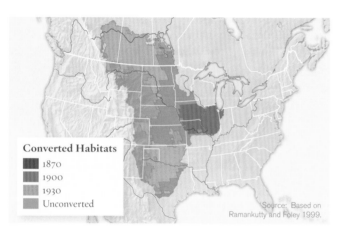

The extinction tipping point. When more than 60 percent of an ecoregion is converted, the number of endangered species declines because species begin to go extinct as habitat disappears.

Converted Habitats
- 1870
- 1900
- 1930
- Unconverted

Source: Based on Ramankutty and Foley 1999.

Lost grasslands. Habitat loss in the North American Great Plains happened in the blink of an ecological eye, as grasslands were converted to farms.

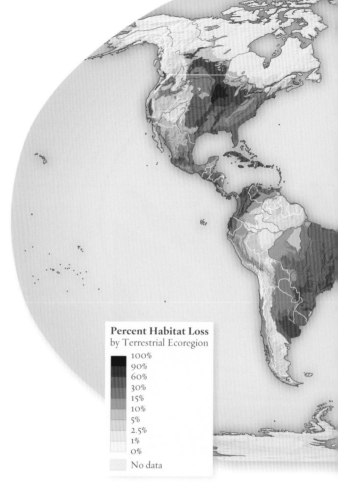

Percent Habitat Loss
by Terrestrial Ecoregion
- 100%
- 90%
- 60%
- 30%
- 15%
- 10%
- 5%
- 2.5%
- 1%
- 0%
- No data

FOR TENS OF THOUSANDS of years, the temperate grasslands of North America sustained massive herds of grazing mammals, such as bison. Then, within just sixty years during the late 1800s and early 1900s, settlers turned one of the world's largest grasslands into cropland. Much of the land that was not plowed under was transformed by overgrazing livestock, and the native prairie was gone. By the dawn of the twenty-first century, less than 1 percent of the original grasslands remained.

Habitat loss is the leading cause of species extinctions, which are now one hundred to one thousand times higher than they would be if so much habitat were not being converted. When animals' homes are converted to farms and cities, they usually cannot just pick up and move, since neighboring habitats either are at capacity or are similarly under development. Scientists predict that a continuing loss of habitat could well lead to the extinctions of half of all species on Earth sometime during the twenty-first century.

Even after much of their habitat is destroyed, many species hang on, sometimes for decades, in the small fragments that are left. In what is referred to as an "extinction debt," even though they may not actually be extinct, habitat and populations become so diminished that it is just a matter of time. Many of the world's natural landscapes are severely fragmented today and carry a heavy extinction debt that will be paid in the decades to come.

As a rule, the most fertile lands are converted first. More than half of all tropical dry forests and temperate mixed forests have already been lost, even as less productive land in deserts, boreal forests, and tundra has largely been spared.

Habitat loss often harms humans as well as plants and animals. When natural landscapes are converted to new uses, they usually provide fewer of the goods and services they once did, from water filtration to carbon sequestration to products such as Brazil nuts gathered from wild trees.

The direct conversion of natural habitat to human land uses is the most obvious form of habitat loss. Other kinds are harder to track. Some are unintended side effects of land and water management or invasive species. One, for example, is when fire is suppressed by forest and range management agencies in an ecosystem that depends on a regular fire cycle. In the case of the western United States, rangeland that is overgrazed by livestock is invaded by cheatgrass—an invasive plant that now covers millions of square kilometers. Where cheatgrass is established, fires occur earlier in the year as well as more frequently, which the native sagebrush habitat simply cannot tolerate.

HABITATS CONVERTED BY HUMANS. High levels of habitat loss correspond with the most fertile soils and dense human populations.

Data sources: Based on JRC 2003; CIESIN et al. 2004.

As human awareness grows about the importance of habitat, efforts are mounting to preserve it. Across the world between 2000 and 2005, a total area almost the size of British Columbia, Canada, was set aside to protect natural landscapes. There are still many good opportunities for conservation. Nearly 20 percent of all ecoregions have less than 1 percent of their land converted. Land management is also improving. Fires intentionally set and carefully controlled can reduce the buildup of fuel for wildfires and restore fire regimes. In the western United States, early detection and elimination of invasive plant species, along with reseeding with native grasses after a fire, planting sagebrush, and implementing better grazing practices, are some of the actions being taken by state and federal agencies to conserve and restore sagebrush habitat.

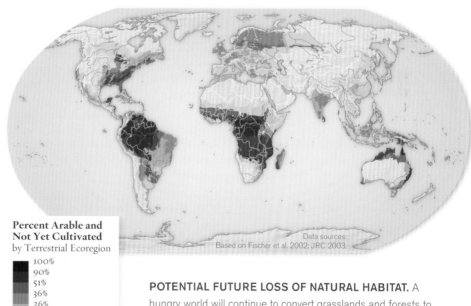

Percent Arable and Not Yet Cultivated
by Terrestrial Ecoregion

- 100%
- 90%
- 51%
- 36%
- 26%
- 16%
- 6%
- 3%
- 0%
- No data

Data sources: Based on Fischer et al. 2002; JRC 2003.

POTENTIAL FUTURE LOSS OF NATURAL HABITAT. A hungry world will continue to convert grasslands and forests to farmland. Almost 70 percent of the arable land not yet converted to agriculture is in tropical grasslands and tropical moist forests, which are also high in biodiversity.

Coastal Development

Reshaping the Seashore

Beachfront property. Tourism and coastal development have transformed coastlines. Thirty years ago, Cancun was a mangrove lagoon.

Redrawing the map. A palm tree-shaped island in Dubai, with hotels and several thousand villas.

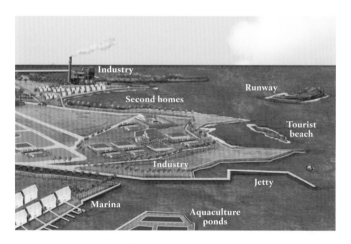

Industry

Second homes

Runway

Tourist beach

Industry

Jetty

Marina

Aquaculture ponds

Hardened coastlines. Salt marshes have been replaced by industrial land and mangroves have been converted to aquaculture ponds. Coastal currents are interrupted by marinas and jetties, while beaches and dunes are transformed by tourism and expanding sprawl.

OFF THE COAST of the small Arab sheikdom of Dubai, developers have built islands in the shape of palm trees. From Hong Kong to the Seychelles, coral reef flats have been converted to airport runway strips. Along the U.S. eastern seaboard, hundreds of kilometers of coasts have been "suburbanized" into small lots with private beachfront yards.

Especially over the past fifty years, ambitious engineers have turned sea into land, and land into marinas, redrawing coastlines and devastating marine habitat. Vast areas of salt marshes in almost every estuary in Northern Europe have been drained and walled off from the sea to create room for farms and industrial complexes. In Southeast Asia and China, vast expanses of aquaculture ponds crowd the coastlines, transforming tidal landscapes with dams and pools.

A few coastal habitats—even some with dense human populations—have escaped the development binge. Sections of the crowded Mediterranean Riviera, for example, have retained their dramatic rocky cliffs and shores, even as hundreds of kilometers of beaches, salt marshes, and estuaries around them have been transformed. But elsewhere in Europe, local governments have built concrete barriers and walls into the sea to control erosion of sandy shores. Developers in the U.S. state of Florida and other resort areas have dumped thousands of tons of sand, and raked beaches to keep up appearances. Such measures send sediments drifting out to smother the seafloor over wide areas, while redirecting coastal currents that erode adjacent shores.

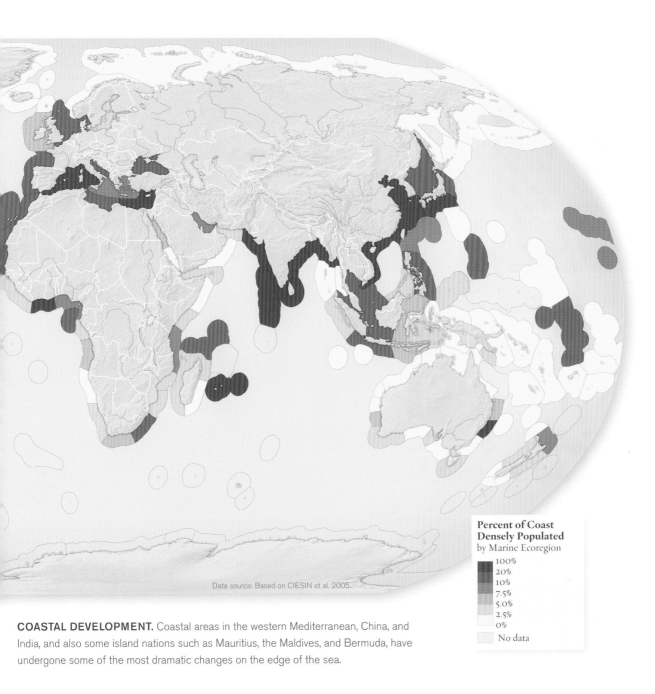

Data source: Based on CIESIN et al. 2005.

Percent of Coast Densely Populated
by Marine Ecoregion

- 100%
- 20%
- 10%
- 7.5%
- 5.0%
- 2.5%
- 0%
- No data

COASTAL DEVELOPMENT. Coastal areas in the western Mediterranean, China, and India, and also some island nations such as Mauritius, the Maldives, and Bermuda, have undergone some of the most dramatic changes on the edge of the sea.

Marine species pay a high price for our remodeling of their homes. Seabird nesting places have been destroyed, while the few remaining marine turtles and the near-extinct monk seal of Western Europe have been hounded out of their last strongholds. Since the 1970s, the last important loggerhead turtle-nesting site in the Mediterranean, on the island of Zakynthos in Greece, has been severely degraded by an accumulation of illegal building of resorts and beach walls, bulldozing of beach sand, and a massive influx of tourists.

Humans increasingly are paying for development's damage to the coasts. The bill is coming due in the decline of fisheries once nourished by salt marshes and coral reefs, reduced water quality, and loss of coastal protection from storms. As engineering projects in one place shift sediment to another, new communities end up obliged to pay for coastal management. And as overzealous tourist developers overbuild resorts, they often end up destroying the natural scenery that drew visitors in the first place.

With a growing awareness of other repercussions, including greater risks of storm damage and increased erosion and pollution, many countries have passed laws requiring new coastal developments to be set back from the seashore. Some governments have invested more broadly with more dramatic goals. Eastern Bangladesh, where some 138,000 people died in a single storm in 1991, has planted more than 900 square kilometers of mangroves, in an effort to prevent erosion and protect people living on the coast.

Bottom Trawling and Dredging
Scouring the Seafloor

Clean sweep.
Creatures living in a diverse seafloor community are left in a barren landscape after the dredge sweeps through the area.

Where's the shrimp?
Up to one-third of all catch thrown back overboard by commercial fisheries in the 1980s and early 1990s came from shrimp trawlers, which continue to be the major source of such discards.

Elliott Norse, MCBI

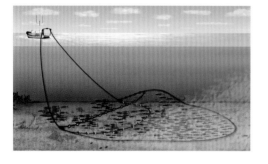

Strip-mining the seafloor. The trawl's heavy gates shove marine creatures into the net, while the net's bottom edge, made of thick metal cable studded with heavy steel balls, crushes everything in its path.

BOTTOM TRAWLING has been called the clear-cutting of the sea, an epithet acknowledging its standing as the most destructive of all fishing methods. With long, heavy nets stretched across gates weighing several tons each, trawlers, and smaller, sharp-toothed dredges, sweep and rake the ocean floor in a relentless hunt for bottom-dwelling species, including scallops, shrimp, cod, and flounder. Few seafood diners appreciate the level of destruction these meals require. The collateral damage of these underwater bulldozers includes the unintended slaughter of so-called bycatch, the fish, mollusks, and turtles

that are subsequently tossed overboard. In shrimp fisheries, the average bycatch weight quadruples that of the shrimp's. Meanwhile, scouring injures seafloor habitats essential for many species to reproduce and grow.

The process indeed compares to clear-cutting a forest, since it wipes out entire systems of interdependent life. Studies on the impact of shrimp trawling in the Great Barrier Reef Marine Park in Australia showed that a single trawl sweep removed up to 25 percent of the bottom-dwelling organisms. Deep-sea coral communities can similarly be devastated in a single sweep,

while repeated trawling actually changes the interplay of marine species, diminishing stocks of commercially valuable fish while clearing the path for small, opportunistic creatures such as sea stars and clams. Over the past thirty years, trawls have increased in size, targeting deeper and more remote locations. Two favorite and over-exploited fish, Chilean seabass and orange roughy, are caught by trawlers operating in the deep waters of the Southern Ocean.

Scientists estimated in 1998 that trawling throughout the world annually disturbs an area of seabed equal to twice the continental United

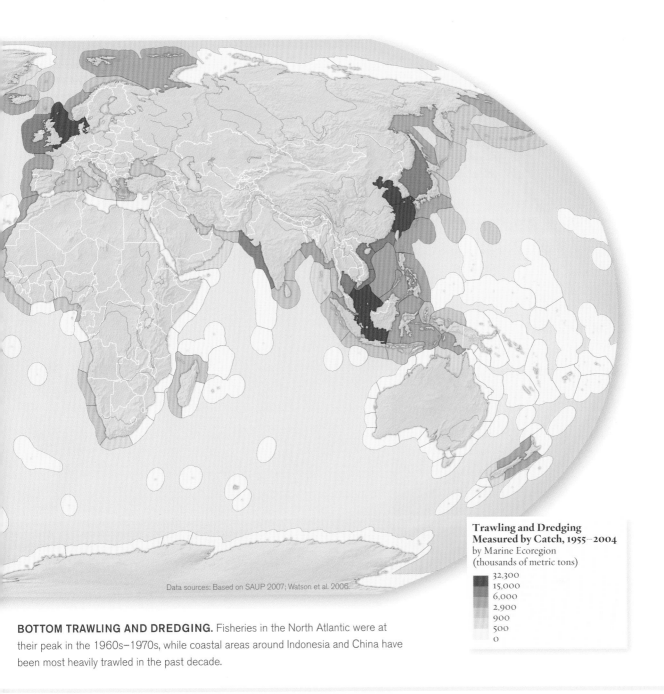

Data sources: Based on SAUP 2007; Watson et al. 2006.

**Trawling and Dredging
Measured by Catch, 1955–2004**
by Marine Ecoregion
(thousands of metric tons)

32,300
15,000
6,000
2,900
900
500
0

BOTTOM TRAWLING AND DREDGING. Fisheries in the North Atlantic were at their peak in the 1960s–1970s, while coastal areas around Indonesia and China have been most heavily trawled in the past decade.

States. In 2002, a more detailed assessment of U.S. waters showed that trawlers have altered an area larger than California. Depending on the location, the impacts of trawling can be relatively light, lasting months or years, or severe, lasting decades and even centuries.

Bottom trawling injures not only marine life but human livelihoods. Industrial trawlers often encroach into fishing grounds near the shore, destroying small-scale fishers' nets, overexploiting commercially valuable fish, and degrading the fishing grounds.

Increased awareness of the toll of trawling and dredging has prompted varied efforts at reform. Trawling has been banned in some sensitive marine areas, including a large portion of Alaska's Aleutian Islands and in more than 2300 square kilometers of deep-sea coral reefs in Canadian waters off Nova Scotia. In 2006, Iceland, Russia, China, and South Korea blocked a United Nations proposal to ban trawling in the high seas, even though the move was backed by important international players, including Australia, the United States, and the European Union. In other countries, such as Norway and Chile, regulations now limit the number of fishing boats and licenses, specify the kinds of nets that can be used, and offer incentives to reduce or eliminate by-catch.

These legal pressures have spurred interest in new technologies, such as a recently designed dredge with swiveling scoops instead of a toothed bar, which can dislodge scallops without touching the seafloor. Another helpful trend is education campaigns by conservation groups about the survival outlook for various marine species and the consequences of the way they are harvested. Organizations like California's Monterey Bay Aquarium publish handy pocket guides, ranking the sustainability of various types of seafood.

Landscape Fragmentation

Going to Pieces

NASA

Bit by bit. Satellite photography reveals patterns of fragmentation, the process of habitat loss that starts with converting a few small patches at first but often continues until only a few small patches of natural habitat are left. In the photographs, green indicates natural cover and pink shows human-dominated land uses.

Rapid encroachment. The landscape in Rondonia, Brazil, shown in these one-hundred-kilometer-wide satellite photographs, is quickly fragmenting as roads, urban areas, and agriculture spread into natural forests.

1989

2001

NASA

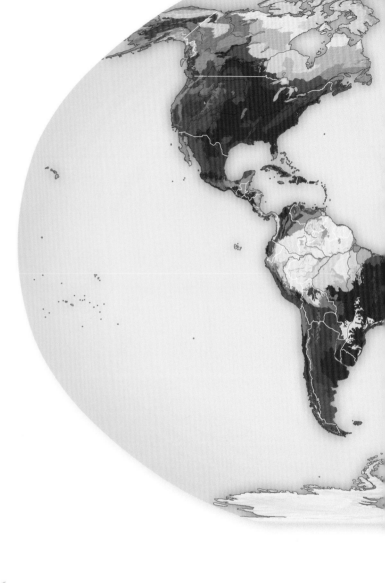

ROADS ARE HABITAT CONNECTORS for people. They connect one part of a habitat, such as a home, to another part, such as a workplace. But for many wild animals, roads (and other development) are barriers instead of connectors. They divide habitat into patches. As the patches get smaller and farther apart, they eventually become too small and too far apart to support the animals that once lived there—even if the patches still have trees and other plants growing on them.

As land gets developed, habitats get broken up into smaller pieces. When the patterns made by development change, the animals that live there change, too. When it comes to conserving biodiversity, how the patches of habitat are arranged on the land and how the pieces are shaped can make or break nature. The patches that are left are called *fragments*, and the process of being broken up is called *landscape fragmentation*.

Patterns made by natural habitat and developed land can be used to gauge the habitat's condition for wildlife. The size of

the patches is important because larger ones provide more habitat for a greater number of species. Many species can survive only in the interior portion of a patch and not along the edge. Ovenbirds, for example, which range across eastern North America, require about ninety hectares of interior forest to nest and raise their young. Additionally, the distance between one patch of habitat and another is important because many species require a home range larger than just a single patch, and they must be able to reach

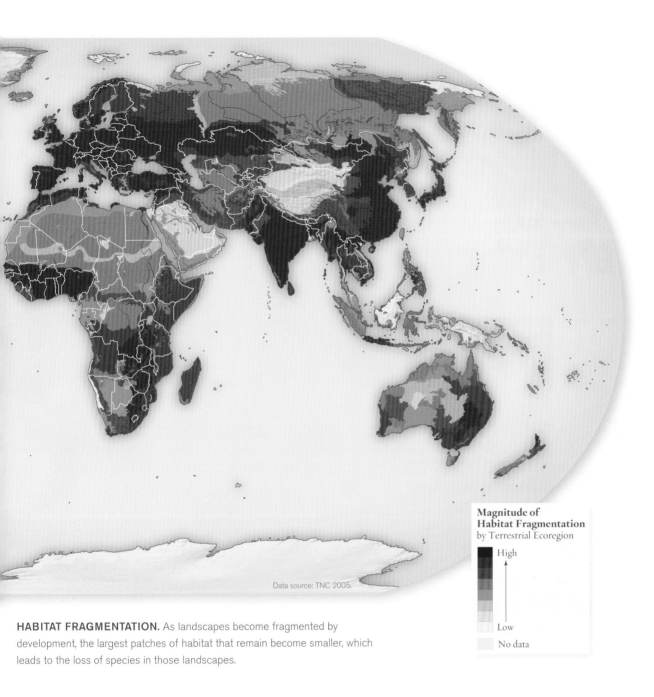

Data source: TNC 2005.

HABITAT FRAGMENTATION. As landscapes become fragmented by development, the largest patches of habitat that remain become smaller, which leads to the loss of species in those landscapes.

Magnitude of Habitat Fragmentation by Terrestrial Ecoregion

High

Low

No data

the nearby patches of habitat to survive. Male hooded warblers, for example, will fly only about 450 meters across open ground to reach the next patch.

Fortunately, there are ways to lessen the effects of landscape fragmentation. Governments, landowners, and private non-profit organizations can conserve the largest remaining patches of habitat before they become fragmented. For example, the Cerrado grasslands of Brazil are rapidly disappearing as the region is converted to massive soybean production. In 2008, the 8,900-hectare

Serra do Tombador Preserve was established by local governments, non-profit conservation groups, and private landowners to keep a large piece of habitat from destruction. Another solution is to connect smaller patches by making corridors between them. In 2007, a corridor for over one thousand endangered Asian elephants in southern India was established by conservation organizations and forestry agencies. Called the "E-D" corridor, it connects two patches of forested elephant habitat that had been

cut off from each other by farms, towns, and roads.

Implementing solutions like these come down to designing how the land is shared by humans and wildlife. Experience shows that as human populations grow and spread out, it is possible to design our environment to sustain rather than diminish nature.

Thwarted Fish Runs

Up against a Wall

An uphill battle. Baby eels migrating upriver are unable to surpass dams, contributing to their declining populations in the United States and Canada. In Europe, eel numbers have hit an all-time low, with less than 1 percent of their populations returning to rivers to mature.

Blowing up Embrey Dam. Demolition experts blasted a thirty-meter hole in the Embrey Dam in the state of Virginia in 2004, thereby opening the Rappahannock River and allowing it to flow uninterrupted for the first time in more than 150 years. The Rappahannock thus became one of the longest free-flowing rivers in the continental United States.

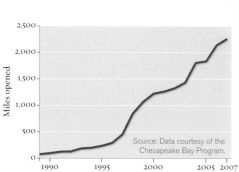

Source: Data courtesy of the Chesapeake Bay Program.

Bringing back the Chesapeake Bay's fish runs. From 1989 to 2007, the Chesapeake Bay states opened up 3,647 kilometers of historic habitat by removing dams and constructing fish passages around existing dams.

UNTIL THE EARLY 1900s, millions of shad, sturgeon, and other migratory fish regularly swam up the rivers of the United States' East Coast to spawn every spring before returning to the sea. The American shad was an especially favored item on regional menus, and its Chesapeake Bay fishery was an important source of regional income. Yet as dams for hydroelectric power were built along the Susquehanna River, they cut off access to the shad's largest spawning grounds. The population plummeted, and by 1994, shad fishing in the Chesapeake Bay had been banned.

Now in the twenty-first century, the thousands of shad and other migratory fish still swimming up the Susquehanna have to overcome four large hydroelectric dams in the river's lower reaches in addition to other challenges like pollution. Despite expenditures by dam owners and state agencies of more than $60 million on fish passages, in 2008, only twenty-one shad managed to swim past the fourth dam to reach their optimal spawning grounds. That represented less than 1 percent of the thousands of fish that had tried and failed.

Migratory fish require varied types of habitats as they feed, mature, and spawn—needs that also vary according to the species. Shad spawn in the slow-moving waters of main river channels or larger tributaries, to avoid the risk of the eggs being swept away by currents. But eels, which spawn at sea and mature in rivers, survive best in the fast and cooler streams of headwaters, where the juveniles can more easily avoid predators. When dams block the routes to preferred

**Degree of Disruption
of Fish Runs**
by Freshwater Ecoregion
Impact level

Severe

↑

Negligible

No data

Data source: Reidy-Liermann et al. (unpublished manuscript).

DISRUPTION OF FISH RUNS. Dams impede access to many river habitats that migratory fish need to feed and reproduce.

habitats, fish make do where they can, but their numbers tend to decline in the process.

Studies highlighting such harm to migratory fish have encouraged conservationists' arguments against the building of new dams, and in some cases have even led to the removal of existing structures. Since 1999, more than 450 dams—many of which had already ceased to operate—have been taken down in the United States, where currently more dams are being removed than built.

In some cases, the dam removals have helped restore traditional migratory fish runs—a celebrated instance being that of the Embrey Dam, built for hydropower in 1910 on the Rappahannock River near Fredericksburg, Virginia. By the 1990s, the dam had become obsolete, and cracks in its structure had made it a safety hazard. Its removal in 2004 reopened hundreds of kilometers of habitat for shad and other fish, which promptly began recolonizing streams that had been out of reach for more than 150 years.

Other ways local, state, and federal governments have helped restore fish runs include retrofitting existing dams with effective fish passages and managing the release of water from dams in ways that mimic natural river flows. None of these river-based strategies can be sufficient in the long run, however, without efforts to restore fish populations at sea by curtailing harvests and managing stocks.

Global Contamination of the Biosphere

JOHN PETERSON MYERS

SCRATCH A SAMPLE OF BARK off any mature tree from virtually any forest in the world—Belize, boreal Canada, the Adirondacks, the Marshall Islands, Tasmania, anywhere near or far. Then challenge a competent analytical chemist to find it free of pesticides or industrial pollutants. They won't.

Take samples of umbilical cord blood from newborn babies and analyze them for contaminants. You will find hundreds.

Measure soils in seemingly pristine cloud forests of Costa Rica where frogs are disappearing. Some pesticide levels will be higher in those cloud forest soils than what you'll find in lowland fields adjacent to the banana plantations where the pesticides are applied.

Examine the blubber of a sperm whale that specializes in feeding hundreds of meters beneath the surface in the mid-Atlantic. It will contain brominated flame retardants, compounds used to make sure the foam in your sofa doesn't burn in the first few seconds after it's hit by a match or cigarette, but known to cause neurological deficits in animals exposed during development.

Sample a polar bear in the Arctic, or an Eskimo. Their contaminant load, also called a "body burden," will be higher for many chemicals than their ursine or human counterparts in temperate or tropical latitudes, even though they are thousands of miles from where the contaminants first entered nature.

Collect fish from rivers downstream of sewage outflows, and you will witness males that have been feminized by compounds that came from the sewage. Measure the sediment in the rivers for those same compounds, and you will observe the chemicals migrating downward toward groundwater, which in many regions will become drinking water. Spread sewage sludge on farmland, and observe the behavior of lambs whose mothers fed on the fertilized grass. It is different.

No matter where you look, you will find the aftermath of a century of prodigious use of synthetic chemicals. Many of these chemicals have helped to make our modern life possible. But startling new science is revealing that some of them are having unintended consequences.

Few of the contaminant levels will be at a concentration that classical toxicology would confirm as certainly toxic. For the most part, they won't be as high as immediately around the facilities where the chemicals are produced. Usually they will be what twenty or even ten years ago would have been called "background levels": high enough to measure with sensitive instruments, but too low to have any biological effect.

Over the past two decades, however, a new generation of toxicology has emerged that challenges this assumption, raising questions about the human and ecological impacts of what now has become pervasive exposure to chemicals that, invented within the past 110 years, are novel additions to the body chemistry of life on Earth. Work by ecological chemists like Thomas Eisner has revealed the evolutionary warfare that has played out between organisms over millennia. One organism develops a new chemical defense. Its predators evolve a response. All that takes many generations. What is new here is that in the blink of an evolutionary eye, human creativity has thrown more than eighty thousand new chemicals into the world's ecosystems, and atmospheric processes, rivers, and ocean currents have spread them everywhere. We are only now witnessing the selective processes that have been set in motion. And they have a long way to go.

Although this new toxicology has many dimensions, central to all of it has been the discovery that some contaminants interfere with the chemical signaling systems that control how cells behave, not by taking traditional toxicological routes like mutation or other types of overt toxicity, but rather by hijacking control of the mechanisms that govern how genes are turned on and off. This new toxicology is revealing that some contaminants can affect cells at doses millions of times below what conventional toxicology had thought necessary. Depending on when during the course of life exposure takes place and which genes are affected, the impacts can be profound.

The poster child of this new toxicology is a molecule called bisphenol A, or BPA. First synthesized in the late 1800s, it has proven to be such a useful compound that annual production around the world now exceeds 2.7 billion kilograms. Work in the 1930s showed that it could cause effects similar to the human hormone estrogen. But assays of the day indicated it was weak compared with estrogen, so it was dropped as a potential synthetic substitute. Then over a decade later, polymer chemists discovered it could be used to make polycarbonate plastic and epoxy resins.

Now polycarbonate plastic and the BPA-based resins are literally everywhere. Polycarbonate water bottles have become wildly popular as sports bottles—rigid, transparent, and often tinted pink or blue or green and emblazoned with the logo of a not-for-profit group supporting nature or fighting breast cancer. Most of today's plastic baby bottles are made out of polycarbonate. Over 50 percent of food cans sold in U.S. supermarkets are lined with BPA-based resins.

Unfortunately, however, the chemical bonds that bind BPA molecules together in polycarbonate and the resins are not stable. They are highly vulnerable to degradation, meaning that despite their seeming rigidity, the bonds break down with normal use. Add a little heat (microwave the baby's formula in plastic or expose a sports bottle to sun), add something acidic (tomato paste in a can) or alcoholic (wine for the hike), and the leaching rate shoots up. It also increases greatly simply with wear and tear.

The widespread use of BPA now means that it can be found in virtually all Americans; in watersheds, especially downstream from landfills; and in the air. The levels in people average in the parts per billion, which to a traditional toxicologist translates to "irrelevant." But scientific research over the past decade, carried out not by traditional toxicologists but instead by endocrinologists—the medical experts who study how hormones work—have revealed a wide range of troubling impacts in animals exposed experimentally to even lower levels than what can be found in the average American today.

Animal experiments have shown that exposure to BPA early during development can cause effects that play out over the life of the animal, including hyperactive behavior, breast and prostate cancer, obesity, uterine fibroids, polycystic ovaries, and errors in cell division that lead to spontaneous miscarriage. In adult rodents, it induces insulin resistance (a precursor to type 2 diabetes) and interferes with the standard medical intervention for prostate cancer.

This science is so new that studies of people are in their infancy, but experts working with BPA have concluded that the cellular and physiological processes affected in animals by the compound are so similar to what happens in people that human impacts are of concern. Tests with cells show that the chemical alters the behavior of over two hundred human genes, including many that are involved in very fundamental physiological processes.

The first major epidemiological study of BPA was published in September 2009. As predicted from animal studies and from experiments with human fat cells, people with elevated BPA levels in their urine—higher than average but still within a range commonly experienced by Americans—are at greater risk to heart disease, heart attacks, and type 2 diabetes.

Impacts on natural systems are also worrisome. One set of experiments shows that BPA and a set of similarly widespread chemicals decrease the efficiency of nitrogen fixation by leguminaceous plants. They interfere with the signaling processes that allow nitrogen-fixing bacteria to enter into their symbiotic relationship with the roots of the host plant. Another series of experiments reveals that, even at extremely low

Ubiquitous contaminants, from litter on isolated beaches to new chemicals in waterways

Mark Godfrey/TNC

Refineries and industrial plants on the Schuylkill River in Philadelphia, Pennsylvania, United States

levels, it causes the ovaries of a common gastropod mollusk to rupture.

Perhaps most worrisome, work with BPA has revealed a huge blind spot in the way that traditional toxicology has been used to establish safety standards for human health and the environment, a blind spot whose implications are not limited to BPA, but instead are relevant to a wide array of chemicals that act like hormones.

Traditional toxicology assumes that "the dose makes the poison": the higher the dose, the bigger the effect. This assumption governs how toxicological testing is done to set health standards. Animal experiments begin at relatively high doses. If effects are detected, work continues at lower and lower doses until no effect is seen. Then a series of safety factors is used to ensure that the acceptable exposure level is a hundred or a

thousand or more times lower than the lowest level shown to cause harm.

Endocrinologists, however, have known for decades that hormones can cause effects at low levels that are completely the opposite of what happens at high doses. With hormone-like substances, high-dose experiments can be useless for predicting what will happen at doses literally a million or more times beneath those exposures. For example, doctors prescribing tamoxifen, an estrogen-

Mark Godfrey/TNC

to BPA at fifty parts per billion of body weight per day. Experiments with animals now show many adverse effects following exposure to levels beneath that standard. And experiments with cells now show that BPA can have profound physiological impacts at levels beneath a part per trillion, far beneath the serum concentrations that would be caused by the "safe" exposure level.

BPA is not alone in its ability to affect gene behavior in animals and people, or in its ubiquitous distribution. Indeed, and unfortunately, the list is long. We have depended on flawed science to protect us and the world's biota from contamination. Hazardous materials have entered into commerce. Global processes have spread them around the world. Now, because of how far and wide these compounds have spread, and because of their manifold impacts on reproduction, immune system function, neurological development, insulin regulation, and other end points that are profoundly important to evolutionary fitness, we are likely to be living in an era of the most rapid rate of molecular evolution of the world's biota that has ever occurred in the history of life on Earth.

How could that be? Two considerations make it inescapable. First, the sheer volume of novel but biologically active chemicals that have been introduced and distributed globally over the past century mean that organisms around Earth have been challenged in unprecedented ways. Second, in people and in animals, there is large genetic variability in defenses against chemical contaminants. Some individuals are relatively insensitive, others much more sensitive. "Natural" selection over generations will decrease the frequency of individuals sensitive to these novel chemicals.

This scenario might be interpreted by some as reassuring—we and the biota will adapt over generations. But inherent in that view are two givens: (1) the process of selection will involve diseases, disabilities, and reduced function (i.e., human and animal suffering), and (2) remaining populations will be less diverse and likely more vulnerable to other environmental changes.

What does this mean for humans and for nature? We don't know with certainty, but clearly it has implications for human health and the survival of species. This new toxicology indicates that one part of getting ahead of humankind's impact on the biota and on ourselves will be to rethink profoundly how we design materials for use in commerce, asking questions about safety before materials enter widespread use. That approach doesn't happen today. Fortunately, a new generation of chemists—green chemists—is focused squarely on this challenge. Finding solutions that work economically and that provide us materials enabling a modern lifestyle without undermining our health will require close collaboration between these new chemists and the health scientists who have opened the window into new toxicology. Hopeful signs indicate that this collaboration has taken root and is growing.

JOHN PETERSON MYERS IS THE CHIEF SCIENTIST AT ENVIRONMENTAL HEALTH SCIENCES.

like bisphenol A, use the drug to treat breast cancer because high doses suppress breast cancer cell proliferation. Low doses, however, can cause breast cancer cell proliferation, an effect known as the "tamoxifen flare."

Many scientific studies have now revealed similar low-dose effects with BPA and other contaminants that behave like hormones. Using the old methods, toxicologists concluded that people could safely be exposed

Freshwater Pollution

Clear but Hazardous

South African River Health

Main rivers
— Largely modified
— Moderately modified
— Intact

Minor rivers
— Largely modified
— Intact

Source: Nel et al. 2004.

SOUTH AFRICAN RIVER HEALTH.
River water quality is often monitored for impacts on human health; this is a rare example of the mapping of freshwater ecosystem health. The rivers of this semiarid country are vulnerable to urban development and agricultural pollutants.

FOR MUCH OF THE NINETEENTH and early twentieth centuries, people in the United States were accustomed to seeing urban rivers catch fire, the flames ignited from deposits of oil and debris. Long before the birth of the modern environmental movement, industrialized countries routinely used their waterways as waste dumps.

In 1969, however, a dramatic fire on the U.S. state of Ohio's Cuyahoga River made national news, obliging government officials to turn their attention to water pollution and leading the way, three years later, to the historic passage of the U.S. Clean Water Act. Since that time, most other industrialized countries have implemented water quality laws, which have helped remove the most visible pollutants from waterways. Yet today,

new and more insidious pollutants threaten most of the world's major rivers and lakes.

Some of these new contaminants are in the form of small amounts of synthetic chemicals, known as endocrine disruptors, which scientists fear may be seriously affecting humans and wildlife when accumulated over time, by interfering with hormones that regulate growth, development, and reproduction. Herbicides, pesticides, and chemicals that make plastics are all washed into waterways from farms and factories and can contain these toxic substances, in addition to dioxin, PCBs, and DDT. These chemicals accumulate in fatty tissue and mother's milk, and can be a danger even if not much is present in nature. Some pesticides are retained in fish bodies in amounts between one thousand and one hundred

thousand times greater than concentrations in the water they inhabit.

Pharmaceuticals meant for humans and livestock have also increasingly been flushed into rivers and lakes, with evidence growing as to their effects. A survey of U.S. rivers in 1999 and 2000 found synthetic hormones in 37 percent of streams, and caffeine in more than half. Synthetic estrogen—both given to livestock and contained in human birth-control pills—has been shown to disrupt amphibian growth and development and is believed to be the reason that 42 percent of male bass sampled recently in a relatively undeveloped portion of the Potomac River were producing eggs.

Water pollution remains most deadly in the developing world, which is beset not

Visuals Unlimited/Corbis

Diffuse sources. Chemical fertilizers and pesticides that run off agricultural fields into nearby lakes and rivers are damaging sensitive ecosystems, and are difficult to intercept.

Down the drain. These pharmaceuticals and other chemicals have been detected in U.S. rivers. Scientists know little about the impacts of this cocktail on nature and humans.

Chemical	Use
Acetaminophen	Pain reliever
Caffeine	Stimulant
Carbamazepine	Anti-convulsive and mood stabilizer
Estrogen	Birth control
Ibuprofen	Pain reliever
Monensin	Antibiotic typically given to cattle
Naproxen	Pain reliever
Prozac	Antidepressant
Trenbolone	Anabolic steroid for humans and cattle
Triclocarban	Disinfectant used in antibacterial soaps

Source Based on Donner et al. 2008 and Kolpin et al. 2002.

Markus Botzek/Corbis

Drug side effects. The amounts of synthetic estrogen from birth control pills and livestock operations found in streams can disrupt growth and development of amphibians, including causing sex changes.

only with these new pollutants but also with older ones stemming from nonexistent or primitive methods of sewage treatment and garbage disposal. Outside the industrial world, less than 10 percent of all sewage and 30 percent of industrial wastes are treated at all before being dumped into lakes and rivers, statistics that help explain why more than one billion people in the developing world lack access to safe drinking water.

Throughout the world, efforts to combat water pollution often begin—and, much too often, end—with addressing what is known as "point" sources: the contaminants flowing through pipes. This is the easiest route to mandatory cleanups: laws can require industries to use helpful technology, and inspectors can check compliance at clearly identifiable sources. Cleaning up "nonpoint"

source pollution—where contaminants drift into waterways from farms and roads—is much more difficult. Integrated and flexible approaches are needed to deal with these increasing challenges.

The Great Lakes, containing 18 percent of the world's surface freshwater, became a major focus of such efforts in the 1970s, when the United States and Canada joined to recognize and wrestle with pollution problems, especially the phosphorus coming from detergents and fertilizers. The Great Lakes Water Quality Agreement, first signed by the two nations in 1972, set up a complex framework for protecting the shared freshwater resources. Coordinated government and partner efforts to cut point and nonpoint sources included banning phosphate

detergents and improving farm practices, including reducing the use of phosphorus fertilizers. In 2007, phosphorus reduction goals for four of the five lakes were met.

With the reduction in one pollutant, though, the effects of persistent toxic chemicals such as PCBs and DDT on wildlife became even more obvious. Zero discharge goals were set for designated chemicals in the late 1970s. The point-source discharge of toxics has decreased, and there is evidence that wildlife like eagles and cormorants are rebounding. Even so, there is still work to be done, as persistent chemicals remain in the ecosystem—still entering from nonpoint sources or just sticking around in sediment, and new pharmaceuticals likely pose new threats.

Nitrogen Pollution

Too Much of a Good Thing

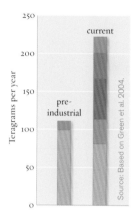

Global sources of nitrogen.
The amount of nitrogen stemming from human activities now exceeds the amount occurring naturally in the environment.

- Human waste
- Fertilizer
- Livestock waste
- Atmospheric deposition
- Fixation by plants

Source: Based on Green et al. 2004.

Toxic tides.
Excess nitrogen in coastal waters can rapidly increase algae growth in surface waters, forming red tides (such as the one shown here) and other toxic algal blooms.

Miriam Godfrey, NIWA

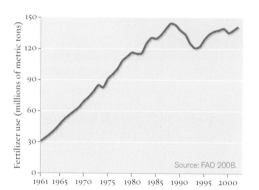

The global rise in fertilizer use.
Global chemical fertilizer use has increased by 450 percent since the 1960s, only dipping after 1990 with the collapse of the Soviet Union.

Source: FAO 2008.

EVERY YEAR, more than two hundred thousand tons of nitrogen waste travels down the Mississippi River into the Gulf of Mexico. Most stems from farm fertilizers, sewage plants, livestock pens, and coal plants throughout the river basin—an area encompassing some 40 percent of the continental United States and part of Canada. Swept into the river by rain and winds, the chemical nutrients ultimately pour into the Gulf of Mexico, overfeeding algae in coastal waters, which bloom, die, and decay, and in the process suck up oxygen from the water, suffocating marine life.

Although nitrogen is vital to all living things, it can be deadly to life when it exceeds natural levels. This is a dark side of the agricultural revolution begun in the 1940s, when new technologies, including mass-produced synthetic fertilizers, greatly increased food production. Humans have doubled the amount of nitrogen in the environment since that time, a trend that continues today as the global population grows, per capita meat consumption rises, and demands mount for crops, livestock feed, and, most recently, biofuels.

These trends have all combined to increase the flow of excess nitrogen to the world's coasts sixfold within the past century, leading to more "dead zones" like the one in the Gulf of Mexico. "Red tides" are also increasingly common in many parts of the world where pollution feeds blooms of floating toxic algae that infect shellfish and sicken or kill

Data source: Based on Green et al. 2004.

**Change in Nitrogen Flow
since Preindustrial Times**
by Marine Ecoregion
(metric tons per year)

1,200,000	↑ increasing
900,000	
200,000	
90,000	
30,000	
0	
-8,299	↓ decreasing
No data	

INCREASE IN NITROGEN FLOW TO THE COASTS. The centers of intensive agriculture and industry in the Northern Hemisphere have produced some of the world's largest modern increases in nutrient pollution.

shellfish-eating creatures, including fish, marine mammals, and humans.

By 2008, the Gulf of Mexico dead zone had grown to equal the size of the U.S. state of New Jersey, damaging regional and commercial fisheries that annually generate more than $2 billion. Appearing anew each spring, the dead zone spreads farther each year along the coasts of Louisiana and Texas; more shellfish are killed, fish swim farther away to escape, and fishing boats must travel ever farther out to sea for their catch.

Because excess nitrogen comes from so many different sources, efforts to address it must take many forms. Cities and industry can improve sewage treatment technologies; conservation groups can set aside undeveloped land as "buffers," and farms can reduce fertilizer use wherever possible, including switching to crops that need less nitrogen or chemical fertilizers. "Nutrient-trading"—an innovative approach aimed at reducing pollution as inexpensively as possible—is another promising strategy, which has been

implemented in several parts of the world in recent years, including the U.S. state of Connecticut. There, beginning in 2002, officials trying to cope with a dead zone in the Long Island Sound have encouraged the state's seventy-nine wastewater plants to buy and sell permits to release nitrogen above a mandated level. By 2006, this effort had helped reduce nitrogen discharges from the region's treatment plants into Long Island Sound by 25 percent from 2001 levels.

Ruin of the Reefs

Fading Jewels, Lost Wealth

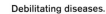

Blowing up livelihoods. "Blast fishing," in which fishers illegally use explosives to kill or stun their prey, is widespread in Southeast Asia. Not only is there collateral fish damage but reefs are also left unable to support future fisheries.

Debilitating diseases. A growing number of diseases have been attacking corals. White-band disease, a slow necrosis that creeps across corals, has virtually stopped new reef growth across the Caribbean.

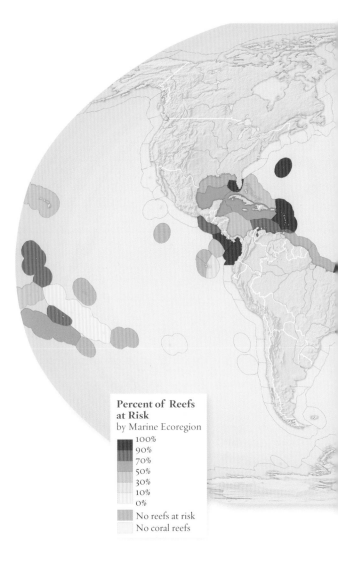

Percent of Reefs at Risk
by Marine Ecoregion

100%
90%
70%
50%
30%
10%
0%
No reefs at risk
No coral reefs

INDONESIA'S CORAL-RINGED Pulau Seribu archipelago stretches through the Java Sea for eighty kilometers north of the capital city of Jakarta. The reefs are legally protected yet still vulnerable to the expanding array of abuses, including overfishing and pollution, that are increasingly depleting the world's marine life. As a result, this chain of tiny islands has come to resemble a giant science exhibit, displaying a gradient of ruin in which the reefs farthest from Jakarta still host abundant life, yet those nearest to the city are dead and barren.

At the turn of the twenty-first century, scientists warned that 48 percent of the world's coral reefs were at risk of being despoiled. In some areas with large coastal populations, such as Jakarta, the percentage exceeded 90 percent. Throughout the world, the coastal development crowding cities, ports, and

tourist resorts right up to the water's edge has devastated fragile coral reefs. People have completely destroyed reefs by building on them or mining them for building stone, or blasting them to bits to clear the way for shipping channels, ports, and marinas.

Pollution flowing from land to sea is a more indirect but just as deadly harm, since nitrogen from sewage and fertilizer feed algae that block out light or grow over the corals, smothering them. Marine pollution, including oil spills, adds to the toll.

Overfishing changes the complex balance of life in the sea. Reefs in Jamaica have lost so many of their larger grazing fish that algae grows almost unchecked, inhibiting the growth of new corals. Predators such as groupers are greatly reduced in numbers on almost all reefs, while sharks, once the top predators, are now ecologically insignificant. Typically, small numbers of these once-

abundant fish remain, and recovery can be swift if reefs are given some respite from hooks, traps, and spears, but in some cases the losses are complete. The Nassau grouper has vanished from large swaths of the Caribbean, while giant clams have not been seen in Fiji's waters for more than fifty years.

Reefs weakened by one threat may be finally driven to collapse by the addition of another—which is what makes the mounting risks from climate change so worrisome. The coral architects of these intricate ecosystems are adapted to warm water but easily harmed by increases of even a degree or two centigrade. As waters have warmed, reefs in many areas of the world have lost the algae that give them their jewel-like colors and have bleached white—an alarm that often presages coral death. Wide areas of Indian Ocean reefs were devastated in this way in

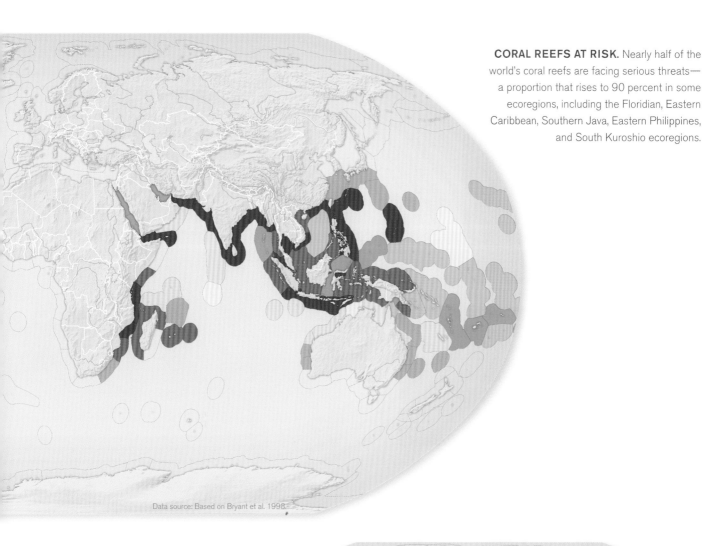

CORAL REEFS AT RISK. Nearly half of the world's coral reefs are facing serious threats—a proportion that rises to 90 percent in some ecoregions, including the Floridian, Eastern Caribbean, Southern Java, Eastern Philippines, and South Kuroshio ecoregions.

Data source: Based on Bryant et al. 1998.

1998, when an El Niño event swept super-warm waters around the world. In 2005, warming brought bleaching and death to the coral reefs of the Caribbean without such an El Niño event. The waters of the world are warming, and such events are projected to become increasingly common.

Conservation groups, governments, and local communities have been working to safeguard coral reefs in recent years by creating hundreds of marine protected areas, ranging from the world's largest marine reserve, in Kiribati's Phoenix Islands, to tiny Apo Island in the Philippines. Some of the most successful reserves, like that off Arnavon Island in the Solomon Islands and off Soufrière in St. Lucia, have been those in which local people are involved and see direct benefits from protection, including more abundant fish supplies and ecotourism.

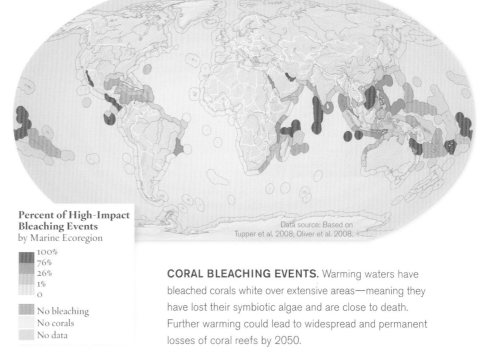

Data source: Based on Tupper et al. 2008; Oliver et al. 2008.

Percent of High-Impact Bleaching Events
by Marine Ecoregion

- 100%
- 76%
- 26%
- 1%
- 0

- No bleaching
- No corals
- No data

CORAL BLEACHING EVENTS. Warming waters have bleached corals white over extensive areas—meaning they have lost their symbiotic algae and are close to death. Further warming could lead to widespread and permanent losses of coral reefs by 2050.

Into the Wild

The Cost of Expanding Human Access

Roads providing access. Monkeys and endangered animals are common in wild-meat markets of western and central Africa, where logging roads penetrate once-remote forests.

Room to roam. A solitary adult male grizzly bear can have a range of over seven hundred square kilometers. Like many large mammals, they are sensitive to human intrusions—whether roads or hunters—and remain only in the least accessible parts of North America.

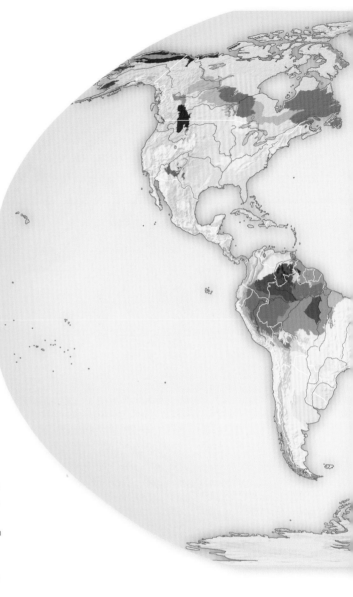

WHEN LOGGERS FIRST BUILT roads through the deep jungles of the Congo, they set off a chain reaction. The new roads opened routes for market hunters to go deeper into the jungle, finding game they could not get to before. Soon trucks traveling in and out were transporting not only logs and woodsmen but the meat of wild pigs, forest antelope, porcupines, reptiles, and our closest living relative, endangered bonobo chimpanzees.

Removing these animals from the forest changes the balance between predators and available prey affecting the web of life; as the forest becomes more accessible to people, its wildness begins to vanish.

The same story is being repeated throughout the world's last wild places, from the Amazon in South America to the Indonesian jungles of Asia—where the last forest sanctuaries of the orangutan are coming under the ax. It happened in nineteenth-century

North America as well, when railroads and roads penetrated the Great Plains, wiping out the wilderness, and again later when the West was finally conquered.

Today, more than 60 percent of all land on Earth is within just ten kilometers of a road. And new roads and airstrips continue to encroach on formerly remote places. As they do, the risks to native species multiply. Wilderness splinters into fragments and

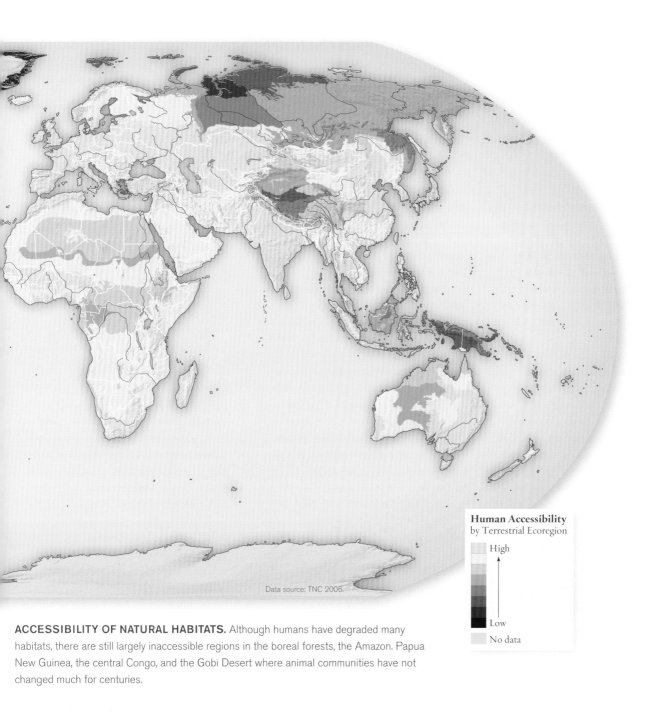

Human Accessibility
by Terrestrial Ecoregion

High

Low

No data

Data source: TNC 2006.

ACCESSIBILITY OF NATURAL HABITATS. Although humans have degraded many habitats, there are still largely inaccessible regions in the boreal forests, the Amazon. Papua New Guinea, the central Congo, and the Gobi Desert where animal communities have not changed much for centuries.

eventually disappears. Settlers bring livestock, invasive plants, pollution, and new germs. It is no coincidence that today the most intact communities of large mammals live in Earth's most remote regions.

Pristine wilderness still exists—in the Arctic, the Tibetan Plateau, and New Guinea's lowland jungles, among other places. But human wanderlust and enterprise, and an ever-expanding population means it is just a matter of time before we gain access

to them. Will we use our access to degrade and destroy, or will we use it to manage and cherish the ancient web of life these places support? The history of conservation shows that we can do the latter, and these untouched places offer that possibility. After all, humans have managed to coexist with wildness in some parts of Earth. One example is the Crown of the Continent ecosystem along the northern Rocky Mountains in

southwestern Alberta, southeastern British Columbia, and northwestern Montana. Here, humans have long had access deep into the wild country for hunting, fishing and some logging, yet the animal communities, which include grizzly bear, lynx, mountain lion, wolf, fox, martin, and wolverine, are in about the same balance as they have been for hundreds of years past.

Poverty and Nature's Services

M. SANJAYAN

HIKING THROUGH THE RAIN FOREST in coastal West Africa, I stumble onto an unfolding scene in a tiny village in Sierra Leone—a country whose inhabitants are among the poorest on Earth despite being surrounded by a wealth of biodiversity.

A ten-year-old boy, skinny and under-nourished, clad only in dingy shorts, crouches over a weak flame, engrossed in his task of burning the fur off a dead monkey.

It is a *Cercopithecus* of some sort, perhaps a white-nosed Guenon.

Holding the monkey carefully in both hands, the boy slowly turns it as its pelt singes and curls into soft gray ash. It is a delicate task, one at which the boy excels. Every so often he uses a piece of tin sheet metal to furiously fan the rain-soaked fire—a smoky mess whose acrid odor hangs in the air.

The monkey is in the process of transitioning from wildlife into food. Soon, it will be dismembered, every bit from nose to tail tip thrown into a pot with some okra, peppers, or other meager vegetables and a small spill of palm oil or peanut oil if available—a West African stew ultimately yielding what I estimate, based on the small crush of spectators hovering expectantly, to be about two tablespoons of meat protein for each person. A small monkey in a big pot.

It is an arresting scene, typical of many I have witnessed in villages around the world. Yet something about this boy and his handiwork prompts me to pull out my small camera and snap a photo—and immediately feel a little shabby about it. The boy just looks up and giggles.

Much later, in the privacy of my tent, with the rain dripping outside, I flick through the pictures on my camera until I come to the one of the boy. This time around, though, it's not the dead monkey that draws my attention. I focus on the sheet of tin.

It's a piece of a signboard—one of many that line rural roads all over the world, proclaiming God, government, or charity. On this one, blue letters framed against a white field proclaim an international hunger-prevention organization, the World Food Programme.

It is a staggering sight. Here is this kid fanning the flames with a sign from a global organization whose mission is to feed people, when in actuality, what he is going to eat today is a monkey from the forest. It is a powerful lesson that for the rural poor, nature continues to provide when governments and charities can't or simply don't.

This is a lesson conservationists can't afford to ignore.

As we begin to better map, quantify, and assign monetary value to nature's services—from water to carbon storage—we need to take into account the roughly one-sixth of the world's population that lives on the very margins of national or global economies and for whom such services are virtually irreplaceable. The value of water to a West African woman trying to prepare a meal is far greater than the value of the same commodity to a woman in southern California trying to fill up her swimming pool.

Valuation of nature's services must properly recognize and incorporate this vast life-sustaining net that nature provides to the poor—and the context in which such provisioning occurs.

As I see it, for the planet's roughly one billion poor rural inhabitants, six basic services currently procured for free from nature provide most of their daily needs:

FRESHWATER is the most obvious, and its procurement is taxing, particularly to women, who bear most of the load. Although taps are sprouting in many rural African villages, few connect to sustainable water sources, and without water, taps don't run. Of course the problem with freshwater is often that it is not found where it is needed most, and large parts of the world now experience acute water shortages. For the poor, natural storage mechanisms such as flowing rivers, lakes, ponds, and rural wells hold freshwater until it is needed. But with habitat alteration, more inland water is moved into the sea faster than it can be used or accessed by the people who need it most. In countries such as Bolivia and Madagascar, the lack of accessible freshwater has been widely implicated in the civil unrest that led to the toppling of elected governments.

FUELWOOD, collected from forests, plantations, or local groves, is indispensible for the heating and cooking needs of 40 percent of rural homes. Its collection is the second-most taxing chore impacting daily life (after water collection), and again, it is women and children who bear the disproportionate burden. Most attempts to stem tropical deforestation have focused on protecting primary forests or watersheds, while the individual (though not cumulatively) small-scale act of collecting sticks for cooking fires has been mostly ignored.

FISHERIES provide more than 20 percent of the protein for people in the world's poorest countries. In southwest Asia's lower Mekong Basin, for example, forty million people benefit from inland fisheries to meet their daily dietary needs and/or provide jobs. For island nations, fishing is often the biggest economic driver and provides subsistence livelihoods to the majority of the population. Given the resource limitations that island nations face, thriving fisheries can be crucial to the well-being of the countries' citizens. Even in places far from the ocean or major freshwater bodies, fish in a dried form is commonly transported well into the interior of continents, especially in Africa.

FERTILITY of soils and natural nutrient cycling provides "fertilizers" for places untouched by the green revolution with far fewer consequences in terms of energy use and nutrient overload. Maintaining fertility also allows for a denser population to coexist without resorting to the sort of wars that have frequented countries of the Rift Valley lake region in Africa, for example, where acute pressures for farmland and dropping productivity of farms remains.

FOREST PRODUCTS, such as honey, meat from forest animals, medicinal plants, fiber, and so forth, have a myriad of uses. Wild animals often provide the only meat protein that is "affordable" to the rural poor. If the species being targeted are relatively common—

Reliance on nature for food in West Africa

say, agricultural pests or species that thrive in disturbed environments—then sustainability can be maintained for a long while. However, it is important to draw a distinction between forest products that are used in local subsistence and those that are exported into the cities for a lucrative trade market. The bush meat crisis, where entire forests are decimated of wildlife, from bats to great apes, is rarely about subsistence consumption but rather about using logging roads, modern transportation networks, and modern tools to supply the luxury demands of people in cities totally removed from the forest.

FODDER in terms of grass and browse for livestock is important in rural communities because trade in meat products is one of the few ways through which the poor can access the global economy. Livestock is the common bank for rural populations. In Kenya, an indigenous herdsman explained to me that he considers the cows to be his savings account, his goats his checking account, and the few chickens that scratch around his village to be cash in the pocket. Depending on his need, he decides what he is going to take to the market and sell.

These "6 Fs" of nature (six free services) are part of the staple packet of goods and services that virtually every rural community depends on. Lose them, and people will suffer.

That night, while looking at the photo of the boy and his soggy fire, I think about returning to the village and bartering for the sign; hanging in my office, it would be a powerful reminder of the insight I gained in his West African village. But though I carry many things that the boy would probably covet, I don't actually have anything of real value to him. No matter what I might offer him, it wouldn't be a fair trade. I don't need the sign. The boy does.

M. SANJAYAN IS A LEAD SCIENTIST AT THE NATURE CONSERVANCY.

Forest Clearing

Uprooting Nature

Ancient sanctuaries.
Some trees in old-growth forests are hundreds of years old. Mixed with young trees, as in this stand of western red cedars in the U.S. state of Idaho, they form complex habitats.

Unstable slopes.
Clear-cut logging can cause landslides and erosion that damage stream and river habitats.

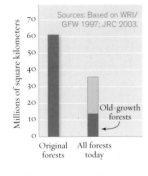

Loss of forests worldwide.
Forests covered just under half of all land on Earth prior to large-scale clearing by humans, which began several thousand years ago and continues today.

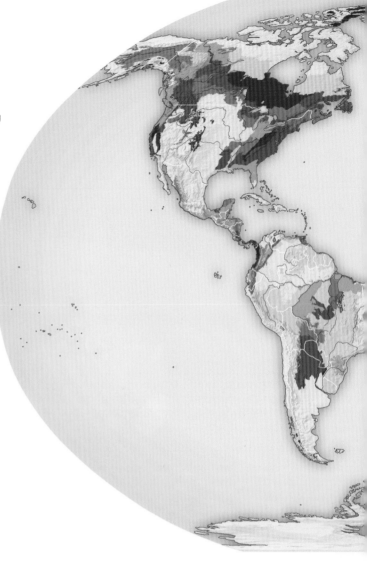

EVERY YEAR, throughout the world, a combined area of forest equal to the size of Germany is cleared to feed modern appetites for paper, cardboard, and lumber. Scientists and conservationists worry that in many places, too much forest is being cut too fast, especially given that it can take a century, or even two, for the trees to grow back and for lost habitat to be restored.

In some cases, this never happens. By 2000, humans had permanently cleared away about 42 percent of Earth's original forests to make room for homes, offices, factories, shops, and farms. About eighty thousand square kilometers of forest—an area about the size of the entire Japanese island of Hokkaido or the U.S. state of Maine—was permanently lost between 1990 and 2000 alone.

Clear-cutting forests, even if they then are left to grow back, can permanently damage habitat. Natural forest is varied in its structure, with patches of large and small trees mixed together, with occasional small openings in the forest canopy, and with the trunks of fallen trees rotting on the forest floor. But when the trees across a region are cut down within a span of even twenty to thirty years, those that grow back are more of a uniform height, and the forest habitat has a uniform structure.

Forest destruction steals creatures' homes and in many cases pushes them toward extinction. The marbled murrelet is a small seabird that, like the salmon, lives at sea but returns inland to breed. It nests in old-growth forests in North America's Pacific Northwest, often in the largest trees. These forests have evolved over centuries into mature and complex habitat relatively untouched by humans. The marbled murrelet has become endangered as old-growth

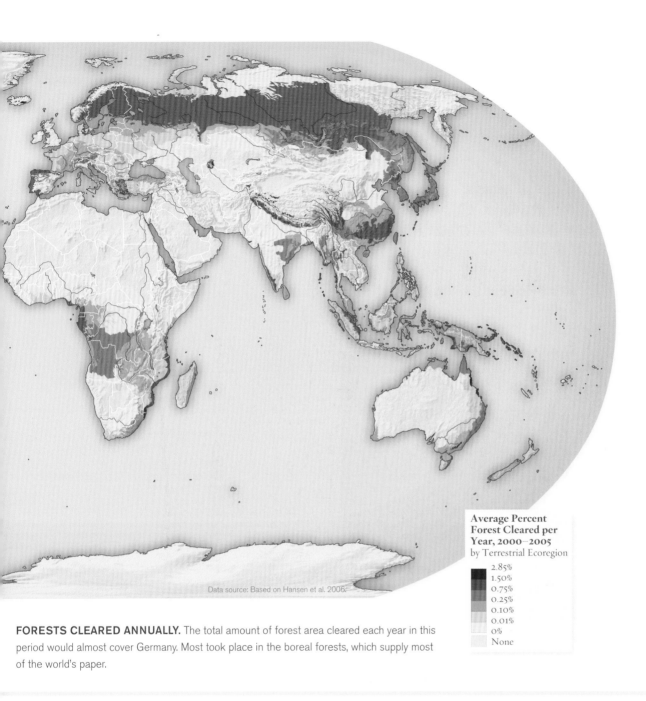

**Average Percent
Forest Cleared per
Year, 2000–2005**
by Terrestrial Ecoregion

- 2.85%
- 1.50%
- 0.75%
- 0.25%
- 0.10%
- 0.01%
- 0%
- None

Data source: Based on Hansen et al. 2006.

FORESTS CLEARED ANNUALLY. The total amount of forest area cleared each year in this period would almost cover Germany. Most took place in the boreal forests, which supply most of the world's paper.

forests have been logged; even if the forest is able to grow back, the young trees are not suitable for their nests.

Deforestation not only directly removes habitat but also increases local soil erosion, releasing sediment once held by tree roots that clogs rivers and lakes—threatening species like the salmon. And globally, deforestation is estimated to be the source of almost 20 percent of the greenhouse gases that cause global warming, since some of the massive amount of carbon absorbed, or "sequestered," as forests grow is released when they are burned or cut down.

As the costs of deforestation have become more widely understood in recent decades, they have inspired a global movement to encourage responsible forestry. Increasingly, private timber companies and government forestry agencies have been working with scientists and conservation organizations to harvest wood in ways intended to guarantee that the forests and their creatures can survive. Increasingly, trees are cut in small patches, in order to leave surrounding habitat intact. Trees cut on steep slopes are removed carefully—sometimes even by helicopter—to prevent landslides.

Encouraging this movement toward wiser stewardship of forest resources is a new industry of consumer watchdogs and certification. People can now buy wood products that are produced responsibly by looking for labels from the Forest Stewardship Council, the Sustainable Forestry Initiative, or the Program for the Endorsement of Forest Certification. The growing recycling industry has been another boon for saving forests. Wood fiber can be recycled as many as seven times as paper and cardboard, each time saving another small part of a forest.

Water Stress
Overused and Undermanaged

A cemetery for ships. Excess demand for irrigation water has turned the Aral Sea into a desert, marked by the rusting hulks of fishing vessels.

Christopher Herwig/Aurora

Last gasps on the Klamath. In 2002, water diversions for farm irrigation from Northern California's Klamath River resulted in the death of more than thirty-three thousand salmon before they could spawn.

AP Photo/Joe Cavaretta

Degree of Water Stress
by Freshwater Ecoregion

- Extreme stress
- High stress
- Moderate stress
- Low or no stress
- Minimal water use
- Unassessed

AS RECENTLY as the 1960s, the Aral Sea was the world's fourth-largest lake, sustaining abundant wildlife and fish and providing livelihoods for some sixty thousand people. Yet over the next four decades, cotton farmers increasingly diverted water from the two principal rivers feeding into the sea, dramatically reducing its volume, hastening the collapse of the fishing industry, and eventually splitting the sea into two shrinking pools. Scientists have predicted the South Aral lake will dry out completely by 2020, while the World Bank has loaned more than $60 million to Kazakhstan for engineering projects to keep water in the North Aral.

The Aral Sea, in fact, is merely an extreme example of a trend with disturbing implications for freshwater environments and the life that depends on them. Drying rivers and disappearing lakes have become increasingly common on every continent, from China's Yellow River to North America's Colorado River to Africa's Lake Chad. The rising demand for freshwater for crops and other human needs is outstripping available supplies, in a phenomenon known as *water stress*. It diminishes not only lakes and rivers but also the water reserves of groundwater aquifers, the majority of which are connected to surface waters. The so-called fossil aquifers, including one beneath the Sahara Desert—formed by rainfall during the last Ice Age—are in even worse shape, since they cannot be replenished.

Already, more than 2.3 billion people throughout the world are suffering due to water stress, a number expected to rise to 3.5 billion by 2025. Agriculture remains the biggest water consumer, representing some 70 percent of global water use. And increasing climate change will likely bring even worse news for water supplies, because temperatures will rise, rainfall may be more unpredictable, and snowmelt may well be reduced.

Water stress causes cascading impacts throughout local economies, reducing hopes for economic development, thwarting food production, driving species to extinction, and leaving people parched. A particularly cruel effect in communities living near the remnants of the Aral Sea has been a rise in respiratory disease, due to air polluted by toxic residues of pesticides in the exposed seabed. Water stress also harms local plants and animals, as lower levels in rivers and lakes increase the water's temperature and salinity and reduce oxygen and the capacity

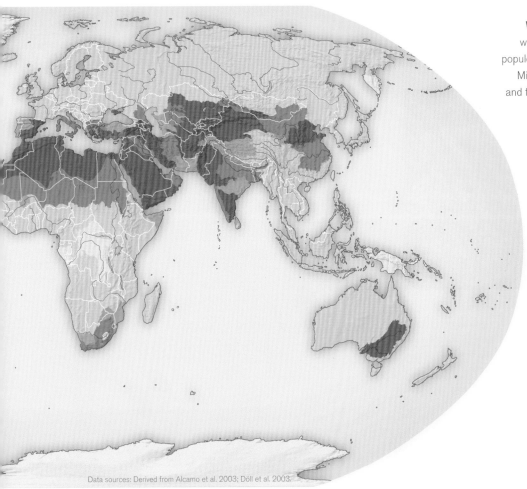

Data sources: Derived from Alcamo et al. 2003; Döll et al. 2003.

WATER STRESS. Human demand for water outstrips natural supply in arid and populous regions like the Mediterranean, the Middle East, Central Asia, much of China, and the western United States. Competition for water is endangering freshwater environments and species.

Data source: Based on Struckmeir & Richts 2007.

of freshwater to dilute pollutants. There are also many regions of the world that have more ample water supplies, such as the eastern United States or central Europe, but pollution and other types of ecosystem degradation can render water supplies unusable, putting people, species, and ecosystems in jeopardy.

To cope with proliferating water stress, a few nations, including South Africa and Australia, limit water withdrawals from rivers during times when low river flows might harm fish that are trying to reach spawning grounds. South Africa has also taken the more aggressive measure of creating "environmental water reserves," which stipulate that river water cannot be diverted or otherwise used if doing so would jeopardize native species and ecosystems.

Dominant Groundwater Feature
by Freshwater Ecoregion

Shallow aquifer
High recharge rate
Low recharge rate

Deep aquifer
High recharge rate
Moderate recharge rate
Low recharge rate

GROUNDWATER AQUIFERS. Overtapping shallow aquifers can rob waterways of flow, disturbing species and river processes. Deep groundwater aquifers, such as the U.S. Ogallala Aquifer, are especially vulnerable as they recharge slowly, if at all.

Overfishing

Emptying the Oceans

Struck down before their prime. Deep-sea fish, such as these yellow-eye rockfish being caught off the coast of Alaska, can take as many as twenty-two years to mature and reproduce. Overfishing can therefore wipe them out in no time. In California, yellow-eye rockfish stocks are not expected to recover until 2074, despite limitations on harvests.

Caught by the billions. Huge hauls of small fish, such as these Jack mackerel being harvested off Chile's coast, are processed and used as feed for livestock, poultry, salmon, and shrimp. Reductions in their stocks deprive larger wild fish of their customary meals.

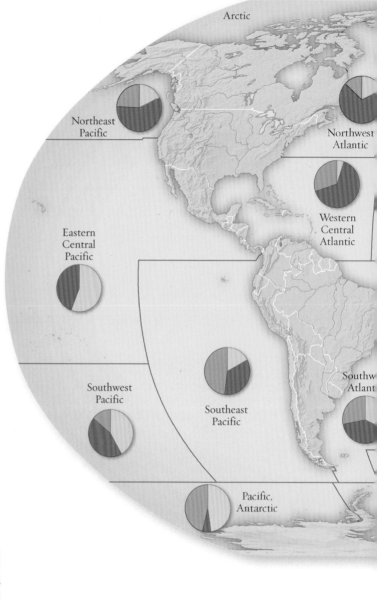

ONLY RELATIVELY recently in human history has fishing become a large-scale enterprise, with thousands of workers in "factory boats" that spend months at a time catching, processing, and freezing fish, and bulldozer-like trawlers scouring the high seas. Over the past half century, expanding markets, new technology boosting ships' range and capacity, and—in the 1960s and 1970s—generous government subsidies for fishing fleets, combined to increase harvests dramatically.

By the 1980s, however, the limits of the oceans' bounty were already becoming clear, as too many boats were traveling ever farther to chase fewer and fewer fish. In 2006, the United Nations reported that just 3 percent of regularly monitored fish stocks remained underexploited. More than half were fully exploited, and one-fourth were overexploited or depleted. In the North Atlantic Ocean, most species of groundfish, including longtime regional favorites such as Atlantic cod, haddock, flounder, and plaice, fell into this last besieged group.

Such popular fare have been caught faster than they can reproduce, especially in the case of slow-maturing species such as groundfish and sharks. This in turn has driven fishing ships to explore more remote and deeper parts of the oceans, in a quest for new commercially viable species that, at least temporarily, has hidden the mounting toll on the oceans from developed-nation consumers who still find plenty of fish, if not always the same species and no longer quite so cheap, in markets and restaurants.

Yet the costs of overfishing are as unavoidable as they are far-reaching. The depletion

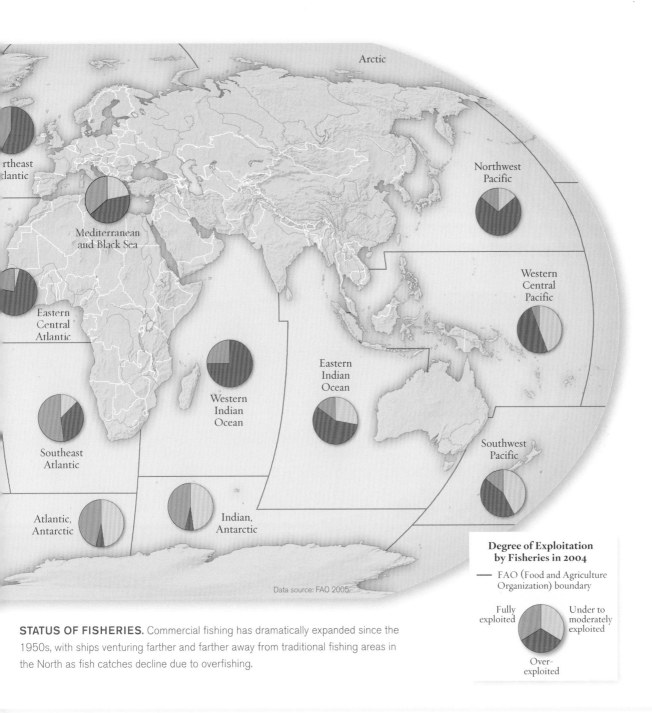

Arctic

Northeast Atlantic

Mediterranean and Black Sea

Northwest Pacific

Western Central Pacific

Eastern Central Atlantic

Western Indian Ocean

Eastern Indian Ocean

Southeast Atlantic

Southwest Pacific

Atlantic, Antarctic

Indian, Antarctic

Data source: FAO 2005.

Degree of Exploitation by Fisheries in 2004

—— FAO (Food and Agriculture Organization) boundary

Fully exploited

Under to moderately exploited

Over-exploited

STATUS OF FISHERIES. Commercial fishing has dramatically expanded since the 1950s, with ships venturing farther and farther away from traditional fishing areas in the North as fish catches decline due to overfishing.

of stocks has gradually driven the industry to seek smaller and younger fish, diminishing the potential for future production. Compounding this is that with the decline of the most prized fish—the large, predatory species such as tuna, cod, or hake—fishers increasingly are switching to species lower in the food chain, such as sardines, that feed on plankton or small invertebrates. This pattern of exploitation, known as "fishing down the food web," risks upsetting the balance of marine life. In the North Atlantic Ocean, for example, only 12 percent of the catch in

the early 1990s was made up of large predatory fish such as cod and hake—down from more than 40 percent four decades earlier.

Managing fish stocks so as to have fish for future generations is a complex and difficult task, requiring not one but a range of solutions. Yet it is not impossible, and scientists and policy makers alike know what it takes. The answers include reductions in the number of boats and in quotas for specific species, restrictions on the size of fish being caught, and temporary bans on fishing in

certain areas. The growing movement to certify fish as sustainably harvested is also promising. In 2006, Pacific cod fishers using long-line freezer ships off the coast of Alaska became the world's first cod fishery to be so certified under the Marine Stewardship Council (MSC). The MSC seal requires fishers to limit damage to marine ecosystems while sustaining production for future generations.

Wildlife Trade

Sold into Extinction

The plight of the pangolin. The scales of the exotic, ant-eating pangolin are a coveted medicinal ingredient in Asia. The trade of this species has decimated wild populations and put the pangolin at risk of extinction.

China's wild-meat markets. At the notorious wild-animal market in Guangzhou, in southern China, more than nine hundred stalls sell thousands of animals, all destined for dinner plates.

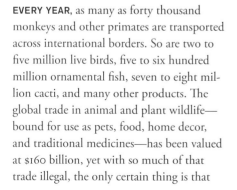

One step forward. Part of a trend of improved enforcement, in January 2008, Thai officials confiscated dead tigers and leopards and three hundred live pangolins bound for Laos after a raid on an illegal operation along the Mekong River.

EVERY YEAR, as many as forty thousand monkeys and other primates are transported across international borders. So are two to five million live birds, five to six hundred million ornamental fish, seven to eight million cacti, and many other products. The global trade in animal and plant wildlife—bound for use as pets, food, home decor, and traditional medicines—has been valued at $160 billion, yet with so much of that trade illegal, the only certain thing is that the total demand is rising together with human populations and incomes.

China, the United States, Japan, and the European Union are the main consumers of these wild creatures and plants, most of which originate in developing countries. But as prosperity increases in the developing world, demand is also rising, multiplying the threats to many species' survival.

The international police agency INTERPOL values the unlawful trade in wildlife, including animals and plants, at more than $20 billion a year, making it the world's biggest source of criminal income after drugs and guns. One of the greatest dangers of the illegal trade is that it tends to target species, such as rhinos, tigers, leopards, and turtles, that are under some legal protection precisely because they are already highly threatened. In some regions, overexploitation and illegal trade are so severe that they have surpassed habitat loss as the most serious threat to species' survival. A

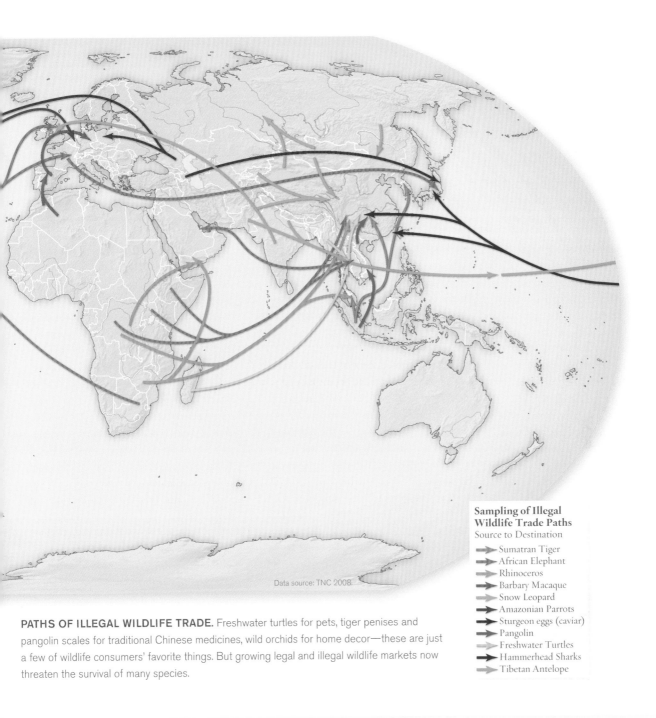

Sampling of Illegal Wildlife Trade Paths
Source to Destination

➤ Sumatran Tiger
➤ African Elephant
➤ Rhinoceros
➤ Barbary Macaque
➤ Snow Leopard
➤ Amazonian Parrots
➤ Sturgeon eggs (caviar)
➤ Pangolin
➤ Freshwater Turtles
➤ Hammerhead Sharks
➤ Tibetan Antelope

Data source: TNC 2008.

PATHS OF ILLEGAL WILDLIFE TRADE. Freshwater turtles for pets, tiger penises and pangolin scales for traditional Chinese medicines, wild orchids for home decor—these are just a few of wildlife consumers' favorite things. But growing legal and illegal wildlife markets now threaten the survival of many species.

comprehensive assessment of the conservation status of the world's mammals in 2008 showed that exploitation is the second-greatest threat affecting over nine hundred mammal species, especially in Asia.

Over the past few years, some countries have been collaborating to crack down on illegal wildlife trade. In 2005, a new international effort—the Association of Southeast Asian Nations Wildlife Enforcement Network (ASEAN-WEN)—began to share intelligence, train judges on existing wildlife

protection laws, and more aggressively pursue illegal traders. For the first time in this region, park rangers and environmental officers coordinated with police, customs and immigration authorities, and INTERPOL to combat illegal trade.

New undercover sting operations, better training of law enforcement agents and prosecutors, and more sophisticated forensics technology and hidden cameras have led to more arrests. Yet a key remaining problem is that, in most countries, the penalties for

buying or selling banned species are too lenient compared to the potential rewards. In 2006, the Thai wildlife crime task force set up by ASEAN-WEN seized 250 shahtoosh shawls, made from the down fur of the critically endangered Tibetan antelope, with a combined value of about $99,500. The traders who pleaded guilty were released after paying a single fine of just $300. Experts believe as many as twenty thousand Tibetan antelopes are poached each year to make the shawls.

Future of Fisheries

JACKIE ALDER
DANIEL PAULY

MORE AND MORE PEOPLE are eating fish. Over the past forty years, the amount of fish caught around the world has tripled, with each person eating nearly twice as much fish. Our consumption of fish has outpaced population as we have increased our incomes and changed our food preferences, especially in our move toward healthier food choices like marine fish. Our demand for fish is expected to continue to increase at about 1.5 percent annually over the coming decades as populations and incomes grow. Meeting this demand will be a challenge, especially since seafood is the fastest-growing food commodity that is traded globally.

Recent assessments warn that many of the world's fisheries continue to decline. While some stocks are rebuilding, the number of overfished or crashed stocks is increasing and outweighs them. One way we can look at how fisheries are changing is to look at how the catch is changing, which can be measured by the mean trophic index (MTI). This is a combined measure of the "trophic level" of fish caught—where they are in the food chain; a higher value indicates more large predators at the top of the food chain. An increasing or unchanged MTI usually indicates that the fisheries are rebuilding or stable; but if the MTI decreases, then it suggests that much of the catch is fish lower down the food web—because larger fish have been overfished—and these are often not the fish of choice among consumers. Today, the majority of fish caught are found lower down the food web despite fishing deeper and farther offshore.

While there is a global creep in the decline of marine fisheries, some species are on a precipitous decline, especially large predators such as the bluefin tuna in the Mediterranean and eastern Atlantic. We

are catching these fish faster than they can reproduce, and we risk losing these majestic fish that can swim across the Atlantic Ocean in less than four weeks.

Climate change is already impacting fish as sea temperatures warm. We are already seeing some fish in the North Sea such as the commercially important wolf fish moving north and being replaced by small and low-value fish such as anchovies and red mullet. Climate change will also reduce or eliminate some habitats for fish. Coral reefs that are home to hundreds of fish, from the small clown fish as seen in *Finding Nemo,* to snappers, a favorite food for many people, may be affected.

Another consequence of climate change is ocean acidification. The oceans naturally absorb carbon dioxide, some of it in the form of carbonic acid. As the amount of the gas has increased in the atmosphere, more is absorbed in the ocean, resulting in the lowering of the pH of ocean water. This development can affect the future of fisheries, because acids dissolve calcium carbonate that form shells and corals. The greatest threat is on coral reefs and cold-water corals. Acidification will have an impact on colder ecosystems first (e.g., the Southern Ocean), particularly through its impact on small calcareous plankton animals that are the foundation of marine food webs, including those supporting exploited fish populations.

Climate change and ocean acidification are long-term threats, but the chronic stress imposed by fishing on marine ecosystems today is more pressing. Addressing the problem of overfishing is not easy since any decision will affect someone through the loss of jobs, profits, or food security. A range of possible strategies could help stem the declines. Many scientists and fisheries managers recommend a mix of solutions, including reducing fishing effort by reducing the number of fishing boats, eliminating perverse subsidies, increasing no-take areas, taking an ecosystem approach to fisheries management, and

using economic incentives such as certification to change fishing practices. Research suggests that waiting too long will leave us with fewer big fish, more small, less appealing fish, a greater reliance on farmed fish, and more vulnerable marine ecosystems.

Although the future of fisheries is far from optimistic, individuals can take several steps to help. Advocating for better fisheries management can encourage politicians to promote or support policies that eliminate perverse capacity building, encourage ecosystem-based management, equitably allocate property rights (especially to small-scale fisheries), reduce fishing effort, and develop networks of marine protected areas. Individual choices can also make a difference—already some buyers, sellers, and consumers are helping improve the sustainable management of fisheries by choosing seafood that is certified as sustainably caught. A number of certification schemes, such as the Marine Stewardship Council, provide valuable information to consumers.

Will eating farmed fish help the plight of marine fisheries? There is no simple answer. While it may seem that consuming farmed fish would reduce the demand on declining wild fisheries, under the current practices of farming marine fish species, little, if anything, has been done to stem the decline of fish stocks. Although aquaculture production is reported to contribute about 40 percent of all seafood produced globally, over two-thirds of that is in China, and only 3 percent are marine fish. The marine species that are farmed in significant quantities include Atlantic salmon, tropical shrimp, and, more recently, bluefin tuna. Salmon has been farmed since the 1970s, yet many stocks on both sides of the Atlantic are considered overfished or collapsed. The bluefin tuna, especially in the eastern Atlantic and the Mediterranean, is at risk of collapse, and many suggest that farming has accelerated their decline in the Mediterranean. In

Commercial salmon fishing, southeastern Alaska, United States

some cases, farmed fish are fed fishmeal and fish oil derived from wild capture fisheries, some of them exploiting stocks that are overfished. Choosing farmed fish that are fed on primarily plant-based diets may be a better choice. Farming of some species such as shrimp can also contribute to the destruction of habitats—for example, when ponds are built where mangroves used to provide important fish nurseries that are key to maintaining wild capture fish populations.

The future of fisheries is not necessarily doom and gloom. Recent work suggests that policies focused on sustainable resource use grounded in ecosystem-based management have the potential to alter the trends. There is potential to move the trends faster toward sustainable resource use when consumers support these policies by choosing sustainable seafood. The key will be to communicate the need for the right policies and for consumers to make the right seafood choices.

JACKIE ALDER IS HEAD OF THE MARINE AND COASTAL BRANCH, UNITED NATIONS ENVIRONMENT PROGRAMME.

DANIEL PAULY IS A PROFESSOR AT THE FISHERIES CENTRE, UNIVERSITY OF BRITISH COLUMBIA.

Fire

Healthy Doses of Destruction

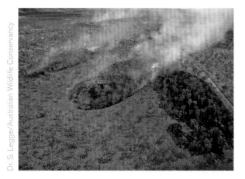

Dr. S. Legge/Australian Wildlife Conservancy

Renewing a landscape with fire. Aerial view of a large-scale controlled burn being conducted at the Mornington Wilderness Sanctuary in Western Australia.

Controlled flames. A prescribed fire being enacted as part of a prairie restoration project along the central Platte River in Nebraska, United States.

Chris Helzer/TNC

Status of Fire Regimes
by Ecoregion

Very degraded 10%
No data 16%
Degraded 52%
Intact 22%

Trends of Fire Regimes
by Ecoregion

No data 16%
Declining 59%
Stable 24%
Improving 1%

Source: Shlisky et al. 2007.

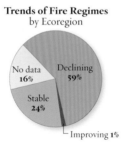

More balance needed. Although degraded systems can potentially be restored, the fire regimes in almost 60 percent of ecoregions are actually declining.

FIRE IS A ROUTINE part of life in many ecosystems, periodically sweeping through grasslands, shrublands, and forests, as it clears away dead material and opens up space for new growth. For some plants, such as the many sugarbush species of South Africa or the giant sequoias of the United States, fire is such a normal part of their ecology that their seeds must be heated to germinate. Fire returns nutrients to the soil and boosts the health of their habitats.

The rate of fire outbreaks, their schedule, and their intensity are factors that make up the so-called *fire regime* prevailing in different habitats. When the fire regime that has prevailed for centuries is disrupted, fires can be too much for one ecosystem, yet not enough for another.

For each ecosystem, just like Goldilocks, the balance of fire has to be "just right." Fire-dependent ecosystems, like the South African Fynbos and the California Chaparral, cannot persist for long without the right kind

of fire at the right time of year in places. Fire-sensitive ecosystems developed in the absence of fire and can be destroyed when fire becomes too frequent, too intense, or too widespread. Examples include tropical rain forests, as well as the deciduous forests of Europe and North America. Fire-independent ecosystems are either too cold, as in the tundra, or too sparse, as in the Sahara Desert, for fires to get started and burn large areas.

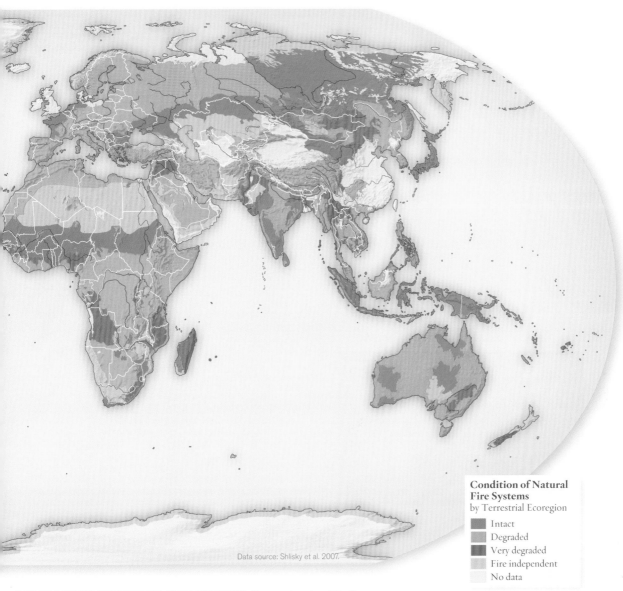

Data source: Shlisky et al. 2007.

Condition of Natural Fire Systems
by Terrestrial Ecoregion

- Intact
- Degraded
- Very degraded
- Fire independent
- No data

DEGRADATION OF NATURAL FIRE SYSTEMS. Too much or too little fire can upset the natural balance of ecosystems. Many of the wildest places on Earth have intact fire regimes, but most ecoregions have degraded fire regimes that could be restored with proper management.

Modern efforts to suppress wildfires may actually be making them more destructive. Dead wood and grass builds up, and when it finally does catch fire, it creates a hot, fast-moving blaze that ends up killing plants that otherwise would survive. Disastrous wildfires in Greece, California, Australia, and Indonesia provide examples of the damage to landscapes and people that is possible when natural fire regimes are disrupted.

When lightning struck the mountains of central Arizona in 1990, for instance, it ignited dead wood that had built up over decades. The subsequent fire claimed six lives, sixty-three homes, and ten thousand hectares—a disaster that might have been avoided if the routine small fires that normally swept the area had not been suppressed, degrading the natural fire regime.

On the other side of the world, farmers have been burning away the humid jungle on the island of Borneo to clear land for crops. These fires frequently flare out of control, destroying vast tracts of rain forest.

In this case the fire-sensitive ecosystem has been degraded by too much fire.

Fire regimes that have been disrupted can often be restored. Carefully controlled fires have been carried out to restore fire-dependent ecosystems, from Guatemala to Australia. On the edges of La Amistad International Park, for example, a fire-sensitive landscape on the border of Costa Rica and Panama, park rangers have burned a buffer zone to keep fires from spreading within the reserve's boundaries.

Dams and Reservoirs

Clogging Earth's Arteries

The long journeys' end. China's Three Gorges Dam has put an end to the migrations of more than forty fish species, including the highly endangered Chinese sturgeon and the Chinese paddlefish.

Brian Richter/TNC

Gone in the blink of an eye. For some twenty million years, the Yangtze River dolphin, or baiji, evolved to live in freshwater. It took fewer than fifty years of human development to drive it to extinction.

Mark Carwardine/Oceans-Image/Photoshot

Degree of Disruption of Natural River Flow by Dams by Major River Basin

- High
- Moderate
- Little or none
- Unassessed basin

THE YANGTZE RIVER emerges from snow and glaciers high in eastern Tibet to travel 6,300 kilometers across China, before spilling out into the East China Sea. Along the way, it supports hundreds of species found nowhere else on Earth, including the prehistoric Chinese alligator and the Yangtze finless porpoise, in addition to the more than four hundred million people living in its basin.

But the river and all the life it supports have changed dramatically since the 1950s, with the construction of more than 45,600 small and large dams. This includes the world's largest river barrier, the 185-meter-high and 2.5-kilometer-wide Three Gorges Dam, which became fully operational in 2009.

The Three Gorges Dam, built primarily for flood control and hydropower, has become a prime target for an international backlash mounting over the toll of dams

to rivers, fish, other animals, and people. Critics brand it a social and environmental disaster that has led to the forced relocation of more than 1.3 million people and hastened the extinction of one of China's unique and most charismatic freshwater mammals, the Yangtze River dolphin.

While dams and their reservoirs have certainly encouraged economic development, by providing hydropower and making farms more productive through irrigation, they also cause irreparable harm to the natural world. In addition to being barriers to migratory fish, dams and their reservoirs turn river fragments into artificial lakes that collect pollutants, sediments, and algae, smothering life adapted to flowing waters. The Three Gorges Dam, for instance, has turned a six-hundred-kilometer stretch of fast-flowing river habitat, a distance equal to half the length of California, into a reservoir

that now accumulates a billion tons of sewage discharge yearly.

Dams and reservoirs also obstruct the normal passage of sediment to downstream habitats such as floodplains, deltas, and estuaries, depriving farmlands of the natural fertilizer in the rich river silt and coastal fisheries of important land-based nutrients. Finally, by dramatically slowing the speed at which water flows downstream, reservoirs rob the river of its natural self-cleaning mechanism affecting people and ecosystems even hundreds of kilometers away. Throughout the world, dams and reservoirs mostly built over the past half century have severely disrupted two-thirds of all large river systems.

The harm done by dams can be minimized by locating dams so as to leave as much free-flowing river as possible, and

Data source: Modified from Nilsson et al. 2005.

building dams that do not require large reservoirs, such as run-of-the-river dams, which use the natural flow of the river instead of stored-up water to operate hydropower turbines. Additionally, operating dams by periodically releasing water from reservoirs to mimic natural river flow and flood patterns can help restore habitat and create conditions to which fish and other species are adapted. An example of this kind of management is the three hundred thousand gallons of water per second released for sixty hours from Glen Canyon Dam on the Colorado River in March 2008. This large release, which mimicked the river's historical spring floods, redistributed sediment to restore sandbars and replenished backwaters that chub and other fish use for spawning and maturing. In addition, sediment deposits along the river created more beach areas for recreational use.

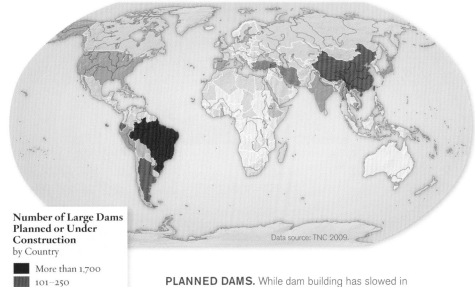

Data source: TNC 2009.

Number of Large Dams Planned or Under Construction
by Country

- More than 1,700
- 101–250
- 51–100
- 21–50
- 11–20
- 5–10
- 1–4
- Insufficient data

PLANNED DAMS. While dam building has slowed in many developed countries, it's continuing apace elsewhere. Dam locations are confidential in many countries, but public records alone indicate that more than two thousand new large dams are in the works.

Sediment Flow

Starving Some Habitats, Smothering Others

Mark Godfrey/TNC

Replenished by sediments. Salt marshes rely on sediments to build up habitats. If starved of deposits, they become vulnerable to erosion and storm damage—threats that will only increase as sea levels rise.

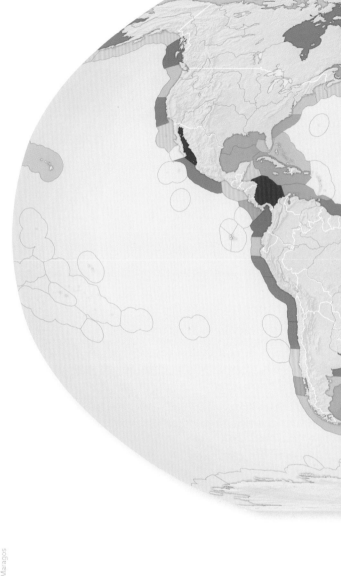

Smothering sensitive life. Coral reefs can be smothered when deforestation and coastal development increase the amount of sediment deposited in coastal waters.

Jim Maragos

AS RIVERS FLOW into the sea, they slow and drop the sediments—mud, sand, and silt—that have washed in along their journeys over land. Those sediments are vital for some habitats, but can spell ruin for others. Salt marshes benefit from soil that brings in nutrients and replenishes earth swept away by tides. But coral reefs and seagrasses suffer when particles block the sun, and they can even be smothered by shifting mud.

Over millions of years, each of the world's coastal environments has adapted to local conditions, including a reliable pattern of sediment flow. Yet humans have steadily been changing these patterns. In some areas, we have increased erosion by clearing forests where roots once held back soil and by disturbing land with farming, mining, and building. Elsewhere, we have built dams that have blocked sediment flow.

Due to increased erosion, the world's rivers on average now annually carry 16 percent

more sediment than in preindustrial times—enough to rebuild China's Great Wall two times over. In Indonesia, land clearing has caused sharp increases in sediment flow, threatening the vast reef systems in the Coral Triangle region and imperiling local economies that rely on those reefs for food and jobs.

While Indonesia's coasts are overburdened by sediment, other regions do not have enough. Globally, dams are holding back

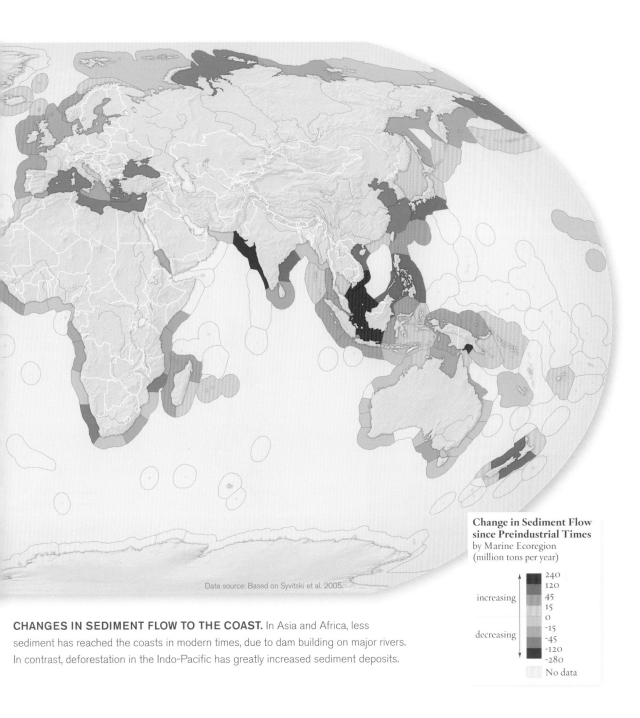

Data source: Based on Syvitski et al. 2005.

Change in Sediment Flow since Preindustrial Times
by Marine Ecoregion
(million tons per year)

increasing	240
	120
	45
	15
	0
decreasing	-15
	-45
	-120
	-280
	No data

CHANGES IN SEDIMENT FLOW TO THE COAST. In Asia and Africa, less sediment has reached the coasts in modern times, due to dam building on major rivers. In contrast, deforestation in the Indo-Pacific has greatly increased sediment deposits.

about 25 percent of the sediment that would otherwise have reached the coast. One effect is that some coastlines are receding, eroded by waves and storms—a trend that may become more destructive as sea levels rise with climate change.

The low-lying marshes of the U.S. Mississippi River Delta have traditionally provided habitat for commercially important fish, while absorbing the impacts of storms from the Gulf of Mexico. But between 1932 and 2000, regional marshes

covering an area approximately the size of the U.S. state of Delaware were lost, due in part to the building of concrete shipping and drainage channels through the delta, which have impeded the flow of sediments that once fed them. This development has increased the vulnerability of southern Louisiana, including the major port of New Orleans, to natural disasters such as Hurricane Katrina in 2005.

Reversing changes in sediment flow can require actions to be taken far from the

coast. Since 2003, Australia's government has worked to limit sediment flow from land-clearing, farming and cattle-grazing that has increased fourfold since Europeans first arrived, threatening the health of the Great Barrier Reef. By 2007, authorities had set up twenty-one pilot projects along the coast, to protect and restore wetlands that help capture the sediment before it reaches the reef, and to reduce erosion through improved land use and agricultural practices.

Melting Ice and Rising Seas

Squeezing the Coasts

THE VARYING THREAT OF SEA-LEVEL RISE.
Areas particularly vulnerable to sea-level rise (in red) on the U.S. eastern seaboard include the low-lying salt marshes around Chesapeake Bay, barrier islands along much of the coast south of New York City, and areas exposed to the full brunt of waves coming off the Atlantic Ocean. Farther north, more steeply rising coasts and rocky shores with high tidal ranges are likely to be less affected.

New York City

Washington, D.C.

ATLANTIC OCEAN

Sea-Level Rise Vulnerability
— Very high
— High
— Moderate
— Low

Data source: Courtesy of U.S. Geological Survey.

Melting away. Polar bears depend on the Arctic Ocean ice pack for hunting. As the Arctic Ocean warms and loses its ice, polar bear populations are declining.

Rinie Van Meurs/Foto Natura/Minden Pictures

IN SEPTEMBER 2007, the summer ice melt in the Arctic Ocean was so extensive that the once-treacherous Northwest Passage from the Atlantic to the Pacific Ocean became ice-free and navigable for the first time in human history. Experts predicted the North Pole itself would be free of ice by 2040. These dramatic changes encouraged shipping companies to anticipate a new trade route that would cut several days from journeys from the Atlantic to the Pacific. They also inspired a scramble to claim mineral rights for the sea floor, opening a new frontier of offshore oil and gas operations.

Yet even as the vanishing sea ice clears the way for expanding commerce, it is greatly increasing the risks of pollution and other damage to once-wild, ice-bound shores. It is also stealing hopes for the survival of an array of unique animals. Polar bears, walrus, and narwhal, bowhead, and beluga whales in the Arctic; and leopard, crabeater, and Weddell seals and Adelie penguins in the Antarctic, hunt, breed, and even sleep on and around the floating blocks of ice. Many less charismatic species are also at risk, notably Antarctic krill—the large, free-swimming shrimp that form "swarms" numbering billions of animals. The total biomass of Antarctic krill has been estimated at five hundred million metric tons—roughly double the weight of all humans on Earth, and for part of each year, these krill depend on algae that live under sea ice. Krill in turn feed penguins, whales, and major fish species, raising the question of what the progressive loss of ice and algae, and ultimately krill, will do to the entire Antarctic food chain.

Melting ice has other, equally ominous impacts. Sea levels are rising as icecaps on Greenland and Antarctica and glaciers elsewhere are retreating and their meltwater flows from land into the ocean. Compounding this process is the gradual expansion of existing ocean water as it warms. Over the course of the twentieth century, sea levels rose about eighteen centimeters as a result of climate change. Scientists have predicted they will climb much more than this and perhaps over a meter by 2100.

Rising seas will have varying impacts throughout the world, with low-lying areas most dramatically affected, since they will be more prone to severe erosion and flooding, especially after heavy storms. But even steeper shores will be affected by changing patterns of erosion. The impacts of sea-level

MORE THAN JUST WARMING WATERS.

As levels of atmospheric carbon dioxide increase, some of the CO₂ is dissolving in seawater and making it more acidic. In the early years of the twenty-first century, scientists discovered that this trend of *ocean acidification* was accelerating. This is particularly worrisome, because as ocean acidity increases, it robs the water of carbonate minerals needed by plankton, corals, and shellfish, possibly inhibiting their growth. A decline of coral reef growth could lead to more coastal erosion, since reefs have provided the important benefit

Oysters

Plankton with carbonate skeleton

Jennifer Molnar

Steve Gschmeissner / Photo Researchers, Inc.

of buffering the impact of waves. Another profound worry has to do with the decline of certain planktonic plants and animals, which may not only interrupt the marine food chain that supports fish and other creatures but also worsen the effects of climate change. These organisms are some of the planet's most abundant species, which under normal circumstances help absorb carbon dioxide. Much remains unknown about the consequences of continued ocean acidification, but no one is arguing in favor of it.

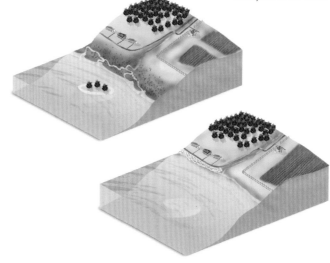

Hemmed in. Coastal habitats can naturally shift and adapt to changing coastlines and rising sea levels. But when roads and buildings get in the way, habitats like salt marshes can't migrate to stay above the tides.

---

rise are further influenced by miniscule geologic movements. Land that is already rising, such as northern Scandinavia, will remain less affected by sea-level rise, while in areas such as the U.S. state of Louisiana, where land is sinking, changes may be more destructive.

To be sure, coastlines have never been stable. Long before humans came on the scene, coastal habitats were adaptable, with mangrove forests, salt marshes, mudflats, and sandy shores shifting and colonizing new areas in response to changes in sea levels. Yet throughout the world today, towns, industries, farms, and aquaculture are blocking the way. In years to come, these coastal environments, with all their vital benefits—including water filtration, storm protection, and fish habitat—may be squeezed out of existence, hemmed in by rising waters and human land uses.

In the most extreme cases, the very land on which humans live will disappear, as is already happening on some low-lying islands. By the first years of the twenty-first century, high tides had washed over much of the small coral atoll of Carteret, off the coast of Papua New Guinea, eroding its coasts and making its wells so salty that islanders were forced to collect rainwater to drink. Traditional crops were no longer able to withstand the salty soils, forcing islanders to substitute them with diets of fish and coconuts.

With climate change under way, scientists and policy makers are investigating mitigation strategies to reduce impacts on people as well as ways to help species and habitats adapt. Many coastal communities will undoubtedly spend spiralling sums "defending" their coastline with walls and barriers, while others will be forced to abandon their land to the sea. But one relatively new practice takes a more measured approach. In eastern England, costly coastal defenses have been taken down in many sites, allowing a controlled reflooding of agricultural land. Rich and diverse salt marshes colonize the former fields and pastures. As the sea floods back, muddy sediments are deposited among the foliage, raising the level of the ground and actually countering the challenge of rising sea levels. These new salt marshes will provide a low-cost critical coastal defense for many years to come.

Disappearing Glaciers

Ice Storage on a Slippery Slope

1940

2006

Unknown photographer, circa 1940

Karen Holzer photo, USGS

Lost treasures. Grinell Glacier in Glacier National Park, Montana, United States. is practically gone, and the stream habitats below will soon be left dry for parts of the year.

Devastation with early rains. Unusually early rain-on-snow flood events in Pakistan and Afghanistan in 2005 killed hundreds, left tens of thousands homeless, and scoured and polluted rivers upon which people depend.

Tariq Mahmood-AFP/Getty Images

Change in Snowmelt Timing, 1975–2040
by Freshwater Ecoregion

- Earlier by over 3 weeks
- Earlier by 2 to 3 weeks
- Earlier by 1 to 2 weeks
- Less than a week changed
- Later by over a week
- Little or no snow
- No data

BY 2030, all the glaciers in the U.S. state of Montana's Glacier National Park will have melted, imperiling the life they have supported for thousands of years.

Warmer temperatures are the main reason for this monumental change. Well into the twentieth century, water flowed steadily all year from the legendary park's Rocky Mountain flanks, despite many months without rain during the summer and fall. The gradual melting of the deep snow that piled up each winter, supplemented by gentle thawing of the ancient glaciers, fed the lowland streams and lakes until winter snowfalls replenished the glaciers and snowpack and restarted the cycle.

Today, however, streams that once flowed year-round run dry in the summer, and spring melt is starting sooner, spelling disaster for a diverse range of plants and animals. Life in snow-fed streams has grown accustomed to patterns of temperature, water quantity, and water clarity. Now there are changes in all three. The bull trout found in the drying creeks of the Montana park could pay a typical price. The fish depends on cool water from the glaciers for spawning in the dry last weeks of summer. Its eggs then incubate until the spring, but they must hatch on time to avoid washing away with the first floods of the snowmelt. A single week's difference in timing can throw everything

off, adding to existing pressures that now threaten the bull trout with extinction.

The bull trout is not alone. At least one in six people on this planet depend on melted snow and ice for water to drink and irrigate farmland. As these reservoirs of ice recede, the hundreds of millions of people they once sustained will very likely need to move elsewhere. Already, in parts of Asia, including Pakistan and Nepal, changes in the rhythms of melting snow are amplifying floods and droughts that kill hundreds and leave thousands starving or homeless every year. In India and Bangladesh, changes to the vast, glacier-fed Ganges and Brahmaputra rivers

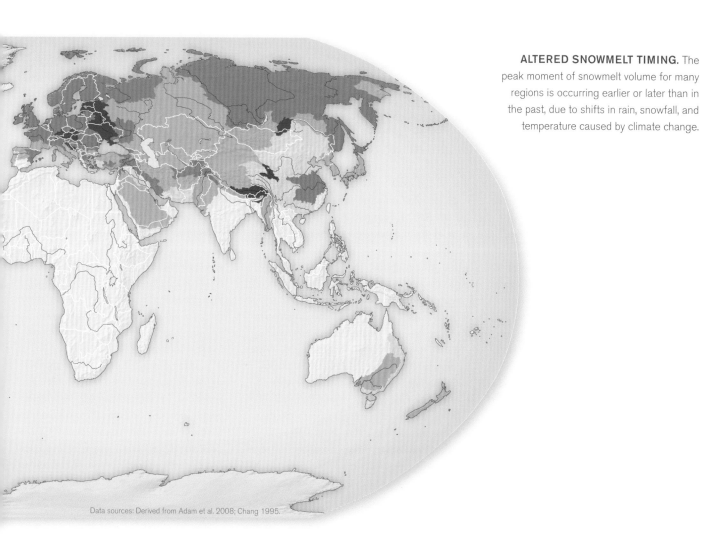

ALTERED SNOWMELT TIMING. The peak moment of snowmelt volume for many regions is occurring earlier or later than in the past, due to shifts in rain, snowfall, and temperature caused by climate change.

threaten to destroy crops on which hundreds of millions of people rely.

The changing rhythm of melting snow and ice is becoming an increasingly urgent problem, spanning regions from the highlands of Tibet to the cosmopolitan city of San Francisco. But solutions are elusive, mainly due to the glacier-like pace of efforts to address climate change. Short-term fixes, such as pumping water out of newly formed glacial lakes before the lake walls burst, have alleviated floods in the mountains of Nepal, Switzerland, and Peru. But any real hope of confronting meltwater problems in the long run will depend on an unprecedented level of global insight and cooperation.

Glaciers of Asia

■ Glacier
— Major river

Elevation
Above 4,000m
Below 4,000m

ASIA'S NATURAL WATER TOWERS. One in four people on Earth live in the basins of major rivers originating in glaciers of the Himalaya Mountains and Tibetan Plateau.

Nature Conservation and Climate Change

JONATHAN M. HOEKSTRA

EVEN AS THE WORLD begins to take more serious action to address global climate change, nature is already feeling the effects. Melting permafrost in Canada has made an entire lake drain away into the ocean. Hotter, drier conditions in the western United States have lengthened the wildfire season by more than two months. Warmer seas are bleaching coral reefs and fueling more powerful hurricanes and cyclones. Species living on mountaintops and near the poles are feeling the heat but have nowhere cooler to go.

People are feeling the heat, too. Bill Gates, in his 2009 annual letter to his philanthropic foundation, observed, "It is interesting how often the impact of climate change is illustrated by talking about the problems the polar bears will face rather than the much greater number of poor people who will die unless significant investments are made to help them." That is a headline story about climate change—the profound impacts that it will have on people around the world.

The World Health Organization estimates that climate change is already causing at least 150,000 premature deaths every year. Impoverished environmental refugees are already fleeing their homes as rising sea levels threaten to inundate islands like Kirabati and low-lying coastal areas like Bangladesh. In Africa, droughts will decrease crop yields and increase water stress for up to 250 million people.

Whether the climate change story is one of rescue or ruin will depend on how human society responds to the challenges before us. How swiftly and decisively will we act to reduce global greenhouse gas emissions and to limit the magnitude of climate change? How will we help people and communities who fall victim to the impacts of climate change?

The conservation of natural habitats needs to be part of our climate change solutions, not just because someone needs to ensure that species and ecosystems survive into the future, but because it offers proven and ready solutions to some of the most serious problems we must confront. By putting nature to work to ensure a more livable and sustainable future for people, conservation strategies can help rein in greenhouse gas emissions and help people resist and recover from unavoidable negative impacts.

Consider options for reducing global greenhouse gas emissions. Almost 20 percent of global greenhouse gas emissions come from the destruction and degradation of forests—more than from all cars, trucks, trains, ships, and airplanes combined. When forests are harvested, burned, or degraded, carbon held in the trees and soil is released to the atmosphere. Every year 12.9 million hectares of forest—an area larger than the U.S. state of New York—are lost to agriculture and urban development, or lost to disease and destructive wildfire. As a consequence of emissions from deforestation, Brazil and Indonesia rank just behind the United States and China as the world's largest greenhouse gas emitters. Canada could join this list if its vast boreal forests are not adequately protected and managed as climate change, insect outbreaks, and wildfire combine to turn these globally significant carbon sinks into a huge carbon source.

Conservation strategies can help reduce and even reverse emissions through improved forest protection, restoration, and management. In 1997, the Bolivian government collaborated with The Nature Conservancy and Fundación Amigos de la Naturaleza to establish the Noel Kempff Mercado Climate Action Project. By protecting 6,000 square kilometers of forest from logging and agricultureal expansion, it will avoid 5.8 million tons of carbon emissions over the next thirty years. Additional projects are under way in Brazil and Indonesia to further demonstrate how forest conservation can measurably reduce greenhouse gas emissions.

Another way to offset carbon emissions is to restore forests that were previously lost. The growing trees absorb carbon dioxide from the atmosphere and store it in their trunks, branches, and roots. Projects in the U.S. state of Louisiana's Tensas River Valley and along California's Garcia River are replanting abandoned agricultural land and heavily logged areas with native trees.

As technical challenges are resolved to ensure reliable accounting of how much carbon is saved or stored in forests, these strategies for avoiding or offsetting emissions could qualify for carbon credit investments in burgeoning carbon markets. Such investments could pay for forest conservation and provide direct economic benefits to forest communities.

Burning of agricultural lands is another significant source of global greenhouse gas emissions. In central Australia, Aboriginal people are using traditional controlled burns to restore rangeland habitat quality. Over time, the frequent, low-intensity fires actually release fewer greenhouse gases than would less frequent, more intense fires. In farmed landscapes, no-till practices can also reduce greenhouse gas emissions from exposed and erosive soils.

Conservation also has very important roles to play in helping people and communities resist and recover from the negative impacts of a changing climate. Warming seas threaten to bleach coral reefs and jeopardize local fisheries on which many island and coastal communities depend. In Kimbe Bay, Papua New Guinea, The Nature Conservancy worked with fishing communities to design and establish a network of marine protected areas that will be able to recover from a bleaching event, and sustain their local fisheries. The science-based resilience principles demonstrated there are now being replicated around the world from the Florida Keys to the western Indian Ocean.

Along the U.S. state of North Carolina's Albemarle Peninsula, last home of the endangered red wolf, rising sea levels are eroding about 7.6 meters of shoreline every year. The restoration and creation of living oyster reefs will protect the shoreline against wave damage and grow as sea level rises. Elsewhere along the U.S. Atlantic and Gulf coasts, barrier islands and coastal marshes are being protected and restored for shoreline protection as alternatives to concrete sea walls.

Ecologically sustainable water management offers effective strategies for securing community water supplies as glaciers melt and droughts intensify because of climate change. Watershed protection helps maintain clean, reliable water supplies and groundwater recharge zones for major metropolitan water supplies such as New York City and Seattle in the United States, Quito in Ecuador, and Bogotá in Colombia. Along China's Yangtze River, floodplain restoration is being evaluated as a cost-effective means of containing periodic floodwaters so that dams and reservoirs can be operated at full capacity for power generation and irrigation purposes.

In arid ecosystems, "grassbanks" set aside certain grazing areas as a community resource in the event of a drought. This strategy is being used to help sustain ranching communities in Montana, as well as pastoralist communities in northern Kenya.

Each of these conservation strategies help people protect their livelihoods and well-being while simultaneously protecting biodiversity and natural ecosystems, at least under the range of climate conditions we currently experience. However, climate change is likely to exacerbate extreme conditions and potentially shift the range of conditions that will be considered "normal" in the future. To ensure that ecosystem-based adaptation strategies remain resilient in the face of changing climate, we need to carefully monitor their effectiveness so that we can tweak them as necessary.

Conservation-based adaptation strategies are not cost-free. It costs money to plant new trees or to restore a barrier island. There are also trade-offs when forest protection or the establishment of marine protected areas or a grassbank require that some land-uses or activities are limited.

But these strategies can be cost-effective compared to technological alternatives. A

Corals resilient to warming waters in Kimbe Bay, Papua New Guinea

Mark Godfrey/TNC

2009 report by McKinsey and Company estimated the cost per ton of carbon abatement in ten different economic sectors. Technological fixes like carbon capture and storage for power plants are expected to cost $38–$56 per ton of carbon sequestered. Meanwhile, sequestering carbon through avoided deforestation and reforestation prices out in the range of $2–$20 per ton of carbon.

Furthermore, ecosystem-based strategies for combating climate change offer other benefits as well, such as sustaining delivery of ecosystem services and supporting local livelihoods. In Vietnam, for example, the Red Cross restored twelve thousand hectares of mangrove forest to provide storm protection for local communities. In addition to saving more than $7 million per year in levee maintenance costs, the project also created livelihoods for people to plant and harvest shellfish amid the restored mangroves.

There will not be one silver bullet solution to reduce global greenhouse gas emissions or to help people deal with every impact of climate change. Challenges of this magnitude

and complexity will require multiple solutions implemented by all countries and sectors of society. Some will be cost-effective. Others will be expensive. Some may depend on technologies yet to be developed. But many are ready now.

Swift action is urgently needed to begin reducing greenhouse gas emissions, and to address emergent climate change impacts. We cannot afford only to wait for tomorrow's technology. Conservation has a tool kit of approaches that are ready to use now. Let's put nature to work.

JONATHAN M. HOEKSTRA IS THE DIRECTOR OF THE NATURE CONSERVANCY'S CLIMATE CHANGE PROGRAM.

Terrestrial Invaders

Unwelcome Guests

NASA

The island of Guam

Mike Trenerry

Invading brown tree snake

Island Marauders. Isolated island ecosystems are vulnerable to invasions by non-native species, which have the advantage of surprise. Invasions can lead to catastrophic losses of biodiversity, often with costs to people as well. The brown tree snake that stowed away to Guam after World War II has caused twelve local bird extinctions and, by climbing onto electric wires and transformers, caused power outages on average every other day. The U.S. government spends millions of dollars each year inspecting outgoing cargo, to prevent new invasions elsewhere.

But the isolation of islands can make it easier to get rid of a harmful species. Using poisoned bait, in 2001, New Zealand successfully eradicated the Norway rat from remote Cambell Island.

Johnny Randall/NC Botanical Garden

Leafy plague. Imported for erosion control, kudzu now blankets large swaths of the southeastern United States.

THE NORWAY RAT is one of history's most intrepid travelers. Originally a native of China, it has exploited the global shipping trade, hitchhiking to Europe and the New World by 1800, and eventually finding its way to every continent except Antarctica.

In 2004, university researchers in New Zealand decided to see just how hard it might be to capture a single rat. They radio-tagged one and released it onto New Zealand's previously rat-free Motuhoropapa Island and went about setting traps. The rat, nicknamed Razza, managed to evade them for a full eighteen weeks, avoiding capture even after it swam to another island, almost half a kilometer away.

From the time the first ships sailed the seas, carrying passengers and cargo, animals, plants, insects, and diseases have hitched rides to new territories. Sometimes, like the rat, they come as stowaways; at other times, people have imported them intentionally. Either way, they have often caused havoc in the process. If they are hardy enough to survive in new territories, they may have two big advantages: they lack natural predators, and their potential prey are unprepared for them.

Such was the fateful case after a wealthy landowner in Australia imported European rabbits for hunting in 1859. The rabbits quickly made themselves at home, destroying habitats and crops with their voracious appetite. Despite a 1,700-kilometer "rabbit-proof" fence built by the government, the rabbits could not be contained. Today they are found across Australia and, with feral cats and foxes, the rabbits have continued to plague Australia, at an annual expense of up to $600 million in control efforts and damage to crops and livestock.

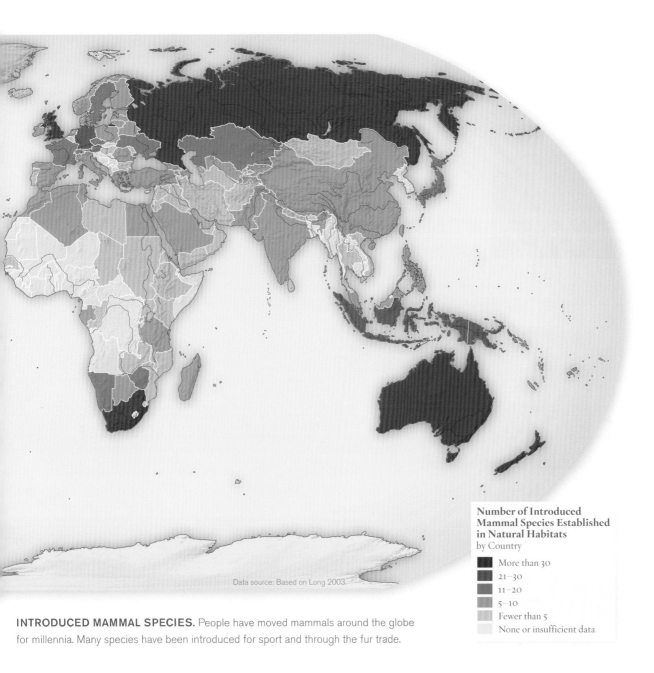

Data source: Based on Long 2003.

Number of Introduced Mammal Species Established in Natural Habitats
by Country

- More than 30
- 21–30
- 11–20
- 5–10
- Fewer than 5
- None or insufficient data

INTRODUCED MAMMAL SPECIES. People have moved mammals around the globe for millennia. Many species have been introduced for sport and through the fur trade.

Mammals are not the only energetic intruders. Kudzu, native to eastern Asia, has become a universal symbol of uncontrolled growth. It grows up to a foot a day, blanketing whatever stands in its path, whether that might be a tree, a house, even a parked car. It can smother and crowd out native plants, while the weight of its vines can be enough to uproot a tree.

Japanese visitors introduced the species to the United States in 1876, at the Centennial Exposition in Philadelphia. U.S. government agencies subsequently promoted the plant to control soil erosion and as pasture for livestock, with the U.S. Soil Erosion Service paying farmers $8 an acre to plant it. Kudzu has since spread throughout the southeastern United States, overrunning native plants and infrastructure and damaging native forests.

Eradicating invasive species can be expensive at best and is frequently impossible, unless the invasion is confined to a small or isolated area. Thus the most effective use of resources against invasions is in efforts to stop them from happening in the first place. Quarantine and cargo inspection requirements and bans on imports of designated species have been among the most helpful tactics against would-be invaders. New Zealand is a leader in these tactics—investing in prevention measures to protect the island nation's economy and habitats from incoming harmful species, as well as funding international efforts like the Pacific Island Initiative that aid invasive species control more broadly in the region.

Freshwater Invaders

Good Intentions with Costly Consequences

Multiplying mussels. Zebra mussels can rapidly multiply in a new habitat and have caused significant damage by covering shoreline habitats and clogging water intake pipes in the U.S. Great Lakes region.

Clogging waterways. Water hyacinth, a fast-growing ornamental plant, can take over waterways by forming dense mats, smothering native species and interfering with navigation.

Unintended consequences. Released into Africa's Lake Victoria, the Nile perch has caused the likely extinction of over one hundred native fish, many of which were found nowhere else on Earth.

THE NILE PERCH, a large, predatory fish native to north and west Africa, was found in East Africa's Lake Victoria in the mid-1950s. Evidence suggests local officials had tried to create a new source of income from the world's largest tropical lake. Lake Victoria was already home to hundreds of native fish species, many found nowhere else on Earth, yet most of them were too small to be commercially valuable outside the region.

By the 1980s, the perch population had exploded. Being new to the lake, the big fish lacked predators and was able to outcompete fish that had evolved there. The new fishery became a lucrative industry, with exports to Europe and beyond. Yet meanwhile the perch transformed the once-complex lake environment, likely driving more than one hundred native fish to extinction and eliminating that dietary staple for thousands of families living on shore.

Throughout the world, more than a thousand freshwater species are known to have been moved to new habitats beyond their native ranges. Many, like the Nile perch, are introduced purposely, to create fish stocks for sport and food. Others escape into natural habitats after being imported for farming or as ornamental species in water gardens and ponds. Still others hitchhike to new habitats by hiding in the hulls of ships or clinging to the bottom of recreational boats moving between lakes and rivers.

Some invasive species, such as the Nile perch, can boost incomes for some, yet whether they are purposely introduced or not, the most harmful newcomers can wreak

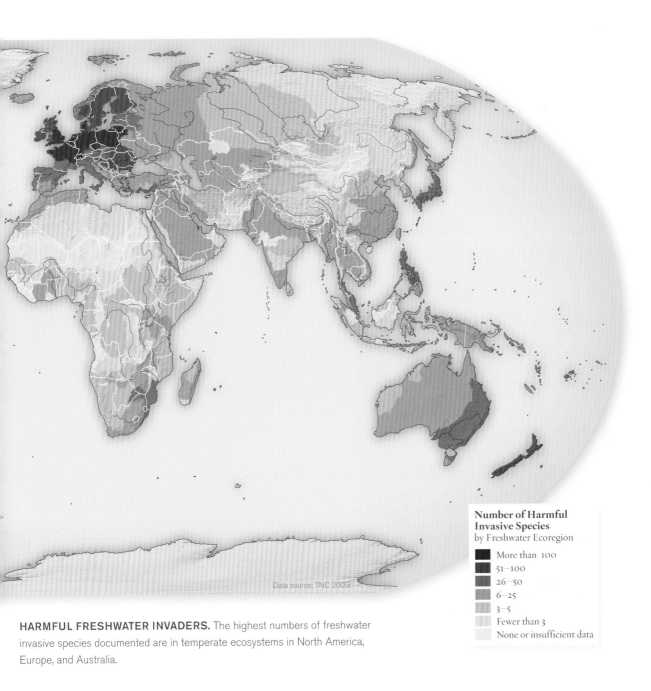

Data source: TNC 2009.

**Number of Harmful
Invasive Species**
by Freshwater Ecoregion

- More than 100
- 51–100
- 26–50
- 6–25
- 3–5
- Fewer than 3
- None or insufficient data

HARMFUL FRESHWATER INVADERS. The highest numbers of freshwater invasive species documented are in temperate ecosystems in North America, Europe, and Australia.

havoc on both local environments and economies. After riding to North America in the ballast water of a large ship circa 1988, the hardy and rapidly multiplying zebra mussel blanketed shorelines, colonizing the insides of pipes and other infrastructure and costing some $100 million worth of damage per year as it has spread from the Great Lakes region across the United States.

It is usually difficult and costly, if not impossible, to get rid of the newcomers once they are established. Such is the case with water hyacinth, an ornamental plant native

to South America that grows rapidly in new environments, forming dense mats that clog waterways and push out native species. In some places, including Florida and Lake Victoria, introduced weevils and moths that eat the hyacinth have helped control the plant. Yet large infestations remain in many other regions of the world.

Prevention strategies are by far the most economical approach in reducing harm from invasive species. In South Africa, conservationists, government officials, and fishermen

have worked together to create markets for native fish species, such as the largemouth yellowfish and smallmouth yellowfish, as an alternative to introducing non-native species for anglers or food. By reintroducing and nurturing the species in designated rivers, they have worked to build up thriving industries of native fish that create jobs while protecting natural environments.

Marine Invaders

Stowaways Attacking Our Coasts

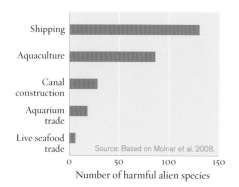

Source: Based on Molnar et al. 2008.

Number of harmful alien species

How they got here.
Shipping and aquaculture are the predominant pathways for marine invaders to reach new habitats.

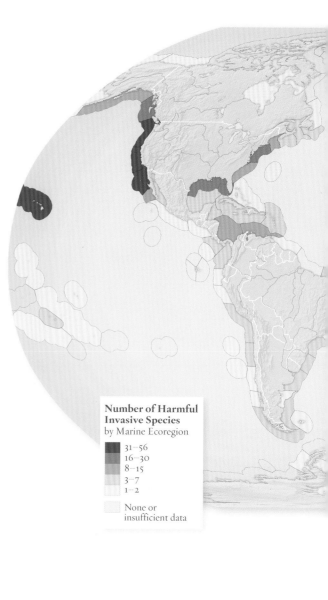

Number of Harmful Invasive Species
by Marine Ecoregion

- 31–56
- 16–30
- 8–15
- 3–7
- 1–2
- None or insufficient data

The "killer algae."
Caulerpa quickly blanketed the seafloor after it was introduced to the Mediterranean Sea, smothering native species and interfering with navigation.

A. Meinesz

THOUSANDS OF SHIPS crisscross the oceans every day, traveling between distant ports. Along with crews, passengers, and freight, most also carry a rich diversity of stowaway species, including zooplankton, algae, crustaceans, and fish. Some of these hitchhikers cling to the ships' hulls. Others ride within the ballast water meant to keep the ship stable on the open ocean. As many as ten thousand species may be found each day on ships traveling throughout the world—making up the main source of non-native species that invade along coastlines.

Aquaculture—the farming of species such as fish, shrimp, shellfish, and seaweed—has been another important source of invasions.

Species are purposefully imported to coastal waters for aquaculture or accidentally released after hitchhiking on farmed species or equipment.

While many species fail to survive in their new homes, some end up proliferating and dominating the area, due to a lack of natural predators and competition. At least one such harmful invader has been discovered in 78 percent of the world's marine ecoregions—and it takes only one to transform an ecosystem.

The case of *Caulerpa taxifolia*, also known as "the killer algae," is a powerful cautionary tale. Native to the Indian Ocean, the soft, green caulerpa is a popular decorative feature in aquariums. In the early 1980s, it arrived in Mediterranean waters, inadvertently released

in wastewater from an aquarium in Monaco. Once there, it rapidly carpeted thousands of hectares of the seafloor, smothering fish habitat, fouling fishing nets, and entangling boat propellers, as it spread from Spain to Croatia. In June 2000, the species was discovered in a Southern California lagoon, prompting the state to ban private possession of it. Over the next six years, diver teams armed with tarps and chlorine managed to eradicate it before it could spread farther.

As the world becomes more connected through trade, more marine species will likely end up in new habitats. Although only a fraction of them will likely go on to dominate these environments, many that do will be impossible to remove. The eradication

HARMFUL MARINE INVADERS.
Temperate coastlines of North America, Europe, and Australia have the most documented invasions. Southeast Asia—with large ports and aquaculture operations—likely harbors more invaders than current data show.

Data source: Based on Molnar et al. 2008.

of caulerpa from California shows success is possible, given early detection and considerable effort and expense. Yet once invasive species spread, it is usually too late to stop them, making it all the more important to prevent them from getting a foothold.

International agreements and some national laws have aimed to limit species transported by shipping, with methods including emptying and replacing ballast water in the open ocean instead of in port to reduce the introduction of species in coastal waters. For other pathways, such as aquaculture, improving management practices, such as carefully cleaning equipment and treating wastewater, can help minimize the number of harmful species introduced.

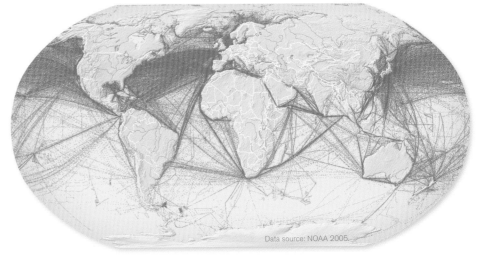

Data source: NOAA 2005.

INCREASING OPPORTUNITIES FOR OPPORTUNISTS.
The risk of invasion is much higher in places with more shipping traffic. Here are shown the paths of several thousand ships in just one year.

Terrestrial Animals at Risk

More in Jeopardy Each Year

At risk of extinction. The number of amphibians, mammals, birds, and reptiles that are threatened and included on IUCN's Red List.

Data source: IUCN 2008.

On the road to recovery. After flirting with extinction, with only twenty-two birds left in the wild in 1982, the California condor is slowly recovering.

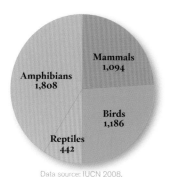

ZSSD/Minden Pictures

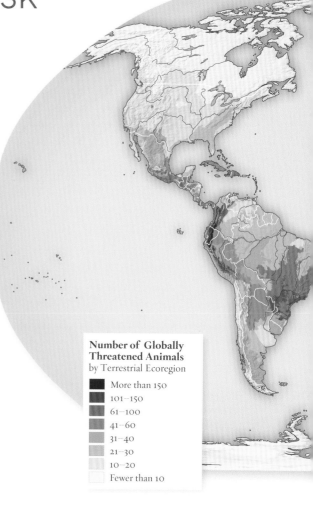

Number of Globally Threatened Animals by Terrestrial Ecoregion

- More than 150
- 101–150
- 61–100
- 41–60
- 31–40
- 21–30
- 10–20
- Fewer than 10

CONSERVATIONISTS SELDOM tire of the story of the California condor's return from the brink of extinction. Despite some less than beguiling attributes—including an appetite for rotting meat and a face only a condor mother could love—North America's largest bird attracted devoted human champions in the early 1980s, when its plight first became known. Ranchers had been shooting condors, wrongly blaming them for killing the carcasses on which they fed. Condors were also being sickened by pesticides and electrocuted on power lines. By 1982, their population in the wild had fallen to just twenty-two individuals.

Beginning that year, ornithologists climbed cliffs to capture the last few wild birds. The condors were then bred in captivity at the Los Angeles Zoo and the San Diego Wild Animal Park. After ten years of these efforts, the captive population stood at sixty-three, and the first few birds were released back into the wild. More than a decade later, condors face old threats and new ones, including the West Nile virus. But by 2007, a dozen wild-hatched birds had fledged, and 128 condors were roaming the skies in the wild.

This dramatic rescue is a showcase of what conservation can do. Yet for every California condor—and bald eagle and peregrine falcon, two other celebrated survivors—more than sixteen thousand species languish on endangered lists. The 2008 Red List of Threatened Species, kept by the International Union for the Conservation of Nature (IUCN), portrayed 5,966 species as threatened out of the nearly 60,000 described vertebrate species on Earth. An additional 2,496 species of invertebrates and 8,457 species of plants were also listed. Only 43 percent of all known vertebrate species, 4 percent of all plants, and less than 0.5 percent of invertebrates were evaluated, meaning many others could be in danger.

In fact, IUCN has estimated that one-third of all amphibian species, one-fourth of all mammals, and more than one in ten birds are sliding toward extinction. And even this estimate connotes only part of the toll on modern animal life. Long before species are technically extinct, they become so rare as to be gone from nature.

The good news is that never before have so many people, organizations, and governments dedicated themselves to stopping this trend and protecting what remains. Beyond species-specific strategies, such as those that worked with the condor, efforts include laws limiting hunting and trading of endangered animals, preservation of habitat as parks and reserves, and even international treaties.

Data sources: Based on WWF WildFinder 2006 and IUCN 2008.

On a local level, environmental groups have organized projects that give communities incentives to protect wildlife and its habitat. An effort to save a small Colombian monkey called the titi has supplied villagers clay stoves that burn wood more efficiently, reducing the demand for wood from nearby forest.

More dramatic results have come from preserving large areas of habitat, which benefits endangered species while keeping others from declining. Most species, particularly predators and large animals, require large, intact areas to sustain healthy populations. Grizzly bears, wolves, mountain lions, and five dozen other mammal species thrive in the 41,000-square-kilometer Glacier-Waterton International Peace Park on the U.S.-Canada border, set aside by an agreement with indigenous leaders, conservation groups, and government officials.

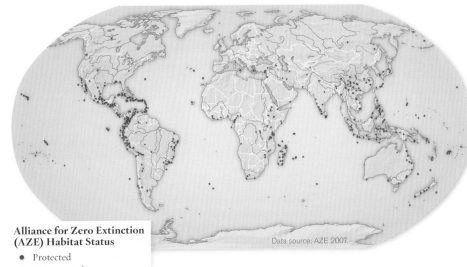

Alliance for Zero Extinction (AZE) Habitat Status
- Protected
- Unprotected

Data source: AZE 2007.

IMMINENT RISK OF EXTINCTION. These sites contain one or more species that are endangered, according to IUCN's Red List, and occur only in that one area. Only about half of the sites are protected.

Freshwater Animals at Risk

Are Their Futures Drying Up?

Number of Globally Threatened Mammal, Bird and Crocodilian Species
by Freshwater Ecoregion

- 12—15
- 9—11
- 6—8
- 3—5
- 1—2
- None or insufficient data

Data source: TNC 2009.

THREATENED FRESHWATER MAMMALS, BIRDS, AND CROCODILIANS. The greatest numbers are found in the Lower Amur River in northern Asia; the Lower Paraná in South America; the Ganges, Brahmaputra, and Irrawaddy rivers in southern Asia; and Indonesia's coastal rivers.

Prehistoric survivors face extinction. With fewer than two hundred individuals of each species remaining in the wild, the Chinese alligator and the gharial of India and Nepal are the most threatened crocodile species.

J. Thorbjarnarson/ Wildlife Conservation Society

Chinese alligator

Michael & Patricia Fogden/ Minden Pictures

Gharial

EVERYONE KNOWS the hippo—the barrel-bodied mammal wallowing in African rivers and wetlands. Yet the animal's fame has not spared it from the fate of thousands of other wetland-loving animal and plant species threatened by human activities. In 2004, with its numbers in precipitous decline, the hippo landed for the first time on the International Union for the Conservation of Nature (IUCN) Red List of globally threatened species.

By the early twenty-first century, nearly one in three of all amphibians and freshwater mammals and almost one in six of all freshwater birds were similarly at risk, according to the Red List, the leading resource on the conservation status of plants and animals. Limited studies suggested that freshwater fish, the most familiar inhabitants of rivers, lakes, and wetlands, were not faring any better. By 2006, 200 out of 522 species of European freshwater fish and one in four in East Africa had joined the Red List.

The plight of these species is directly related to the decline and loss of their freshwater homes, degraded by by-products of human development that include pollution, competition for water from nearby farms, the breakup of rivers by dams, and the introduction of invasive species. Animals living in these bodies of water are particularly vulnerable because they are often so accessible. This applies not only to fish but also to big mammals like the hippo, which increasingly has been hunted for its meat and ivory teeth.

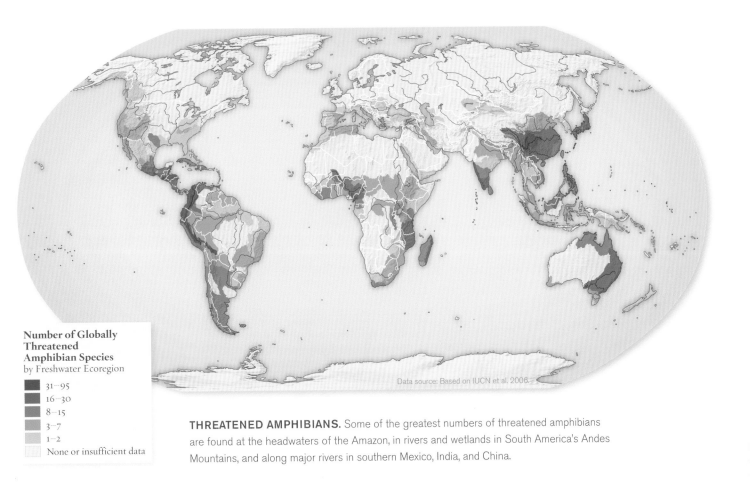

Number of Globally Threatened Amphibian Species
by Freshwater Ecoregion

- 31—95
- 16—30
- 8—15
- 3—7
- 1—2
- None or insufficient data

Data source: Based on IUCN et al. 2006.

THREATENED AMPHIBIANS. Some of the greatest numbers of threatened amphibians are found at the headwaters of the Amazon, in rivers and wetlands in South America's Andes Mountains, and along major rivers in southern Mexico, India, and China.

Cyril Ruoso/ JH Editorial/Minden Pictures

Pygmy hippopotamus

Timothy Boucher

Common hippopotamus

A threatened African icon. Both the common hippopotamus and its more reclusive cousin, the pygmy hippo, are now threatened with extinction because of habitat loss and hunting for their meat and ivory.

Turtles are also in particular danger. In 2004, some 40 percent of the more than 240 freshwater turtle species were threatened with extinction, primarily due to hunting for food, the pet trade, and ingredients for traditional Chinese medicine. Growing appetites for turtle meat in China, Japan, Korea, and Taiwan have accelerated hunting in Southeast Asia, where wild populations are imperiled despite some new efforts to limit trade.

Crocodiles offer a lonely success story. Back in 1971, these freshwater reptiles had been hunted nearly to extinction, with all twenty-three species ranked as threatened. But then, in a unique collaboration, conservationists and leaders of the reptile-skin and leather industry worked to restore habitat and limit hunting. After more than thirty years, one-third of the crocodile species has recovered in the wild, with another third sufficiently abundant to support well-regulated annual harvests. Seven species are still at risk, including the odd-looking gharial, with its narrow, knobby snout, of which

fewer than two hundred adults remain in the wild. Yet overall, no other group of vertebrate animals has undergone such an improvement in its conservation status.

The crocodile success was chiefly inspired by concern that continued overhunting could destroy a profitable business. Because not all freshwater species share the dubious privilege of such dedicated vested interests, their survival in the wild requires new and vigorous efforts to limit hunting and protect habitats.

Marine Animals at Risk

Sea Life Unraveling

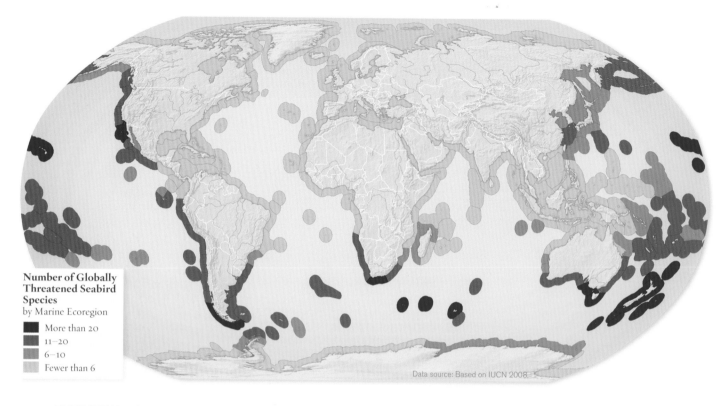

Number of Globally Threatened Seabird Species
by Marine Ecoregion

- More than 20
- 11–20
- 6–10
- Fewer than 6

Data source: Based on IUCN 2008.

THREATENED SEABIRDS. The greatest diversity of seabirds is found in the Southern Hemisphere, so the concentration of threatened seabirds there is expected. Many are threatened by invasive species such as rats and cats on the islands where they nest, others by unsustainable fishing.

Just three decades between discovery and extinction.
Modern humans first set eyes on the Steller's sea cow, a relative of the manatee, in 1741, when a Russian ship was stranded on a frozen island of the North Pacific. Only half the sailors survived, sustaining themselves by feeding on local mammals, including the sea cow. Hearing tales of the delicious meat, other hunters flocked to the island. The last giant sea cow was killed in 1768.

GREAT WHALES were the first major victims of industrial fishing, hunted down to the brink of extinction since the eighteenth century. Next came sea lions and several species of seals, followed by the collapse, by the first decade of the new millennium, of many of the world's most familiar fish stocks, such as tuna, cod, swordfish, and grouper.

Overharvesting for general consumption has been the greatest threat to most marine species. Others have succumbed to growing luxury markets, claiming bluefin tuna, prized for sushi; pipefish, key ingredients of traditional Chinese medicine; and the Bangaii cardinalfish, a treasured feature in aquariums. Such elite tastes have been especially devastating for sharks in all the world's oceans over the past two decades. As East Asia's economies have grown, so have appetites for shark fin soup, a delicacy in such urgent demand that it has led to thirty-five shark species being listed as threatened. Often, sharks are stripped of their fins and then discarded in the sea to die.

Most conspicuous by their absence have been sea turtles, once among the major grazing animals in tropical seas. In the early 1700s, Caribbean waters harbored an estimated one hundred million green and hawksbill turtles, a population reduced over the next two centuries to roughly 1 percent of its earlier size.

Seabirds have similarly declined in many oceans, less as a result of hunting than of wider patterns of change, including an increase in introduced species, such as rats and cats, that feed on eggs and chicks on nesting islands. The albatross, which spends

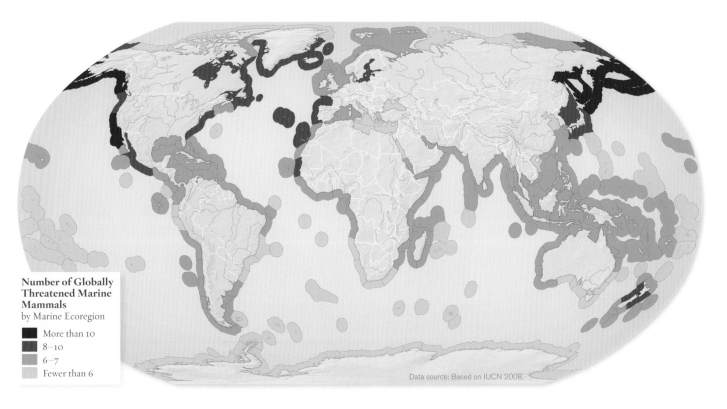

Number of Globally Threatened Marine Mammals
by Marine Ecoregion

- More than 10
- 8–10
- 6–7
- Fewer than 6

Data source: Based on IUCN 2008.

THREATENED MARINE MAMMALS. The preponderance of threatened marine mammal species in the Northern Hemisphere reflects the longer history of exploitation and relatively sophisticated hunting technologies.

Jürgen Freund/NPL/Minden Pictures

Shark finning. A delicacy in soup in East Asia, shark fins are removed, and, in many cases, the carcass (or even a still-living but finless and dying shark) is discarded. Thirty-five shark species are now threatened as a result.

Lynn McBride/TNC

Victims of their own popularity. Uncontrolled harvesting for the aquarium trade jeopardizes charismatic fish. The Australian government regulates collection of this rare leafy sea dragon, while twelve related species of seahorse and pipefish are on the brink of extinction.

most of its life at sea, has suffered a particularly precipitous fall. These large-winged birds—some species have wing spans of more than 3.4 meters—have been caught in the hooks of long-lining vessels that ply the Southern Ocean, where most albatrosses can be found.

As so often happens, the toll on marine life has rebounded to humans. Fishing ships have had to pay more and travel farther for an ultimately reduced catch. Exotic species such as the napoleon wrasse, bumphead parrotfish, goliath grouper, and giant

clam have all rapidly joined the list of threatened species.

Efforts to reduce fishing impacts are almost as old as fishing itself but in recent decades have led to pioneering policies including the creation of marine protected areas, as well as technological innovations. In the late 1980s, the United States required that all shrimp trawlers be fitted with turtle excluder devices (TEDs), which allow large animals such as turtles to escape from shrimp nets. Some countries fishing in the

Southern Ocean have more recently agreed to measures aimed specifically at reducing albatross losses, including requirements that fishers cast lines at night, hang streamers to scare the birds off, and use weighted lines that sink more rapidly and keep tempting bait out of sight. To give the big birds a fighting chance in the long run, however, vessels from all countries fishing in this ocean will have to collaborate—a huge challenge in international waters where no one government has jurisdiction.

5

Taking Action

To keep every cog and wheel is the first precaution of intelligent tinkering.

—ALDO LEOPOLD, *A SAND COUNTY ALMANAC*

MUCH OF THE CONSERVATION MOVEMENT in the twentieth century focused on keeping all of nature's cogs and wheels—the species that make up every natural community and ecosystem. Growing human populations and accelerating natural resource consumption drove habitat loss at an unprecedented pace and pushed iconic species like pandas, tigers, gray wolves, and whales to the brink of extinction.

In response, conservationists rallied to set aside lands and waters to provide species with the space they needed to survive and to protect them from human encroachment. They lobbied governments to establish national parks and wildlife refuges, and to protect other public lands from excessive development. Organizations like The Nature Conservancy established networks of private nature reserves to ensure that rare species and communities were not lost.

This emphasis on habitat protection has been remarkably successful. When Aldo Leopold wrote *A Sand County Almanac* in 1949, there were fewer than four thousand protected areas that covered around one-tenth of 1 percent of the world's land area. Today, there are more than one hundred thousand protected areas around the world that span more than 14 percent of the land area, and nearly 3 percent of coastal waters. These protected areas give hope that many species will have the space they need to survive into the future.

But simply setting aside habitat is not enough. Water, air, birds, and fish still move back and forth across the boundaries of nature reserves, in and out of protected space. So, too, do pollution and invasive species. And global threats like climate change know no boundaries at all. Effective conservation requires that broad threats are systematically addressed, and that habitat protection is integrated with land use and water management across the larger landscape.

More important, for conservation to be successful and effective in the twenty-first century, it must shift from protecting nature *from* people to protecting nature *for* people. The Millennium Ecosystem

Assessment documented the many benefits that nature provides to people: pollinating crops, supporting fisheries, delivering clean, dependable water supplies, preventing soil erosion, and protecting against storm damage and floods. Instead of trying to isolate protected areas from the surrounding landscape, conservation must contribute to the well-being and sustainability of human communities by helping protect natural ecosystems and the benefits that they provide to people.

This section of the atlas examines global progress in habitat protection and explores some of the strategies that promise to continue conservation progress into the future. Maps of habitat protection on land, at sea, and in freshwater show the global extent of protected areas and reveal outstanding gaps. Other pages feature conservation strategies that have the greatest potential for addressing major threats and advancing conservation in a way that will sustain nature and people.

Protected Areas on Land

Triumph for Nature

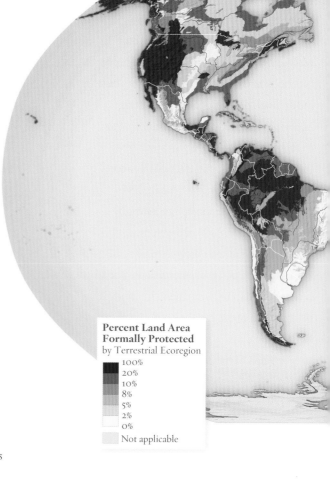

Living with nature.
Bogd Khan Mountain in Mongolia is one of the world's first protected areas. A small number of nomads live within its boundaries following traditional livestock practices.

The rise of habitat protection over time.
International conservation agreements such as the Convention on Biological Diversity have driven the recent global rise in habitat protection.

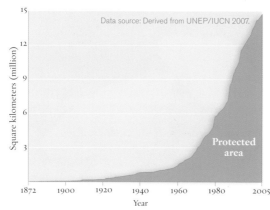

Data source: Derived from UNEP/IUCN 2007.

Protected area

Percent Land Area Formally Protected
by Terrestrial Ecoregion
- 100%
- 20%
- 10%
- 8%
- 5%
- 2%
- 0%
- Not applicable

RISING FROM THE VAST STEPPES, Bogd Khan Mountain is a place sacred to Mongolia's nomadic people. It was protected from human exploits more than seven hundred years ago by Genghis Khan, and officially protected by the emperor of Manchur in 1778, making it one of the oldest protected natural areas in the world.

Since then, people have established more than a hundred thousand protected areas around the world to protect natural habitats and natural resources from damage or development. The modern habitat protection movement started in 1903 when U.S. president Theodore Roosevelt established Yellowstone National Park. Habitat protection increased most dramatically at the end of the twentieth century, spurred by international conservation agreements such as the

Convention on Biological Diversity under which 168 countries agreed to protect at least 10 percent of their natural ecosystems. The result has been the unprecedented protection of natural landscapes, including over 38 percent of the Amazon's tropical forest—almost 2.4 million square kilometers across nine countries.

All together, the world's protected areas cover more than 14 percent of the land, an area larger than Brazil and China combined. This makes habitat protection one of the major land uses on the planet after agriculture. However, not all habitat types benefit from the same level of protection. Temperate grasslands, like those in Mongolia, have less than 5 percent of their total area protected. In contrast, tropical moist forests (including rain forests) have three times as much habitat protection.

Protected areas benefit nature by providing home, space, and refuge for species, and by keeping the fabric of natural ecosystems intact. They also benefit people by protecting sacred sites such as Bogd Khan Mountain, preserving places of exceptional scenic beauty like Yellowstone National Park, maintaining open spaces for hiking, hunting, and recreation, and managing valuable natural resources such as timber and rangeland.

Despite the remarkable progress in establishing protected areas, there are still important challenges to effective habitat protection. Threats such as invasive species and altered fire regimes do not stop at park boundaries and cannot be managed in isolation from the surrounding landscape. Another challenge is to avoid "paper parks" that are protected on paper but lack adequate management

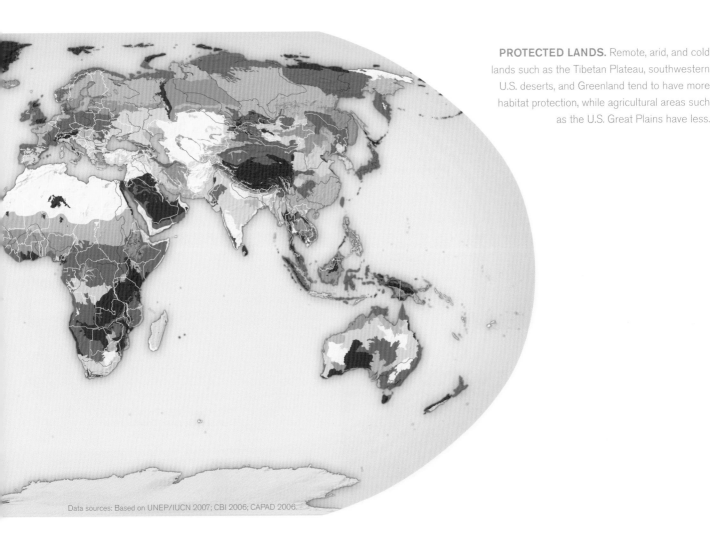

Data sources: Based on UNEP/IUCN 2007; CBI 2006; CAPAD 2006.

to protect habitats and natural resources from unauthorized development or resource extraction. At the same time, effective park management needs to address legitimate access and use by people who might have been displaced when protected areas were established. This requires that protected areas also be managed in a way that recognizes the needs of surrounding communities.

Habitat protection in Mongolia offers a promising example for the future. The Mongolian people have already protected nearly 14 percent of their country's natural habitat, and they are committed to protecting at least 30 percent by 2030. Even more, they are ensuring that adequate funding and management programs will preserve the vast grassland steppes that sustained nomadic cultures of Mongolia for centuries and now for future generations to come.

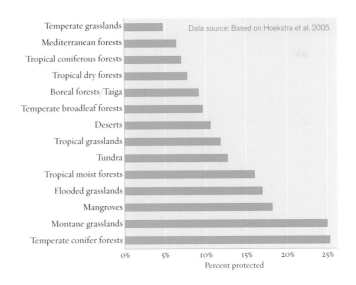

Data source: Based on Hoekstra et al. 2005.

Disparities in protection between biomes. Rain forests (tropical moist forests) and temperate coniferous forests have had three and five times more habitat protected, respectively, than temperate grasslands.

Protecting Rivers, Lakes, and Wetlands

Thinking beyond Park Boundaries

Scott Warren

Extraordinary diversity. Brazil's Pantanal includes jaguars, giant otters, and the lesser anteater, as well as more than 650 species of birds. These wetlands are protected under the Ramsar Convention.

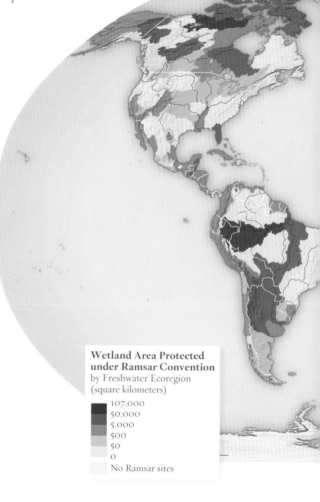

Wetland Area Protected under Ramsar Convention
by Freshwater Ecoregion (square kilometers)

- 107,000
- 50,000
- 5,000
- 500
- 50
- 0
- No Ramsar sites

Timothy Boucher

Dirk Roux

Monitoring fish to conserve elephants. The Mozambique tilapia is one of the species monitored in South Africa's Kruger National Park to assess the condition of the rivers that sustain all other park species. Regular monitoring of freshwater species is now standard practice for park managers.

FROM THE EVERGLADES in the United States to the Bangweulu swamps of Zambia, large wetlands have become as famous for their fragility as for their exotic array of wildlife. Brazil's Pantanal—one of the world's most biologically diverse landscapes—spans 170,000 square kilometers and harbors species including giant river otters, jaguars, and parrots, yet it is threatened by human activities including forest clearing, river dredging for navigation, wildlife poaching, overfishing, and pollution from farms, mining, and urban waste.

World leaders officially recognized the value and vulnerability of wetlands in 1971, when 158 nations signed a conservation

treaty specifically aimed at protecting them. Over the next thirty-seven years, 1,828 wetland sites covering 169 million hectares of both coastal and freshwater wetlands have been designated under the Ramsar Convention—so named for the city in Iran where it was signed—to be protected from development, pollution, and other dangers.

Complicating this effort, however, is that there is no similar scheme of protection for rivers that feed into such wetlands. Conserving rivers is in fact a far more daunting task, because they typically flow over large areas of land and cannot be fenced in. Instead, protecting rivers requires a range of coordinated efforts influencing activities on adjacent land, such as zoning rules

limiting land uses, regulation of pesticides on nearby farms, and maintenance of trees and other vegetation along the riverbanks. A few countries, including the United States, Australia, Canada, and South Africa, have programs that officially designate rivers as qualifying for protection from pollution and dam construction.

In recent decades, scientists and conservation-minded officials have attracted increasing support for wetlands and river protection by bringing attention to the financial value of benefits including water filtration and recreation opportunities. A showcase of this strategy is South Africa's Kruger National Park, created in 1926 to help preserve large

Data source: Based on UNEP/IUCN 2007.

mammals such as elephants and rhinos. The reserve is crossed from west to east by five rivers that carry sediments and pollutants from upstream activities such as irrigated agriculture, mining, and dense townships. In the 1960s, three of Kruger's rivers stopped flowing during part of the year, threatening the survival of the animals living in the park, as well as tourist revenues and jobs. The reserve's managers rose to the challenge, reaching out to upstream communities to talk about their water use and its impact on the park and regularly monitoring water quality and riparian vegetation within the park to inform day-to-day management activities.

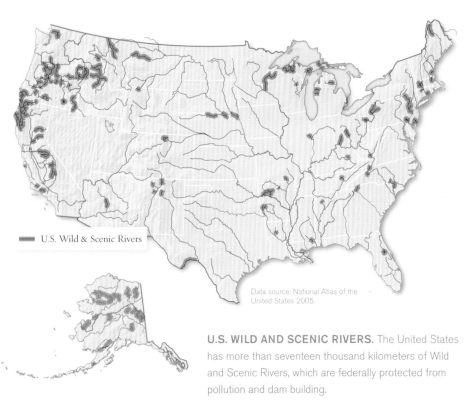

═══ U.S. Wild & Scenic Rivers

Data source: National Atlas of the United States 2005.

U.S. WILD AND SCENIC RIVERS. The United States has more than seventeen thousand kilometers of Wild and Scenic Rivers, which are federally protected from pollution and dam building.

Marine Protected Areas

Oases for Fish and People

Protected waters.
Papahanaumokuakea Marine National Monument covers the entirety of the northwestern Hawaiian Islands, where the rare Hawaiian monk seal can survive and breed unmolested.

Frans Lanting

Land-sea linkages.
The land and the surrounding waters of Australia's Macquarie Island have been strictly protected to maintain the critical habitats at this interface, like king penguin nesting grounds.

Konrad Wothe/Minden Pictures

Mark Godfrey/TNC

Don't ask us—ask them!
While fishers are often skeptical of advice from "outsiders," increasingly conservation organizations are supporting the transfer of lessons learned, fisher-to-fisher—to share the positive benefits of closing off some areas to fishing.

RISING OFF THE COAST of northeastern Australia, the Great Barrier Reef is far and away the world's largest coral reef, stretching through clear, shallow waters for more than two thousand kilometers. It is a natural wonder that attracts more than two million visitors annually, and, in 2007, some $4.5 billion in tourist revenues.

Recognizing the value of the site, one of the great global centers of marine biodiversity, Australia's federal government in the late 1970s established the Great Barrier Reef Marine Park, in an area nearly the size of

Germany. This was marine protection on an unprecedented scale. But as with many other large marine parks, the Great Barrier Reef was zoned into sectors to allow for activities ranging from recreational fishing to scientific research. Today more than one-third of its area is closed to fishing. The results of this protection have been seen in the sustained good health of the reef, the large numbers of fish, the relatively quick recovery from storms, and a continuingly stable source of income from fishing within carefully managed areas.

In addition to implementing these restrictions, park management has worked closely

with adjacent coastal communities and local authorities to influence agricultural practices and urban planning, in order to reduce impacts from sediments and pollution being swept onto the reef.

The benefits that can be accrued from marine protected areas have also been widely reported from much smaller sites. Beginning in 1985, a tiny reserve next to Apo Island in the Philippines was closed to fishing. Adjacent fishing communities subsequently enjoyed a substantial improvement in fish catches, as the large fish in the reserve have restocked the surrounding waters. The

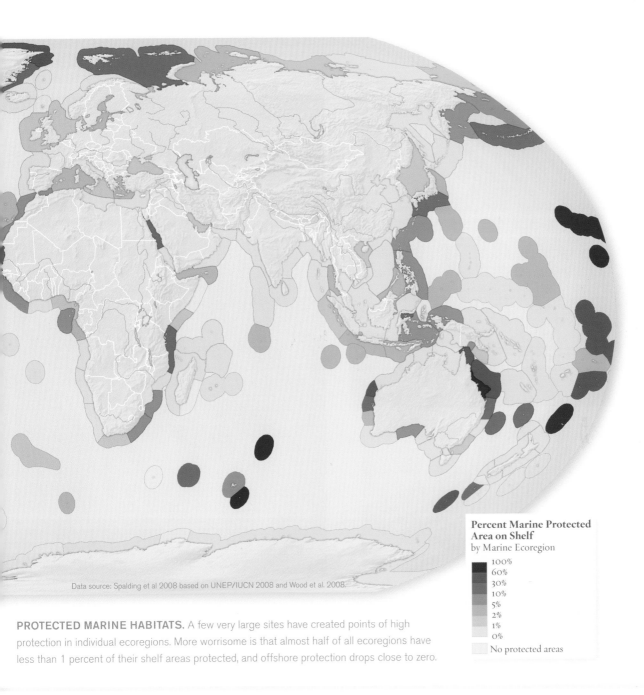

Data source: Spalding et al 2008 based on UNEP/IUCN 2008 and Wood et al. 2008.

Percent Marine Protected Area on Shelf
by Marine Ecoregion

100%
60%
30%
10%
5%
2%
1%
0%

No protected areas

PROTECTED MARINE HABITATS. A few very large sites have created points of high protection in individual ecoregions. More worrisome is that almost half of all ecoregions have less than 1 percent of their shelf areas protected, and offshore protection drops close to zero.

success story of Apo Island has since been spread and imitated around the world.

Although marine protected areas can be a boon for fishers (and for fish), they have also quite often offered further benefits, in the form of tourism and recreation, as well as support for important habitats such as mangroves, coral reefs, and coastal marshes that in turn help protect human communities from the impacts of storms and rising sea levels.

By 2008, a total of 5,045 marine protected areas had been established throughout the world's oceans. Most were small and near the coasts, yet a few, like the Great Barrier

Reef, were giants, the size of nations. These include tropical sites such as the Phoenix Islands Protected Area in Micronesia, Papahanaumokuakea Marine National Monument in Hawaii, and the Galápagos Marine Park, in addition to large tracts of polar seas around Macquarie Island Marine Park, Heard and MacDonald Islands Marine Reserve, and Northeast Greenland National Park.

The scientific evidence from the parks has been extraordinarily encouraging. Overall, throughout the world, marine protected areas have yielded substantial benefits not

only for nature but for people's livelihoods, sustenance, and safety.

Yet though the rate of protection has increased, in 2008, marine parks covered only about 4 percent of the world's continental shelves (by contrast some 14 percent of the world's land surface is protected). Furthermore, this protection is not evenly distributed, with about half of all marine ecoregions having less than one percent protection and the deep ocean almost entirely unprotected. Given that each ecoregion is home to communities found nowhere else, such low levels of protection are of grave concern.

Protecting Nature's Services

Dividends from the Wealth of Nature

Nature's many services.
These include mangroves supporting fisheries, honeybees pollinating crops and flowers, and forests filtering water.

NATURE SUSTAINS people's lives with food and water, but the bounty does not stop there. Mangrove forests and coral reefs protect low-lying coasts from storm damage while serving as nurseries for young fish. Honeybees and other insects pollinate important crops, such as apples and coffee. Tree roots filter rainwater and hold the soil in place on steep slopes, preventing erosion and mudslides. Scientists call these daily labors "ecosystem services," since most require an entire and intact system of life to do the job.

Trying to value this work in dollars is a controversial and challenging exercise, because sustaining lives is arguably priceless. But that has not stopped economists and

ecologists from coming up with estimates. The most famous one, published by ecological economist Robert Costanza and colleagues in 1997, puts the value of Earth's services at $33 trillion a year, a figure greater than the annual output of all the world's economies combined.

Scientists agree more readily about the statistics showing the contributions of these services to human well-being—such as the fact that, throughout the world, ocean and freshwater fisheries provide more than 15 percent of the protein in people's diets and provide jobs for about thirty-eight million workers.

In Africa and South Asia, rural families derive more than 20 percent of their household

income from wild foods, fuelwood, timber, and other forest products. Many poor communities, such as remote fishing villages in the Solomon Islands, depend almost entirely on small-scale fishing and local agriculture for their subsistence.

For most of human history, nature's benefits were seemingly free and inexhaustible. But as human numbers increase and resource consumption accelerates, limits are coming into view. We have started to squander our enormous natural inheritance, spending down the principal instead of living on the dividends alone so as to ensure continued wealth for future generations.

In 2005, the Millennium Ecosystem Assessment—the first global survey of

CARBON SEQUESTRATION: NEW VALUE FOR AN OLD SERVICE. Photosynthesis—the way plants grow by using sunlight—has long provided people with food and timber. Today, photosynthesis is also fueling an emerging market for a natural service to confront global climate change. Forests, grasslands, wetlands, soil, and phytoplankton in the ocean absorb carbon dioxide as they grow, storing it to make new material, in a process known as *carbon sequestration*. The importance of this role is highlighted by the fact that nearly 20 percent of climate-warming greenhouse gas emissions are due to deforestation that releases stored carbon back into the atmosphere.

As government regulations in Europe and elsewhere place limits on the total amount of greenhouse gas emissions that will be allowed, and as international climate change treaties recognize the value of forests for carbon sequestration, vigorous new "carbon-trading" markets are emerging. People throughout the world are already paying groups to plant trees to "offset" their personal carbon emissions. Larger companies, eager to reduce their carbon footprint in anticipation of regulatory actions, have helped to fund forest conservation in Bolivia's Noel Kempff Mercado National Park and forest restoration in the Lower Mississippi Valley of the southern United States. In 2008, global carbon markets were valued at nearly $118 billion. However, these investments are not without risk or worry. They will not be successful if protecting one forest simply results in another forest being cut, or if a protected forest is later cut down or burns. Nonetheless, conservationists and carbon entrepreneurs are working to prove that forest conservation can be a durable and profitable part of the climate change solution.

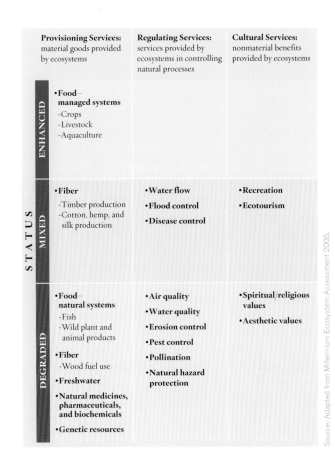

Source: Adapted from Millennium Ecosystem Assessment 2005.

The status of nature's service. Many services from natural systems are in decline, while those from some managed systems thrive.

nature's services—reported that more than 60 percent of services evaluated were in global decline, due to overexploitation and other unsustainable practices, and warned of significant consequences for human well-being. Among the most devastating of these is that declining water quality has left more than one billion people struggling for access to safe drinking water from streams, lakes and wells.

At times throughout history, people have exploited one of nature's services to the detriment of others, with disastrous costs. The 1920s North American wheat boom spurred homesteaders to plow up the U.S. western states' shortgrass prairie, trading grazing resources for crop production. Too late,

settlers realized that they had unwittingly sacrificed two other natural services—soil stability and drought resistance—as "black blizzards" blew away more than 90 million acres of the world's most fertile topsoil and drove more than 2.5 million people to flee the ecological disaster now known as the Dust Bowl. Today in northwestern China, a modern dust bowl is turning millions of acres of grasslands into desert every year and costing the Chinese economy billions of dollars in lost crop production.

The more hopeful news is that new awareness of the value of "natural capital" has prompted major investments in the wealth of nature throughout the world. Major

cities, from New York City and Seattle to Quito and Bogotá, are securing clean and reliable municipal water supplies by protecting and maintaining upper watersheds in natural conditions. In other places, including even parts of Oklahoma once scourged by the Dust Bowl, farmers are adopting no-till methods that protect against soil loss. Even such small and remote places as Solomon Island villages are creating marine protected areas to safeguard important fish nurseries, with the added benefit of tourist income from foreign visitors who come to dive among the healthy coral reefs.

Convergent Conservation

SCOTT A. MORRISON

TO A VISITOR from central Chile, the scrublands outside my home in coastal California would look strikingly familiar. So, too, for the visitor from southwestern Australia. Or from South Africa, or the Mediterranean Basin. That my chaparral would evoke their matorral or kwongan, their fynbos or maquis is a happenstance millions of years in the making. What unites these disparate places are climatic conditions not found on the other 98 percent of Earth's land surface: wet mild winters and warm dry summers. Over untold millennia that distinctive "Mediterranean" climate oriented the evolutionary trajectories of the plants and animals that occur there in a common direction, with an extraordinary consequence: the alignment of form and function, structure and strategy of largely unrelated species, occupying opposite sides of the planet.

Ecologists refer to this phenomenon as *convergent evolution*: species exposed to similar environments acquire comparable traits along different evolutionary pathways. Examples abound: marsupials that look and behave like mammals of other continents; distant flowers, similarly shaped, conforming to complementary adaptations of pollinators that in one case may be a bird and in another a moth. Like roots to water, evolutionary lineages seek perfection for persisting in the particular conditions of particular places and among the particular others that co-occur. So assemble the species that comprise the natural communities characteristic of the landscapes in which we live. And where similar environmental conditions occur elsewhere on the planet, those evolutionary tendencies repeat and create patterns in the mosaic that is our natural world: the Earth's biomes, each a collection of correlated communities, each of those a unique assemblage of species. It is these patterns among species that create patterns across places. The natural communities that comprise the world's biomes, although importantly idiosyncratic in detail, are functionally quite similar. And it is

that similarity that connects what is local and familiar with what is distant and otherwise foreign.

Human livelihoods have also been organized by such environmental forces. Our ancestors that lived in the world's deserts, for example, came upon similar behavioral strategies for thriving in the extremity and unpredictability of that biome. Whether we look across societies at the edge of the ice or in the heart of the forests, we see cultural convergence in adaptation to the conditions and resources available in such places. And as humans exploited those resources, we ourselves became a driving environmental force. We converted natural habitat to human land uses and altered to varying degrees the nature that remained. We changed how fires burn, how waters flow, and how species interact. And in cascading consequence, we watched the rare be replaced by the common and the unique disappear.

Similar ecosystems unravel in similar ways. So, the emergent pattern across biomes today is one of alarmingly convergent *extinction*: the tendency to lose the endemic, the wide-ranging, the specialist, the predator, the species of the commons we use as commodity. Today, the fates of deep-rooted evolutionary lineages are being decided by the cumulative consequence of such unspectacular decisions as where we place our homes, how we use water, what we decide to buy. Yet, could it be that in that very mundane similarity of threats to diversity across a biome there is an opportunity to improve our effectiveness as conservationists? After all, if we are all confronting similar challenges, perhaps we might—through more purposefully *collective* effort—sooner and more efficiently find ways of addressing those challenges.

In another corner of the world, I most surely have counterparts working to solve conservation problems that are more similar than not to those I'm working on here in California. Across any biome, a multitude of conservation strategies are being designed and tested. Some will succeed; some will fail. Either way, conservation colleagues from elsewhere would surely benefit from the lessons learned. Communication of

successful innovations (and, just as important, failures) could inform actions in places where the systems and challenges are similar. Indeed, if we were to plan and implement our individual conservation efforts as if they were treatments in a vast collaborative experiment in conservation practice, we might sooner elucidate ways of increasing the return on investment of ever-insufficient conservation resources. Each of our efforts could be informing another's. Each success could be positioned to advance the next.

And from that vantage of looking across our collective efforts we might more readily diagnose gaps in our own local conservation capacities. Where I work, for example, a lack of a particular expertise or regulatory framework or some other factor may be limiting the rate that conservation outcomes can be achieved. Perhaps conservation colleagues from elsewhere have implemented a strategy that, if applied in my region, could overcome those limitations and transform the enabling conditions for conservation—like a market-based incentive that converts a driver of threat into a force for conservation. Let's learn how they did it and apply it as a model.

We need each other's innovations if we are to deliver what biodiversity conservation demands: greater protection of diversity within areas that have explicit protected status, and greater conservation of diversity outside of those areas. We need places for the plants and animals that can persist only where humans mostly are not. While some of those places are already secured, in no biome is the existing network of formally protected areas adequately representative of the diversity of its natural communities. Ensuring that the world's reserve network captures the full complement of its natural systems is a necessity that unites our individual local efforts into a global, collaborative imperative.

But biodiversity conservation cannot rely on formal protected areas alone. Nature is not so tidily bounded in parks or reserves. Not only are too many species found only outside those areas; the processes that maintain the ecological function of reserves and the viability of species occur at far greater

A California rancher and a Mongolian herder share lessons in grassland conservation.

scales. While protected areas provide an essential foundation, lasting conservation relies on our ability also to protect biodiversity where people live. And how to accomplish that is one of the greatest challenges of our day.

Fortunately, the growing recognition of this necessity is coinciding with a growing awareness of the reliance of human well-being on functional ecosystems. This interdependence—of society on functional ecosystems, of ecosystem functions on native diversity, and, increasingly, of ecosystem functions on human management—should lead us to seek convergent *strategies* that protect biodiversity while meeting other societal goals. Especially in this world of globalizing economies, increasing population, diminishing resources, and accelerating climatic flux, conservation cannot be considered to be an activity separate from our day-to-day affairs. We need human enterprise to be compatible with the protection of ecological function and the persistence of native species. Figuring out how to mainstream conservation into our livelihoods and economies—such that by going about our everyday business we effect conservation—is surely beyond the wherewithal of any of us acting alone. If we are going to increase the

pace, scale, and effectiveness of conservation, we must align efforts.

The enormity and urgency of the conservation imperative requires that we be especially efficient with always limited conservation resources. We cannot afford to reinvent wheels or miss opportunities to scale up the impact of our efforts. Just as we need a global network of formally protected natural areas, we need a networked global community of conservation practitioners. The greater that network, the more audacious can be our conservation goals—because we will be more likely generating new approaches and alliances to achieve them.

Simply sharing what works in one region with those who might use it in another is a good place to start.

This atlas is a guidebook for the convergence of conservation effort. By illustrating similarities in natural communities and socio-ecological challenges, it highlights where there may be especially promising opportunity for collaboration on conservation solutions. Great efficiency and economy of scale might be realized if we communicate with others working on very similar threats in very similar systems. Convergent conservation stems from an explicit understanding of how individual conservation efforts

complement those of others—geographically, ecologically, socially, economically, and strategically. Every once in a while, one of us will hit on a truly transformative strategy. Convergent conservation is the replication—with some local adaptation, of course—of that catalytic conservation concept.

On another side of the planet, I imagine a colleague looking out across a conservation landscape that looks remarkably similar to my own. In a distant future, others will look at these same places and see something perhaps similar—or perhaps something greatly diminished. Which future it will be is largely ours to decide. Yes, those unique evolutionary lineages of the plants and animals that surround us have persisted through the ebbs and flows of eons past. But this moment—today—is where that past and all possible futures converge. That continuity—that convergence—is ours, in partnership, to ensure. No matter where we are in the world or what the origins of our conservation ethic, let us be oriented by that awareness and be accountable to make those connections.

SCOTT A. MORRISON IS THE DIRECTOR OF CONSERVATION SCIENCE FOR THE NATURE CONSERVANCY'S CALIFORNIA CHAPTER.

International Cooperation

Saving the Whales—and More

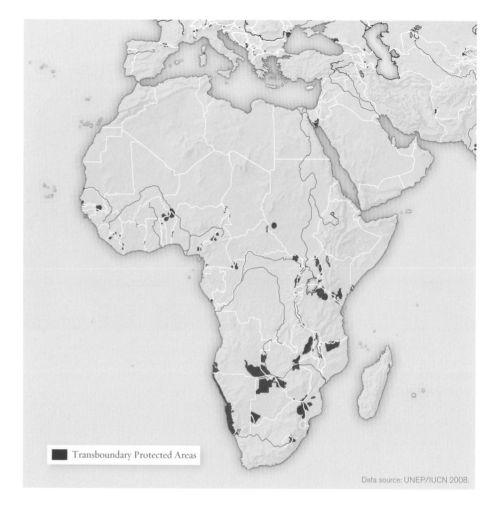

TRANSBOUNDARY PROTECTED AREAS. Globally, there are 227 protected area complexes that traverse international boundaries. Many are managed cooperatively, such as the Kgalagadi Transfrontier Park between South Africa and Botswana, where ancient migrations of animals like wildebeest are able to continue.

Transboundary Protected Areas

Data source: UNEP/IUCN 2008.

IN THE EARLY 1980s, the world's great whales had arrived at the brink of extinction. Hunted for centuries, they were finally no match for modern explosive harpoons and factory ships that could process whale meat far out at sea. Yet even as populations plummeted, hunters had no incentive to call off the chase—if they did not hunt whales, they reasoned, someone else would.

The whales were caught in a classic environmental dilemma, known as the "tragedy of the commons." The problem arises when a finite resource is shared without restrictions, allowing individuals to take more than their share. Natural resources may seem like an unlimited buffet—until limits abruptly come into view.

Individual nations have passed thousands of laws to protect common resources such as clean air and water. Yet the past few decades have made it increasingly clear that many precious environmental goods are shared by more than one country. Animals roam back and forth across boundaries. Fish travel the ungoverned open ocean. Particulate air pollution wafts from Beijing to San Francisco.

Awareness of this interdependence has led to new international cooperation. Sometimes it is as simple as two countries agreeing on the boundaries of a nature reserve, as South Africa and Mozambique have done, since 2001, with the Greater Limpopo Transfrontier Park. The new reserve joined the previously separate Kruger and Limpopo national parks in a collaboratively managed superpark, allowing animals to move freely across the borders.

More complex issues have loomed when countries have joined to manage rivers, with their upstream-downstream dilemmas of pollution, dam building, and irrigation. In 1998, the Danube River Protection Convention came into force, joining fourteen nations lining the path of Europe's largest river. This convention, managed by an international commission, has encouraged the building of sewage treatment plants, the restoration of floodplain habitats, increased levels of scientific monitoring, education programs, and even the celebration of Danube Day, on June 29.

Collaboration raises the bar of what conservation can accomplish. Countries working together can learn from one another's experiences, pool resources, and minimize the chances that their efforts will be undermined. The International Whaling Commission was established by whaling nations in 1946 to better manage the industry in the face

RESTRICTIONS ON ILLEGAL TRADE. Many species have been driven to the brink of extinction by heavy demand from international markets. The Convention on International Trade in Endangered Species, signed by 174 countries, includes restrictions or outright bans in the trade of certain animal products, including a complete ban on elephant ivory trade in 1990. In a powerful symbolic gesture, the year before some ten metric tons of confiscated elephant ivory were burned in Kenya. The ban on this trade led to a dramatic decline in poaching, and populations are recovering in some areas of southern Africa.

Walls of death banned. Drift nets are long, unselective nets that can be tens of kilometers in length and are indiscriminate, catching everything in their paths. Relatively rapid action by the international community led to a global ban on the use of large-scale pelagic drift nets in the high seas in 1992. More recently (2002), the European Union went further by banning all drift net use by EU vessels in their own territorial waters. Drift net fishing still continues, but this intervention has prevented a much larger disaster.

Burning confiscated tusks

Victory at sea. As whaling progressed from a hazardous activity restricted to coastal waters to a highly mechanized industry, whales' numbers collapsed in every corner of the globe. Thanks to international cooperation, whaling has largely ceased.

of spiraling declines of whale populations. For forty years it appeared to make little progress, but its members joined in a historic agreement in 1986 that ultimately saved the whales. They mandated a moratorium on whaling—a ban on whale capture, with only minor exceptions for research and for traditional small-scale hunts by indigenous peoples. This agreement was intended to give the whale stocks a chance to recover and to enable the development of more sustainable management plans for future whaling. In 2009, the moratorium was still in place.

The ban has not been easy, nor has it been completely effective. Three nations—Japan, Iceland, and Norway—have continued lower levels of whaling while, together with others, have also pressed for the ban to end. Other countries have sought a permanent

halt. But overall the moratorium has been respected for more than twenty years, in which time species including the humpback, gray, and bowhead whales have annually increased in numbers, even as others, such as the northern right whale, remain in peril of extinction.

Since then, there have been other signal gains from international cooperation. Among the most celebrated of which is the Montreal Protocol, the 1989 treaty that stopped production of chemicals that were destroying the ozone layer and threatening humans and other animals with cancer from ultraviolet rays.

As the risks of global climate change became more apparent, the United Nations used the Montreal model to inspire another consensus, the Framework Convention on

Climate Change, which led to the treaty signed in Kyoto in 1997 and went into effect in 2005. But until a comprehensive international climate agreement is successfully ratified and implemented by all major greenhouse gas emitters, the world's climate stability will remain virtually ungoverned and in question. Another example of the persistence of the tragedy of the commons is the high seas, where fish stocks—yet another unmonitored buffet—were plummeting from overharvesting. There will never be any force equal to the force of nature—even in its weakened modern state—to convince people to put differences aside to help preserve Earth's life-support systems. The tide of destruction to our natural systems could well end up threatening civilizations—or else it may finally inspire people to rise above human nature.

Greening the Marketplace
Certifiably Profitable

Bird-friendly beans. Coffee grown in the shade (above), under a canopy of trees, not only tastes better but conserves habitat for birds and other species. Most coffee today comes from sun-soaked plantations (right), unnatural settings that require large amounts of fertilizers and pesticides. But specialty coffees are growing in popularity and are now certified according to a wide array of standards, including "shade grown" and "Fair Trade," and sold at premium prices.

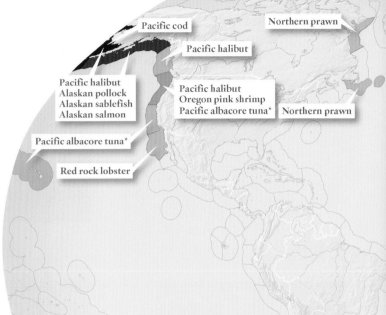

Pacific cod

Pacific halibut

Northern prawn

Pacific halibut
Alaskan pollock
Alaskan sablefish
Alaskan salmon

Pacific halibut
Oregon pink shrimp
Pacific albacore tuna*

Northern prawn

Pacific albacore tuna*

Red rock lobster

Scallop

*Certified by United States fisheries only

Kinder, gentler tuna fishing. "Longline" tuna-catching methods, which can have thousands of baited hooks on a mechanized line as long as eighty kilometers, can kill many young tuna, sea turtles, sharks, and seabirds. Encouraged by new consumer demand, some fishers have switched to more environmentally friendly methods, such as individually manned poles and lines. In 2007, the American Albacore Fishing Association's U.S. Pacific albacore tuna fishery, which has always used pole and line methods, was the first of its kind to win MSC certification.

CHOICES, CHOICES. Paper or plastic—or the reusable fabric tote bag. The Hummer or the hybrid. The Chilean seabass or the responsibly caught wild Alaska salmon. There is always room for improvement, but consumers today are more educated than ever before about their impacts on a besieged natural world. And big corporations are fighting to convince them that their products are environmentally benign.

But how do you tell the green from the greenwashed? This, increasingly, is the job of a rapidly growing global industry of certifiers that now monitors and labels a host of industries, from forestry to furniture to farming to fishing. At their best, these government agencies and independent watchdogs can assure consumers that products were produced according to national or global sustainability standards, as verified by a professional and independent auditor.

A tour of the local grocery store turns up labels galore. Coffee may be "shade grown"; tuna, "dolphin safe"; bananas, "organic"; breakfast cereal, "GMO free." You can now buy paper marked according to its recycled-materials content and appliances government certified as energy efficient.

All these options can at times bewilder even the savviest shopper. With new eligible products and labels appearing all the time, it is hard, without reading a lot of fine print, to figure out which claims can be trusted. But two non-profit, international certifiers that so far have endured years of scrutiny now oversee a growing share of the planet's

Tesoros Del Sol organic Coffee: tesdelsol.com

Danny Lehman/Corbis

NOAA

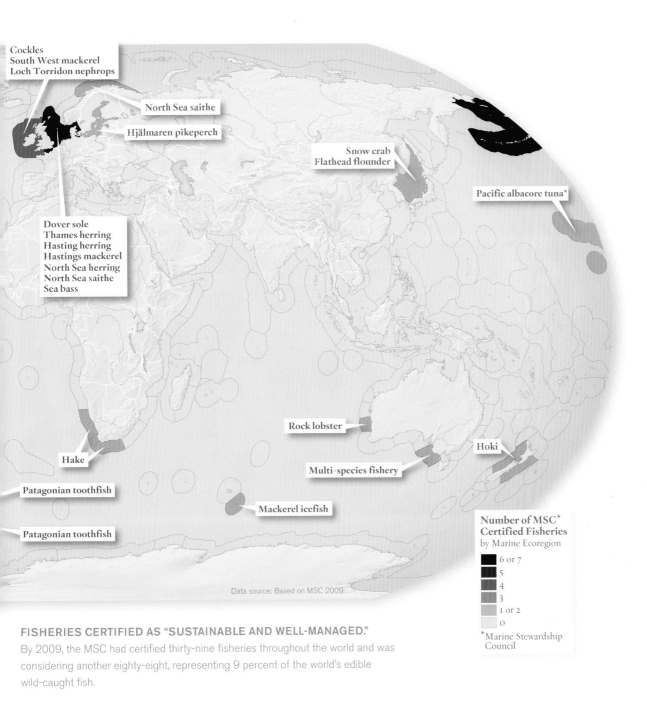

Cockles
South West mackerel
Loch Torridon nephrops

North Sea saithe

Hjälmaren pikeperch

Snow crab
Flathead flounder

Pacific albacore tuna*

Dover sole
Thames herring
Hasting herring
Hastings mackerel
North Sea herring
North Sea saithe
Sea bass

Rock lobster

Hoki

Hake

Multi-species fishery

Patagonian toothfish

Mackerel icefish

Patagonian toothfish

Data source: Based on MSC 2009.

Number of MSC* Certified Fisheries
by Marine Ecoregion

- 6 or 7
- 5
- 4
- 3
- 1 or 2
- 0

*Marine Stewardship Council

FISHERIES CERTIFIED AS "SUSTAINABLE AND WELL-MANAGED."
By 2009, the MSC had certified thirty-nine fisheries throughout the world and was considering another eighty-eight, representing 9 percent of the world's edible wild-caught fish.

timber and fishing industries. They are the Forest Stewardship Council, formed in 1993 by environmental groups and timber industry representatives, and the Marine Stewardship Council (MSC), initially set up in 1997 as a partnership between Unilever, previously the world's biggest buyer of seafood, and the conservation group World Wildlife Fund.

The MSC has been an independent agency since 1999. Its mission is to counter overfishing and other destructive fishing practices that are threatening marine environments and fishing livelihoods. To win certification, fisheries must undergo extensive evaluations to ensure they are well managed and environmentally sustainable. At the supermarket, the fish and fish products from a certified fishery carry the distinctive blue MSC label that lets consumers know the fish were caught with less harm to the environment and other marine species. As of 2009, more than two thousand MSC-labeled seafood products were available at supermarkets in thirty-six countries worldwide.

In many cases, certified products cost more money, because firms that are managed sustainably may entail higher production costs. Bottom trawling is a relatively cheap way to catch seafood, for instance, but it passes the costs on in the destruction it wreaks on the seabed. The new certification industry is expanding its niche, however, in hopes that eventually consumer demand for certified products will push entire industries to take better care of nature.

Collaborative Solutions

Problem-Solving Partnerships

Working in communities. Community Markets for Conservation (COMACO) works in Zambia with local people to move away from destructive activities like poaching and toward sustainable practices like organic crops.

WHITE-SAND BEACHES, lush jungles, and rich marine life make the Caribbean island of St. Lucia a paradise for tourists and anglers. So much so that Soufrière, one of its historic communities, came close to being loved to death. As so often happens when natural resources are at once both limited and popular, a turf war broke out between the coastal community's two biggest boosters. Visitors' yachts were mooring in prime fishing locations, while fishers were depleting the waters of the marine life the tourists had traveled far to see. It was plainly bad for business on both sides.

Beginning in 1995, however, Soufrière turned itself into a rare exception to the old, familiar story of the slow ruin of beautiful places. That is when the Caribbean Natural Resources Institute and some other institutions like the Department of Fishing and the

Soufrière Regional Development Foundation proposed a new strategy by which the fishers and tourism industry would join in the establishment of the Soufrière Marine Management Area. Unlike a typical marine protected area, the new cooperative has been run by an advisory committee composed of representatives of twenty-two groups with interests in the local resources.

The collaborative management of natural resources has become more common throughout the world since the early 1990s, as evidence has accumulated that traditional, "top-down" methods have failed in complicated situations such as Soufriere's turf war. The pioneering Agenda 21 document that emerged from the 1992 Earth Summit in Rio de Janeiro endorsed an inclusive approach to solving such complex development problems as land use and coastal development,

setting a precedent for the management of future resource conflicts.

In recent years, conservation groups have joined in a varied array of collaborative efforts. In some cases, big non-profit environmental organizations have teamed up with former foes, such as oil or timber corporations, to share resources and strategies for mutual benefit: the environmental groups pointing the way to more sustainable approaches, and the corporations scoring points with an environmentally concerned public.

Another increasing area of cooperation is within individual governments. Ministries or agencies that previously routinely ignored the ecological consequences of their action have been coordinating efforts as never before. A case in point is the U.S. National Invasive Species Council, established in 1999 and led by the departments of Agriculture,

UNEXPECTED PARTNERS The future of many American rivers rests with the U.S. Army Corps of Engineers. The Army Corps is the nation's largest water manager, operating more than six hundred dams that provide benefits such as flood risk management, water supply, hydropower, navigation, and recreation.

This extensive network of dams, most of which was built between 1930 and 1970, has substantially changed our rivers, by holding back water and altering natural flow patterns. Natural flows are critical to the long-term health of our rivers, floodplains, and estuaries, as well as to the ability of these systems to provide economically important services such as natural flood attenuation, water purification, commercial and recreational fisheries, and ecotourism.

In July 2002, the Army Corps collaborated with The Nature Conservancy in launching the Sustainable Rivers Project to change how Army Corps dams are operated to restore rivers, floodplains, and estuaries. This work involves defining and returning "environmental flows" to rivers—flows that mimic key aspects of free-flowing rivers, such as natural periods of low flow or seasonal flooding of wetlands where fish can spawn. The project has engaged hundreds of scientists from dozens of institutions, including state and federal natural resource agencies, nongovernmental organizations, and the nation's colleges and universities. The Sustainable Rivers Project now represents the largest coordinated environmental flow project in the world, involving work on thirty-six Army Corps dams in eight river basins as of 2009. The project's ultimate goal is to demonstrate a new, ecologically sensitive model for water management—one built upon deep collaboration between engineers and ecologists.

Restoring a river's rhythm. Government agencies and conservation organizations collaborate to return natural flows to the Savannah River, Georgia, United States.

Commerce, and the Interior, with members ranging from the departments of Defense and Homeland Security to the National Aeronautics and Space Administration (NASA) and the Environmental Protection Agency (EPA). The council was designed to coordinate the federal response to the threat of invasive species to the U.S. economy and environment, with each of its members making specific contributions. The U.S. Coast Guard, for instance, under the Department of Homeland Security, has been charged with combating aquatic invasive species transported via ballast water, while NASA has applied its extensive satellite technologies in mapping and monitoring the spread of invasive species. Into the future, the council will continue to integrate the efforts of its many member agencies in hopes of eventually stopping the spread of invasive species.

Especially since the 1990s, important new partnerships have also been forged between environmental groups and people living on the land the groups seek to protect. In the early days of the environmental movement, many groups interested in protecting nature thought it possible to fence off land or otherwise restrict access. But subsequent experience has shown that is usually impossible and not always effective in conserving resources. Since then, the big international environmental groups have dedicated more effort into working with local people and in many cases trying to provide alternative income sources, such as artisan furniture manufacture or ecotourism, as incentives to steer them away from exhausting local natural resources.

In Zambia, one such organization, Community Markets for Conservation

(COMACO), began working with rural subsistence farmers in 2001 to promote and subsidize sustainable farming practices, while reducing the poaching of local wildlife. Individuals in the community who join COMACO are trained in organic farming practices and band together to form co-ops. COMACO then buys their products at above-market-value prices and sells them in Zambian outlets. The catch? Prospective members must first turn in their poaching equipment. Over the program's first seven years, more than forty thousand snares were turned in, while some former poachers even signed up to be trained as wildlife guides, having learned to value nature instead of destroying it. As in the other instances of this new model of collaboration, enlightened self-interest has played a key role.

Conservation on Our Watch

GRETCHEN C. DAILY
MARILYN CORNELIUS
CHARLES J. KATZ, JR.
BRIAN SHILLINGLAW

HOWEVER MEASURED—in dollars raised or hectares saved—conservation has always been a race to buy time. Now it needs to be about more, addressing head-on the root problem: that conservation too often is seen as being in conflict with human development. How do we practice effective, enduring conservation in a world of growing numbers and aspirations of people? We need to change our approaches quickly if we are to do anything more than temporarily slow the pace of biodiversity loss in a few places.

What can conservation do to address the real struggle and win the race? We identify three core areas of focus in this promising time of innovation.

First, we must move past what author Michael Rosenzweig has called our "Noah's Ark" view of the world. Our conservation strategy has been to secure as large and as biodiverse a fleet of arks—"protected areas"—as possible and to bolster that fleet through restoration of some currently unseaworthy vessels. But unlike the floodwaters of the Bible story, current threats to biodiversity won't quickly recede.

In that light, how many species might a fleet of arks sustain over the long term? Maybe 5 percent. Even if this estimate is off by a factor of three, we must accept the reality that protected areas can be only one small part of a much larger agenda. Abandon them? Absolutely not—many species will survive nowhere else. But we must abandon our false expectations of them. We need to seize the chance to preserve biodiversity and the benefits it confers on society *within* a sea of humanity, before it is too late. We need to harmonize production and conservation. Partnerships with farmers, ranchers, foresters, and (even!) real estate developers will result in more productive and participatory conservation efforts.

Second, there is no way for conservation to grow in effectiveness if we think of our work as based on charity alone. We need to transform the way people think about the environment, so that conservation is appreciated for its vital role in achieving the needs and aspirations of people everywhere. Conservation practitioners are demonstrating the value of ecosystems as capital assets, communicating the vital roles these assets play in supporting human well-being, and opening new revenue streams to fund conservation. We need to build on the momentum and confidence generated and bring these successes to scale. We need to enable decision makers to quantify the importance of natural capital, assess trade-offs, and create ways to invest strategically in conservation and development.

Third, it is stunning to recognize how white and Western the dominant forces in conservation are today. In the United States, for instance, people of color constitute about 33 percent of the population but make up only about 10 percent of the staff and board members of natural resource organizations, despite the major roles that people of color have played in the many phases and forms of conservation in this country. In our day, we must integrate others so as not to pursue a narrow solution to a broad and complex problem. We need representation and participation from the myriad ethnicities and cultures of the world if we are to understand the many values surrounding nature and the tremendous traditional knowledge and practices relevant to conservation today. This achievement can occur by educating conservation practitioners about indigenous, traditional, and modern conservation approaches that could be integrated formally into current practice; cultivating capacity; and supporting a cadre of leaders worldwide who would implement conservation in their home regions.

Globally, some of the most successful, enduring, and inspiring conservation traditions come from regions of the world rarely given scientific attention and encompassing cultures and worldviews that Westerners barely know. The same is true for the most recent of innovations. Payments for ecosystem services, pioneered in Costa Rica, have taken off in China, Latin America, Southeast Asia, and southern Africa. To succeed in our mission, the conservation movement must fully involve and incorporate leaders and devoted practitioners in the full diversity of human communities.

Conservation has achieved breathtaking successes and has established approaches that must endure. We need to sustain reserves and philanthropy, while expanding our ranks to include diverse founders whose narratives are yet unknown to the greater conservation community. That in itself is a challenge. Yet to achieve even the most modest of goals in the future, we must seek to make conservation mainstream—economically attractive and commonplace worldwide.

The Real Struggle

The ways in which conservation must change follow naturally from looking at the world's ecosystems and their biodiversity as capital assets. If properly managed, they yield a flow of vital services, including the provision of goods (e.g., seafood and timber), life-support processes (climate stabilization and water purification), cultural benefits (sense of place, inspiration), and the conservation of options (genetic diversity for future use).

Relative to other forms of capital, however, that embodied in ecosystems is poorly understood, scarcely monitored, routinely undervalued, and undergoing rapid degradation and depletion. Often the importance of ecosystem services—and the mangroves, wetlands, and other natural capital underpinning their production—is widely appreciated only upon their loss, such as in the aftermath of the Asian tsunami or Hurricane Katrina. Continuing rapid growth in the size and per capita consumption of the human population make these circumstances especially dangerous: the liquidation of ecosystem capital is intensifying just when the need for it is reaching all-time highs.

Our most fundamental struggle is to awaken people to the connections between conservation and human well-being. Services provided by ecosystems are becoming scarce, and scarcity confers economic value. Momentum is building behind the use of ecosystem service approaches to support biodiversity, stabilize climate, filter water, control floods, enhance soil fertility, offer human enjoyment, and sustain traditional culture—all with an economic justification.

Valuing nature, and acting in accordance with those values, makes conservation relevant in people's day-to-day lives—in the midst of human enterprise, in the heart of the economy, and among the full spectrum of people dependent on Earth's lands and waters. Revealing the value of nature, in economic and broader cultural terms, opens the possibility of taking conservation to scale—and of reaching, geographically, into all places and ways of thinking that can advance conservation.

Conservation on Our Watch

Many people who have pursued lifetime careers in conservation say they feel a rebirth of the movement today—a surge of creativity, energy, inspiration, and engagement with "new" kinds of people testing out bold new ideas, daunting or not!

Embracing the complexity—and diversity, both biological and cultural—of the world is the only viable path forward. For too long the conservation movement has been running away from people and communities in the race to save nature. We know now that we can protect more—hopefully much more—by running with people, toward the shared goal of understanding the values of nature and aligning incentives with their protection.

Planting a tree in Jaguari watershed, Brazil

GRETCHEN C. DAILY IS A PROFESSOR AT STANFORD UNIVERSITY AND CHAIR OF THE NATURAL CAPITAL PROJECT.

MARILYN CORNELIUS IS A DOCTORAL STUDENT IN THE EMMETT INTERDISCIPLINARY PROGRAM ON ENVIRONMENT AND RESOURCES (E-IPER), STANFORD UNIVERSITY.

CHARLES J. KATZ, JR. IS ON THE BOARD OF ADVISERS OF THE WOODS INSTITUTE FOR THE ENVIRONMENT AND STANFORD'S SCHOOL OF EARTH SCIENCES AND ON THE WASHINGTON BOARD OF TRUSTEES, THE NATURE CONSERVANCY.

BRIAN SHILLINGLAW IS AN E-IPER AND STANFORD LAW SCHOOL GRADUATE, NOW MANAGER OF POLICY AND REGULATORY AFFAIRS WITH NEW FORESTS, INC.

Rule of Law

Protecting the Commons

Dave Currie

Trying to make a comeback. The Kirtland's warbler and American alligator are two of the species benefiting from federal protection under the U.S. Endangered Species Act.

Hugo Arnal/TNC

IN **528 AD**, the Roman emperor Justinian declared that his empire's rivers, streams, and surrounding lands should be protected, because, together with the air, running water, the sea and seashore, they were "common to all mankind." It was a novel idea at the time: that the state should help protect nature as opposed to private property. But for the next 1,500 years, Justinian's code would be echoed in the laws and regulations of countries throughout the world.

Skip ahead to 1962, when Rachel Carson's landmark book *Silent Spring* exposed the growing threats to human health and the environment from pesticides. The book drew U.S. attention as never before to a clear conflict between private industry and common welfare, and it helped gather force for an environmental movement that would

formally be launched with demonstrations by twenty million people on the first Earth Day, on April 22, 1970.

Throughout the next decade, private groups increased pressure on governments to respond to urban smog, polluted rivers and beaches, and other environmental issues. And governments did indeed respond—with a wave of groundbreaking legislation, including, in the United States, the Clean Water Act, the Clean Air Act, and the creation of the federal Environmental Protection Agency. The new laws set strict rules to reduce pollution, particularly the "point source" discharges from industrial plants and cities. And they achieved some remarkable success, reducing organic waste discharges into rivers and lakes by 98 percent from industrial sources and by 46 percent from public waste treatment facilities.

To be sure, the U.S. laws have been less effective in combating "nonpoint" pollution sources, such as fertilizers and chemicals draining from farmland. The health of U.S. rivers and lakes has also been damaged by excessive withdrawal of water for irrigation, as well as from dredging riverbeds or forcing flows into fixed channels. A federally sponsored assessment in 2002 indicated that more than 40 percent of sampled rivers and streams in the United States were "impaired" as habitats for wildlife.

Other countries, including South Africa, have developed more far-reaching legislation for sustaining their rivers and lakes, with measures that not only reduce pollution but ensure that sufficient water remains in the river for freshwater animals and plants, as well as downstream communities.

TRADING POLLUTION. In the early 1990s, a bold experiment in a new market for dirty air proved it possible to help both the environment and the economy at the same time. The 1990 amendments to the Clean Air Act established a market to combat the problem of acid rain, principally from emissions of sulfur dioxide (SO_2) from U.S. power plants.

Here's how it worked: the U.S. Environmental Protection Agency (EPA) set a new limit on SO_2 emissions and gave electrical utilities throughout the country permits to emit SO_2, which they could buy and sell with others in the industry. Companies with more efficient power plants could reduce emissions below their targets and sell their unused permits. The firms with less efficient plants found it more economical to buy permits than to replace older equipment. Eventually the permits were being traded like pork bellies, with speculators entering the market to bet on future prices.

Mark Godfrey/TNC

The system has been termed "cap and trade," because the initial limit, or cap, motivates the trade. The system has been successful in cutting overall emissions at the lowest cost. By the spring of 2000, the market had grown to nearly $3 billion, and firms had achieved their pollution reductions at one-tenth of the predicted cost.

Today the largest cap and trade system in the world is the European Union Emission Trading Scheme, which puts a cap on greenhouse gas emissions. It is being hailed as a model that could be rolled out to a global system as one of the measures to reduce climate change.

Enforcement with teeth. For laws like the U.S. Clean Water Act to be effective, they need to be enforced, backed by a functioning justice system, and have sufficient punitive measures to discourage lawbreaking.

Mark Godfrey/TNC

Environmentalists have also campaigned to defend threatened wildlife. One of their major achievements was the 1973 U.S. Endangered Species Act. Stricter than similar legislation in other countries, this law requires the development of recovery plans for creatures and plants on a list of threatened species, and to ensure the protection of those species' "critical habitats." In August 2009, approximately 1,320 species were listed under this act; and although more are added each year, 93 percent of listed species have stable or increasing populations. Species such as the Florida panther, the whooping crane, and the black-footed ferret have all started to come back from the brink of extinction, while a few, ranging from the American alligator to the diminutive alpine flower Robbins' cinquefoil, have recovered sufficiently to be taken off the list.

Fish are another common resource where the need for regulation and harvest limits has become increasingly clear. In the absence of laws and monitoring, the harvesting of fish becomes a winner-take-all affair that turns into a loss for all parties concerned, once the fish are depleted. If managed well, fishing industries are often receptive to regulations, provided they see equality of treatment and the long-term benefits. Regulations may include limiting the size and number of fish that can be caught, banning destructive technologies, and setting times and places for when harvests are allowed. They may also include incentives, such as provisions of individual quotas to fishers, who may then either fish up to their limit or sell their rights to someone else.

Alaska's salmon fishery leads the field, with innovative management policies including restrictions on access and gear type used, and real-time-based management of the fishery by local biologists that allows them to open or close the fishery on a daily basis depending on the condition of salmon runs.

The most colossal test to date of the power of the rule of law has surely come with the threat of climate change. As with other past environmental dilemmas, this one sets in stark relief the public's interest in a stable climate against private gain from the continued burning of fossil fuels, such as oil, gas, and coal. Reducing greenhouse gas emissions will ultimately require a package of national and international strategies, including taxes, investments, incentives, and a variety of laws, large and small. And it will tax legislators' imaginations, courage, and resourcefulness as never before.

Individual Action

Parting the Waters

Love Affair with Nature. That was the name of the event on Valentine's Day, 2007, when one hundred couples were joined by volunteers to plant mangroves on the day of a mass wedding in the Philippines.

BIBLICAL LORE says that back when the Israelites were fleeing Egypt, pursued by the pharaoh's army, the Lord provided a miracle by parting the waters of the Red Sea to let them cross. But a lesser-known Jewish story is that the sea did not begin to part until one man, Nachshon ben Aminadav, took the first step, wading in until the waters reached his chin.

Most progress begins just this way, with a single spark of courage, leading to a first step. Despite the vast scale of the problems facing the planet, people have proven repeatedly that individual actions can make a profound difference.

Such endeavors can take many forms: from small, day-to-day decisions about purchases of food, clothing, and appliances, to involvement with citizens' groups and environmental campaigns. Such actions can move individuals from being net contributors to environmental problems to being a part of the solution. And as efforts grow to many millions of concerned citizens, so industries and politicians begin to change.

Some of these first steps have been truly heroic—and have been recognized accordingly. Every year since 1990, environmental crusaders from throughout the world have been honored in San Francisco, California, with the Goldman Environmental Prize. One such recipient was Tarcísio Feitosa da

Silva from Altamira, Brazil, who led efforts to protect vast areas of tropical forest in a remote, lawless region, in the face of death threats. Another was Olya Melen, a crusading attorney from Ukraine, who managed to suspend construction of a massive canal that would have cut through the heart of the Danube Delta, one of the world's most important wetlands. Yet another was Tsetsegee Munkhbayar from Mongolia, who worked with government and grassroots groups to shut down destructive mining operations along the country's scarce waterways. In many cases, governments colluding with industry persecute activists who stick their necks out to defend environmental resources.

Peter Dombrovskis © Liz Dombrovskis

Mark D. Spalding

Each year thousands
of volunteers give
their time to support
conservation projects
around the world.

THE POWER OF ONE PICTURE. In 1978, the Tasmanian Hydro Electric Commission announced a plan to build a dam on the Gordon River in Tasmania, Australia. Initial opinion polls showed hearty local support for the project, which was billed as bringing jobs and development.

Over the next five years, however, a protest movement formed, led by the Tasmanian Wilderness Society. A powerful weapon in the protest was this spectacular photo, entitled *Morning Mist, Rock Island Bend, Franklin River,* by Peter Dombrovskis, which was published in newspaper ads with the simple caption "Could you vote for a party that would destroy this?"

In June 1980, some ten thousand people marched through the streets of Tasmania's state capital to protest the planned dam, in the largest protest in the state's history. After more large rallies and protests, in 1983 the dam project was finally abandoned. During the campaign, the area received United Nations recognition as a World Heritage site.

Mark Godfrey/TNC

International recognition and support become all the more important in such cases.

But environmental defense does not always have to be confrontational. The expanding global movement to buy land to preserve it has often been supported by governments. In the United Kingdom in 2008, nearly 6 percent of the population had joined the National Trust, making donations for land purchases and giving voice to a powerful constituency in favor of conservation. In just one of its campaigns, the National Trust purchased almost 10 percent of the coastlines of England, Wales, and Northern Ireland. Statistics for The Nature Conservancy are even more remarkable: by 2009, working with partners in more than thirty countries,

it had contributed significantly to protecting some 480,000 square kilometers of land, an area larger than Sweden.

For millennia, people have been inspired by their faith to conserve nature, with many world religions seeing the natural world as a reflection of divine providence. The Abrahamic faiths (Christianity, Judaism, and Islam) share a common story of the creation of the world and all celebrate the "goodness" and beauty of nature. Hinduism teaches the sanctity of all living creatures, while Buddhism emphasizes simplicity and appreciation of the natural cycle of life. In modern times, many religious leaders have sought to revitalize and stress these traditions.

A proclamation by the Dalai Lama against wearing animal fur led to a dramatic cessation of the demand for tiger fur among Tibetan Buddhists and threw a critical lifeline to tiger populations across India. Religious leaders have also begun speaking out more forcefully about the threat of climate change, with Pope John Paul II first talking about the crisis of the greenhouse effect in 1990.

Meanwhile, millions of people throughout the world have contributed to saving nature by joining beach cleanups, tracking wild birds, monitoring streams, and installing solar power and windmills in their homes. All of them share the spirit of Nachshon, who dared to take that first, liberating step.

Restoring Nature

Mending the Web of Life

Restoring the Kennebec River. The removal of the aging Edwards dam in the U.S. state of Maine has returned the natural river flows to the Kennebec River, allowing migrating fish to once again swim upstream to their old stomping grounds, providing fishing opportunities for humans and wildlife.

Before

After

CONSERVATIONISTS historically have focused their efforts on preserving untrammeled landscapes. Yet increasingly, they have also been obliged to restore injured environments. The damage may have occurred in many ways and taken many different forms. Rivers may have been blocked by dams; the natural cycle of fire may have been altered in grasslands; coral reefs may have been broken by trampling from swimmers and boat anchors. Often nature can heal itself, if left undisturbed, but sometimes human hands are needed to undo the damage first, before a habitat can be restored to health.

Sometimes restoring a habitat involves reintroducing a key species, as U.S. government wildlife biologists did in 1995, when they brought back wolves to Yellowstone National Park in what began the first step in a major revival of that ecosystem. Seven decades earlier, wolves had been almost exterminated from the area by federal agriculture authorities and bounty hunters, setting off a chain of unanticipated destructive consequences. In the absence of wolves, the elk population exploded, eventually numbering about twenty thousand. The elk ate too much of the park's grasses, bushes, and trees,

Lupines

Lupines of the Kitty Todd Preserve. Regular fires are set on this Ohio, United States, preserve to restore prairie and woodland habitats, because without fire, plants like the wild lupine will not grow; and without the lupine, the endangered Karner's butterfly can't exist.

Karner's blue butterfly

Before

After

Coral reef restoration in the Red Sea, Israel. Corals are first grown in a coral nursery and then transplanted onto reefs where corals have died out due to both development on land and recreational activities in the water.

particularly on river banks, leaving little food for other animals, such as beavers. The subsequent disappearance of beaver ponds meant there were fewer places with soggy soil for grizzly bears to dig for roots.

Once the wolves were back and keeping elk in check, Yellowstone's willow and aspen trees came back, as did other vegetation along stream banks and, eventually, also beavers. The willows shade the water in the stream,

keeping it cooler, which is healthier for fish. Meanwhile, the wolves were also contributing to the survival of eagles, ravens, magpies, grizzlies, coyotes, and foxes, which all fed on the remains of large animals killed by the new predators. Restoring wolves to Yellowstone actually restored an entire ecosystem.

Sometimes the physical damage to land, water, or seafloor is so great that the cost of

restoration exceeds the budgets of governments and non-profit groups, which must make the difficult choice between costly cleanups and less expensive efforts to prevent the damage in the first place. Yet the diminishing global supply of healthy nature has left one certainty: that there will long be a role for habitat restoration.

6

Conclusion
Our Future, Our Choices

THE WORLD IS STILL a magical, complex, vibrant place. Nature still fills us with awe and wonder.

As the great eighteenth-century explorer and scientist Alfred Russell Wallace first noted, there is order in this complexity. But there is more. Wallace would have regarded it as barely worth saying, but in a changing world it is all too important: nature and diversity are everywhere. We cannot simply train our sights on a few locations in the tropics if we want to secure a future for nature. By the same token, nature's gifts to humanity are widely distributed, from food and timber to pollution regulation and coastal protection. We have everything to gain from taking a comprehensive view to conserving nature.

Unfortunately, nature is under siege like never before. The threats, too, are complex, all too often stirred into synergies as one problem builds on another. Overarching most of nature's challenges are three broad drivers: population growth, overconsumption, and climate change. Globally, the world population now exceeds 6.7 billion people, and the rate of growth is staggering. Our ever-growing numbers place an increasing demand on the planet—for food, clothing, drinking water, and the resources to deal with our waste. Although 6.7 billion is no small number, there might be space for these people were it not for the second half of the equation: overconsumption. As populations have grown, so have expectations.

Human inventiveness has created many luxuries and apparent necessities in the past century: cars, trains, and air travel; mobile phones, televisions, and disposable diapers; heated pools, air conditioning, and imported food. All come from somewhere.

From growing population and consumption comes a list of direct threats: pollution, deforestation, overfishing, invasive species, and broken rivers. This book's maps tease apart many of these issues, but we must not forget that many threats are related to, and build on, one another. Each turn of the page paints a broader picture of the magnitude of the changes that are taking place. Climate change is a problem singled out for special attention. Although, like other threats, it is driven by population growth and consumption, it can now be considered a driver of change in its own right, its impacts diffuse yet ubiquitous. There are real fears that it may begin to accelerate beyond our direct influence, as rising temperatures and melting ice create feedbacks that exacerbate the problem.

The situation is serious and the future can look bleak, but this atlas holds another lesson. The maps can be seen in many ways as a series of symptoms and a diagnosis. In the past we might have looked on aghast as poorly planned activities led to unforeseen consequences. Today we stand at a unique point in history, where we understand what is happening.

We can even model and predict the consequences of future actions. But we are not helpless physicians facing an incurable patient. We have a broad and improving array of interventions we can call into play. We can prevent the spread of these problems, and we can even restore the damage. We now have the capacity to drive change in a positive direction.

Just as nature itself is complex and interconnected, and so are the threats now facing nature, then so too must be our responses. Science and data lie at the heart of our understanding, and they are critical in developing a response, but for the latter we must call in people and politics. To act at the scale necessary, we need to bring together diverse partners and look for incentives and actions that benefit both people and nature.

Conservation tools are wide ranging. The rule of law is critical—singling out species and places for protection lies at the heart of many conservation actions. On land, and increasingly in the oceans, protected areas already play a crucial role, not only protecting habitats and the species they encompass but also the essential goods and services they supply to people. Many are places where people continue to make a living, but in sustainable ways. Some protect vital water resources that support agriculture or urban populations downstream; others support fishers who find growing catches in adjacent waters. Laws have set limits to hunting or fishing, often to protect the livelihoods of those who hunt and fish. Laws also have set limits on pollution, helped bring back species from

the brink of extinction, and helped secure the futures of millions of people who depend on nature for their very survival.

Some of the largest threats cannot be handled by the boundaries of protected areas or even by the actions of individual governments. They require truly global collaboration, and even here we have tools available. International agreements have already helped to stem the demise of the world's great whales, to ban the chemicals that were destroying the ozone in the upper atmosphere, and to reduce the flow of trade in many endangered species. Similar collaboration will be central to reducing greenhouse gas emissions.

Trade and free markets have played a significant role in shaping the modern world, with patterns of demand creating the impacts of supply. Now these same markets are being seen as a critical part of the solution. Trading in rights to pollute sounds counterproductive, but limiting the stock of permitted pollution actually creates powerful incentives to reduce toxic wastes in efficient ways. Such trading has been invaluable in the United States as a means of reducing acid rain, and it could be central to solving the challenge of climate change. At smaller scales, the privatization of once-common resources has been a powerful tool in managing fisheries, and the ancient concept of private property has been central to the efforts of many conservation organizations in purchasing large tracts of land where nature protection can be assured.

As individuals, we, too, have a role. After all, many human influences on nature are nothing more than the accumulation of

tiny pinpricks: the individual actions of 6.7 billion people. Sometimes our influence is direct—we chop down a tree, catch a fish, or dump our waste—but more often than not our actions are remote. Our lives, particularly in the developed world, have become disconnected from nature. We are often unaware of the origins of our food or the fate of our waste. We purchase without knowing and dispose without caring. Increasingly, however, we are becoming aware of the challenges facing the planet. Individually, we are making informed choices about how to live our lives. We are also contributing to wider movements, through local communities or large nongovernmental organizations. We are demanding changes from politicians, from companies, from stores. Increasing numbers of us are also choosing to become directly involved: planting native species, uprooting invasive weeds, cleaning trash off beaches and coral reefs.

Information, science, and informed response lie at the heart of this book. Without them we could look on only from the sidelines. With them we can grasp the problem, anticipate the future, evaluate trade-offs, and craft comprehensive solutions. This book paints a picture of our world as it is today—and offers a glimpse of what it may look like in the future if we continue down our current path. We are the first generation that can predict the future of the world with some accuracy. We can also choose to shape that future. What will these maps look like in the future? It is ours to decide.

Appendices

Terrestrial Ecoregions

NEARCTIC REALM

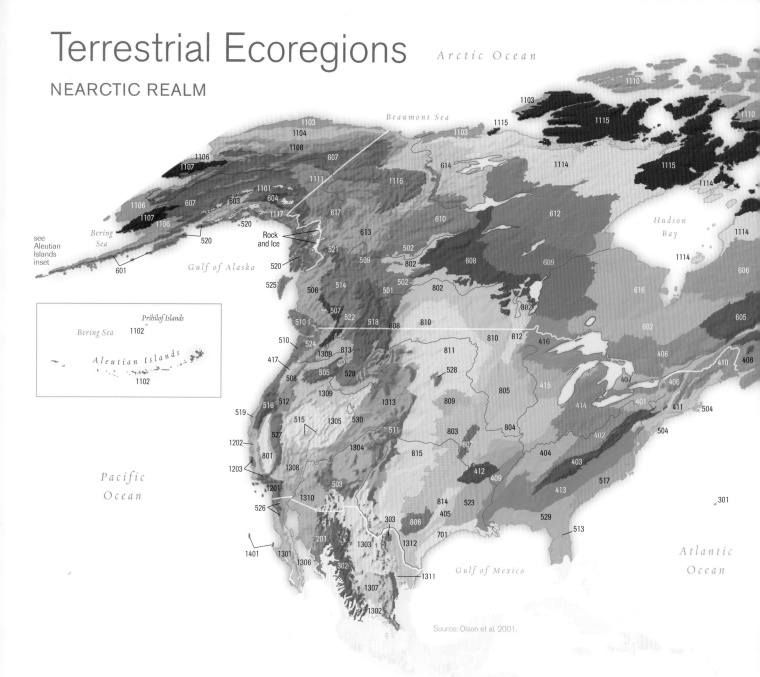

Source: Olson et al. 2001.

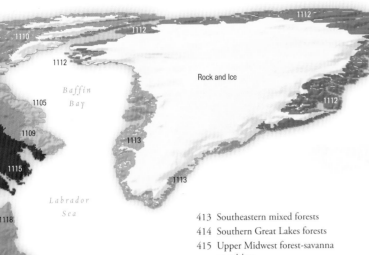

Baffin
Bay

Rock and Ice

Labrador
Sea

Tropical & Subtropical Dry Broadleaf Forests

201 Sonoran-Sinaloan transition subtropical dry forest

Tropical & Subtropical Coniferous Forests

301 Bermuda subtropical conifer forests

302 Sierra Madre Occidental pine-oak forests

303 Sierra Madre Oriental pine-oak forests

Temperate Broadleaf & Mixed Forests

401 Allegheny Highlands forests

402 Appalachian mixed mesophytic forests

403 Appalachian-Blue Ridge forests

404 Central U.S. hardwood forests

405 East Central Texas forests

406 Eastern forest-boreal transition

407 Eastern Great Lakes lowland forests

408 Gulf of St. Lawrence lowland forests

409 Mississippi lowland forests

410 New England-Acadian forests

411 Northeastern coastal forests

412 Ozark Mountain forests

413 Southeastern mixed forests

414 Southern Great Lakes forests

415 Upper Midwest forest-savanna transition

416 Western Great Lakes forests

417 Willamette Valley forests

Temperate Coniferous Forests

501 Alberta Mountain forests

502 Alberta-British Columbia foothills forests

503 Arizona Mountains forests

504 Atlantic coastal pine barrens

505 Blue Mountains forests

506 British Columbia mainland coastal forests

507 Cascade Mountains leeward forests

508 Central and Southern Cascades forests

509 Central British Columbia Mountain forests

510 Central Pacific coastal forests

511 Colorado Rockies forests

512 Eastern Cascades forests

513 Florida sand pine scrub

514 Fraser Plateau and Basin complex

515 Great Basin montane forests

516 Klamath-Siskiyou forests

517 Middle Atlantic coastal forests

518 North Central Rockies forests

519 Northern California coastal forests

520 Northern Pacific coastal forests

521 Northern transitional alpine forests

522 Okanogan dry forests

523 Piney Woods forests

524 Puget lowland forests

525 Queen Charlotte Islands

526 Sierra Juárez and San Pedro Mártir pine-oak forests

527 Sierra Nevada forests

528 South Central Rockies forests

529 Southeastern conifer forests

530 Wasatch and Uinta montane forests

Boreal Forests/Taiga

601 Alaska Peninsula montane taiga

602 Central Canadian Shield forests

603 Cook Inlet taiga

604 Copper Plateau taiga

605 Eastern Canadian forests

606 Eastern Canadian Shield taiga

607 Interior Alaska-Yukon lowland taiga

608 Mid-Continental Canadian forests

609 Midwestern Canadian Shield forests

610 Muskwa-Slave Lake forests

611 Newfoundland Highland forests

612 Northern Canadian Shield taiga

613 Northern Cordillera forests

614 Northwest Territories taiga

615 South Avalon-Burin oceanic barrens

616 Southern Hudson Bay taiga

617 Yukon Interior dry forests

Tropical & Subtropical Grasslands, Savannas & Shrublands

701 Western Gulf coastal grasslands

Temperate Grasslands, Savannas, & Shrublands

801 California Central Valley grasslands

802 Canadian Aspen forests and parklands

803 Central and Southern mixed grasslands

804 Central forest-grasslands transition

805 Central tall grasslands

806 Edwards Plateau savanna

807 Flint Hills tall grasslands

808 Montana Valley and Foothill grasslands

809 Nebraska Sand Hills mixed grasslands

810 Northern mixed grasslands

811 Northern short grasslands

812 Northern tall grasslands

813 Palouse grasslands

814 Texas blackland prairies

815 Western short grasslands

Tundra

1101 Alaska-St. Elias Range tundra

1102 Aleutian Islands tundra

1103 Arctic coastal tundra

1104 Arctic foothills tundra

1105 Baffin coastal tundra

1106 Beringia lowland tundra

1107 Beringia upland tundra

1108 Brooks-British Range tundra

1109 Davis Highlands tundra

1110 High Arctic tundra

1111 Interior Yukon-Alaska alpine tundra

1112 Kalaallit Nunaat high arctic tundra

1113 Kalaallit Nunaat low arctic tundra

1114 Low Arctic tundra

1115 Middle Arctic tundra

1116 Ogilvie-MacKenzie alpine tundra

1117 Pacific Coastal Mountain icefields and tundra

1118 Torngat Mountain tundra

Mediterranean Forests, Woodlands, & Shrub

1201 California coastal sage and chaparral

1202 California interior chaparral and woodlands

1203 California montane chaparral and woodlands

Deserts & Xeric Shrublands

1301 Baja California desert

1302 Central Mexican matorral

1303 Chihuahuan desert

1304 Colorado Plateau shrublands

1305 Great Basin shrub steppe

1306 Gulf of California xeric scrub

1307 Meseta Central matorral

1308 Mojave desert

1309 Snake-Columbia shrub steppe

1310 Sonoran desert

1311 Tamaulipan matorral

1312 Tamaulipan mezquital

1313 Wyoming Basin shrub steppe

Mangrove

1401 Northwest Mexican Coast mangroves

Terrestrial Ecoregions
NEOTROPIC REALM

Tropical & Subtropical Moist Broadleaf Forests

101 Araucaria moist forests
102 Atlantic Coast restingas
103 Bahia coastal forests
104 Bahia interior forests
105 Bolivian Yungas
106 Caatinga Enclaves moist forests
107 Caqueta moist forests
108 Catatumbo moist forests
109 Cauca Valley montane forests
110 Cayos Miskitos-San Andrés and Providencia moist forests
111 Central American Atlantic moist forests
112 Central American montane forests
113 Chiapas montane forests
114 Chimalapas montane forests
115 Chocó-Darién moist forests
116 Cocos Island moist forests
117 Cordillera La Costa montane forests
118 Cordillera Oriental montane forests
119 Costa Rican seasonal moist forests
120 Cuban moist forests
121 Eastern Cordillera real montane forests
122 Eastern Panamanian montane forests
123 Fernanda de Noronha-Atol das Rocas moist forests
124 Guayanan Highlands moist forests
125 Guianan moist forests
126 Gurupa varzea

127 Hispaniolan moist forests
128 Iquitos varzea
129 Isthmian-Atlantic moist forests
130 Isthmian-Pacific moist forests
131 Jamaican moist forests
132 Japurá-Solimoes-Negro moist forests
133 Juruá-Purus moist forests
134 Leeward Islands moist forests
135 Madeira-Tapajós moist forests
136 Magdalena Valley montane forests
137 Magdalena-Urabá moist forests
138 Marajó varzea
139 Maranhão Babaçu forests
140 Mato Grosso tropical dry forests

Source: Olson et al. 2001.

141 Monte Alegre varzea
142 Napo moist forests
143 Negro-Branco moist forests
144 Northeastern Brazil restingas
145 Northwestern Andean montane forests
146 Oaxacan montane forests
147 Orinoco Delta swamp forests
148 Pantanos de Centla
149 Paramaribo swamp forests
150 Paraná-Paraíba interior forests
151 Pernambuco coastal forests
152 Pernambuco interior forests
153 Peruvian Yungas
154 Petén-Veracruz moist forests
155 Puerto Rican moist forests
156 Purus varzea
157 Purus-Madeira moist forests
158 Rio Negro campinarana
159 Santa Marta montane forests
160 Serra do Mar coastal forests
161 Sierra de los Tuxtlas
162 Sierra Madre de Chiapas moist forest
163 Solimões-Japurá moist forest
164 South Florida rocklands
165 Southern Andean Yungas
166 Southwest Amazon moist forests
167 Talamancan montane forests
168 Tapajós-Xingu moist forests
169 Tepuis
170 Tocantins-Araguaia-Maranhão moist forests
171 Trinidad and Tobago moist forests
172 Trinidade-Martin Vaz Islands tropical forests
173 Uatuma-Trombetas moist forests
174 Ucayali moist forests
175 Venezuelan Andes montane forests
176 Veracruz moist forests
177 Veracruz montane forests
178 Western Ecuador moist forests
179 Windward Islands moist forests
180 Xingu-Tocantins-Araguaia moist forests
181 Yucatán moist forests

Tropical & Subtropical Dry Broadleaf Forests

201 Apure-Villavicencio dry forests
202 Atlantic dry forests
203 Bahamian dry forests
204 Bajío dry forests
205 Balsas dry forests
206 Bolivian montane dry forests
207 Cauca Valley dry forests
208 Cayman Islands dry forests
209 Central American dry forests
210 Chaco
211 Chiapas Depression dry forests

212 Chiquitano dry forests
213 Cuban dry forests
214 Ecuadorian dry forests
215 Hispaniolan dry forests
216 Islas Revillagigedo dry forests
217 Jalisco dry forests
218 Jamaican dry forests
219 Lara-Falcón dry forests
220 Leeward Islands dry forests
221 Magdalena Valley dry forests
222 Maracaibo dry forests
223 Marañón dry forests
224 Panamanian dry forests
225 Patía Valley dry forests
226 Puerto Rican dry forests
227 Sierra de la Laguna dry forests
228 Sinaloan dry forests
229 Sinu Valley dry forests
230 Southern Pacific dry forests
231 Trinidad and Tobago dry forests
232 Tumbes-Piura dry forests
233 Veracruz dry forests
234 Windward Islands dry forests
235 Yucatán dry forests

Tropical & Subtropical Coniferous Forests

301 Bahamian pine forests
302 Belizian pine forests
303 Central American pine-oak forests
304 Cuban pine forests
305 Hispaniolan pine forests
306 Miskito pine forests
307 Sierra de la Laguna pine-oak forests
308 Sierra Madre de Oaxaca pine-oak forests
309 Sierra Madre del Sur pine-oak forests
310 Trans-Mexican Volcanic Belt pine-oak forests

Temperate Broadleaf & Mixed Forests

401 Juan Fernández Islands temperate forests
402 Magellanic subpolar forests
403 San Félix-San Ambrosio Islands temperate forests
404 Valdivian temperate forests

Tropical & Subtropical Grasslands, Savannas, & Shrublands

701 Arid Chaco
702 Beni savanna
703 Campos Rupestres montane savanna
704 Cerrado
705 Clipperton Island shrub and grasslands
706 Córdoba montane savanna

707 Guyanan savanna
708 Humid Chaco
709 Llanos
710 Uruguayan savanna

Temperate Grasslands, Savannas, & Shrublands

801 Argentine Espinal
802 Argentine Monte
803 Humid Pampas
804 Patagonian grasslands
805 Patagonian steppe
806 Semi-arid Pampas

Flooded Grasslands & Savannas

901 Central Mexican wetlands
902 Cuban wetlands
903 Enriquillo wetlands
904 Everglades
905 Guayaquil flooded grasslands
906 Orinoco wetlands
907 Pantanal
908 Paraná flooded savanna
909 Southern Cone Mesopotamian savanna

Montane Grasslands & Shrublands

1001 Central Andean dry puna
1002 Central Andean puna
1003 Central Andean wet puna
1004 Cordillera Central páramo
1005 Cordillera de Mérida páramo
1006 Northern Andean páramo
1007 Santa Marta páramo
1008 Southern Andean steppe
1009 Zacatonal

Mediterranean Forests, Woodlands, & Shrub

1201 Chilean matorral

Deserts & Xeric Shrublands

1301 Araya and Paria xeric scrub
1302 Aruba-Curaçao-Bonaire cactus scrub
1303 Atacama desert
1304 Caatinga
1305 Cayman Islands xeric scrub
1306 Cuban cactus scrub
1307 Galápagos Islands xeric scrub
1308 Guajira-Barranquilla xeric scrub
1309 La Costa xeric shrublands
1310 Leeward Islands xeric scrub
1311 Malpelo Island xeric scrub
1312 Motagua Valley thornscrub
1313 Paraguana xeric scrub
1314 San Lucan xeric scrub

1315 Sechura desert
1316 Tehuacán Valley matorral
1317 Windward Islands xeric scrub
1318 St. Peter and St. Paul rocks

Mangrove

1401 Alvarado mangroves
1402 Amapa mangroves
1403 Bahamian mangroves
1404 Bahia mangroves
1405 Belizean Coast mangroves
1406 Belizean Reef mangroves
1407 Bocas del Toro-San Bastimentos Island-San Blas mangroves
1408 Coastal Venezuelan mangroves
1409 Esmeraldes-Pacific Colombia mangroves
1410 Greater Antilles mangroves
1411 Guianan mangroves
1412 Gulf of Fonseca mangroves
1413 Gulf of Guayaquil-Tumbes mangroves
1414 Gulf of Panama mangroves
1415 Ilha Grande mangroves
1416 Lesser Antilles mangroves
1417 Magdalena-Santa Marta mangroves
1418 Manabí mangroves
1419 Maranhao mangroves
1420 Marismas Nacionales-San Blas mangroves
1421 Mayan Corridor mangroves
1422 Mexican South Pacific Coast mangroves
1423 Moist Pacific Coast mangroves
1424 Mosquitia-Nicaraguan Caribbean Coast mangroves
1425 Northern Dry Pacific Coast mangroves
1426 Northern Honduras mangroves
1427 Pará mangroves
1428 Petenes mangroves
1429 Piura mangroves
1430 Río Lagartos mangroves
1431 Río Negro-Río San Sun mangroves
1432 Río Piranhas mangroves
1433 Rio São Francisco mangroves
1434 Southern Dry Pacific Coast mangroves
1435 Tehuantepec-El Manchón mangroves
1436 Trinidad mangroves
1437 Usumacinta mangroves

Terrestrial Ecoregions
PALEARCTIC REALM

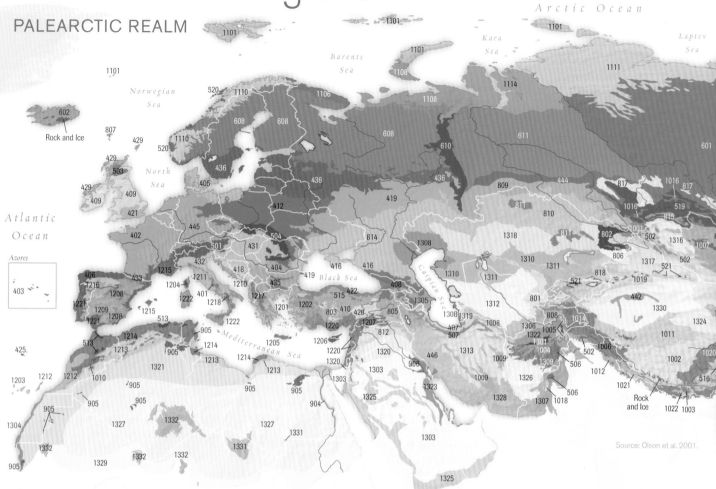

Source: Olson et al. 2001.

Tropical & Subtropical Moist Broadleaf Forests

101 Gizhou Plateau broadleaf and mixed forests

102 Yunnan Plateau subtropical evergreen forests

Temperate Broadleaf & Mixed Forests

401 Appenine deciduous montane forests

402 Atlantic mixed forests

403 Azores temperate mixed forests

404 Balkan mixed forests

405 Baltic mixed forests

406 Cantabrian mixed forests

407 Caspian Hyrcanian mixed forests

408 Caucasus mixed forests

409 Celtic broadleaf forests

410 Central Anatolian deciduous forests

411 Central China loess plateau mixed forests

412 Central European mixed forests

413 Central Korean deciduous forests

414 Changbai Mountains mixed forests

415 Changjiang Plain evergreen forests

416 Crimean Submediterranean forest complex

417 Daba Mountains evergreen forests

418 Dinaric Mountains mixed forests

419 East European forest steppe

420 Eastern Anatolian deciduous forests

421 English Lowlands beech forests

422 Euxine-Colchic deciduous forests

423 Hokkaido deciduous forests

424 Huang He Plain mixed forests

425 Madeira evergreen forests

426 Manchurian mixed forests

427 Nihonkai evergreen forests

428 Nihonkai montane deciduous forests

429 North Atlantic moist mixed forests

430 Northeast China Plain deciduous forests

431 Pannonian mixed forests

432 Po Basin mixed forests

433 Pyrenees conifer and mixed forests

434 Qin Ling Mountains deciduous forests

435 Rodope montane mixed forests

436 Sarmatic mixed forests

437 Sichuan Basin evergreen broadleaf forests

438 South Sakhalin-Kurile mixed forests

439 Southern Korea evergreen forests

440 Taiheiyo evergreen forests

441 Taiheiyo montane deciduous forests

442 Tarim Basin deciduous forests and steppe

443 Ussuri broadleaf and mixed forests

444 West Siberian broadleaf and mixed forests

445 Western European broadleaf forests

446 Zagros Mountains forest steppe

Temperate Coniferous Forests

501 Alps conifer and mixed forests

502 Altai montane forest and forest steppe

503 Caledon conifer forests

504 Carthian montane conifer forests

505 Da Hinggan-Dzhagdy Mountains conifer forests

506 East Afghan montane conifer forests

507 Elburz Range forest steppe

508 Helanshan montane conifer forests

509 Hengduan Mountains subalpine conifer forests

510 Hokkaido montane conifer forests

511 Honshu alpine conifer forests

512 Khangai Mountains conifer forests

513 Mediterranean conifer and mixed forests

514 Northeastern Himalayan subalpine conifer forests

515 Northern Anatolian conifer and deciduous forests

516 Nujiang Langcang Gorge alpine conifer and mixed forests

517 Qilian Mountains conifer forests

518 Qionglai-Minshan conifer forests

519 Sayan montane conifer forests

520 Scandinavian coastal conifer forests

521 Tian Shan montane conifer forests

Boreal Forests/Taiga

601 East Siberian taiga

602 Iceland boreal birch forests and alpine tundra

603 Kamchatka-Kurile meadows and sparse forests

604 Kamchatka-Kurile taiga

605 Northeast Siberian taiga

606 Okhotsk-Manchurian taiga

607 Sakhalin Island taiga

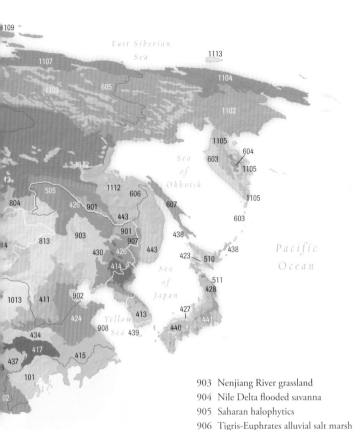

1017 Southeast Tibet shrub and meadows
1018 Sulaiman Range alpine meadows
1019 Tian Shan montane steppe and meadows
1020 Tibetan Plateau alpine shrub and meadows
1021 Western Himalayan alpine shrub and meadows
1022 Yarlung Zambo arid steppe

Tundra

1101 Arctic desert
1102 Bering tundra
1103 Cherskii-Kolyma mountain tundra
1104 Chukchi Peninsula tundra
1105 Kamchatka Mountain tundra and forest tundra
1106 Kola Peninsula tundra
1107 Northeast Siberian coastal tundra
1108 Northwest Russian-Novaya Zemlya tundra
1109 Novosibirsk Islands arctic desert
1110 Scandinavian Montane Birch forest and grasslands
1111 Taimyr-Central Siberian tundra
1112 Trans-Baikal Bald Mountain tundra
1113 Wrangel Island arctic desert
1114 Yamalagydanskaja tundra

Mediterranean Forests, Woodlands, & Shrub

1201 Aegean and Western Turkey sclerophyllous and mixed forests
1202 Anatolian conifer and deciduous mixed forests
1203 Canary Islands dry woodlands and forests
1204 Corsican montane broadleaf and mixed forests
1205 Crete Mediterranean forests
1206 Cyprus Mediterranean forests
1207 Eastern Mediterranean conifer-sclerophyllous-broadleaf forests
1208 Iberian conifer forests
1209 Iberian sclerophyllous and semi-deciduous forests
1210 Illyrian deciduous forests
1211 Italian sclerophyllous and semi-deciduous forests
1212 Mediterranean acacia-argania dry woodlands and succulent thickets
1213 Mediterranean dry woodlands and steppe
1214 Mediterranean woodlands and forests
1215 Northeastern Spain and Southern France Mediterranean forests
1216 Northwest Iberian montane forests
1217 Pindus Mountains mixed forests
1218 South Appenine mixed montane forests
1219 Southeastern Iberian shrubs and woodlands
1220 Southern Anatolian montane conifer and deciduous forests
1221 Southwest Iberian Mediterranean sclerophyllous and mixed forests
1222 Tyrrhenian-Adriatic sclerophyllous and mixed forests

Deserts & Xeric Shrublands

1301 Afghan Mountains semi-desert
1302 Alashan Plateau semi-desert
1303 Arabian Desert and East Sahero-Arabian xeric shrublands
1304 Atlantic coastal desert
1305 Azerbaijan shrub desert and steppe
1306 Badkhiz-Karabil semi-desert
1307 Baluchistan xeric woodlands
1308 Caspian lowland desert
1309 Central Afghan Mountains xeric woodlands
1310 Central Asian northern desert
1311 Central Asian riparian woodlands
1312 Central Asian southern desert
1313 Central Persian desert basins
1314 Eastern Gobi desert steppe
1315 Gobi Lakes Valley desert steppe
1316 Great Lakes Basin desert steppe
1317 Junggar Basin semi-desert
1318 Kazakh semi-desert
1319 Kopet Dag semi-desert
1320 Mesopotamian shrub desert
1321 North Saharan steppe and woodlands
1322 Paromisus xeric woodlands
1323 Persian Gulf desert and semi-desert
1324 Qaidam Basin semi-desert
1325 Red Sea Nubo-Sindian tropical desert and semi-desert
1326 Rigestan-North Pakistan sandy desert
1327 Sahara desert
1328 South Iran Nubo-Sindian desert and semi-desert
1329 South Saharan steppe and woodlands
1330 Taklimakan desert
1331 Tibesti-Jebel Uweinat montane xeric woodlands
1332 West Saharan montane xeric woodlands

903 Nenjiang River grassland
904 Nile Delta flooded savanna
905 Saharan halophytics
906 Tigris-Euphrates alluvial salt marsh
907 Ussuri-Wusuli meadow and forest meadow
908 Yellow Sea saline meadow

Montane Grasslands & Shrublands

1001 Altai alpine meadow and tundra
1002 Central Tibetan Plateau alpine steppe
1003 Eastern Himalayan alpine shrub and meadows
1004 Ghorat-Hazarajat alpine meadow
1005 Hindu Kush alpine meadow
1006 Karakoram-West Tibetan Plateau alpine steppe
1007 Khangai Mountains alpine meadow
1008 Kopet Dag woodlands and forest steppe
1009 Kuhrud-Kohbanan Mountains forest steppe
1010 Mediterranean High Atlas juniper steppe
1011 North Tibetan Plateau-Kunlun Mountains alpine desert
1012 Northwestern Himalayan alpine shrub and meadows
1013 Ordos Plateau steppe
1014 Pamir alpine desert and tundra
1015 Qilian Mountains subalpine meadows
1016 Sayan Alpine meadows and tundra

608 Scandinavian and Russian taiga
609 Trans-Baikal conifer forests
610 Urals montane tundra and taiga
611 West Siberian taiga

Temperate Grasslands, Savannas, & Shrublands

801 Alai-Western Tian Shan steppe
802 Altai steppe and semi-desert
803 Central Anatolian steppe
804 Daurian forest steppe
805 Eastern Anatolian montane steppe
806 Emin Valley steppe
807 Faroe Islands boreal grasslands
808 Gissaro-Alai open woodlands
809 Kazakh forest steppe
810 Kazakh steppe
811 Kazakh upland
812 Middle East steppe
813 Mongolian-Manchurian grassland
814 Pontic steppe
815 Sayan Intermontane steppe
816 Selenge-Orkhon forest steppe
817 South Siberian forest steppe
818 Tian Shan foothill arid steppe

Flooded Grasslands and Savannas

901 Amur meadow steppe
902 Bohai Sea saline meadow

Terrestrial Ecoregions
AFROTROPIC REALM

Tropical & Subtropical Moist Broadleaf Forests

101 Albertine Rift montane forests
102 Atlantic Equatorial coastal forests
103 Cameroonian Highlands forests
104 Central Congolian lowland forests
105 Comoros forests
106 Cross-Niger transition forests
107 Cross-Sanaga-Bioko coastal forests
108 East African montane forests
109 Eastern Arc forests
110 Eastern Congolian swamp forests
111 Eastern Guinean forests
112 Ethiopian montane forests
113 Granitic Seychelles forests
114 Guinean montane forests
115 Knysna-Amatole montane forests
116 KwaZulu-Cape coastal forest mosaic
117 Madagascar lowland forests
118 Madagascar subhumid forests
119 Maputaland coastal forest mosaic
120 Mascarene forests
121 Mount Cameroon and Bioko montane forests
122 Niger Delta swamp forests
123 Nigerian lowland forests
124 Northeastern Congolian lowland forests
125 Northern Zanzibar-Inhambane coastal forest mosaic
126 Northwestern Congolian lowland forests
127 São Tomé and Principe moist lowland forests
128 Southern Zanzibar-Inhambane coastal forest mosaic
129 Western Congolian swamp forests
130 Western Guinean lowland forests

Tropical & Subtropical Dry Broadleaf Forests

201 Cape Verde Islands dry forests
202 Madagascar dry deciduous forests
203 Zambezian Cryptosepalum dry forests

Tropical & Subtropical Grasslands, Savannas, & Shrublands

701 Angolan Miombo woodlands
702 Angolan Mopane woodlands
703 Ascension scrub and grasslands
704 Central Zambezian Miombo woodlands
705 East Sudanian savanna
706 Eastern Miombo woodlands
707 Guinean forest-savanna mosaic
708 Itigi-Sumbu thicket
709 Kalahari Acacia-Baikiaea woodlands
710 Mandara Plateau mosaic
711 Northern Acacia-Commiphora bushlands and thickets
712 Northern Congolian forest-savanna mosaic
713 Sahelian Acacia savanna
714 Serengeti volcanic grasslands
715 Somali Acacia-Commiphora bushlands and thickets
716 Southern Acacia-Commiphora bushlands and thickets
717 Southern Africa bushveld
718 Southern Congolian forest-savanna mosaic
719 Southern Miombo woodlands
720 St. Helena scrub and woodlands
721 Victoria Basin forest-savanna mosaic
722 West Sudanian savanna
723 Western Congolian forest-savanna mosaic
724 Western Zambezian grasslands
725 Zambezian and Mopane woodlands
726 Zambezian Baikiaea woodlands

Temperate Grasslands, Savannas & Shrublands

801 Al Hajar Al Gharbi montane woodlands
802 Amsterdam and Saint-Paul Islands temperate grasslands
803 Tristan da Cunha-Gough Islands shrub and grasslands

Flooded Grasslands & Savannas

901 East African halophytics
902 Etosha Pan halophytics
903 Inner Niger Delta flooded savanna
904 Lake Chad flooded savanna
905 Saharan flooded grasslands
906 Zambezian coastal flooded savanna
907 Zambezian flooded grasslands
908 Zambezian halophytics

Montane Grasslands & Shrublands

1001 Angolan montane forest-grassland mosaic
1002 Angolan scarp savanna and woodlands
1003 Drakensberg alti-montane grasslands and woodlands
1004 Drakensberg montane grasslands, woodlands and forests
1005 East African montane moorlands
1006 Eastern Zimbabwe montane forest-grassland mosaic
1007 Ethiopian montane grasslands and woodlands
1008 Ethiopian montane moorlands
1009 Highveld grasslands
1010 Jos Plateau forest-grassland mosaic
1011 Madagascar ericoid thickets
1012 Maputaland-Pondoland bushland and thickets
1013 Ruwenzori-Virunga montane moorlands
1014 South Malawi montane forest-grassland mosaic
1015 Southern Rift montane forest-grassland mosaic

Mediterranean Forests, Woodlands, & Shrub

1201 Albany thickets
1202 Lowland fynbos and renosterveld
1203 Montane fynbos and renosterveld

Deserts & Xeric Shrublands

1301 Aldabra Island xeric scrub
1302 Arabian Peninsula coastal fog desert
1303 East Saharan montane xeric woodlands
1304 Eritrean coastal desert
1305 Ethiopian xeric grasslands and shrublands
1306 Gulf of Oman desert and semi-desert
1307 Hobyo grasslands and shrublands
1308 Ile Europa and Bassas da India xeric scrub
1309 Kalahari xeric savanna
1310 Kaokoveld desert
1311 Madagascar spiny thickets
1312 Madagascar succulent woodlands
1313 Masai xeric grasslands and shrublands
1314 Nama Karoo
1315 Namib desert
1316 Namibian savanna woodlands
1317 Red Sea coastal desert
1318 Socotra Island xeric shrublands
1319 Somali montane xeric woodlands
1320 Southwestern Arabian foothills savanna
1321 Southwestern Arabian montane woodlands
1322 Succulent Karoo

Mangrove

1401 Central African mangroves
1402 East African mangroves
1403 Guinean mangroves
1404 Madagascar mangroves
1405 Southern Africa mangroves

Red Sea

Gulf of Aden

Gulf of Guinea

Atlantic Ocean

Indian Ocean

Tristan da Cunha-Gough Islands

803

Amsterdam and Saint-Paul Islands

802

Source: Olson et al. 2001.

Terrestrial Ecoregions

INDO-MALAY REALM

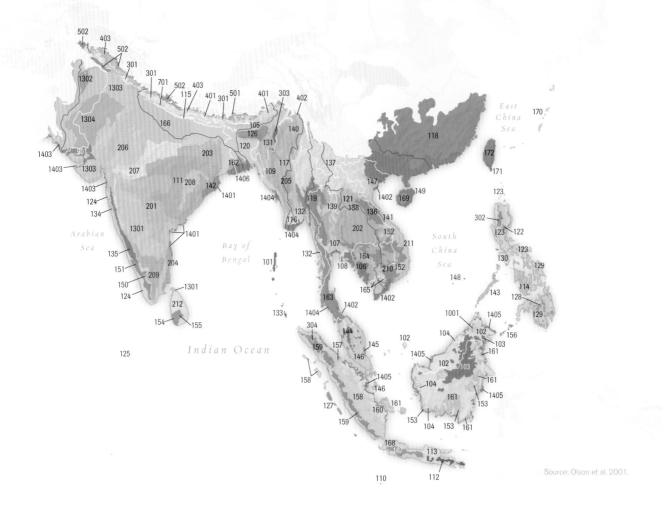

Source: Olson et al. 2001.

Tropical & Subtropical Moist Broadleaf Forests

101 Andaman Islands rain forests
102 Borneo lowland rain forests
103 Borneo montane rain forests
104 Borneo peat swamp forests
105 Brahmaputra Valley semi-evergreen forests
106 Cardamom Mountains rain forests
107 Chao Phraya freshwater swamp forests
108 Chao Phraya lowland moist deciduous forests
109 Chin Hills-Arakan Yoma montane forests
110 Christmas and Cocos Islands tropical forests
111 Eastern highlands moist deciduous forests
112 Eastern Java-Bali montane rain forests
113 Eastern Java-Bali rain forests
114 Greater Negros-Panay rain forests
115 Himalayan subtropical broadleaf forests
116 Irrawaddy freshwater swamp forests
117 Irrawaddy moist deciduous forests
118 Jian Nan subtropical evergreen forests
119 Kayah-Karen montane rain forests
120 Lower Gangetic Plains moist deciduous forests
121 Luang Prabang montane rain forests
122 Luzon montane rain forests
123 Luzon rain forests
124 Malabar Coast moist forests
125 Maldives-Lakshadweep-Chagos Archipelago tropical moist forests
126 Meghalaya subtropical forests
127 Mentawai Islands rain forests
128 Mindanao montane rain forests
129 Mindanao-Eastern Visayas rain forests
130 Mindoro rain forests
131 Mizoram-Manipur-Kachin rain forests
132 Myanmar coastal rain forests
133 Nicobar Islands rain forests
134 North Western Ghats moist deciduous forests
135 North Western Ghats montane rain forests
136 Northern Annamites rain forests
137 Northern Indochina subtropical forests
138 Northern Khorat Plateau moist deciduous forests
139 Northern Thailand-Laos moist deciduous forests
140 Northern Triangle subtropical forests
141 Northern Vietnam lowland rain forests
142 Orissa semi-evergreen forests
143 Palawan rain forests
144 Peninsular Malaysian montane rain forests
145 Peninsular Malaysian peat swamp forests
146 Peninsular Malaysian rain forests
147 Red River freshwater swamp forests
148 South China Sea Islands
149 South China-Vietnam subtropical evergreen forests
150 South Western Ghats moist deciduous forests
151 South Western Ghats montane rain forests
152 Southern Annamites montane rain forests
153 Southwest Borneo freshwater swamp forests
154 Sri Lanka lowland rain forests
155 Sri Lanka montane rain forests
156 Sulu Archipelago rain forests
157 Sumatran freshwater swamp forests
158 Sumatran lowland rain forests
159 Sumatran montane rain forests
160 Sumatran peat swamp forests
161 Sundaland heath forests
162 Sundarbans freshwater swamp forests
163 Tenasserim-South Thailand semi-evergreen rain forests
164 Tonle Sap freshwater swamp forests
165 Tonle Sap-Mekong peat swamp forests
166 Upper Gangetic Plains moist deciduous forests
167 Western Java montane rain forests
168 Western Java rain forests
169 Hainan Island monsoon rain forests
170 Nansei Islands subtropical evergreen forests
171 South Taiwan monsoon rain forests
172 Taiwan subtropical evergreen forests

Tropical & Subtropical Dry Broadleaf Forests

201 Central Deccan Plateau dry deciduous forests
202 Central Indochina dry forests
203 Chhota-Nagpur dry deciduous forests
204 East Deccan dry-evergreen forests
205 Irrawaddy dry forests
206 Khathiar-Gir dry deciduous forests
207 Narmada Valley dry deciduous forests
208 Northern dry deciduous forests
209 South Deccan Plateau dry deciduous forests
210 Southeastern Indochina dry evergreen forests
211 Southern Vietnam lowland dry forests
212 Sri Lanka dry-zone dry evergreen forests

Tropical & Subtropical Coniferous Forests

301 Himalayan subtropical pine forests
302 Luzon tropical pine forests
303 Northeast India-Myanmar pine forests
304 Sumatran tropical pine forests

Temperate Broadleaf & Mixed Forests

401 Eastern Himalayan broadleaf forests
402 Northern Triangle temperate forests
403 Western Himalayan broadleaf forests

Temperate Coniferous Forests

501 Eastern Himalayan subalpine conifer forests
502 Western Himalayan subalpine conifer forests

Tropical & Subtropical Grasslands, Savannas, & Shrublands

701 Terai-Duar savanna and grasslands

Flooded Grasslands & Savannas

901 Rann of Kutch seasonal salt marsh

Montane Grasslands & Shrublands

1001 Kinabalu montane alpine meadows

Deserts & Xeric Shrublands

1301 Deccan thorn scrub forests
1302 Indus Valley desert
1303 Northwestern thorn scrub forests
1304 Thar desert

Mangrove

1401 Goadavari-Krishna mangroves
1402 Indochina mangroves
1403 Indus River Delta-Arabian Sea mangroves
1404 Myanmar Coast mangroves
1405 Sunda Shelf mangroves
1406 Sundarbans mangroves

Terrestrial Ecoregions

AUSTRALASIA, OCEANIA, & ANTARCTICA REALMS

AUSTRALASIA

Tropical & Subtropical Moist Broadleaf Forests

101 Admiralty Islands lowland rain forests

102 Banda Sea Islands moist deciduous forests

103 Biak-Numfoor rain forests

104 Buru rain forests

105 Central Range montane rain forests

106 Halmahera rain forests

107 Huon Peninsula montane rain forests

108 Japen rain forests

109 Lord Howe Island subtropical forests

110 Louisiade Archipelago rain forests

111 New Britain-New Ireland lowland rain forests

112 New Britain-New Ireland montane rain forests

113 New Caledonia rain forests

114 Norfolk Island subtropical forests

115 Northern New Guinea lowland rain and freshwater swamp forests

116 Northern New Guinea montane rain forests

117 Queensland tropical rain forests

118 Seram rain forests

119 Solomon Islands rain forests

120 Southeastern Papuan rain forests

121 Southern New Guinea freshwater swamp forests

122 Southern New Guinea lowland rain forests

123 Sulawesi lowland rain forests

124 Sulawesi montane rain forests

125 Trobriand Islands rain forests

126 Vanuatu rain forests

127 Vogelkop montane rain forests

128 Vogelkop-Aru lowland rain forests

Tropical & Subtropical Dry Broadleaf Forests

201 Lesser Sundas deciduous forests

202 New Caledonia dry forests

203 Sumba deciduous forests

204 Timor and Wetar deciduous forests

Temperate Broadleaf & Mixed Forests

401 Chatham Island temperate forests

402 Eastern Australian temperate forests

403 Fiordland temperate forests

404 Nelson Coast temperate forests

405 Northland temperate forests

406 Northland temperate kauri forests

407 Rakiura Island temperate forests

408 Richmond temperate forests

409 Southeast Australia temperate forests

410 Southland temperate forests

411 Tasmanian Central Highland forests

412 Tasmanian temperate forests

413 Tasmanian temperate rain forests

414 Westland temperate forests

Tropical & Subtropical Grasslands, Savannas, & Shrublands

701 Arnhem Land tropical savanna

702 Brigalow tropical savanna

703 Cape York tropical savanna

704 Carpentaria tropical savanna

705 Einasleigh upland savanna

706 Kimberly tropical savanna

707 Mitchell grass downs

708 Trans Fly savanna and grasslands

709 Victoria Plains tropical savanna

Temperate Grasslands, Savannas & Shrublands

801 Cantebury-Otago tussock grasslands

802 Eastern Australia mulga shrublands

803 Southeast Australia temperate savanna

Montane Grasslands & Shrublands

1001 Australian Alps montane grasslands

1002 Central Range sub-alpine grasslands

1003 Southland montane grasslands

Tundra

1101 Antipodes Subantarctic Islands tundra

Mediterranean Forests, Woodlands, & Shrub

1201 Coolgardie woodlands

1202 Esperance mallee

1203 Eyre and York mallee

1204 Jarrah-Karri forest and shrublands

1205 Kwongan heathlands

1206 Mount Lofty woodlands

1207 Murray-Darling woodlands and mallee

1208 Naracoorte woodlands

1209 Southwest Australia savanna

1210 Southwest Australia woodlands

Deserts & Xeric Shrublands

1301 Carnarvon xeric shrublands

1302 Central Ranges xeric scrub

1303 Gibson desert

1304 Great Sandy-Tanami desert

1305 Great Victoria desert

1306 Nullarbor Plains xeric shrublands

1307 Pilbara shrublands

1308 Simpson desert

1309 Tirari-Stuart stony desert

1310 Western Australian Mulga shrublands

Mangrove

1401 New Guinea mangroves

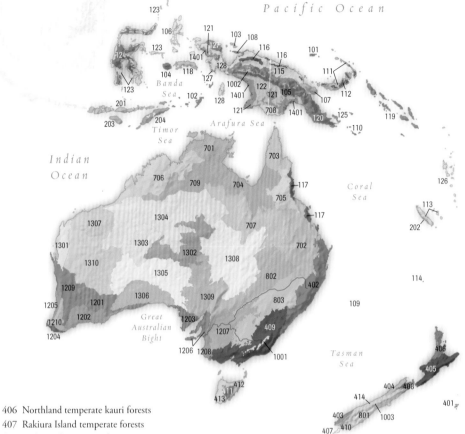

Source: Olson et al. 2001.

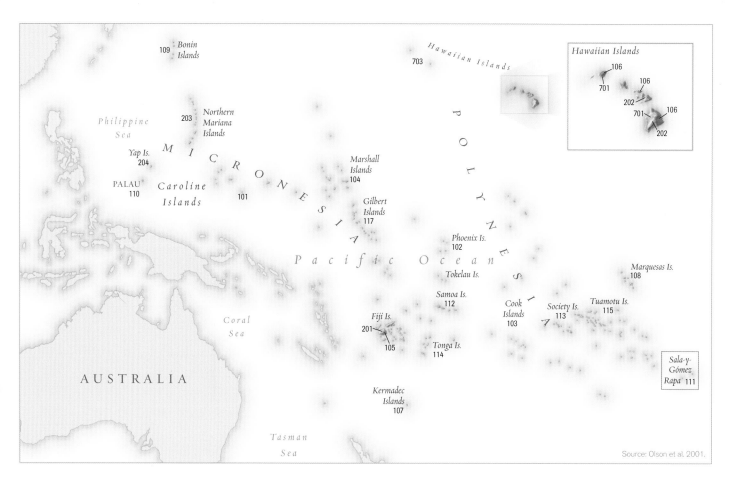

Source: Olson et al. 2001.

OCEANIA

Tropical & Subtropical Moist Broadleaf Forests

101 Carolines tropical moist forests
102 Central Polynesian tropical moist forests
103 Cook Islands tropical moist forests
104 Eastern Micronesia tropical moist forests
105 Fiji tropical moist forests
106 Hawaii tropical moist forests

107 Kermadec Islands subtropical moist forests
108 Marquesas tropical moist forests
109 Ogasawara subtropical moist forests
110 Palau tropical moist forests
111 Rapa Nui and Sala-y-Gomez subtropical broadleaf forests
112 Samoan tropical moist forests
113 Society Islands tropical moist forests
114 Tongan tropical moist forests

115 Tuamotu tropical moist forests
116 Tubuai tropical moist forests
117 Western Polynesian tropical moist forests

Tropical & Subtropical Dry Broadleaf Forests

201 Fiji tropical dry forests
202 Hawaii tropical dry forests
203 Marianas tropical dry forests
204 Yap tropical dry forests

Tropical & Subtropical Grasslands, Savannas, & Shrublands

701 Hawaii tropical high shrublands
702 Hawaii tropical low shrublands
703 Northwestern Hawaii scrub

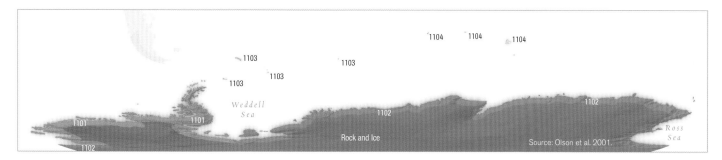

Source: Olson et al. 2001.

ANTARCTICA

Tundra

1101 Marielandia Antarctic tundra
1102 Maudlandia Antarctic desert
1103 Scotia Sea Islands tundra
1104 Southern Indian Ocean Islands tundra

Freshwater Ecoregions

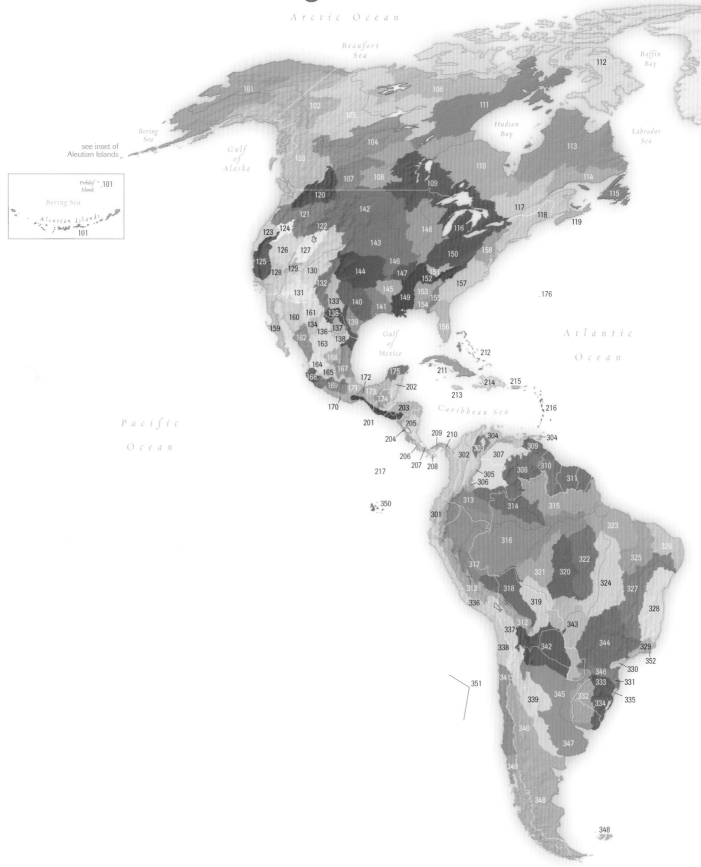

Source: Abell et al. 2008.

NEARCTIC

101 Alaskan coastal
102 Upper Yukon
103 Alaska and Canada Pacific coastal
104 Upper Mackenzie
105 Lower Mackenzie
106 Central Arctic coastal
107 Upper Saskatchewan
108 Middle Saskatchewan
109 English-Winnipeg Lakes
110 Southern Hudson Bay
111 Western Hudson Bay
112 Canadian Arctic Archipelago
113 Eastern Hudson Bay-Ungava
114 Gulf of St. Lawrence coastal drainages
115 Canadian Atlantic islands
116 Laurentian Great Lakes
117 St. Lawrence
118 Northeast United States and southeast Canada Atlantic drainages
119 Scotia-Fundy
120 Columbia glaciated
121 Columbia unglaciated
122 Upper Snake
123 Oregon and northern California coastal
124 Oregon lakes
125 Sacramento-San Joaquin
126 Lahontan
127 Bonneville
128 Death Valley
129 Vegas-Virgin
130 Colorado
131 Gila

132 Upper Rio Grande-Bravo
133 Pecos
134 Rio Conchos
135 Lower Rio Grande-Bravo
136 Cuatro Ciénegas
137 Rio Salado
138 Río San Juan (Mexico)
139 West Texas Gulf
140 East Texas Gulf
141 Sabine-Galveston
142 Upper Missouri
143 Middle Missouri
144 U.S. southern plains
145 Ouachita Highlands
146 Central prairie
147 Ozark Highlands
148 Upper Mississippi
149 Lower Mississippi
150 Teays-Old Ohio
151 Cumberland
152 Tennessee
153 Mobile Bay
154 West Florida Gulf
155 Apalachicola
156 Florida peninsula
157 Appalachian piedmont
158 Chesapeake Bay
159 Southern California coastal-Baja California
160 Sonora
161 Guzmán-Samalayuca
162 Sinaloa
163 Mayran-Viesca
165 Lerma-Chapala
166 Llanos El Salado
176 Bermuda

NEOTROPIC

164 Rio Santiago
167 Pánuco
168 Ameca-Manantlán
169 Rio Balsas

170 Sierra Madre del Sur
171 Papaloapan
172 Coatzacoalcos
173 Grijalva-Usumacinta
174 Upper Usumacinta
175 Yucatan
201 Chiapas-Fonseca
202 Quintana Roo-Motagua
203 Mosquitia
204 Estero Real-Tempisque
205 San Juan (Nicaragua/Costa Rica)
206 Chiriqui
207 Isthmus Caribbean
208 Santa Maria
209 Chagres
210 Rio Tuira
211 Cuba-Cayman Islands
212 Bahama Archipelago
213 Jamaica
214 Hispaniola
215 Puerto Rico-Virgin Islands
216 Windward and Leeward Islands
217 Cocos Island (Costa Rica)
301 North Andean Pacific Slopes-Rio Atrato
302 Magdalena-Sinu
303 Maracaibo
304 South America Caribbean Drainages-Trinidad
305 Orinoco High Andes
306 Orinoco piedmont
307 Orinoco Llanos
308 Orinoco Guiana Shield
309 Orinoco delta and coastal drainages
310 Essequibo
311 Guianas
312 Amazonas High Andes
313 Western Amazon piedmont
314 Rio Negro
315 Amazonas Guiana Shield
316 Amazonas lowlands

317 Ucayali-Urubamba piedmont
318 Mamore-Madre de Dios piedmont
319 Guapore-Itenez
320 Tapajos-Juruena
321 Madeira Brazilian Shield
322 Xingu
323 Amazonas estuary and coastal drainages
324 Tocantins-Araguaia
325 Parnaiba
326 Northeastern Caatinga and coastal drainages
327 S. Francisco
328 Northeastern Mata Atlantica
329 Paraiba do Sul
330 Ribeira de Iguape
331 Southeastern Mata Atlántica
332 Lower Uruguay
333 Upper Uruguay
334 Laguna dos Patos
335 Tramandai-Mampituba
336 Central Andean Pacific slopes
337 Titicacaz
338 Atacama
339 Mart Chiquita-Salinas Grandes
340 Cuyan-Desaguadero
341 South Andean Pacific slopes
342 Chaco
343 Paraguay
344 Upper Parana
345 Lower Parana
346 Iguassu
347 Bonaerensean drainages
348 Patagonia
349 Valdivian lakes
350 Galapagos Islands
351 Juan Fernández Island
352 Fluminense

Freshwater Ecoregions

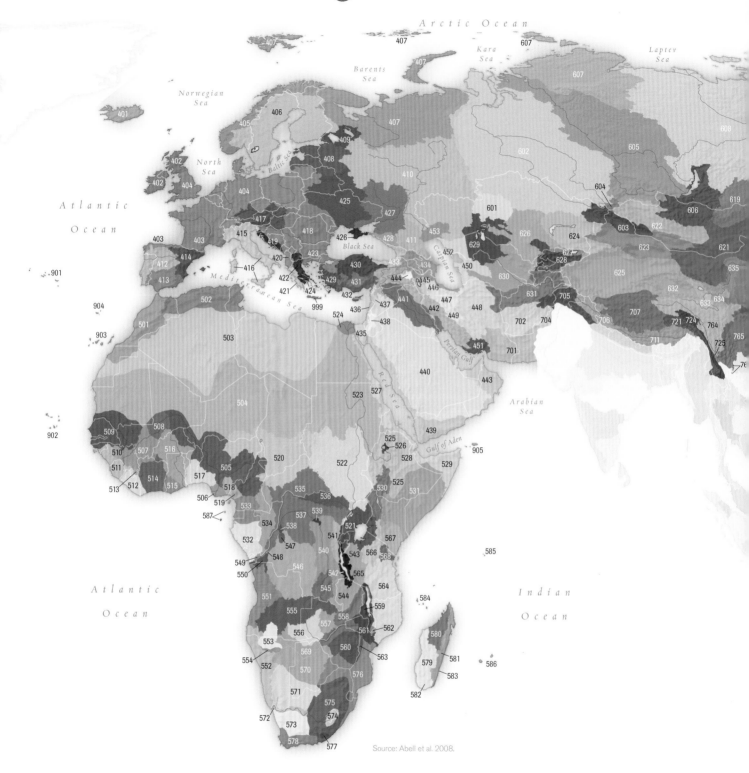

Source: Abell et al. 2008.

536 Uele
537 Cuvette Centrale
538 Tumba
539 Upper Congo rapids
540 Upper Congo
541 Albertine highlands
542 Lake Tanganyika
543 Malagarasi-Moyowosi
544 Bangweulu-Mweru
545 Upper Lualaba
546 Kasai
547 Mai Ndombe
548 Malebo Pool
549 Lower Congo rapids
550 Lower Congo
551 Cuanza
552 Namib
553 Etosha
554 Karstveld sink holes
555 Zambezian headwaters
556 Upper Zambezi floodplains
557 Kafue
558 Middle Zambezi-Luangwa
559 Lake Malawi
560 Zambezian Highveld
561 Lower Zambezi
562 Mulanje
563 Eastern Zimbabwe Highlands
564 Coastal East Africa
565 Lake Rukwa
566 Southern Eastern Rift
567 Tana, Athi and coastal drainages
568 Pangani
569 Okavango
570 Kalahari
571 Southern Kalahari
572 Western Orange
573 Karoo
574 Drakensberg-Maloti highlands
575 Southern Temperate Highveld
576 Zambezian Lowveld
577 Amatolo-Winterberg highlands
578 Cape Fold
579 Western Madagascar
580 Northwestern Madagascar
581 Madagascar eastern highlands
582 Southern Madagascar
583 Madagascar eastern lowlands
584 Comoros-Mayotte
585 Seychelles
586 Mascarenes
587 S. Tome and Principe-Annobon
902 Cape Verde
905 Socotra

PALEARCTIC

401 Iceland-Jan Mayen
402 Northern British Isles
403 Cantabric Coast-Languedoc

AFROTROPIC

439 Southwestern Arabian coast
443 Oman Mountains
505 Lower Niger-Benue
506 Niger Delta
507 Upper Niger
508 Inner Niger Delta
509 Senegal-Gambia
510 Fouta-Djalon
511 Northern Upper Guinea
512 Southern Upper Guinea
513 Mount Nimba
514 Eburneo
515 Ashanti
516 Volta
517 Bight drainages
518 Northern Gulf of Guinea drainages-Bioko
519 Western equatorial crater lakes
520 Lake Chad
521 Lake Victoria basin
522 Upper Nile
525 Ethiopian Highlands
526 Lake Tana
528 Northern Eastern Rift
529 Horn of Africa
530 Lake Turkana
531 Shebelle-Juba
532 Ogooue-Nyanga-Kouilou-Niari
533 Southern Gulf of Guinea drainages
534 Sangha
535 Sudanic Congo-Oubangi

404 Central and Western Europe
405 Norwegian Sea drainages
406 Northern Baltic drainages
407 Barents Sea drainages
408 Southern Baltic lowlands
409 Lake Onega-Lake Ladoga
410 Volga-Ural
411 Western Caspian drainages
412 Western Iberia
413 Southern Iberia
414 Eastern Iberia
415 Gulf of Venice drainages
416 Italian peninsula and islands
417 Upper Danube
418 Dniester-Lower Danube
419 Dalmatia
420 Southeast Adriatic drainages
421 Ionian drainages
422 Vardar
423 Thrace
424 Aegean drainages
425 Dnieper-South Bug
426 Crimea peninsula
427 Don
428 Kuban
429 Western Anatolia
430 Northern Anatolia
431 Central Anatolia
432 Southern Anatolia
433 Western Transcaucasia
434 Kura-South Caspian drainages
435 Sinai
436 Coastal Levant
437 Orontes
438 Jordan River
440 Arabian interior
441 Lower Tigris and Euphrates
442 Upper Tigris and Euphrates
444 Lake Van
445 Orumiyeh
446 Caspian highlands
447 Namak
448 Kavir and Lut Deserts
449 Esfahan
450 Turan Plain
451 Northern Hormuz drainages
452 Caspian marine
453 Volga Delta-Northern Caspian drainages
501 Atlantic northwest Africa
502 Mediterranean northwest Africa
503 Sahara
504 Dry Sahel
523 Lower Nile
524 Nile Delta
527 Western Red Sea drainages
601 Irgyz-Turgai
602 Ob
603 Upper Irtysh
604 Chuya

605 Yenisei
606 Lake Baikal
607 Taimyr
608 Lena
609 Kolyma
610 Anadyr
611 East Chukotka
612 Koryakia
613 Kamchatka and Northern Kurils
614 Okhotsk Coast
615 Coastal Amur
616 Lower Amur
617 Middle Amur
618 Argun
619 Shilka (Amur)
620 Songhua Jiang
621 Inner Mongolia endorheic basins
622 Western Mongolia
623 Dzungaria
624 Balkash-Alakul
625 Tarim
626 Lower and Middle Syr Darya
627 Lake Issyk Kul-Upper Chu
628 Northern central Asian highlands
629 Aral Sea drainages
630 Middle Amu Darya
631 Upper Amu Darya
632 Qaidan
633 Upper Huang He
634 Upper Huang He corridor
635 Huang He Great Bend
636 Lower Huang He
637 Liao He
638 Eastern Yellow Sea drainages
639 Southeastern Korean peninsula
640 Hamgyong-Sanmaek
641 Sakhalin, Hokkaido, and Sikhote-Alin coast
642 Honshu-Shikoku-Kyushu
643 Biwa Ko
701 Baluchistan
702 Helmand-Sistan
704 Yaghistan
705 Indus Himalayan foothills
706 Upper Indus
707 Tibetan Plateau endorheic drainages
711 Upper Brahmaputra
721 Upper Salween
724 Upper Lancang (Mekong)
725 Er Hai
762 Yunnan lakes
764 Upper Yangtze
765 Middle Yangtze
766 Lower Yangtze
901 Azores
903 Canary Islands
904 Madeira Islands

Freshwater Ecoregions

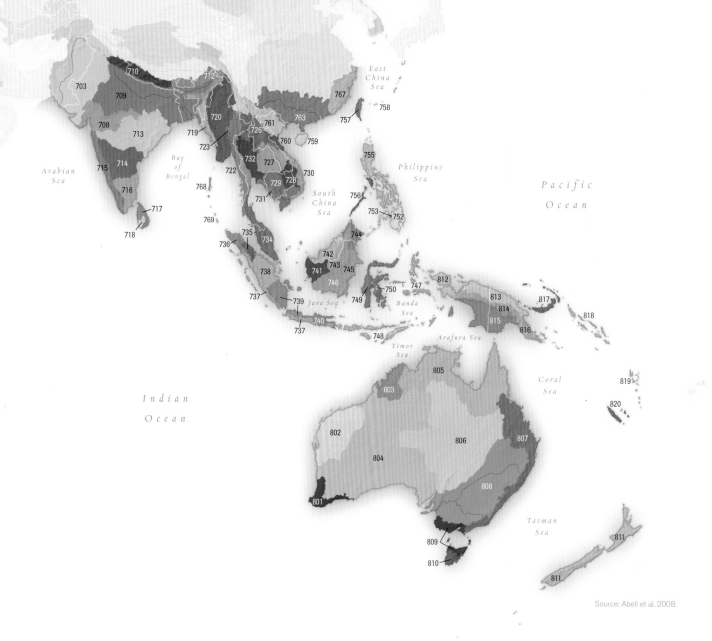

Source: Abell et al. 2008.

AUSTRALASIA

747 Malukku
748 Lesser Sunda Islands
749 Sulawesi
750 Malili lakes
751 Lake Poso
801 Southwestern Australia
802 Pilbara
803 Kimberley
804 Paleo
805 Arafura-Carpentaria
806 Lake Eyre basin
807 Eastern Coastal Australia
808 Murray-Darling
809 Bass Strait drainages
810 Southern Tasmania
811 New Zealand
812 Vogelkop-Bomberai
813 New Guinea north coast
814 New Guinea central mountains
815 Southwest New Guinea-Trans-Fly
    lowland
816 Papuan Peninsula
817 Bismarck Archipelago
818 Solomon Islands
819 Vanuatu
820 New Caledonia

INDO-MALAY

703 Lower and Middle Indus
708 Namuda-Tapi
709 Ganges delta and plain
710 Ganges Himalayan foothills
712 Middle Brahmaputra
713 Northern Deccan Plateau
714 Southern Deccan Plateau
715 Western Ghats
716 Southeastern Ghats
717 Sri Lanka dry zone
718 Sri Lanka wet zone
719 Chin Hills-Arakan coast
720 Sitang-Irawaddy
722 Lower and Middle Salween
723 Inle Lake
726 Lower Lancang (Mekong)
727 Khorat Plateau (Mekong)
728 Kratie-Stung Treng (Mekong)
729 Mekong delta
730 Southern Annam
731 Eastern Gulf of Thailand
    drainages
732 Chao Phraya
733 Mae Khlong
734 Malay Peninsula eastern slope
735 Northern central Sumatra-western
    Malaysia

736 Aceh
737 Indian Ocean slope of Sumatra
    and Java
738 Southern central Sumatra
739 Southern Sumatra-western Java
740 Central and eastern Java
741 Kapuas
742 Northwestern Borneo
743 Borneo highlands
744 Northeastern Borneo
745 Eastern Borneo
746 Southeastern Borneo
752 Mindanao
753 Lake Lanao
755 Northern Philippine Islands
756 Palawan-Busuanga-Mindoro
757 Western Taiwan
758 Eastern Taiwan
759 Hainan
760 Northern Annam
761 Song Hong
763 Xi Yiang
767 Coastal Fujian-Zeijang
768 Andaman Islands
769 Nicobar Islands

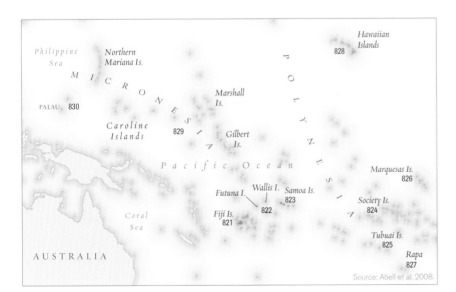

OCEANIA

821 Fiji
822 Wallis-Futuna
823 Samoas
824 Society Islands
825 Tubuai Islands
826 Marquesas Islands
827 Rapa
828 Hawaiian Islands
829 East Caroline Islands
830 West Caroline Islands

Marine Ecoregions

ARCTIC REALM

Arctic

1 North Greenland
2 North and East Iceland
3 East Greenland shelf
4 West Greenland shelf
5 Northern Grand Banks Southern Labrador
6 Northern Labrador
7 Baffin Bay-Davis Strait
8 Hudson Complex
9 Lancaster Sound
10 High Arctic Archipelago
11 Beaufort-Amundsen-Viscount Melville-Queen Maud
12 Beaufort Sea continental coast and shelf
13 Chukchi Sea
14 Eastern Bering Sea
15 East Siberian Sea
16 Laptev Sea
17 Kara Sea
18 North and east Barents Sea
19 White Sea

TEMPERATE NORTHERN ATLANTIC REALM

Northern European Seas

20 South and west Iceland
21 Faroe Plateau
22 Southern Norway
23 Northern Norway and Finnmark
24 Baltic Sea
25 North Sea
26 Celtic Seas

Lusitanian

27 South European Atlantic shelf
28 Saharan upwelling
29 Azores Canaries Madeira

Mediterranean Sea

30 Adriatic Sea
31 Aegean Sea
32 Levantine Sea
33 Tunisian Plateau/Gulf of Sidra
34 Ionian Sea
35 Western Mediterranean
36 Alboran Sea

Cold Temperate Northwest Atlantic

37 Gulf of St. Lawrence Eastern Scotian shelf
38 Southern Grand Banks South Newfoundland
39 Scotian shelf
40 Gulf of Maine/Bay of Fundy
41 Virginian

Warm Temperate Northwest Atlantic

42 Carolinian
43 Northern Gulf of Mexico

Black Sea

44 Black Sea

TEMPERATE NORTHERN PACIFIC REALM

Cold Temperate Northwest Pacific

45 Sea of Okhotsk
46 Kamchatka shelf and coast
47 Oyashio Current
48 Northeastern Honshu
49 Sea of Japan/East Sea
50 Yellow Sea

Warm Temperate Northwest Pacific

51 Central Kuroshio Current
52 East China Sea

Cold Temperate Northeast Pacific

53 Aleutian Islands
54 Gulf of Alaska
55 North American Pacific fjordland
56 Puget Trough/Georgia Basin
57 Oregon, Washington, Vancouver coast and shelf
58 Northern California

Warm Temperate Northeast Pacific

59 Southern California Bight
60 Cortezian
61 Magdalena transition

TROPICAL ATLANTIC REALM

Tropical Northwestern Atlantic

62 Bermuda
63 Bahamian
64 Eastern Caribbean
65 Greater Antilles
66 Southern Caribbean
67 Southwestern Caribbean
68 Western Caribbean
69 Southern Gulf of Mexico
70 Floridian

North Brazil Shelf

71 Guianan
72 Amazonia

Tropical Southwestern Atlantic

73 Sao Pedro and Sao Paulo Islands
74 Fernando de Naronha and Atoll das Rocas
75 Northeastern Brazil
76 Eastern Brazil
77 Trindade and Martin Vaz Islands

St. Helena and Ascension Islands

78 St. Helena and Ascension Islands

West African Transition

79 Cape Verde
80 Sahelian upwelling

Gulf of Guinea

81 Gulf of Guinea west
82 Gulf of Guinea upwelling
83 Gulf of Guinea central
84 Gulf of Guinea islands
85 Gulf of Guinea south
86 Angolan

WESTERN INDO-PACIFIC REALM

Red Sea and Gulf of Aden

87 Northern and central Red Sea
88 Southern Red Sea
89 Gulf of Aden

Somali/Arabian

90 Arabian (Persian) Gulf
91 Gulf of Oman
92 Western Arabian Sea
93 Central Somali coast

Western Indian Ocean

94 Northern Monsoon Current coast
95 East African coral coast
96 Seychelles
97 Cargados Carajos/Tromelin Island
98 Mascarene Islands
99 Southeast Madagascar
100 Western and northern Madagascar
101 Bight of Sofala/Swamp coast
102 Delagoa

West and South Indian Shelf

103 Western India
104 South India and Sri Lanka

Central Indian Ocean Islands

105 Maldives
106 Chagos

Bay of Bengal

107 Eastern India
108 Northern Bay of Bengal

Andaman

109 Andaman and Nicobar Islands
110 Andaman Sea coral coast
111 Western Sumatra

CENTRAL INDO-PACIFIC REALM

South China Sea

112 Gulf of Tonkin
113 Southern China
114 South China Sea oceanic islands

Sunda Shelf

115 Gulf of Thailand
116 Southern Vietnam
117 Sunda Shelf/Java Sea
118 Malacca Strait

Java Transitional

119 Southern Java
120 Cocos-Keeling/Christmas Island

South Kuroshio

121 South Kuroshio

Tropical Northwestern Pacific

122 Ogasawara Islands
123 Mariana Islands
124 East Caroline Islands
125 West Caroline Islands

Western Coral Triangle

126 Palawan/north Borneo
127 Eastern Philippines
128 Sulawesi Sea/Makassar Strait
129 Halmahera

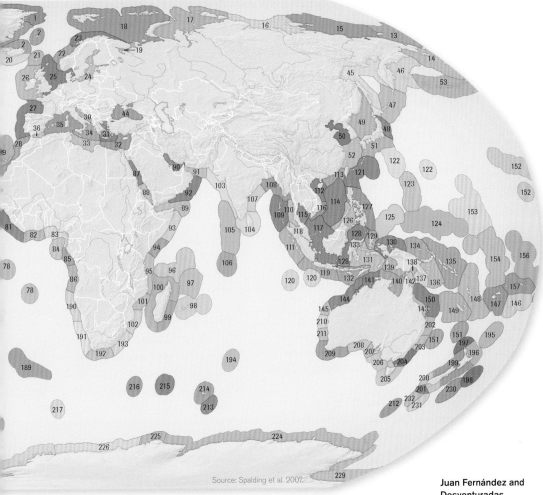

Source: Spalding et al. 2007.

Foreword: Ehrlich

REFERENCE

Ehrlich, P. R., and A. H. Ehrlich. 2008. *The Dominant Animal: Human Evolution and the Environment.* Washington, DC: Island.

CHAPTER 1

Introduction

REFERENCES

Clode, D., and R. O'Brien. 2001. Why Wallace drew the line: A re-analysis of Wallace's bird collections in the Malay Archipelago and the origins of biogeography. In *Faunal and Floral Migrations and Evolution in SE Asia-Australasia: Proceedings of the 38th U.S. Rock Mechanics Symposium, Washington DC, July 7–10, 2001,* ed. I. Metcalfe, J. M. B. Smith, M. Morwood, and I. Davidson. Orlando, FL: CRC Press.

Dunn, R. R. 2004. Blurring Wallace's Line. *Natural History* (September). www4.ncsu.edu/~rrdunn/BlurringWallace%27sLine.pdf.

UN Environment Programme (UNEP). 2003. *Global Deserts Outlook.* Ed. Exequiel Ezcurra. www.globio.info/press/Global%20Deserts%20Outlook.pdf.

Wallace, A. R. 1876. *The Geographical Distribution of Animals: With a Study of the Relations of Living and Extinct Faunas as Elucidating the Past Changes of the Earth's Surface.* London: Macmillan.

Wolf, B. O., and C. Martinez del Rio. 2003. How important are columnar cacti as sources of water and nutrients for desert consumers? A review. *Isotopes in Environmental and Health Studies* 39, no. 1: 53–67.

World Resources Institute—Global Forest Watch. 1997. Data on original and frontier forests' extent. Available at www.globalforestwatch.org. Washington, DC: World Resources Institute. Digital media.

Essay: Ricketts

REFERENCES

Coad, L., N. D. Burgess, L. Fish, C. Ravilious, C. Corrigan, H. Pavese, A. Granziera, and C. Besançon. 2008. Progress towards the Convention on Biological Diversity terrestrial 2010 and marine 2012 targets for protected area coverage. *Parks* 17: 35–42.

Hoekstra, J. M., T. M. Boucher, T. H. Ricketts, and C. Roberts. 2005. Confronting a biome crisis: Global disparities of habitat loss and protection. *Ecology Letters* 8: 23–29.

Kambem-Toham, A., A. W. Adeleke, N. D. Burgess, R. Carroll, J. D'Amico, E. Dinerstein, D. M. Olson, and L. Some. 2003. Forest conservation in the Congo basin. *Science* 299: 346.

Lamoreux, J. F., J. C. Morrison, T. H. Ricketts, D. M. Olson, E. Dinerstein, M. W. McKnight, and H. H. Shugart. 2006. Global tests of biodiversity concordance and the importance of endemism. *Nature* 440: 212–214.

Millennium Ecosystem Assessment. 2005. *Ecosystems and Human Well-being: Synthesis.* Washington, DC: Island.

Mittermeier, R. A., P. Robles-Gil, M. Hoffmann, J. D. Pilgrim, T. M. Brooks, C. G. Mittermeier, J. L. Lamoreux, and G. Fonseca, eds. 2004. *Hotspots Revisited: Earth's Biologically Richest and Most Endangered Ecoregions.* Mexico City: CEMEX.

Olson, D. M., and E. Dinerstein. 1998. The Global 200: A representation approach to conserving the Earth's most biologically valuable ecoregions. *Conservation Biology* 12: 502–515.

Rosenzweig, M. L. 1995. *Species Diversity in Space and Time.* Cambridge: Cambridge University Press.

Terrestrial Ecoregions, Realms, and Biomes

ECOREGION AND BIOME MAPS DATA SOURCE

Olson, D. M., E. Dinerstein, E. D. Wikramanayake, N. D. Burgess, G. V. N. Powell, E. C. Underwood, J. A. D'Amico, et al. 2001. Terrestrial ecoregions of the world: A new map of life on earth. *BioScience* 51: 933–938.

TECHNICAL NOTES

"Terrestrial Ecoregions of the World" (Olson et al. 2001) is a global standard for conservation planning on land. An *ecoregion* is defined as a large area of land that contains a geographically distinct assemblage of natural communities that share a large majority of their species and ecological dynamics, share similar environmental conditions, and interact ecologically in ways that are critical for their long-term persistence. There are 825 terrestrial ecoregions across the globe. Olson et al. (2001) report three underlying approaches in melding information from the many antecedents: (1) delineate biogeographic boundaries that are yet not well represented, (2) provide an even expression of biogeographic representation, and (3) match the boundaries and units of adjacent types as much as possible. See Olson et al. (2001) for a list of biogeographic divisions used to derive ecoregional boundaries. For downloadable versions of ecoregions: www.worldwildlife.org/science/data/item1872.html.

Freshwater Ecoregions and Basins

ECOREGION MAP DATA SOURCE

Abell, R., M. L. Thieme, C. Revenga, M. Bryer, M. Kottelat, N. Bogutskaya, B. Coad, et al. 2008. Freshwater ecoregions of the world: A new map of biogeographic units for freshwater biodiversity conservation. *BioScience* 58: 403–414.

TECHNICAL NOTES

"Freshwater Ecoregions of the World" (FEOW) is the first global biogeographic regionalization of Earth's freshwater biodiversity (see Abell et al. 2008). It was a collaborative effort jointly led and funded by The Nature Conservancy and World Wildlife Fund, which included over 250 experts and contributors (www.feow.org). A *freshwater ecoregion* is a large area encompassing one or more freshwater systems that contains a distinct assemblage of natural freshwater communities and species. Each of the 426 ecoregions has a distinct evolutionary history and/or ecological process that produced a unique species composition. The freshwater species, dynamics, and environmental conditions within a given ecoregion are more similar to each other than to those of surrounding ecoregions. The freshwater ecoregion boundaries were delineated using the best available regional information and expert opinion describing freshwater biogeography, defined broadly to include the influences of phylogenetic history, palaeogeography, and ecology. We restricted our analyses to information describing freshwater fish species distributions, with a few exceptions for extremely data-poor regions and inland seas, where some invertebrates and brackish-water fish were considered, respectively. In general, though not always, ecoregions correspond with hydrological basins (or watersheds).

RIVER BASIN MAP DATA SOURCE

World Resources Institute (WRI). 2003. UPDATE of Revenga, C., S. Murray, J. Abramovitz, and A. Hammond. 1998. *Watersheds of the World: Ecological Value and Vulnerability.* Washington, DC: World Resources Institute.

TECHNICAL NOTES

River basin boundaries are based on a revised version of *Watersheds of the World: Ecological Value and Vulnerability* (WRI 2003). For more information and a complete list of major basins: http://earthtrends.wri.org. Basins were derived from the Major Watersheds of the World data set distributed on the GlobalARC CD-ROM by the U.S. Army Corps of Engineers Construction Engineering Research Laboratories (CERL) and the EROS Data Center HYDRO1k basin boundaries developed at the U.S. Geological Survey (USGS) (http://edcdaac.usgs.gov/gtopo30 /hydro/). The CERL basins were digitally derived using ETOPO5, five-minute gridded elevation data, and known locations of rivers. The HYDRO1k is a geographic database derived from the USGS's thirty-arc-second digital elevation model of the world (GTOPO30). Because of the low resolution of the elevation data used to derive the CERL base data layer, boundaries are coarse, and an effort was made to refine the basin boundaries as follows. WRI revised and checked basin boundaries by overlaying ArcWorld 1:3 million rivers. In cases where rivers (except canals) crossed basin boundaries, the boundary was edited using a one-kilometer digital elevation model as a guide and redrawing the boundaries along identifiable ridges. In some cases, polygons were split to separate sub-basins.

Marine Ecoregions, Provinces, and Realms

ECOREGION AND REALM MAPS DATA SOURCE

Spalding, M. D., H. E. Fox, G. R. Allen, N. Davidson, Z. A. Ferdaña, M. Finlayson, B. S. Halpern, et al. 2007. Marine ecoregions of the world: A bioregionalization of coast and shelf areas. *BioScience* 57: 573–583.

TECHNICAL NOTES

Marine ecoregions, provinces, and realms (Spalding et al. 2007, www.nature.org/meow) in these maps are drawn out to an offshore boundary that approximates two hundred nautical miles. This is a convention applied for easy visualization of information at global scales (in these maps and throughout this book). In reality, these biogeographic units refer to continental shelf areas only. These are defined as areas of waters and sea bed to a depth of two hundred meters.

The definitions of these biogeographic units, according to Spalding et al. (2007), are as follows.

Realm: "Very large regions of coastal, benthic, or pelagic ocean across which biotas are internally coherent at higher taxonomic levels, as a result of a shared and unique evolutionary history."

Provinces: "Large areas defined by the presence of distinct biotas that have at least some cohesion over evolutionary time frames. Provinces will hold some level of endemism, principally at the level of species. Although historical isolation will play a role, many of these distinct biotas have arisen as a result of distinctive abiotic features that circumscribe their boundaries. These may include geomorphological features (isolated island and shelf systems, semi-enclosed seas); hydrographic features (currents, upwellings, ice dynamics); or geochemical influences (broadest-scale elements of nutrient supply and salinity)."

Ecoregions: "Areas of relatively homogeneous species composition, clearly distinct from adjacent systems. The species composition is likely to be determined by the predominance of a small number of ecosystems and/or a distinct suite of oceanographic or topographic features. The dominant biogeographic forcing agents defining the ecoregions vary from location to location but may include isolation, upwelling, nutrient inputs, freshwater influx, temperature regimes, ice regimes, exposure, sediments, currents, and bathymetric or coastal complexity."

Essay: Christensen

REFERENCES

Cannon, S. F. 1978. *Science in Culture: The Early Victorian Period.* New York: Science History Publications.

Cosgrove, D. 2001. *Apollo's Eye: A Cartographic Genealogy of the Earth in the Western Imagination.* Baltimore: Johns Hopkins University Press.

Godlewska, A. M. C. 1999. From enlightenment vision to modern science? Humboldt's visual thinking. In *Geography and Enlightenment*, ed. D. N. Livingstone and C. W. J. Withers. Chicago: University of Chicago Press.

Pratt, M. L. 1993. *Imperial Eyes: Travel Writing and Transculturation.* New York: Routledge.

Sachs, A. 2006. *The Humboldt Current: Nineteenth-Century Exploration and the Roots of American Environmentalism.* New York: Viking.

von Humboldt, A. 1805. *Essai sur la géographie des plantes; accompagné d'un tableau physique des régions équinoxiales, fondé sur des mesures exécutées, depuis le dixième degré de latitude boréale jusqu'au dixième degré de latitude australe, pendant les années 1799, 1800, 1801, 1802 et 1803.* Par Al. de Humboldt et A. Bonpland. Rédigé par Al. de Humboldt. Paris: Levrault, Schoell.

———. 1825. *De quelques phénomènes physi-

ques et géologiques qu'offrent les Cordillères des Andes de Quito et la partie occidentale de l'Himalaya. Annales des sciences naturelles.* Paris: Chez Béchet Jeune, Librarie de l'Académie Royale de Médecine.

———. 1995. *Personal Narrative of a Journey to the Equinoctial Regions of the New Continent.* New York: Penguin Books.

———. 1997. *Cosmos: A Sketch of a Physical Description of the Universe.* Translated from the German by E. C. Otté; introduction by Michael Dettelbach. Baltimore: Johns Hopkins University Press.

CHAPTER 2

Habitats Introduction

TERRESTRIAL HABITAT FIGURE SOURCE

Myers, N., and J. Kent. 2005. *The New Atlas of Planet Management.* Berkeley: University of California Press.

REFERENCES

Funch, P., and R. M. Kristensen. 1995. Cycliophora is a new phylum with affinities to Entoprocta and Ectoprocta. *Nature* 378: 711–714 (doi: 10.1038/37871a0).

Whittaker, R. H. 1975. *Communities and Ecosystems.* New York: Macmillan.

Forests and Woodlands

FOREST AREA MAP DATA SOURCES

Center for International Earth Science Information Network (CIESIN), International Food Policy Research Institute (IFPRI), the World Bank, and Centro Internacional de Agricultura Tropical (CIAT). 2004. Global Rural-Urban Mapping Project (GRUMP): Urban Extents, Columbia University Palisades, New York, USA. Available at http://sedac.ciesin.columbia.edu/ gpw/. Digital media.

Joint Research Centre of the European Commission (JRC). 2003. *GLC 2000: Global Land Cover Mapping for the Year 2000.* Ispra, Italy: European Commission Joint Research Centre, Institute for Environment and Sustainability. Available at www-tem.jrc.it/ glc2000. Digital media.

TECHNICAL NOTES

We derived the forest map from forest and woodland classes of the Global Land Cover 2000 data set (JRC 2003) with areas of human habitation and infrastructure from the Global Rural-Urban Mapping Project database (CIESIN et al. 2004) removed. We applied a zonal sum procedure to those data to show the amount of forest by ecoregion.

REFERENCES

World Wildlife Fund. 2006. WildFinder: Database of species distributions, ver. Jan-06. Available at www.gis.wwf.org/WildFinder. Digital media.

World Resources Institute—Global Forest Watch. 1997. Data on original and frontier forests' extent. Available at www.globalforestwatch.org. Washington, DC: World Resources Institute. Digital media.

Grasslands

GRASSLAND AREA MAP DATA SOURCES

Center for International Earth Science Information Network (CIESIN), International Food Policy Research Institute (IFPRI), the World Bank, and Centro Internacional de Agricultura Tropical (CIAT). 2004. Global Rural-Urban Mapping Project (GRUMP): Urban Extents, Columbia University Palisades, New York, USA. Available at http://sedac.ciesin.columbia.edu/gpw/. Digital media.

Joint Research Centre of the European Commission (JRC). 2003. Global Land Cover 2000 database. Ispra, Italy: European Commission Joint Research Centre, Institute for Environment and Sustainability. Available at www-tem.jrc.it/glc2000. Digital media.

TECHNICAL NOTES

We derived the grasslands map from grassland classes of the Global Land Cover 2000 data set (JRC 2003) with areas of human habitation and infrastructure from the Global Rural-Urban Mapping Project database (CIESIN et al. 2004) removed. We applied a zonal sum procedure to those data to show the amount of forest by ecoregion.

PRECIPITATION FIGURE DATA SOURCE

Hijmans, R. J., S. E. Cameron, J. L. Parra, P. G. Jones, and A. Jarvis. 2005. Very high resolution interpolated climate surfaces for global land areas. *International Journal of Climatology* 25:1965–1978. Data available at www.worldclim.org.

TECHNICAL NOTES

We calculated the values shown in the figure using a zonal mean procedure, taken as the average annual precipitation (Hijmans et al. 2005) of the regions of deserts, grasslands, and forests presented in this atlas.

REFERENCES

Ramankutty, N., and J. A. Foley. 1999. Estimating historical changes in global land cover: Croplands from 1700 to 1992. *Global Biogeochemical Cycles* 13: 997–1028. Available at www.sage.wisc.edu.

The Nature Conservancy (TNC). 2007. *Mongolia: Grassland without Fences in the Land of the Eternal Blue Sky.* Arlington, VA: Author.

Deserts and Aridlands

ARIDLAND AREA MAP DATA SOURCES

Center for International Earth Science Information Network (CIESIN), International Food Policy Research Institute (IFPRI), the World Bank, and Centro Internacional de Agricultura Tropical (CIAT). 2004. Global Rural-Urban Mapping Project (GRUMP): Urban Extents, Columbia University Palisades, New York. Available at http://sedac.ciesin.columbia.edu/gpw/.

Hijmans, R. J., S. E. Cameron, J. L. Parra, P. G. Jones, and A. Jarvis. 2005. Very high resolution interpolated climate surfaces for global land areas. *International Journal of Climatology* 25: 1965–1978. Available at www.worldclim.org.

Joint Research Centre of the European Commission (JRC). 2003. Global Land Cover 2000 database. Ispra, Italy: European Commission Joint Research Centre, Institute for Environment and Sustainability. Available at www.gvm.sai.jrc.it/glc2000/defaultGLC2000.htm.

Kottek, M., J. Grieser, C. Beck, B. Rudolf, and F. Rubel. 2006. World map of the Köppen-Geiger climate classification updated. *Meteorologische Zeitschrift* 15: 259–263.

TECHNICAL NOTES

We derived the aridlands map by first developing a raster-based mask of arid climates from the Köppen-Geiger climate classification (Kottek et al. 2006) using ArcInfo GIS software. We applied the mask to the GLC 2000 global land cover, and then extracted sparse vegetation classes. For example, pockets of forested land occurring within Köppen-Geiger arid climate regions were excluded. Areas of human habitation and infrastructure were also removed from the map, leaving only natural desert lands. Finally, we applied a zonal sum procedure to the raster map to calculate the percentage of arid land per ecoregion.

REFERENCES

Ezcurra, E., ed. *Global Deserts Outlook*. Nairobi: United Nations Environment Programme. Available at www.unep.org/geo/gdoutlook/.

Millennium Ecosystem Assessment. 2005. *Ecosystems and Human Well-being: Desertification Synthesis.* Washington, DC: World Resources Institute.

Rivers and Wetlands

RIVER AND WETLAND AREA MAP DATA SOURCES

ESRI 1992 and 2005. ESRI ArcWorld Database [CD] and ESRI Data & Maps [CD]. Redlands, CA: Environmental Systems Research Institute. Digital media.

Lehner, B., and P. Döll. 2004. Development and validation of a global database of lakes, reservoirs and wetlands. *Journal of Hydrology* 296: 1–22.

TECHNICAL NOTES

The abundance of rivers and wetlands describes the degree to which a freshwater ecoregion is covered with these habitats. We calculated this abundance by combining selected classes of the Global Lakes and Wetlands Database (Level 3 of Lehner and Döll 2004), together with ESRI Rivers (2005) and the perennial rivers from ArcWorld 1:3million (ESRI 1992), all gridded to one-kilometer cell resolution. It should be noted that some ecoregions (e.g., Australia's Arafura and Carpentaria Drainages and Great Diving Range on the northern and eastern coasts) are dominated by small rivers and streams that are not reflected properly in global river and wetland data sets; thus, abundance in these ecoregions may be underrepresented. We classified an ecoregion as "dominated by lakes and reservoirs" when it met thresholds set by regions of known lake and reservoir dominance versus river and wetland dominance. Known ecoregions were used to determine the algorithms to set the cutoffs between abundance classes.

REFERENCES

International Union for Conservation of Nature (IUCN). 2008. The IUCN Red List of Threatened Species: Mekong catfish. Profile available at www.iucnredlist.org/details/15944.

Lutz, K., Connecticut River program director, The Nature Conservancy, personal communication, January 2008.

Mekong River Commission Secretariat Web site. Viewed January 2008. Available at www.mrcmekong.org/about_mekong/about_mekong.htm.

Mosepele, K., P. B. Moyle, G. S. Merron, D. Purkey, and B. Mosepele. 2009. Fish, floods, and ecosystem engineers: Aquatic conservation in the Okavango Delta, Botswana. *BioScience* 59: 53–64.

Revenga, C., J. Brunner, N. Henninger, K. Kassem, and R. Payne. 2000. *Pilot Analysis of Global Ecosystems: Freshwater Systems.* Washington, DC: World Resources Institute.

Sverdrup-Jensen, S. 2002. *Fisheries in the Lower Mekong Basin: Status and Perspective.* MRC Technical Paper No. 6. Phnom Penh, Cambodia: Mekong River Commission.

Ward, J. V. 1998. Riverine landscapes: Biodiversity patterns, disturbance regimes, and aquatic conservation. *Biological Conservation* 83: 269–278.

Lakes

LAKE AREA MAP DATA SOURCE

Lehner, B., and P. Döll. 2004. Development and validation of a global database of lakes, reservoirs and wetlands. *Journal of Hydrology* 296: 1–22.

TECHNICAL NOTES

We calculated the percentage of the ecoregion that is covered by lakes and reservoirs using lake and reservoir polygons from the Global Lakes and Wetlands Database (GLWD) (Lehner and Döll 2004). This database represents the best available source for lakes and wetlands on a global scale (1:1 to 1:3 million resolution). The GLWD contains shoreline polygons of the 3,067 largest lakes (surface area greater than or equal to 50 km²) and 654 largest reservoirs (storage capacity greater than or equal to 0.5 km³) worldwide, as well as shoreline polygons of approximately 250,000 smaller lakes, reservoirs, and rivers (surface area greater than or equal to 0.1 km²). For our calculations, only lake and reservoir polygons were used. It was not possible to separate natural lake polygons from reservoirs.

REFERENCES

LakeNet. 2008. Web site. Available at www.worldlakes.org.

Lehman, J. T. 1986. Control of eutrophication in Lake Washington. Pages 301–316 in *Ecological Knowledge and Environmental Problem-Solving.* Washington, DC: National Academy of Sciences Press.

NatureServe. 2004. Downloadable animal data sets, NatureServe Central Databases. Available at www.natureserve.org/getData/dataSets/watershedHucs/index.jsp.

Ramsar Convention. 2007. Extraordinary new Ramsar sites in Nepal. Available at www.ramsar.org/wn/w.n.nepal_4new.htm.

Russian Ministry of Natural Resources. 2007. Lake Baikal Protection fact sheet. Administered by Rosprirodnadzor (Russian Nature Protection and Oversight Inspectorate). Available in Russian at www.geol.irk.ru/baikal/baikal.htm.

Seal Conservation Society. 2001. Species information pages: Baikal seal. Available at www.pinnipeds.org/species/baikal.htm.

Caves and Karst

KARST AREA MAP DATA SOURCE

Williams, P. W., and D. C. Ford. 2006. Global distribution of carbonate rocks. *Zeitschrift für Geomorphologie*, Suppl. 147: 1–2.

TECHNICAL NOTES

We derived the percentage area of ecoregions that may contain karst from the global karst data set by Williams and Ford (2006). The global karst data set was an update of a previous version from Williams and Ford that was released in 2005 by Carbon, Hydrology, and Global Environmental Systems (CHANGES), a collaboration of the International Geoscience Programme (IGCP) and sponsored by the UN Educational, Scientific and Cultural Organization (UNESCO) and the International Union of Geological Sciences. We summarized the global karst polygons by calculating the percentage area of ecoregions covered by karst. Total karst area generally reflects the distribution of karst cave systems and thus serves as a proxy of potential cave habitats. This proxy is supported by knowledge that larger cave systems usually indicate higher biodiversity and that karst biodiversity is most abundant in midlatitude temperate regions, as displayed in the map.

REFERENCES

Graening, G. O., M. E. Slay, A. V. Brown, and J. B. Koppelman. 2006. Status and distribution of the endangered Benton Cave crayfish, *Cambarus aculabrum* (Decapoda: Cambaridae). *Southwestern Naturalist* 51, no. 3: 376–439.

Gulden, B. 2009. World's longest underwater caves. National Speleological Society Geo2 Committee, Huntsville, AL, USA. Available at www.caverbob.com/uwcave.htm.

International Union for Conservation of Nature (IUCN). 2008. The IUCN Red List of Threatened Species: Aigamas cave catfish profile. Available at www.iucnredlist.org/details/63363.

Proudlove, G. 2006. *Subterranean Fishes of the World: An Account of the Subterranean (Hypogean) Fishes Described Up to 2003 with a Bibliography 1541–2004.* Moulis, France: International Society for Subterranean Biology.

Quintana Roo Speleological Survey. 2009. List of long underwater caves in Quintana Roo, Mexico. Available at www.caves.org/project/qrss/qrlong.htm.

Williams, P. W., and D. C. Ford. 2006. Global distribution of carbonate rocks. *Zeitschrift für Geomorphologie*, Suppl. 147: 1–2.

Essay: McCormick

REFERENCE

Hoekstra, J. M., T. M. Boucher, T. H. Ricketts, and C. Roberts. 2005. Confronting a biome crisis: Global disparities of habitat loss and protection. *Ecology Letters* 8: 23–29.

Coasts and Shelves

KELP AND UPWELLING MAPS DATA SOURCE

The Nature Conservancy (TNC). 2007. Data on upwellings and kelp communities compiled from multiple sources. Unpublished, The Nature Conservancy, Arlington, Virginia, USA.

TECHNICAL NOTES

There were no global maps summarizing the distribution of upwellings or of kelp communities, so we developed estimates of abundance of kelp forests of the importance of large-scale continuous and predictable/seasonal upwellings. Originally we gathered this information at an ecoregional scale, but we decided to summarize to province due to concerns about fine-scale accuracy. Where information was not readily available, provinces were labeled "no data." Many of the oceanic islands were marked as having no data on upwellings; in fact, upwelling can be an important feature on the leeward side of oceanic islands, but data for specific islands were not readily available.

We used the following data sources:

Robinson, A. R., and K. H. Brink, eds. 1998. *The Global Coastal Ocean, Regional Studies and Syntheses.* New York: Wiley.

———, eds. 2006. *The Global Coastal Ocean: Interdisciplinary Regional Studies and Syntheses.* Cambridge, MA: Harvard University Press.

Sheppard, C., ed. 2000a. *Seas at the Millennium: An Environmental Evaluation, Volume 1: Regional Chapters: Europe, the Americas and West Africa.* Oxford: Elsevier Science.

———, ed. 2000b. *Seas at the Millennium: An Environmental Evaluation, Volume 2: Regional Chapters: The Indian Ocean to the Pacific.* Oxford: Elsevier Science.

————, ed. 2000c. *Seas at the Millennium: An Environmental Evaluation, Volume 3: Global Issues and Processes.* Oxford: Elsevier Science.

REFERENCES

Brumbaugh, R. D., and C. Toropova. 2008. Economic valuation of ecosystem services: A new impetus for shellfish restoration? *Basins and Coasts* 2: 8–15.

Food and Agriculture Organization of the United Nations (FAO). 2007. *The State of the World's Fisheries and Aquaculture 2006.* Rome: Author.

Levinton, J. 2001. *Marine Biology: Function, Biodiversity, Ecology.* New York: Oxford University Press.

Penven, P., V. Echevin, J. Pasapera, F. Colas, and J. Tam. 2005. Average circulation, seasonal cycle, and mesoscale dynamics of the Peru Current System: A modeling approach. *Journal of Geophysical Research* 110, C10021 (doi: 10.1029/2005JC002945).

Stow, D. 2004. *Encyclopedia of the Oceans.* Oxford: Oxford University Press.

Coral Reefs

CORAL AREA MAP DATA SOURCES

UNEP World Conservation Monitoring Centre (UNEP-WCMC). 2003. Global 1 km raster data on coral reef locations, v.7.0. Cambridge: Author. Digital media.

A published version of these data was produced in the following work:

Spalding M. D., C. Ravilious, and E. P. Green. 2001. *World Atlas of Coral Reefs.* Berkeley: University of California Press.

TECHNICAL NOTES

We extracted coral reefs from version 7.0 of the global one-kilometer raster data set compiled by the UNEP-WCMC update of 2003 (for more information about the source data set, e-mail spatialanalysis@unep-wcmc.org), which is almost entirely identical to the data published in the *World Atlas of Coral Reefs* (Spalding et al. 2001). They represent a combination of line and polygon information converted to a one-kilometer grid to smooth data originally drawn at different scales. We made minor modifications to the global map, by removing reef areas from West Africa and the Leeuwin and Southern California Bight ecoregions. The latter represents erroneous data, but other areas, while having some reef-building corals, lack true reef structures (original sources used by UNEP-WCMC were highly schematic sketches of possible locations for reef-building corals). A further modification we made was the addition of a nominal small reef area to the Marquesas ecoregion; limited areas of fringing reefs are found around these islands, but no maps were available when the global map was compiled (more information about corals in these modified regions can be found in Spalding et al. 2001).

CORAL SPECIES RICHNESS MAP DATA SOURCE

Veron, J. E. N. 2000. *Corals of the World.* Townsville: Australian Institute of Marine Science.

TECHNICAL NOTES

Stony coral range maps have been drawn by Veron (2000), who kindly made available to us range maps for 794 species. We laid these range maps over the ecoregions to derive a species total for each ecoregion. Note that these stony corals have a wider range than coral reefs. The large physical structures of coral reefs only develop where such corals survive in sufficient densities (and usually diversity) over the long time scales it takes for such structures to form.

REFERENCES

Spalding, M. D., C. Ravilious, and E. P. Green. 2001. *World Atlas of Coral Reefs.* Berkeley: University of California Press.

Veron, J. E. N. 1995. *Corals in Space and Time: The Biogeography and Evolution of the Scleractinia.* Sydney: University of New South Wales Press.

————. 2000. *Corals of the World.* Townsville: Australian Institute of Marine Science.

Wilkinson, C. 2008. *Status of Coral Reefs of the World: 2008.* Townsville, Australia: Global Coral Reef Monitoring Network and Reef and Rainforest Research Centre.

Mangrove Forests

MANGROVE AREA MAP DATA SOURCES

UNEP World Conservation Monitoring Centre (UNEP-WCMC). 1997. Data on mangrove extent, v.3.0. Cambridge: Author. Digital media.

A published version of these data was produced in the following work:

Spalding, M. D., F. Blasco, and C. D. Field. 1997. *World Mangrove Atlas.* Okinawa, Japan: International Society for Mangrove Ecosystems.

TECHNICAL NOTES

We extracted mangrove forest extents from version 3.0 of the global polygon data set compiled by UNEP-WCMC in collaboration with the International Society for Mangrove Ecosystems (ISME) 1997 (for more information about the source data set, e-mail spatialanalysis@unep-wcmc.org). These are almost entirely the same data that were published in the first *World Mangrove Atlas* (Spalding et al. 1997). We updated this information to include eleven island ecoregions for which no mapped data were available, but where mangroves occur with low mangrove coverage. Information on these was drawn from new work to be included in the publication of a new *World Mangrove Atlas* (Spalding et al. Forthcoming).

MANGROVE SPECIES RICHNESS MAP DATA SOURCE

Spalding, M. D., M. Kainuma, L. Collins. Forthcoming. *World Mangrove Atlas.* London: Earthscan, with International Society for Mangrove Ecosystems, Food and Agriculture Organization of the United Nations, UNEP-WCMC, The Nature Conservancy, United Nations Scientific and Cultural Organisation, United Nations University.

TECHNICAL NOTES

We derived mangrove species diversity information from new maps of the individual ranges for sixty-five mangrove species that will be published in Spalding et al. (forthcoming). These range maps were overlain on ecoregion maps and species totals calculated for each.

REFERENCES

Alongi, D. M. 2008. Mangrove forests: Resilience, protection from tsunamis, and responses to global climate change. *Estuarine, Coastal and Shelf Science* 76: 1–13.

Chan, H. T. 1996. Mangrove reforestation in peninsular Malaysia: A case study of Matang. Pages 64–75 in *Restoration of Mangrove Ecosystems,* ed. C. Field. Okinawa, Japan: International Society for Mangrove Ecosystems (ISME).

Danielsen, F., M. K. Sørensen, M. F. Olwig, V. Selvam, F. Parish, N. D. Burgess, T. Hiraishi, et al. 2005. The Asian tsunami: A protective role for coastal vegetation. *Science* 310: 643.

Duke, N. C., J. O. Meynecke, S. Dittmann, A. M. Ellison, K. Anger, U. Berger, S. Cannicci, et al. 2007. A world without mangroves? *Science* 317: 41–42.

Spalding, M. D., M. Kainuma, and L. Collins. Forthcoming. *World Mangrove Atlas.* London: Earthscan, with International Society for Mangrove Ecosystems, Food and Agriculture Organization of the United Nations, UNEP World Conservation Monitoring Centre, The Nature Conservancy, United Nations

Scientific and Cultural Organisation, United Nations University.

Seagrass Beds

SEAGRASS ABUNDANCE AND SPECIES RICHNESS MAPS DATA SOURCES

Green E. P., and F. T. Short. 2003. *World Atlas of Seagrasses*. Berkeley: University of California Press.

UNEP World Conservation Monitoring Centre (UNEP-WCMC). 2005. Data on extent and location of seagrass beds, v.2.0. Cambridge: Author. Digital media.

TECHNICAL NOTES

We extracted seagrasses from version 2.0 of the global polygon and point data set that was compiled by UNEP-WCMC in 2005 (for more information about the source data set, e-mail spatialanalysis@unep-wcmc.org). These same data were originally published in the *World Atlas of Seagrasses* (Green and Short 2003; see, in particular, the chapter by Spalding et al. 2003). The source data for the habitat map were a mix of point and polygon information gathered from a major literature review as well as from national-level mapping programs. The habitat distribution information was of varying consistency, with likely gaps in information-poor regions. It was not possible to generate accurate area estimates from such data. Instead, we used the data, combined with expert knowledge of patterns of abundance and paucity, to develop a semiquantitative estimate of abundance by province that gives a broadly accurate picture of habitat abundance. We developed the species diversity map from range maps drawn for fifty-five species. The four species from the genus *Ruppia* were not mapped because these are not always reported and are often found outside seagrass habitat.

REFERENCES

Spalding, M. D., M. L. Taylor, C. Ravilious, F. T. Short, and E. P. Green. 2003. Global overview: the distribution and status of seagrasses. Pages 5–26, 262–286 in *World Atlas of Seagrasses*, ed. E. P. Green and F. T. Short. Berkeley: University of California Press.

Salt Marshes

SALT MARSH AREA MAP DATA SOURCE

The Nature Conservancy (TNC) and UNEP World Conservation Monitoring Centre (UNEP-WCMC). 2007. Draft global database and GIS on salt marshes. Unpublished, TNC, Arlington, Virginia, USA; and UNEP-WCMC, Cambridge.

TECHNICAL NOTES

We compiled a global database on salt marshes in collaboration with UNEP-WCMC and with input from Paul Adam, University of New South Wales, Australia.

In this database, habitat abundance was estimated using the array of point locations and GIS data holdings from this database and were broadly based on abundance as a proportion of the total coastline length in each ecoregion. Salt marshes were poorly covered in the literature for some parts of the Arctic coastline and from wide areas of the tropics where salt marshes were often overlooked or classified within mangrove areas. While efforts were made to target data searching for these regions, there may still be some underestimation.

REFERENCES

Adam, P. 1990. *Saltmarsh Ecology*. Cambridge: Cambridge University Press.

———. 2002. Saltmarshes in a time of change. *Environmental Conservation* 29: 39–61.

Ramsar Sites Database. 2008. Ramsar site information available at www.wetlands.org/rsis/. Wageningen, The Netherlands: Wetlands International.

High Seas and Deep Oceans

COLD-WATER CORALS MAP DATA SOURCES

Freiwald, A., J. H. Fosså, A. Grehan, T. Koslow, and J. M. Roberts. 2004. *Cold-Water Coral Reefs*. Cambridge: UNEP-WCMC.

UNEP World Conservation Monitoring Centre (UNEP-WCMC). 2005. Global point data set on location of cold-water corals, v.2.0. Cambridge: Author. Digital media.

TECHNICAL NOTES

We extracted cold-water corals from version 7.0 of the global point data set compiled by UNEP-WCMC in 2005, sourced from A. Freiwald, Alex Rogers, Jason Hall-Spencer, and other contributors (for more information about the source data set, e-mail spatialanalysis@unep-wcmc.org). These are almost entirely the same data as were published in Freiwald et al. (2004) and show point locations of known cold-water coral communities. These source data were derived from field sampling, with undoubtedly a strong bias introduced by the sampling procedure. It is likely that many more such communities exist than were recorded here. Where locations occur in tropical waters, they are typically in deep waters, but they may be relatively close to shallow tropical coral reefs.

SEAMOUNTS AND VENTS MAP DATA SOURCES

Kitchingman, A., and S. Lai. 2004. Inferences on potential seamount locations from mid-resolution bathymetric data. Pages 7–12 in *Seamounts: Biodiversity and Fisheries*, ed. T. Morato and D. Pauly. Vancouver: Fisheries Centre, University of British Columbia.

Ramirez-Llodra, E., and M. C. Baker. 2006. Data on the location of hydrothermal vents. Biogeography of Chemosynthetic Ecosystems (ChEss) Project, www.noc.soton.ac.uk/chess.

TECHNICAL NOTES

Locations of seamounts are from Kitchingman and Lai (2004) and were developed from a global GIS-based analysis, which identifies a total of fourteen thousand seamounts. There is no strict definition of what constitutes a seamount, but this data set was conservative and excludes longer ridge-type formations or lower features. Some authors have suggested there may be a total of fifty thousand or more.

Locations of hydrothermal vents were generously provided by Eva Ramirez-Llodra and Maria C. Baker of the Biogeography of Chemosynthetic Ecosystems (ChEss) Project. The locations of many of these communities closely follow tectonic plate boundaries of spreading midocean ridges and back-arc basins. The points on the map represent only known locations; thousands more such communities are yet to be discovered.

OCEAN TRENCH MAP DATA SOURCE

National Geophysical Data Center (NGDC) and ESRI. 2004. *Global Digital Elevation Model (ETOPO2)*. Redlands, CA: Authors. Digital media.

TECHNICAL NOTES

We used a global bathymetric map (NGDC and ESRI 2004) to plot ocean areas with depths greater than 6,500 meters. Such depths are only found in isolated plate-margin trenches. This isolation has created high levels of endemism, with species restricted to single trenches only. Even at these great depths there is further stratification of communities by depth, and these trench communities are not populated by homogeneous faunas.

REFERENCES

Freiwald, A., J. H. Fosså, A. Grehan, T. Koslow, and J. M. Roberts. 2004. *Cold-Water Coral Reefs*. Cambridge: UNEP-WCMC.

Grassle, J. F., and N. J. Maciolek. 1992. Deep-sea species richness: Regional and local diversity estimates from quantitative bottom samples. *American Naturalist* 139: 313–341.

Halpern, B. S., S. Walbridge, K. A. Selkoe, C. V. Kappel, F. Micheli, C. D'Agrosa, J. F. Bruno, et al. 2008. A global map of human impact on marine ecosystems. *Science* 319: 948–952.

Tyler, P. A. 2003. *Ecosystems of the Deep Oceans.* Amsterdam: Elsevier.

Vinogradova, N. G. 1997. Zoogeography of the abyssal and hadal zones. *Advances in Marine Biology* 32: 325–387.

CHAPTER 3

Species Introduction

TREE OF LIFE FIGURE DATA SOURCE

Chapman, A. D. 2005. Numbers of living species in Australia and the world. Report for the Department of the Environment and Heritage, Canberra, Australia.

International Union for Conservation of Nature (IUCN), Conservation International, and NatureServe. 2006. Global Amphibian Assessment. www.iucnredlist.org/amphibians. Digital media.

TECHNICAL NOTES

The number of species in different taxonomic groups were from Chapman (2005) with data for amphibians from IUCN (2006). For well-studied vertebrate taxa (i.e., mammals, birds, and reptiles), we used the number of described species as reported by Chapman (2005). For other taxa, we used Chapman's estimated numbers. See Chapman (2005) for more details about how each estimate was derived as well as for primary sources. Not all taxa are reported in this tree. Consequently, numbers may not add up precisely to overall estimates for higher taxa.

REFERENCES

Chapman, A. D. 2005. Numbers of living species in Australia and the World. Report for the Department of the Environment and Heritage, Canberra, Australia.

Estes, J. A., and J. F. Palmisano. 1974. Sea otters: Their role in structuring nearshore communities. *Science* 185: 1058–1060.

Maddison, D. R., and K.-S. Schulz, eds. 2007. The Tree of Life Web project. http://tolweb.org.

Millennium Ecosystem Assessment. 2005. *Ecosystems and Human Well-being: Synthesis.* Washington, DC: Island.

Wilcove, D. S., D. Rothstein, J. Dubow, A. Phillips, and E. Losos. 1998. Quantifying threats to imperiled species in the United States. *BioScience* 48: 607–615.

Plants

PLANT SPECIES RICHNESS MAP DATA SOURCE

Kier, G., J. Mutke, E. Dinerstein, T. H. Ricketts, W. Ku, H. Kreft, and W. Barthlott. 2005. Global patterns of plant diversity and floristic knowledge. *Journal of Biogeography* 32: 1107–1116.

TECHNICAL NOTES

Kier et al. (2005) estimated the number of plant species in each terrestrial ecoregion.

CENTERS FOR PLANT DIVERSITY MAP DATA SOURCE

World Wide Fund for Nature (WWF) and International Union for Conservation of Nature (IUCN). 1994–1997. *Centres of Plant Diversity: A Guide and Strategy for Their Conservation.* 3 vols. Gland, Switzerland: Author.

REFERENCES

Archibold, O. W. 1995. *Ecology of World Vegetation.* London: Chapman & Hall.

Cowling, R., and M. J. Samways. 1994. Predicting global patterns of endemic plant species richness. *Biodiversity Letters* 2: 127–131.

Goldblatt, P., and J. C. Manning. 2002. Plant diversity of the Cape region of southern Africa. *Annals of the Missouri Botanical Garden* 89: 281–302.

Ramankutty, N., and J. A. Foley. 1999. Estimating historical changes in global land cover: Croplands from 1700 to 1992. *Global Biogeochemical Cycles* 13: 997–1028. Available at www.sage.wisc.edu.

Freshwater Fish

FISH SPECIES RICHNESS MAP DATA SOURCE

Abell, R., M. L. Thieme, C. Revenga, M. Bryer, M. Kottelat, N. Bogutskaya, B. Coad, et al.. 2008. Ecoregions of the world: A new map of biogeographic units for freshwater biodiversity conservation. *BioScience* 58, no. 5: 403–414.

TECHNICAL NOTES

The map of freshwater fish species richness—the number of species present in each ecoregion—was generated from a variety of sources by Abell et al. (2008). Only species using freshwater for at least a portion of their life cycles, as identified using the habitat assignments in FishBase, are included. For the United States, NatureServe provided presence/absence data for individual species, coded to eight-digit hydrologic unit codes (HUCs); these HUC occurrences were then translated into ecoregions, and the data

were manually cleaned of erroneous occurrences derived from species introductions and problematic records. For all other ecoregions, species lists were provided by experts based on published literature as well as from gray literature and unpublished sources. Abell et al. (2008) generated data on fish species for some small islands using FishBase and then augmented where possible with information from published literature. For a small number of ecoregions, it was impossible to generate species lists; therefore, richness estimates are provided instead. Extirpated species are included in these tallies, but confirmed extinct species, as determined by the Committee on Recently Extinct Organisms (data provided by Ian Harrison), and introduced and undescribed species are excluded.

MIGRATORY FISH MAP DATA SOURCE

The Nature Conservancy (TNC). 2009. Data on migratory fish compiled from multiple sources. Unpublished, The Nature Conservancy, Arlington, Virginia, USA.

TECHNICAL NOTES

We derived the map of long-distance migrant (LDM) fish—the number of LDM species per ecoregion—from published literature, online databases (NatureServe), and expert inquiries. Potadromous, anadromous, amphidromous, and catadromous fish species were judged to be LDMs if they made regular journeys (i.e., for breeding, dispersal, feeding) of at least a hundred kilometers or more in freshwater. These species were then assigned to ecoregions based on the fish species lists database from Abell et al. (2008). Although we used many resources, two key data sources for the map were the following:

Carolsfeld, J., B. Harvey, C. Ross, and A. Baer, eds. 2003. *Migratory Fishes of South America: Biology, Fisheries and Conservation Status.* Washington, DC: International Bank for Reconstruction and Development and the World Bank.

Lucas, M. C., and E. Baras. 2001. *Migration of Freshwater Fishes.* London: Blackwell Science.

REFERENCES

Abell, R., M. L. Thieme, C. Revenga, M. Bryer, M. Kottelat, N. Bogutskaya, B. Coad, et al. 2008. Ecoregions of the world: A new map of biogeographic units for freshwater biodiversity conservation. *BioScience* 58, no. 5: 403–414.

Bain, M. B., N. Haley, D. L. Peterson, K. K. Arend, K. E. Mills, and P. J. Sullivan. 2007. Recovery of a US endangered fish. *PLoS*

ONE 2, no. 1: e168 (doi:10.1371/journal. pone.0000168).

Food and Agriculture Organization of the United Nations. 2007. *State of the World Fisheries and Aquaculture 2006.* Rome: Fisheries and Aquaculture Department, FAO.

Knapp, A., C. Kitschke, and S. von Meibom, eds. 2006. *Proceedings of the International Sturgeon Enforcement Workshop to Combat Illegal Trade in Caviar.* Workshop 27–29 June 2006, Brussels, Belgium. Prepared by TRAFFIC Europe for the European Commission, Brussels.

Pikitch, E. K., P. Doukakis, L. Lauck, P. Chakrabarty, and D. L. Erickson. 2005. Status, trends and management of sturgeon and paddlefish. *Fish and Fisheries* 6: 233–265.

Stone, R. 2002. Caspian ecology teeters on the brink. *Science* 295: 430–433.

Amphibians

AMPHIBIAN SPECIES RICHNESS MAP DATA SOURCE

International Union for Conservation of Nature (IUCN), Conservation International, and NatureServe. 2006. Global Amphibian Assessment. www.iucnredlist.org/amphibians. Digital media.

TECHNICAL NOTES

We calculated the number of amphibian species per freshwater ecoregion using species range maps of the Global Amphibian Assessment (GAA, www.iucnredlist.org/amphibians) (IUCN et al. 2006). The 2006 GAA assessed 5,918 amphibian species and provided distribution maps for 5,640 of those species. When a range overlapped several ecoregions, we counted species as present in all those ecoregions that had part of the range. This may have resulted in an overestimate of species numbers in some ecoregions, especially those that are long and narrow in shape. This is particularly true for the Amazonas High Andes ecoregion (312), where the mountain range has been used as a range boundary for hundreds of species. Distribution maps from the GAA represent the "extent of occurrence" for each species—that is, the area contained within the shortest continuous imaginary boundary, which can be drawn to encompass all the known, inferred, or projected sites of present occurrence of a taxon. Because of the conservative approach taken in the GAA to mapping species, the ranges for many species are likely to be minimum estimates. The GAA followed a rule of allowing interpolation of occur-

rence between known locations if the ecological conditions seem appropriate, but not permitting extrapolation beyond known locations. Some species are therefore almost certain to occur much more widely than the GAA has mapped. Because of this, some regions were recorded as having much lower numbers. Finally, the percentage of data-deficient species (23.4 percent) were very high compared to other taxa in the GAA.

AMPHIBIAN THREAT MAP DATA SOURCE

Stuart, S. N., J. S. Chanson, N. A. Cox, B. E. Young, A. S. L. Rodrigues, D. L. Fischman, and R. W. Waller. 2004. Status and trends of amphibian declines and extinctions worldwide. *Science* 306: 1783–1786. Reprinted with permission from AAAS.

TECHNICAL NOTES

The map is figure 1 of Stuart et al. (2004): "Geographical pattern of the dominant causes of rapid decline in amphibian species: overexploited (shades of blue); reduced-habitat (shades of green); and enigmatic-decline (shades of red). Where two threat types overlap in the same 1-cell, the color referring to the threat type with the larger number of rapidly declining species in that cell is indicated on the map. Intermediate colors are shown in cases of equal numbers of species experiencing two types of decline in the same cell, as shown in the key. Darker colors correspond to larger numbers of rapidly declining species of any type (not just of the dominant type in the cell in question)."

REFERENCES

AmphibiaWeb. 2009. Information on amphibian biology and conservation [Web application]. AmphibiaWeb, Berkeley, CA. Available at http://amphibiaweb.org.

International Union for Conservation of Nature (IUCN), Conservation International, and NatureServe. 2008. Global Amphibian Assessment: Summary of key findings and habitat preferences [Web application]. Gland, Switzerland: IUCN. Available at www .iucnredlist.org/amphibians.

National Science Foundation. 2008. Frog vs. trout. In *Ecology of Infectious Diseases: A Special Report* [Web application]. Arlington, Virginia: Author. Available at www.nsf.gov/ news/special_reports/ecoinf/vs.jsp.

Pounds, J. A., M. R. Bustamante, L. A. Coloma, J. A. Consuegra, M. P. L. Fogden, P. N. Foster, E. La Marca, et al. 2006. Widespread amphibian extinctions from epidemic disease driven by global warming. *Nature* 439: 161–167.

Reptiles

TERRESTRIAL REPTILE SPECIES RICHNESS MAP DATA SOURCE

World Wildlife Fund (WWF). 2006. WildFinder: Database of species distributions, ver. Jan-06. Available at www.gis.wwf .org/WildFinder. Digital media.

TECHNICAL NOTES

We compiled data on terrestrial lizards and snakes by querying the WWF WildFinder database for species occurrences by ecoregion of the following taxonomic groups: Sauria, Serpentes, Amphisbaenia, and Rhynchocephalia. The WWF WildFinder database is a spatially explicit online database of vertebrate species occurrences by ecoregion.

FRESHWATER REPTILE RICHNESS MAP DATA SOURCE

The Nature Conservancy (TNC) and World Wildlife Fund (WWF). 2009. Data on freshwater reptiles compiled from multiple sources. Unpublished, The Nature Conservancy, Arlington, Virginia, USA.

TECHNICAL NOTES

We generated the map of freshwater turtle and crocodilian species richness—the number of species present in each ecoregion—from species distribution maps, primarily drawing on the sources listed below.

Distribution maps for 260 freshwater turtle species were provided by Buhlmann et al. (2007). The original distribution maps represented coarse ranges of where species were thought to be present in the wild; however, they were not exact ranges. Buhlmann et al. compiled data from museum and literature records. They correlated verified locality points with GIS-defined hydrologic unit codes (HUCs) and subsequently created "projected" distribution maps for each species by selecting additional HUCs that were representative of similar habitats, elevations, and physiographic regions as the HUCs with the verified point localities. The amount of information available varied by species, as some species and regions are better studied than others. In addition, many species names, especially in the tropics, actually represent complexes of several turtle species that have not yet been disaggregated.

In developing our map, when a range overlapped several ecoregions, we counted species as present in all those ecoregions that had part of the range. Some ecoregions with a long and narrow shape may have an overestimation of species in our map given the way the range polygons were drawn. This is particularly true in the Amazonas High Andes ecoregion (312), where the mountain range has been used as a range boundary for hundreds of species.

For crocodilians, species range maps are from the IUCN-SSC Crocodile Specialist Group and Britton (2007). Species range maps were assessed visually, and species presence was assigned to ecoregions. When a range overlapped several ecoregions, we counted the species as present in all ecoregions of range overlap.

The following were our primary data sources:

Britton, A. 2007. Information on crocodilian species distributions. Available at www.flmnh .ufl.edu/cnhc/csl.html.

Buhlmann, K. A., T. B. Akre, J. B. Iverson, D. Karapatakis, R. A. Mittermeier, A. Georges, G. J. Rhodin, P. P. van Dijk, and J. W. Gibbons. 2007. A global analysis of tortoise and freshwater turtle distributions. Data from the preliminary results of the Global Reptile Assessment. International Union for Conservation of Nature–Species Survival Commission (IUCN-SSC), Conservation International/Center for Applied Biological Science (CI/CABS), and Savannah River Ecology Laboratory, University of Georgia, Aiken, South Carolina, USA.

International Union for Conservation of Nature (IUCN)–SSC Crocodile Specialist Group Web site. 2008. Available at http://iucncsg .org/ph1/modules/Home/.

REFERENCES

Autumn, K. 2006. How gecko toes stick. *American Scientist* 94: 124–132.

Baille, J. E. M., C. Hilton-Taylor, and S. N. Stuart, eds. 2004. *2004 Red List of Threatened Species: A Global Species Assessment.* Gland, Switzerland: IUCN.

Jørgensen, C. B. 1998. Role of urinary and cloacal bladders in chelonian water economy: historical and comparative perspectives. *Biological Reviews of the Cambridge Philosophical Society* 73: 347–366.

Leslie, A. J., and J. R. Spotila. Alien plant threatens Nile crocodile *(Crocodylus niloticus)* breeding in Lake St. Lucia, South Africa. *Biological Conservation* 98, no. 3: 347–355.

Nagy, K. A. 2002–2003. Dry, dry again. *Natural History* 111, no. 10: 50–55. Available at www.naturalhistorymag.com/1202/1202_ feature2.html.

Smithsonian National Zoological Park. 2009. Komodo dragon fact sheet. Available at http://nationalzoo.si.edu/Animals/ ReptilesAmphibians/Facts/FactSheets/ Komododragon.cfm.

Uetz, P., et al. The Reptile Database. Available at www.reptile-database.org.

Essay: Wikelski and Wilcove

REFERENCES

Alerstam, T., M. Hake, and N. Kjellén. 2006. Temporal and spatial patterns of repeated migratory journeys by ospreys. *Animal Behaviour* 71: 555–566.

Hoover, J. P. 2003. Decision rules for site fidelity in a migratory bird, the prothonotary warbler. *Ecology* 84: 416–430.

Wilcove, D. 2008. *No Way Home: The Decline of the World's Great Animal Migrations.* Washington, DC: Island Press.

Birds

TERRESTRIAL BIRD SPECIES RICHNESS MAP DATA SOURCE

World Wildlife Fund (WWF). 2006. WildFinder: Database of species distributions, ver. Jan-06. Available at www.gis.wwf.org/ WildFinder. Digital media.

TECHNICAL NOTES

We compiled data on terrestrial birds by querying the WWF WildFinder database for species occurrences by ecoregion. The WWF WildFinder database is a spatially explicit online database of vertebrate species occurrences by ecoregion.

FRESHWATER BIRD SPECIES RICHNESS MAP DATA SOURCE

The Nature Conservancy (TNC). 2009. Data on freshwater birds by freshwater ecoregion. Unpublished data compiled from multiple sources, The Nature Conservancy, Arlington, Virginia, USA.

TECHNICAL NOTES

Freshwater obligate birds include those species that need freshwater habitats for breeding (e.g., ducks, herons) or feeding (i.e., birds that depend almost exclusively on food found in freshwater habitats, such as freshwater fish, mollusks, and crustaceans). In all, 815 bird species were found to meet this criterion, with almost all bird families represented. We mapped freshwater bird species to freshwater ecoregions with the following procedures: for North and South America, NatureServe GIS data were summarized by freshwater ecoregion; for Africa, distribution maps presented in *Birds of Africa* (Brown et al. 1982–1997) were used to assign species

to freshwater ecoregion by hand; for Asia and Australia, data were summarized using a grid system of bird species derived from the terrestrial ecoregion WildFinder data set. Literature sources used to determine whether a species was considered a freshwater bird included the following:

Beehler, B., T. K. Pratt, and D. A. Zimmerman. 1986. *Birds of New Guinea.* Princeton, NJ: Princeton University Press.

Brown, L., E. Urban, and K. Newman. 1982. *The Birds of Africa, Volume 1: Ostriches and Birds of Prey.* London: Academic Press.

Byers, C., and U. Olsson. 1995. *Sparrows and Buntings.* Boston: Houghton Mifflin.

Clement, J. 2000. *Thrushes.* Princeton, NJ: Princeton University Press.

Curson, J. 1994. *New World Warblers.* London: Christopher Helm.

Del Hoyo, J., A. Elliott, and D. A. Christie. 2000. *Handbook of Birds of the World: Vols. 1 –13.* Barcelona: Lynx.

Feare, C., A. Craig, C. Shields, and K. Komolphalin. 1999. *Starlings and Mynas.* London: Christopher Helm.

Fry, C. H., and S. Keith. 2000. *The Birds of Africa, Volume 6: Picathartes to Oxpeckers.* London: Academic Press.

Fry, C. H., S. Keith, and E. Urban. 1988. *The Birds of Africa, Volume 3: Parrots to Woodpeckers.* London: Academic Press.

Fry, C. H., S. Keith, E. Urban, and M. Woodcock. 2004. *The Birds of Africa, Volume 7: Sparrows to Buntings.* London: Christopher Helm.

Harris, T., and K. Franklin. 2000. *Shrikes and Bush-shrikes.* London: Christopher Helm.

Jaramillo, A., and P. Burke. 1999. *New World Blackbirds.* Princeton, NJ: Princeton University Press.

Keith, S., E. K. Urban, and C. H. Fry. 1992. *The Birds of Africa, Volume 4: Broadbills to Chats.* London: Academic Press.

MacKinnon, J., and K. Phillipps. 1993. *Birds of Borneo, Java, Sumatra and Bali.* Oxford: Oxford University Press.

———. 2000. *Birds of China.* Oxford: Oxford University Press.

Mullarney, K., L. Svensson, D. Zetterstrom, and P. J. Grant. 1990. *Birds of Europe.* Princeton, NJ: Princeton University Press.

Ridgely, R. S., T. F. Allnutt, T. Brooks, D. K. McNicol, D. W. Mehlman, B. E. Young, and J. R. Zook. 2007. *Digital Distribution Maps of the Birds of the Western Hemisphere.* Version 3.0. Arlington, Virginia: NatureServe.

Ridgely, R., and G. Tudor. 1989. *Birds of South America, Volume 1*. Austin: University of Texas Press.

———. 1994. *Birds of South America, Volume 2*. Austin: University of Texas Press.

Robson, C. 2000. *Birds of South-east Asia*. Princeton, NJ: Princeton University Press.

Simpson, N. J., and N. Day, 2004. *Birds of Australia*. Princeton, NJ: Princeton University Press.

Urban, E. K., C. H. Fry, and S. Keith. 1986. *The Birds of Africa, Volume 2: Game Birds to Pigeons*. London: Academic Press.

———. 1997. *The Birds of Africa, Volume 5: Thrushes to Puffback Flycatchers*. London: Academic Press.

SEABIRD SPECIES RICHNESS MAP DATA SOURCE

Harrison, P. 1983. *Seabirds: An Identification Guide*. London: Christopher Helm.

TECHNICAL NOTES

Using the distribution maps for seabirds from Harrison (1983), we visually mapped each of the 312 seabirds to one or more marine ecoregions. Only breeding ranges (including breeding sites) were used; migration routes and casual or vagrant records were excluded.

REFERENCES

Baillie, J. E. M., C. Hilton-Taylor, and S. N. Stuart, eds. 2004. *2004 IUCN Red List of Threatened Species: A Global Species Assessment*. Gland, Switzerland: IUCN. Available at www.iucnredlist.org.

Çagan H. S., G. C. Daily, and P. R. Ehrlich. 2004. Ecosystem consequences of bird declines. *PNAS* 101: 18042–18047.

Cavitt, J. F., and C. A. Haas. 2000. Brown thrasher *(Toxostoma rufum)*. Number 557 in *The Birds of North America*, ed. A. Poole and F. Gill. Philadelphia: Birds of North America.

Gill, R. E., Jr., T. Piersma, G. Hufford, R. Servranckx, and A. Riegen. 2005. Crossing the ultimate ecological barrier: Evidence for an 11,000-km-long nonstop flight from Alaska to New Zealand and eastern Australia by bar-tailed godwits. *Condor* 107: 1–20.

Sekercioglu, C. 2006. Increasing awareness of avian ecological function. *Trends in Ecology & Evolution* 21: 464–471.

U.S. Fish and Wildlife Service. 2006. *2006 National Survey of Fishing, Hunting, and Wildlife–Associated Recreation*. Washington, DC: U.S. Fish and Wildlife Service. Available at www.2010census.biz/prod/2008pubs/fhw06-nat.pdf.

———. 2008. Bald eagle recovery plan. Available at www.fws.gov/Midwest/eagle/recovery/recovery.html.

Van Bael, S. A., J. D. Brawn, and S. K. Robinson. 2003. Birds defend trees from herbivores in a Neotropical forest canopy. *Proceedings of the National Academy of Sciences* 100: 8304–8307.

Mammals

TERRESTRIAL MAMMAL SPECIES RICHNESS MAP DATA SOURCE

World Wildlife Fund (WWF). 2006. WildFinder: Database of species distributions, ver. Jan-06. Available at www.gis.wwf.org/WildFinder. Digital media.

TECHNICAL NOTES

We compiled data on terrestrial mammals by querying the WWF WildFinder database for species occurrences by ecoregion. The WWF WildFinder database is a spatially explicit online database of vertebrate species occurrences by ecoregion.

MARINE MAMMAL SPECIES RICHNESS MAP DATA SOURCE

Jefferson, T. A., S. Leatherwood, and M. A. Webber. 1993. *Marine Mammals of the World*. Nairobi: United Nations Environment Programme; Rome: Food and Agriculture Organization of the United Nations.

UNEP World Conservation Monitoring Centre (UNEP-WCMC). 2008. Data on marine mammal ranges, v.1.0. Cambridge: Author. Digital media.

TECHNICAL NOTES

We extracted marine mammals from version 1.0 of the global polygon data set compiled by UNEP-WCMC from the publication *Marine Mammals of the World* (Jefferson et al. 1993) (for more information about the UNEP-WCMC source data set, e-mail spatialanalysis@unep-wcmc.org). There were 118 species in the data set (including cetaceans, sirenians, pinnipeds, and other marine carnivores). These included coastal and high seas species, although the latter may only occasionally venture onto continental shelf areas. It is likely that total diversity is underestimated for the Southern Ocean Realm, particularly the sub-Antarctic islands, because certain species in this realm did not have full polygon range maps. We used the range maps to calculate the number of species per marine ecoregion.

FRESHWATER MAMMAL SPECIES RICHNESS MAP DATA SOURCE

The Nature Conservancy (TNC). 2009. Data on freshwater mammals by freshwater ecoregion. Unpublished data compiled from multiple sources. The Nature Conservancy, Arlington, Virginia, USA.

TECHNICAL NOTES

Freshwater mammals include aquatic or semi-aquatic species that spend a considerable amount of time in freshwater to feed and that usually live in the riparian vegetation close to rivers, lakes, marshes, swamps, and other freshwater habitats. We used species range maps, visual assessment of locations based on literature descriptions, and expert opinion to assign mammal species presence to ecoregions. Literature sources used to determine whether a species is considered a freshwater mammal include the following:

Kingdon, J. 1997. *The Kingdon Field Guide to African Mammals*. London: Academic Press.

Nowak, R. M. 1999. *Walker's Mammals of the World, Vols. 1 and 2*. 6th ed. Baltimore: Johns Hopkins University Press.

Revenga, C., and Y. Kura. 2003. *Status and Trends of Inland Water Biodiversity*. CBD Technical Papers Series No. 11. Montreal: Secretariat of the Convention on Biological Diversity.

Wilson, D. E., and D. M. Reeder, eds. 2005. *Mammal Species of the World*. 3rd ed. Baltimore: Johns Hopkins University Press.

The following experts were also consulted: Paul Racey, cochair, International Union for Conservation of Nature–Species Survival Commission (IUCN-SSC) Chiroptera Specialist Group, was consulted to identify freshwater bats; Jim Conroy, chair, IUCN-SSC Otter Specialist Group, was consulted on taxonomic issues regarding otters; and Giovanni Amori, chair, IUCN-SSC Rodent Specialist Group, was consulted regarding freshwater rodents.

Rodents make up at least 50 percent of all mammal species, and this percentage is probably underestimated given that every year more than thirty to forty new rodent species are recognized. In general, rodents are a poorly studied group; therefore, the number of species considered "freshwater rodents" in this data set is underestimated, and the species numbers are likely to be much higher.

Range species maps and distribution information for individual species were obtained from multiple sources, including the following:

African Mammal Databank (www.gisbau
.uniroma1.it/amd.php).

InfoNatura (www.natureserve.org/
infonatura/).

International Union for Conservation of
Nature (IUCN), 2007 European Mammal
Assessment (http://ec.europa.eu/environment/
nature/conservation/species/ema/).

North American Mammals, National Museum
of Natural History, Smithsonian Institution
(www.mnh.si.edu/mna/).

The 2007 IUCN Red List of Threatened Species
(www.redlist.org).

Reeves, R. R., B. D. Smith, E. A. Crespo, and
G. Notarbartolo di Sciara, comps. 2003.
*Dolphins, Whales and Porpoises: 2002–2010
Conservation Action Plan for the World's
Cetaceans.* IUCN-SSC Cetacean Specialist
Group. Gland, Switzerland: IUCN (www
.iucn.org/dbtw-wpd/edocs/2003-009.pdf).

Stone, R. 1995. *Eurasian Insectivores and Tree
Shrews: Status Survey and Conservation Action
Plan.* IUCN-SSC Insectivore, Tree Shrew,
and Elephant Shrew Specialist Group. Gland,
Switzerland: IUCN.

IUCN–Species Survival Commission (SSC)
Otter Specialist Group (www.otterspecialist-
group.org).

IUCN-SSC Cat Specialist Group (www
.catsg.org/catsgportal/20_catsg-website/home/
index_en.htm).

Veron, G., et al. 2006. A reassessment of the
distribution and taxonomy of the endangered
otter civet *Cynogale bennettii* (Carnivora,
Viverridae) of South-east Asia. *Oryx* (doi:
10.1017/S0030605306000068).

Bats of China (www.bio.bris.ac.uk/research/
bats/China percent20bats/index.htm#).

Australian Platypus Conservancy (www
.platypus.asn.au).

Department of the Environment, Water, Heritage,
and the Arts. 2008. *Xeromys myoides* in Species
Profile and Threats Database, Department of
the Environment, Water, Heritage and the Arts,
Canberra (www.environment.gov.au/sprat).

Riverine Rabbit Conservation Project (www
.riverinerabbit.co.za).

Also used was personal communication
from Fernando Rosas, INPA, Laboratorio
de Mamíferos Aquáticos, Manaus, Brazil;
and Paulo Petry, TNC South America
Conservation Region.

REFERENCES

Bulte E., R. Damania, and G. Kooten 2007.
The effects of one-off ivory sales on elephant
mortality. *Journal of Wildlife Management* 71,
no. 2: 613–618.

Dublin H. T., T. Milliken, and R. F. W. Barnes.
1995. *Four Years after the CITES Ban: Illegal
Killing of Elephants, Ivory Trade and Stockpiles.
Report of the IUCN-SSC African Elephant
Specialist Group.* Gland, Switzerland: World
Conservation Union.

Ivory Trade Review Group (ITRG). 1989. *The
ivory trade and the future of the African elephant: Interim report. Mimeograph.* Gaborone,
Botswana: Author.

Kielan-Jaworowska, Z., R. Cifelli, and L.
Zhe-Xi. 2004. *Mammals from the Age of
Dinosaurs: Origins, Evolution, and Structure.*
New York: Columbia University Press.

Smithsonian Institution. 2008. Web site, photographs of the new Kenneth E. Behring Family
Hall of Mammals, "Morgie." Available at
www.mnh.si.edu/mammals/mammalpictures/
morgie.htm.

Wilson, D. E., and D. M. Reeder, eds. 2005.
Mammal Species of the World. 3rd ed.
Baltimore: Johns Hopkins University Press.

Endemic Species

TERRESTRIAL ENDEMIC SPECIES RICHNESS MAP DATA SOURCE

World Wildlife Fund (WWF). 2006.
WildFinder: Database of species distributions,
ver. Jan-06. Available at www.gis.wwf.org/
WildFinder. Digital media.

TECHNICAL NOTES

The number of terrestrial endemic species refers
to the number of endemic mammals, birds, and
reptiles in each terrestrial ecoregion. We compiled data on these endemic species by querying
the WWF WildFinder database for their occurrences by ecoregion. The WWF WildFinder
database is a spatially explicit online database of
vertebrate species occurrences by ecoregion.

FRESHWATER ENDEMIC SPECIES RICHNESS MAP DATA SOURCE

The Nature Conservancy (TNC) 2009. Data
on freshwater endemic species by ecoregion.
Unpublished data compiled from multiple
sources. The Nature Conservancy, Arlington,
Virginia, USA.

TECHNICAL NOTES

The map of the number of freshwater endemic
species shows the number of endemic fish,
freshwater turtles, crocodiles, and amphibians
found in each freshwater ecoregion. To calculate
the total number of endemic species by ecoregion, we simply added the number of endemic

species in these four taxonomic groups. Fish en-
demics are from Abell et al. (2008). Extirpated
fish species are included in these tallies, but
resolved extinct species, as determined by the
Committee on Recently Extinct Organisms,
and introduced species are excluded. Data on
amphibian species were generated from distribution maps for 5,640 amphibian species gathered
by the Global Amphibian Assessment (IUCN et
al. 2006). Data on freshwater turtles were generated from species distribution maps provided
by Dr. Kurt A. Buhlmann, the Savannah River
Ecology Laboratory, University of Georgia,
United States; and the International Union
for Conservation of Nature–Species Survival
Commission (IUCN-SSC) and Conservation
International/Center for Applied Biodiversity
Science (CI/CABS) Global Reptile Assessment
(preliminary results).

For both amphibians and turtles, species
distribution maps were used to determine endemism by ecoregion. If at least 90 percent of a
species' range occurred in only one ecoregion,
that species was said to be endemic. Some ecoregions with a long and narrow shape may have
an overestimation of species given the way the
range polygons were drawn. This is particularly
true for the Amazonas High Andes ecoregion
(312), where the mountain range has been used
as a range boundary for hundreds of species.
The two ecoregional endemic crocodiles were
the Cuban crocodile (*Crocodylus rhombifer*) in the
Cuba–Cayman Islands ecoregion (211), and the
Chinese alligator (*Alligator sinensis*) in the Lower
Yangtze ecoregion (766). These were added to the
total tally for the respective ecoregions.

Our primary data sources for the maps were
the following:

Abell, R., M. L. Thieme, C. Revenga, M. Bryer,
M. Kottelat, N. Bogutskaya, B. Coad, et al.
2008. Freshwater ecoregions of the world: A
new map of biogeographic units for freshwater biodiversity conservation. *BioScience* 58,
no. 5: 403–414.

Buhlmann, K. A., T. B. Akre, J. B. Iverson, D.
Karapatakis, R. A. Mittermeier, A. Georges,
A. G. J. Rhodin, P. P. van Dijk, and J. W.
Gibbons. 2007. A global analysis of tortoise
and freshwater turtle distributions. Data
from the preliminary results of the Global
Reptile Assessment. International Union for
Conservation of Nature–Species Survival
Commission (IUCN-SSC), Conservation
International/Center for Applied Biodiversity
Science (CI/CABS), and Savannah River

Ecology Laboratory, University of Georgia, Athens, Georgia, USA.

International Union for Conservation of Nature (IUCN), Conservation International, and NatureServe. 2006. Global Amphibian Assessment. Available at www.iucnredlist.org/ amphibians. Digital media.

REFERENCES

Abell, R., M. L. Thieme, C. Revenga, M. Bryer, M. Kottelat, N. Bogutskaya, B. Coad, et al. 2008. Freshwater ecoregions of the world: A new map of biogeographic units for freshwater biodiversity conservation. *BioScience* 58, no. 5: 403–414.

Alliance for Zero Extinction (AZE). 2007. AZE Site and Species Database, GIS data. Available at www.zeroextinction.org.

Darwall, W. 2008. Cichlid species information. Unpublished data, Freshwater Biodiversity Unit, IUCN, Cambridge.

Durrell Wildlife Conservation Trust. 2008. Mauritius Kestrel Web page. Available at www.durrell.org/Animals/Birds/ Mauritius-Kestrel/.

International Union for Conservation of Nature (IUCN). 2008. 2008 IUCN Red List of Threatened Species. Available at www .iucnredlist.org.

Shapiro, B., D. Sibthorpe, A. Rambaut, J. Austin, G. M. Wragg, O. R. P. Bininda-Emonds, P. L. M. Lee, and A. Cooper. 2002. Flight of the dodo. *Science* 295, no. 5560: 1683.

The Peregrine Fund. 2003. Mauritius Kestrel Conservation Project. Available at www .peregrinefund.org/conserve_category.asp ?category=Mauritius%20Kestrel.

Evolutionary Distinction

PHYLOGENETIC DIVERSITY MAP DATA SOURCE

The Nature Conservancy (TNC). 2006. Unpublished data on phylogenetic diversity by terrestrial ecoregion. The Nature Conservancy, Arlington, Virginia, USA.

TECHNICAL NOTES

We calculated the phylogenetic diversity of vertebrate species by terrestrial ecoregion using Faith's (1992) statistical model of $PD = \Sigma D_{ij}$, where PD is a phylogenetic diversity score, and ΣD_{ij} is the sum of the pairwise distances for the minimum spanning distance among a selected set of species (i.e., the species occurring in an ecoregion) on a taxic cladogram of all vertebrate species worldwide, using WWF's WildFinder database.

We used the following data sources:

Faith, D. P. 1992. Conservation evaluation and phylogenetic diversity. *Biological Conservation* 61: 1–10.

World Wildlife Fund. 2006. WildFinder: Database of species distributions, ver. Jan-06. Available at gis.wwf.org/WildFinder. Digital media.

TREE OF LIFE FIGURE DATA SOURCE

World Wildlife Fund. 2006. WildFinder: Database of species distributions, ver. Jan-06. Available at www.gis.wwf.org/WildFinder. Digital media.

TECHNICAL NOTES

We drew the cladogram using the taxonomic information (class, order, family, genus, species) included in the WildFinder database (2006) for the Angolan Scarp ecoregion in Africa.

REFERENCES

International Union for Conservation of Nature (IUCN). 2008. IUCN Red List of Threatened Species. Available at www.redlist.org.

World Wildlife Fund. 2006. WildFinder: Database of species distributions, ver. Jan-06. Available at www.gis.wwf.org/WildFinder.

Zoological Society of London (ZSL). 2008. EDGE (Evolutionarily distinct and globally endangered) of Existence Web site. Available at www.edgeofexistence.org.

Essay: Mock

REFERENCES

Hayes, T., and E. Ostrom. 2005. Conserving the world's forests: Are protected areas the only way? *Indiana Law Review* 38: 595–617.

Lopez-Feldman, A., J. Mora, and J. E. Taylor. 2006. Does natural resource extraction mitigate poverty and inequality? Evidence from rural Mexico. Paper presented at the International Association of Agricultural Economists Conference, Gold Coast, Australia, August 12–18, 2006. Available at http://ageconsearch .umn.edu/bitstream/25765/1/cp060070.pdf.

Vedeld, P., A. Angelsen, E. Sjaastad, and G. K. Berg. 2004. *Counting on the Environment: Forest Incomes and the Rural Poor.* Washington, DC: World Bank.

World Resources Institute (WRI) in collaboration with United Nations Development Programme, United Nations Environment Programme, and World Bank. 2005. *World Resources 2005: The Wealth of the Poor—Managing Ecosystems to Fight Poverty.* Washington, DC: WRI.

World Resources Institute (WRI) in collaboration with United Nations Development Programme, United Nations Environment Programme, and World Bank. 2008. *World Resources 2008: Roots of Resilience—Growing the Wealth of the Poor.* Washington, DC: WRI.

CHAPTER 4

A World of Change Introduction

HUMAN IMPACT MAP DATA SOURCES

Halpern, B. S., S. Walbridge, K. A. Selkoa, C. V. Kappel, F. Micheli, C. D'Agrosa, J. F. Bruno, et al. 2008. A global map of human impact on marine ecosystems. *Science* 319: 948–952.

Sanderson, E. W., M. Jaiteh, M. A. Levy, K. H. Redford, A. V. Wannebo, and G. Woolmer. 2002. The human footprint and the last of the wild. *BioScience* 52: 891–904.

TECHNICAL NOTES

The human footprint on land combines maps and data about human population density, cities and settlements, agriculture, and roads and other transportation networks to depict the imprint of human activity across the globe. This map was developed by Eric Sanderson and colleagues from the Wildlife Conservation Society and Columbia University's Earth Institute (Sanderson et al. 2002).

The human impact analysis in the oceans combined maps and data about fishing, pollution, climate change, and invasive species and considers their differential impact on multiple marine ecosystems, leading to a summary map of the distribution and magnitude of anthropogenic threats in the oceans. This map was developed by Ben Halpern from the University of California, Santa Barbara, and colleagues from ten other universities, conservation organizations, and government agencies (Halpern et al. 2008).

We combined these two separate analyses into the single composite map shown. While not direct measures of impacts, these analyses are a good predictor of where people and our activities are changing the planet.

REFERENCES

Food and Agriculture Organization of the United Nations (FAO). 2008. Forestry Database. Available at www.fao.org/forestry/ databases/en.

Food and Agriculture Organization of the United Nations (FAO), Fisheries and Aquaculture Department. 2009. *The State of World Fisheries and Aquaculture 2008.* Rome:

FAO. Available at ftp://ftp.fao.org/docrep/fao/011/i0250e/i0250e.pdf.

Intergovernmental Panel on Climate Change. 2007. *Climate Change 2007: Synthesis Report.* Contribution of Working Groups I, II, and III to the Fourth Assessment Report of the Intergovernmental Panel on Climate Change. Core Writing Team, R. K. Pachauri and A. Reisinger, eds. Geneva: Author.

Lawton, J. H., and R. M. May, eds. 1995. *Extinction Rates.* New York: Oxford University Press.

Postel, S. L., G. C. Daily, and P. R. Ehrlich. 1996. Human appropriation of renewable freshwater. *Science* 271:785–788.

Human Population

HUMAN POPULATION DENSITY AND GROWTH MAPS DATA SOURCES

Center for International Earth Science Information Network (CIESIN), Columbia University; and Centro Internacional de Agricultura Tropical (CIAT). 2005. Gridded Population of the World Version 3 (GPWv3). Socioeconomic Data and Applications Center (SEDAC), Columbia University Palisades, New York. Available at http://sedac.ciesin.columbia.edu/gpw. Digital media.

United Nations Population Division (UNPD). 2007. Global population, largest urban agglomerations and cities of largest change. World Urbanization Prospects: The 2007 Revision Population Database. Available at http://esa.un.org/unup/index.asp.

TECHNICAL NOTES

We summarized human population density and growth data by ecoregion using the Gridded Population of the World database and projections for 2015 (CIESIN et al. 2005). For population density, the mean for each ecoregion was extracted using a zonal statistics algorithm. Projected population growth was calculated by summing population data by ecoregion for each of the two time periods (2000 and 2015) and then calculating the difference to estimate growth. We also displayed the size and projected growth of major urban centers based on data from UNPD (2007).

POPULATION GROWTH FIGURE DATA SOURCE

United Nations Department of Economic and Social Affairs: Population Division (www.un.org/esa/population/unpop.htm). 2008. World population prospects: The 2008

revision. Available at http://esa.un.org/unpp/index.asp.

REFERENCES

Grown, C., G. R. Gupta, and A. Kes. 2006. Taking action to empower women: UN Millennium Project report on education and gender equality. *Global Urban Development* 2, no. 1 (March): 1–19. Available at www.globalurban.org/GUDMag06Vol2Iss1/Grown,%20Gupta,%20&%20Kes%20PDF.pdf.

International Conference on Population and Development (ICPD). 1994. Cairo, Egypt. Available at www.iisd.ca/Cairo.html.

United Nations Population Division. 2007. World urbanization prospects: The 2007 Revision Population Database. Available at http://esa.un.org/unup/index.asp.

Consuming Nature

HUMAN APPROPRIATION MAP DATA SOURCES

Imhoff, M. L., L. Bounoua, T. Ricketts, C. Loucks, R. Harriss, and W. T. Lawrence. 2004a. Human Appropriation of Net Primary Productivity (HANPP). Data distributed by the Socioeconomic Data and Applications Center (SEDAC). Available at http://sedac.ciesin.columbia.edu/es/hanpp.html.

TECHNICAL NOTES

We derived the map showing the amount of carbon fixed by photosynthesis and then consumed by humans from Imhoff et al. (2004a). A zonal sum procedure was applied to the gridded version of those data to summarize by ecoregion.

WATER CONSUMPTION MAP DATA SOURCE

Food and Agriculture Organization of the United Nations (FAO). 2008. Aquastat. Available at www.fao.org/nr/water/aquastat/dbases/index.stm.

TECHNICAL NOTES

We produced the map showing the amount of water withdrawn each year by country using data from the UN Food and Agriculture Organization's Aquastat database (FAO 2008) on the annual quantity of freshwater withdrawn for agricultural, industrial, and domestic purposes by country. This data source included renewable freshwater resources as well as eventual overextraction of renewable groundwater or withdrawal of fossil groundwater and eventual use of desalinated water or treated wastewater. It did not include other categories of water use, such as for cooling of power plants, mining, recreation, navigation, fisheries, and so forth—all of which have a very low net consumption rate.

ECOLOGICAL FOOTPRINT FIGURE DATA SOURCE

Ewing B., S. Goldfinger, M. Wackernagel, M. Stechbart, S. M. Rizk, A. Reed, and J. Kitzes. 2008. *The Ecological Footprint Atlas 2008.* Oakland, CA: Global Footprint Network.

FOOTPRINT BY INCOME FIGURE DATA SOURCE

World Wide Fund for Nature (WWF), Zoological Society of London, and Global Footprint Network. 2006. *Living Planet Report 2006.* Gland, Switzerland: WWF International. Available at www.footprintnetwork.org/download.php?id=303.

TECHNICAL NOTES

Dotted lines in graph reflect estimates due to dissolution of the Soviet Union.

REFERENCE

Imhoff, M., L. Bounoua, T. H. Ricketts, C. J. Loucks, R. Harriss, W. T. Lawrence. 2004b. Global patterns in human consumption of net primary productivity. *Nature* 429: 870–873.

Climate Change

CLIMATE CHANGE MAP DATA SOURCE

National Center for Atmospheric Research (NCAR). 2008–2009. Geographic Information System Initiative. Available at www.gisclimatechange.org. Digital media.

TECHNICAL NOTES

We gridded monthly air temperatures for 1870 through 1880 and 1990 through 2000 to a one-kilometer global resolution. Grids of the monthly temperatures for each year were then averaged, and those temperature values were averaged for the 1870–1880 and 1990–2000 decades. Grids of the annual average temperatures for the 1870–1880 decade were subtracted from the average temperatures for the 1990–2000 decade.

GREENHOUSE GAS FIGURE DATA SOURCE

Intergovernmental Panel on Climate Change (IPCC). 2007. *Climate Change 2007: Synthesis Report.* Contribution of Working Groups I, II, and III to the Fourth Assessment Report of the Intergovernmental Panel on Climate Change. Core Writing Team, R. K. Pachauri and A. Reisinger, eds. Geneva: Author.

REFERENCES

Friedman, L. 2009. Coming soon: Mass migrations spurred by climate change. *New York Times*, March 2.

Intergovernmental Panel on Climate Change (IPCC). 2007. *Climate Change 2007: The*

Physical Science Basis. Geneva: World Meteorological Organization and United Nations Environment Programme.

McKinsey and Company. 2009. *Pathways to a Low-Carbon Economy.* Available at www.mckinsey.com/globalGHGcostcurve.

McMichael, A. J., D. H. Campbell-Lendrum, C. F. Corvalán, A. K. Githeko, J. D. Scheraga, and A. Woodward, eds. 2003. *Climate Change and Human Health: Risks and Responses.* Geneva: World Health Organization.

Pfeffer, W. T., J. T. Harper, and S. O'Neal. 2008. Kinematic Constraints on Glacier Contributions to 21st Century Sea-level Rise. *Science* 321:1340-1343.

Sokolov, A. P., P. H. Stone, C. E. Forest, R. Prinn, M. C. Sarofim, M. Webster, S. Paltsev, et al. 2009. Probabilistic forecast for 21st century climate based on uncertainties in emissions (without policy) and climate parameters. *Journal of Climate.* (DOI: 10.1175/2009JCLI2863.1).

Tans, P. 2009. NOAA/ESRL. Available at www.esrl.noaa.gov/gmd/ccgg/trends/index.html#global.

Essay: Cohen

POPULATION TRAJECTORIES FIGURE DATA SOURCE

United Nations Population Division (UNPD). 2005. *World Population Prospects: The 2004 Revision, Volume 1: Comprehensive Tables.* ST/ESA/SER.A/244. Department of Economic and Social Affairs. New York: United Nations.

REFERENCES

Burnett, V. 2007. Under new program, workers get from Africa to Spain without risking lives at sea. *International Herald Tribune*, August 10. Available at www.iht.com/articles/2007/08/10/europe/spain.php.

Cohen, J. E. 1995. *How Many People Can the Earth Support?* New York: Norton.

———. 2005 Human population grows up. *Scientific American* 293, no. 3 (September): 48–55.

EU abandons Morocco fish talks. 2001. Available at http://news.bbc.co.uk/2/hi/africa/1296678.stm.

Judah, T. 2001. The battle for West Africa's fish. Available at http://news.bbc.co.uk/2/hi/africa/1464966.stm.

———. 2001. West Africa's delicate fishing balance. Available at http://news.bbc.co.uk/2/hi/africa/1467652.stm.

Lebreton, J.-D. 2007. Dynamique des populations et biodiversité. Available at www.academie-sciences.fr/conferences/seances_solennelles/pdf/discours_Lebreton_19_06_07.pdf.

Peters, R. H. 1983. *The Ecological Implications of Body Size.* Cambridge: Cambridge University Press.

Savage, V. M., J. F. Gillooly, J. H. Brown, G. B. West, and E. L. Charnov. 2004. Effects of body size and temperature on population growth. *American Naturalist* 163: 429–441 (doi: 10.1086/381872).

Tschakert, P. 2007. Views from the vulnerable: Understanding climatic and other stressors in the Sahel. *Global Environmental Change* 17, nos. 3–4: 381–396 (doi:10.1016/j.gloenvcha.2006.11.008).

United Nations IRIN Humanitarian Information Unit. 2006. Senegal: For out-of-work fishermen, migration offers hope and ready cash. Available at http://medilinkz.org/news/news2.asp?NewsID=16121.

United Nations Office for West Africa. 2007. *Urbanization and Insecurity in West Africa: Population Movements, Mega Cities and Regional Stability.* UNOWA Issue Papers October 2007. Available at www.un.org/unowa/unowa/studies/urbanization_and_insecurity_in_wa_en.pdf.

United Nations Population Division. 2005. *World Population Prospects: The 2004 Revision, Volume 1: Comprehensive Tables.* ST/ESA/SER.A/244. Department of Economic and Social Affairs. New York: United Nations.

Westhead, J. 2000. West African fishing under threat: Traditional canoes are no match for the trawlers. Available at http://news.bbc.co.uk/2/hi/africa/944696.stm.

Habitat Loss on Land

HABITAT LOSS MAP DATA SOURCES

CIESIN (Center for International Earth Science Information Network), IFPRI (International Food Policy Research Institute), the World Bank; and CIAT (Centro Internacional de Agricultura Tropical). 2004. Global Rural-Urban Mapping Project (GRUMP): Urban extents, Columbia University Palisades, New York, USA. Available at http://sedac.ciesin.columbia.edu/gpw/. Digital media.

Joint Research Centre of the European Commission (JRC). 2003. GLC 2000: Global Land Cover Mapping for the Year 2000. Ispra, Italy: European Commission Joint Research Centre, Institute for Environment and Sustainability. Available at www-tem.jrc.it/glc2000. Digital media.

TECHNICAL NOTES

We derived data on the amount of habitat lost from the Global Land Cover 2000 (JRC 2003), which is based on satellite imagery; the Global Rural-Urban Mapping Project (CIESIN et al. 2004); and a global coverage of roads and railroads compiled from ESRI Digital Chart of the World. While the data tell us how much land has been converted from a natural state to a human-altered state for 2000, it does not tell us about any specific type of habitat that has been lost, what it was converted to, how long ago it was converted, or the extent to which the human land use still supports some biodiversity. Because the satellite-derived data are observations made around 2000, they do not reflect ongoing rates of habitat loss.

ARABLE LAND MAP DATA SOURCES

Fischer, G., H. van Velthuizen, S. Medow, and F. Nachtergaele. 2002. *Global Agro-ecological Assessment* [CD]. Rome: Food and Agriculture Organization of the United Nations; and Laxenburg, Austria: International Institute for Applied Systems Analysis.

Joint Research Centre of the European Commission (JRC). 2003. GLC 2000: Global Land Cover Mapping for the Year 2000. Ispra, Italy: European Commission Joint Research Centre, Institute for Environment and Sustainability. Available at www-tem.jrc.it/glc2000. Digital media.

TECHNICAL NOTES

We developed the map of arable land not yet converted to agriculture from data provided by Fischer et al. (2002). Our map was produced by modeling the moderate- to high-yielding climate-soil envelopes for nine major world crops and projecting those areas geographically in regions that are not classified as urban or agricultural by JRC (2003). It represented rain-fed agriculture only, so the area of arable land is likely underestimated. It also does not account for changing future demands for irrigated agriculture that are driven by national policy and finance.

GREAT PLAINS HABITAT LOSS MAP DATA SOURCE

Ramankutty, N., and J. A. Foley. 1999. Estimating historical changes in global land cover: Croplands from 1700 to 1992. *Global Biogeochemical Cycles* 13: 997–1028. Available at www.sage.wisc.edu.

EXTINCTION TIPPING POINT FIGURE
DATA SOURCES

Joint Research Centre of the European Commission (JRC). 2003. GLC 2000: Global Land Cover Mapping for the Year 2000. Ispra, Italy: European Commission Joint Research Centre, Institute for Environment and Sustainability. Available at www-tem.jrc.it/glc2000. Digital media.

World Wildlife Fund (WWF). 2006. WildFinder: Database of species distributions, ver. Jan-06. Available at www.gis.wwf.org/WildFinder. Digital media.

TECHNICAL NOTES

We created the figure showing the relation between habitat lost and endangered species by querying the WWF WildFinder database (2006) for data on endangered species per ecoregion. A second-order polynomial line was then fit to a scatter graph of the amount of habitat lost and the number of endangered species per ecoregion.

REFERENCES

Lawton, J. H., and R. M. May, eds. 1995. *Extinction Rates*. New York: Oxford University Press.

Millennium Ecosystem Assessment. 2005. *Ecosystems and Human Well-being: Desertification Synthesis*. Washington, DC: World Resources Institute.

Pimm, S. L., and P. Raven. 2000. Biodiversity: Extinction by numbers. *Nature* 403: 843.

Sage, C. 2006. *Prairie: A Natural History*. Vancouver, Canada: Greystone Books.

Schachner, L. J., R. N. Mack, and S. J. Novak. 2008. *Bromus tectorum* (poaceae) in midcontinental United States: Population genetic analysis of an ongoing invasion. *American Journal of Botany* 95, no. 12: 1584–1595.

Tilman, D., R. M. May, C. L. Lehman, and M. A. Nowak. 1994. Habitat destruction and the extinction debt. *Nature* 371: 65–66.

UN Environment Programme (UNEP)/International Union for Conservation of Nature (IUCN). 2004. *Protected Areas Extracted from the 2004 World Database on Protected Areas (WDPA)*. The WDPA is a joint product of UNEP and the IUCN, prepared by UNEP-WCMC and the IUCN WCPA working with Governments, the Secretariats of MEAs, and collaborating NGOs. For further information, contact protectedareas@unep-wcmc.org or go to www.WDPA.org.

Wilson, E. O. 1989. Threats to biodiversity. *Scientific American* 261: 108–117.

Coastal Development

COASTAL DEVELOPMENT MAP DATA SOURCE

Center for International Earth Science Information Network (CIESIN), Columbia University; and Centro Internacional de Agricultura Tropical (CIAT). 2005. Gridded Population of the World Version 3 (GPWv3), Socioeconomic Data and Applications Center (SEDAC), Columbia University Palisades, New York. Available at http://sedac.ciesin.columbia.edu/gpw. Digital media.

TECHNICAL NOTES

The map shows the proportion of coastline (from the shore to within five kilometers of the coast) in each ecoregion where there are more than five hundred persons per square kilometer. By focusing attention on a narrow coastal strip, we believe that we are capturing areas with the highest likelihood of significant losses of intertidal and adjacent habitats as a result of building, dredging, land reclamation, and other forms of coastal engineering. It does not, of course, measure areas of coastal development per se and does not capture areas where aquaculture, agriculture, or low-density tourism have impacts.

REFERENCES

French, P. W. 2006. Managed realignment: The developing story of a comparatively new approach to soft engineering. *Estuarine, Coastal and Shelf Science* 67: 409–423.

MEDASSET. n.d. Mediterranean Association to Save the Sea Turtles Web site. Available at www.medasset.org/cms/.

Salahuddin, B. 2006. *The Marine Environmental Impacts of Artificial Island Construction*. Dubai, UAE: Nicholas School of the Environment and Earth Sciences. Available at http://hdl.handle.net/10161/104.

Spalding, M. D., M. Kainuma, and L. Collins. Forthcoming. *World Mangrove Atlas*. London: Earthscan, with International Society for Mangrove Ecosystems, Food and Agriculture Organization of the United Nations, UNEP World Conservation Monitoring Centre, The Nature Conservancy, United Nations Scientific and Cultural Organisation, United Nations University.

Bottom Trawling and Dredging

TRAWLING MAP DATA SOURCES

Sea Around Us Project (SAUP). 2007. Global fisheries database. Available at www.seaaroundus.org. Vancouver: Fisheries Center, University of British Columbia.

Watson, R., C. Revenga, and Y. Kura. 2006a. Fishing gear associated with global marine catches I: Database development. *Fisheries Research* 79: 97–102.

TECHNICAL NOTES

The map shows trawling and dredging fishing pressure by marine ecoregion between 1955 and 2004, using fish and shellfish catch data from the University of British Columbia (SAUP 2007). Our analysis of the catch data was limited to species caught by bottom trawl or dredge gear (Watson et al. 2006a). We calculated the annual total tonnage of catch for all species caught by these gears in each ecoregion. To account for recovery of benthic systems over time, we applied a decay factor of 2 percent for each year before 2004 to the total catch (implying a full recovery in fifty years). We then calculated the cumulative total catch for each ecoregion (including the decay function) across all years (1955–2004).

REFERENCES

Kura, Y., C. Revenga, E. Hoshino, and G. Mock. 2004. *Fishing for Answers: Making Sense of the Global Fish Crisis*. Ed. G. Mock and C. Revenga. Washington, DC: World Resources Institute.

Marine Conservation Biology Institute (MCBI) and Deep Sea Conservation Coalition. 2005. debunking claims of sustainability: High seas bottom trawl red herrings. MCBI and Deep Sea Conservation Coalition. Available at www.mcbi.org/publications/pub_pdfs/DSCC_RedHerrings.pdf.

Marine Conservation Biology Institute (MCBI) and Oceania. 2005. Deep sea coral protection around the world. Available at www.mcbi.org/what/what_pdfs/Coral_International_Protections.pdf.

National Research Council (NRC). 2002. *Effects of Trawling and Dredging on Seafloor Habitat*. Washington, DC: National Academy Press. Available at http://books.nap.edu.

Norse, E. 2008. Bottom trawling impacts on ocean clearly visible from space. *Marine Conservation Biology News*, February 18. Available at www.mcbi.org/news/trawling_18feb2008.htm.

Poiner, I., J. Glaister, R. Pitcher, C. Burridge, T. Wassenberg, N. Gribble, B. Hill, et al. 1998. *The Environmental Effects of Prawn Trawling in the Far Northern Section of the Great Barrier Reef Marine Park: 1991–1996: Final Report to GBRMPA and FRDC*. Queensland, Australia: CSIRO Division of Marine

Research, Queensland Department of Primary Industries Report.

Watling, L., and E. A. Norse. 1998. Disturbance of the seabed by mobile fishing gear: A comparison with forest clear-cutting. *Conservation Biology* 12, no. 6: 1180–1197.

Watson, R., C. Revenga, and Y. Kura. 2006b. Fishing gear associated with global marine catches II: Trends in trawling and dredging. *Fisheries Research* 79: 103–111.

Landscape Fragmentation

HABITAT FRAGMENTATION MAP DATA SOURCE

The Nature Conservancy (TNC). 2005. Unpublished data on landscape fragmentation by terrestrial ecoregion. The Nature Conservancy, Arlington, Virginia, USA.

TECHNICAL NOTES

We considered agriculture, urban infrastructure, roads, and railroads as "fragmenting" features to the landscape and areas not converted to agriculture, urban infrastructure, roads, or railroads as "nonfragmented" terrestrial landscape patches. We used input spatial data from JRC's GLC 2000 (2003), CIESIN et al. (2004), Defense Mapping Agency (1992), and South American Conservation Region (2005). To produce the data, we constructed a global map grid of fragmenting features (Mollweide projection, based on the WGS 1984 datum; 1 km² resolution); this grid was then combined with the GLC 2000, adding a new "fragmenting features" class to the GLC 2000 map. We then extracted a window around the area of each ecoregion in a way that avoided truncating landscape patches with the ecoregion boundary, and measured landscape fragmentation characteristics using Fragstats (McGarigal et al. 2002). The map shows one of these characteristics: the largest patch size by ecoregion. The primary resources we used to develop this map were the following:

CIESIN (Center for International Earth Science Information Network), IFPRI (International Food Policy Research Institute), the World Bank, and CIAT (Centro Internacional de Agricultura Tropical). 2004. Global Rural-Urban Mapping Project (GRUMP): Urban Extents, Columbia University Palisades, New York, USA. Available at http://sedac.ciesin .columbia.edu/gpw/. Digital media.

Defense Mapping Agency. 1992. *Digital Chart of the World* [4 CDs]. Updated 1996. Fairfax, VA: Author.

Joint Research Centre of the European Commission (JRC). 2003. GLC 2000: Global Land Cover Mapping for the Year 2000. Ispra, Italy: European Commission Joint Research Centre, Institute for Environment and Sustainability. Available at www-tem.jrc .it/glc2000. Digital media.

McGarigal, K., S. A. Cushman, M. C. Neel, and E. Ene. 2002. *FRAGSTATS: Spatial Pattern Analysis Program for Categorical Maps.* Amherst: University of Massachusetts. Available at www.umass.edu/landeco/research/ fragstats/fragstats.html.

South American Conservation Region. 2005. Vías de Sur America. Geographic Information System data set. The Nature Conservancy, Arlington, Virginia, USA.

REFERENCES

Burke, D. M., and E. Nol. 2000. Landscape and fragment size effects on reproductive success of forest-breeding birds in Ontario. *Ecological Applications* 10, no. 6: 1749–1761.

Lindenmayer, D. B., and J. Fischer. 2006. *Habitat Fragmentation and Landscape Change.* Washington, DC: Island.

Norris, D. R., and B. J. M. Stutchbury. 2001. Extraterritorial movements of a forest songbird in a fragmented landscape. *Conservation Biology* 15, no. 3: 729–736.

Science Daily. 2007. Wildlife corridor gives endangered elephants in India passage between reserves. December 21. Available at www.sciencedaily.com/releases/2007/12/ 071220212827.htm.

Thwarted Fish Runs

FISH RUN DISRUPTION MAP DATA SOURCE

Reidy-Liermann, C. A., C. Nilsson, J. Robertson, and R. Ng. Dam obstruction among the world's freshwater ecoregions and implications for global freshwater fish diversity. Unpublished manuscript.

TECHNICAL NOTES

The level of disruption of fish runs was determined by Reidy-Liermann et al. (unpublished) by calculating the average proportion of undammed distance among the longest connected freshwater pathways (including lakes) in each ecoregion, regardless of stream order. This metric considered *only* the five longest water courses or river segments between or without dams. Depending on the confidence in the underlying dam and reservoir data, ecoregions without known dams may have been deemed either as fully free-flowing or as having insufficient data.

When dams data were deemed unreliable for a river, those dams were excluded from the analysis, so results tend to underestimate actual river obstruction.

CHESAPEAKE BAY FIGURE DATA SOURCE

Chesapeake Bay Program. 2007. Data for miles opened to migratory fish. Available at www.chesapeakebay.net/status_fishpassage .aspx?menuitem=19701.

REFERENCES

Allen, N., and C. Augsburger. 2004. USACE sets the Rappahannock River free. *Engineer*, October–December, 16–17.

American Rivers. 2007. *Dam Removal Summary 1999–2008.* Available at www.americanrivers. org/site/DocServer/DAMS_SLATED_FOR _REMOVAL_IN_2008.pdf?docID=8501.

Blankenship, K. 2002. New York releases American shad larvae on Susquehanna. *Bay Journal*, July–August. Available at www .bayjournal.com/article.cfm?article=707.

———. 2006. Shad runs down around Bay; good egg production aids stocking efforts. *Bay Journal*, July–August. Available at www .bayjournal.com/article.cfm?article=2856.

Chesapeake Bay Program. 2008. Information on American shad management and Fish Passage Restoration. Available at www.chesapeakebay .net/fishpassage.aspx?menuitem=14762.

Dekker, W. 2003. Eels in crisis. *ICES Newsletter* 40: 10–11. International Council for the Exploration of the Sea Copenhagen, Denmark. Available at www.ices.dk/marineworld/eel.asp.

Feeney, B. 2004. Embrey Dam removal opens 100s of miles of river to fish. *Bay Journal*, April. Available at www.bayjournal.com/ article.cfm?article=1253.

Pennsylvania Fish and Boat Commission. 2009. Data on American shad counts for dam passage on the Susquehanna River. Available at www.fish.state.pa.us/shad_susq.htm.

Essay: Myers

REFERENCES

Colborn, T., D. Dumanoski, and J. P. Myers. 1996. *Our Stolen Future.* New York: Dutton.

de Boer, J., P. G. Wester, H. J. C. Klamer, W. E. Lewis, and J. P. Boon. 1998. Do flame retardants threaten ocean life? *Nature* 394: 28–29.

Lang, I. A., T. S. Galloway, A. Scarlett, W. E. Henley, M. Depledge, R. B. Wallace, and D. Melzer. 2008. Association of urinary bisphenol: A concentration with medical disorders and laboratory abnormalities in adults.

Journal of the American Medical Association 300: 1303–1310.

Myers, J. P. 2006. Good genes gone bad. *American Prospect*, April. Available at www .prospect.org/cs/articles?articleId=11315.

Simonich, S. L., and R. A. Hites. 1995. Global distribution of persistent organochlorine compounds. *Science* 269: 1851–1854.

Vom Saal, F. S., T. B. T. Akingbemi, S. M. Belcher, L. S. Birnbaum, D. A. Crain, M. Eriksen, F. Farabollini, et al. 2007. Chapel Hill bisphenol A expert panel consensus statement: Integration of mechanisms, effects in animals and potential to impact human health at current levels of exposure. *Reproductive Toxicology* 24: 131–138.

Watters, E. 2006. DNA is not destiny. *Discover*, November. Available at http://discovermagazine .com/2006/nov/cover.

Freshwater Pollution

SOUTH AFRICA RIVERS MAP SOURCE

Nel, J. L., D. J. Roux, G. Maree, C. J. Kleynhans, J. Moolman, B. Reyers, M. Rouget, and R. M. Cowling. 2007. Rivers in peril inside and outside protected areas: A systematic approach to conservation assessment of river ecosystems. *Diversity and Distributions* 13: 341–352.

PHARMACEUTICAL TABLE DATA SOURCES

Donn, J., Mendoza, M., and J. Pritchard. 2008. AP IMPACT: Pharmaceuticals found in drinking water, affecting wildlife and maybe humans. Associated Press, March 9.

Kolpin, D. W., E. T. Furlong, M. T. Meyer, E. M. Thurman, S. D. Zaugg, L. B. Barber, and H. T. Buxton. 2002. Pharmaceuticals, hormones, and other organic wastewater contaminants in U.S. streams, 1999–2000: A national reconnaissance. *Environmental Science and Technology* 36: 1202–1211.

REFERENCES

Kolpin, D. W., E. T. Furlong, M. T. Meyer, E. M. Thurman, S. D. Zaugg, L. B. Barber, and H. T Buxton. 2002. Pharmaceuticals, hormones, and other organic wastewater contaminants in U.S. streams, 1999–2000: A national reconnaissance. *Environmental Science and Technology* 36: 1202–2111.

Pettersson I., A. Arukwe, K. Lundstedt-Enkel, A. S. Mortensen, and C. Berg. 2006. Persistent sex-reversal and oviducal agenesis in adult *Xenopus (Silurana) tropicalis* frogs following larval exposure to the environmental pollutant ethynylestradiol. *Aquatic Toxicology* 79, no. 4: 356–365.

Tyler, C. R., S. Jobling, and J. P. Sumpter. 1998. Endocrine disruption in wildlife: A critical review of the evidence. *Critical Reviews in Toxicology* 28, no. 4: 319–361.

World Health Organization (WHO) and United Nations Children's Fund (UNICEF). 2004. Meeting the MDG drinking water and sanitation target: A mid-term assessment of progress. WHO/UNICEF Joint Monitoring Programme for Water Supply and Sanitation. Available at http://whqlibdoc.who.int/ publications/2004/9241562781.pdf.

Nitrogen Pollution

NITROGEN FLOW MAP DATA SOURCE

Green, P. A., C. J. Vörösmarty, M. Meybeck, J. N. Galloway, B. J. Peterson, and E. W. Boyer. 2004. Pre-industrial and contemporary fluxes of nitrogen through rivers: A global assessment based on typology. *Biogeochemistry* 68, no. 1: 71–105.

TECHNICAL NOTES

The map shows the estimated change in coastal discharge of dissolved inorganic nitrogen (DIN) between preindustrial and contemporary times by marine ecoregion. We calculated this change using data from Green et al. (2005), which was developed using land surface runoff models that included agriculture, livestock, human sewage, and atmospheric deposition sources of DIN. The original spatial data set assigned discharge values to coastal pixels, and we summed the value of pixels within each ecoregion for each time period. We then calculated ecoregional values by subtracting preindustrial sums from contemporary values.

NITROGEN SOURCES FIGURE DATA SOURCE

Green, P. A., C. J. Vörösmarty, M. Meybeck, J. N. Galloway, B. J. Peterson, and E. W. Boyer. 2004. Pre-industrial and contemporary fluxes of nitrogen through rivers: A global assessment based on typology. *Biogeochemistry* 68, no. 1: 71–105.

GROWTH IN FERTILIZER USE FIGURE DATA SOURCE

Food and Agriculture Organization of the United Nations (FAO). 2008. FAOSTAT Online Statistical Service. Rome: FAO. Available at http://faostat.fao.org/default.aspx.

REFERENCES

Connecticut Department of Environmental Protection (CT DEP). 2007. Connecticut Water Quality Trading Program awarded first EPA "Blue Ribbon" award. Available at www .ct.gov/dep/cwp/view.asp?A=2794&Q=398204.

Food and Agriculture Organization of the United Nations (FAO). 2006. Livestock impacts on the environment. Available at www .fao.org/ag/magazine/0612sp1.htm.

Howarth, R. W., D. Anderson, T. Church, H. Greening, C. Hopkinson, W. Juber, N. Marcus, et al. 2000. *Clean Coastal Waters: Understanding and Reducing the Effects of Nutrient Pollution*. Washington, DC: Committee on the Causes and Management of Coastal Eutrophication, Ocean Studies Board and Water Science and Technology Board, Commission on Geosciences, Environment and Resources, National Research Council, National Academy of Sciences.

Mitsch, W. J., J. W. Day Jr., J. W. Gilliam, P. M. Groffman, D. L. Hey, G. W. Randall, and N. Wang. 2001. Reducing nitrogen loading to the Gulf of Mexico from the Mississippi River Basin: Strategies to counter a persistent ecological problem. *BioScience* 51: 373–388.

Ruin of the Reefs

CORAL REEFS AT RISK MAP DATA SOURCE

Bryant, D., L. Burke, J. McManus, and M. Spalding. 1998. *Reefs at Risk: A Map-Based Indicator of Threats to the World's Coral Reefs*. Washington, DC: World Resources Institute, International Center for Living Aquatic Resources Management, UNEP World Conservation Monitoring Centre and United Nations Environment Programme.

TECHNICAL NOTES

The original Reefs at Risk indicator was devised by Bryant et al. (1998) with considerable expert consultation and utilized multiple global data layers to develop separate threat layers measuring coastal development, marine-based pollution, overexploitation and destructive fishing, and inland pollution and erosion. There are areas where particular elements of the model were not as effective, but it has proved a valuable generic tool that has led to further regional studies for Southeast Asia and for the Caribbean that followed the same basic principles, with only minor amendments to the model.

Bryant et al. (1998) used the combined threat layers to derive a simple three-point threat index (low, medium, or high) for each reef pixel (4 × 4 km). In the present map, we used these to generate the proportion of reefs threatened (medium or high threat) by ecoregion.

Although data were available for a few ecoregions in temperate ecoregions and in West

Africa, these were deliberately excluded because these are not true coral reefs and the findings would be misleading. Being based on proportions, the map gives equal weighting to regions with very few reefs and those where reefs are dominant ecosystems. For example, around the Gulf of Aden and much of the Indian subcontinent, coral reefs are relatively rare habitats. These are indeed areas of grave concern, but the relatively low total area of reefs in these regions makes them a marginally lower point of concern than the extensive and diverse areas that are singled out in the text.

CORAL BLEACHING MAP DATA SOURCE

Oliver, J. K., R. Berkelmans, and C. M. Eakin. 2008. Coral bleaching in space and time. Pages 21–39 in *Coral Bleaching: Patterns, Processes, Causes and Consequences*, ed. M. van Oppen and J. M. Lough. Berlin: Springer.

Tupper, M., A. Tewfik, M. K. Tan, S. L. Tan, L. H. Teh, M. J. Radius, and S. Abdullah. 2008. ReefBase: A global information system on coral reefs. Available at www.reefbase.org.

TECHNICAL NOTES

Data on coral bleaching is derived from ReefBase and represents bleaching from a single year (1998). This was the worst bleaching event on record, linked to an El Niño year. It was also very well monitored, partly because of its unprecedented nature. Bleaching has remained widespread since that time in locations around the world. The data was generously provided by Jamie Oliver from a subset that was prepared for another publication (Oliver et al. 2008), and we have only made minor corrections to errors for the Seychelles in this data set. Bleaching reports in ReefBase were derived from a broad range of sources, but each has been assigned a standardized bleaching score (none, low, medium, high). Because reports of no bleaching were rare within this data set, it was impossible to use it to assess presence or absence; however, we decided that a crude measure of the scale of intensity of bleaching could be gauged by looking at the proportion of "high"-intensity events in relation to the total reports.

REFERENCES

Bryant, D., L. Burke, J. McManus, and M. Spalding. 1998. *Reefs at Risk: A Map-Based Indicator of Threats to the World's Coral Reefs.* Washington, DC: World Resources Institute, International Center for Living Aquatic Resources Management, UNEP World Conservation Monitoring Centre and United Nations Environment Programme.

Burke, L., and J. Maidens. 2004. *Reefs at Risk in the Caribbean.* Washington, DC: World Resources Institute.

Burke, L., L. Selig, and M. Spalding. 2002 *Reefs at Risk in Southeast Asia.* Washington, DC: World Resources Institute.

Into the Wild

ACCESSIBILITY MAP DATA SOURCE

The Nature Conservancy (TNC). 2006. Geographic information system data set: Human accessibility into wild lands. The Nature Conservancy, Arlington, Virginia, USA.

TECHNICAL NOTES

The human accessibility map provides an index of the level of effort it would take for a human on foot to access any given square kilometer of nonconverted land from existing infrastructure. We calculated human accessibility from a one-square-kilometer spatial grid of the terrestrial world consisting of a cost surface where the value of each cell was derived from topographic slope, vegetation type, and vegetation density. We developed a second matching spatial grid of infrastructure, depicting roads, railroads, navigable rivers, cities, and towns. Then we calculated a least cost path from each noninfrastructure grid cell to infrastructure grid cells. Agricultural areas were given a cost value of zero. Accessibility scores for ecoregions were taken as the mean human access value per ecoregion.

The amount of the terrestrial world falling within ten kilometers of a road was calculated from a base map of roads from the Digital Chart of the World (Defense Mapping Agency 1992) that had been variously updated with more recent road maps. Roads were buffered by ten kilometers, and the total buffered area was divided by the total terrestrial area. The 61 percent figure is likely conservative.

Data and resources used in development of this data set include the following:

CIESIN (Center for International Earth Science Information Network), IFPRI (International Food Policy Research Institute), the World Bank; and CIAT (Centro Internacional de Agricultura Tropical). 2004. Global Rural-Urban Mapping Project (GRUMP): Urban Extents, Columbia University Palisades, New York, USA. Available at http://sedac.ciesin .columbia.edu/gpw/. Digital media.

Defense Mapping Agency. 1992. *Digital Chart of the World* [4 CDs]. Updated 1996. Fairfax, VA: Author.

GLOBE Task Team and others, eds. 1999. The Global Land One-kilometer Base Elevation (GLOBE) Digital Elevation Model, Version 1.0. Boulder, CO: National Oceanic and Atmospheric Administration, National Geophysical Data Center. Available at www .ngdc.noaa.gov/mgg/topo/globe.html.

Hansen, M., R. DeFries, J. R. Townshend, M. Carroll, C. Dimiceli, and R. Sohlberg. 2006. Vegetation Continuous Fields MOD44B, 2001 Percent Tree Cover, Collection 4, University of Maryland, College Park, Maryland, USA. Available at http://glcf.umiacs.umd.edu/index .shtml. Digital media.

Joint Research Centre of the European Commission (JRC). 2003. GLC 2000: Global Land Cover Mapping for the Year 2000. Ispra, Italy: European Commission Joint Research Centre, Institute for Environment and Sustainability. Available at www-tem.jrc .it/glc2000. Digital media.

South American Conservation Region. 2005. Vías de Sur America. Geographic Information System data set. The Nature Conservancy, Arlington, Virginia, USA.

REFERENCES

Bennett, E., H. Eves, J. Robinson, D. Wilcove. 2002. Why is eating bushmeat a biodiversity crisis? *Conservation in Practice* 3, no. 2: 28–29.

Blake, S., S. Strindberg, P. Boudjan, C. Makombo, I. Bila-Isia, O. Ilambu, F. Grossmann, et al. 2007. Forest elephant crisis in the Congo Basin. *PLoS Biology* 5: 0001–0009.

Dupain, J., and L. Van Elsacker. 2002. Status of the proposed Lomako Forest Bonobo Reserve: A case study of the bushmeat trade. Pages 259–273 in *All Apes Great and Small, Volume 1: African Apes*, ed. B. M. F. Galdikas, N. E. Briggs, L. K. Sheeran, G. L. Shapiro, and J. Goodall. New York: Kluwer Academic/Plenum.

Morrison, J. C., W. Sechrest, E. Dinerstein, D. Wilcove, and J. F. Lamoreaux. 2007. Persistence of large mammal faunas as indicators of global human impacts. *Journal of Mammalogy* 88, no. 6: 1363–1380.

Peres, C. A., J. Barlow, and W. A. Laurance. 2006. Detecting anthropogenic disturbance in tropical forests. *Trends in Ecology & Evolution* 21: 227–229.

Essay: Sanjayan

REFERENCES

Chen, S., and M. Ravallion. 2004. *How Have the World's Poorest Fared since the Early 1980s?*

Policy Research Paper 3341. Washington, DC: World Bank.

Mekong River Commission Secretariat Web site. Viewed January 2008. Available at www.mrcmekong.org/about_mekong/about_mekong.htm.

United Nations Department of Economic and Social Affairs. 2007. *The Millennium Development Goals Report 2007*. Available at www.un.org/millenniumgoals/pdf/mdg2007.pdf.

World Health Organization. 2008. Availability and consumption of fish. Available at www.who.int/nutrition/topics/3_foodconsumption/en/index5.html

Forest Clearing

FOREST CLEARING MAP DATA SOURCE

Hansen, M., R. DeFries, J. R. Townshend, M. Carroll, C. Dimiceli, and R. Sohlberg. 2006. Vegetation Continuous Fields MOD44B, 2001 Percent Tree Cover, Collection 4, University of Maryland, College Park, Maryland, USA. Available at http://glcf.umiacs.umd.edu/index.shtml. Digital media.

TECHNICAL NOTES

We produced the map of forest clearing using Vegetation Continuous Field (VCF) data (Hansen et al. 2006). We assembled VCF files by year for 2000 through 2005 by realm. These data sets were resampled to one-kilometer ground resolution and merged into a global product by year. We then subtracted data from 2001 from 2000 data; this process was applied to all subsequent years. The derived, differenced data sets were averaged to obtain an annual average for years 2000–2005.

LOSS OF FOREST FIGURE DATA SOURCE

Joint Research Centre of the European Commission (JRC). 2003. GLC 2000: Global Land Cover Mapping for the Year 2000. Ispra, Italy: European Commission Joint Research Centre, Institute for Environment and Sustainability. Available at www-tem.jrc.it/glc2000. Digital media.

World Resources Institute—Global Forest Watch. 1997. Original and frontier forests' extent data. Geographic information system data set. Washington, DC: World Resources Institute. Available at www.globalforestwatch.org.

TECHNICAL NOTES

We summed spatial data showing the extent of original forests, all forests today, and remaining old growth forests to derive the number of square kilometers of each.

REFERENCES

Bourdages, J. 1993. *Paper Recycling in Canada: A New Reality*. Government of Canada report. Available at http://dsp-psd.tpsgc.gc.ca/Collection-R/LoPBdP/BP/bp356.htm.

Food and Agriculture Organization of the United Nations (FAO). 2008. Forestry database. Available at www.fao.org/forestry/databases/en.

Hamer, T. E., and S. K. Nelson. 1995. Characteristics of marbled murrelet nest trees and nesting stands. In *Ecology and Conservation of the Marbled Murrelet*, eds. C. J. Ralph, G. L. Hunt Jr., M. G. Raphael, and J. F. Piatt. USDA Forest Service Gen. Tech. Rep. PSW-152. Albany, CA: USDA Forest Service.

Hansen, M., R. DeFries, J. R. Townshend, M. Carroll, C. Dimiceli, and R. Sohlberg. 2006. Vegetation Continuous Fields MOD44B, 2001 Percent Tree Cover, Collection 4, University of Maryland, College Park, Maryland. Available at http://glcf.umiacs.umd.edu/index.shtml. Digital media.

Intergovernmental Panel on Climate Change (IPCC). 2007. *Climate Change 2007: Synthesis Report*. Contribution of Working Groups I, II, and III to the Fourth Assessment Report of the Intergovernmental Panel on Climate Change. Core Writing Team, R. K. Pachauri and A. Reisinger, eds. Geneva: Author.

Water Stress

WATER STRESS MAP DATA SOURCES

Alcamo, J., P. Döll, T. Henrichs, F. Kaspar, B. Lehner, T. Rösch, and S. Siebert. 2003. Development and testing of the WaterGAP 2 global model of water use and availability. *Hydrological Sciences Journal* 48, no. 3: 317–338.

Döll, P., F. Kaspar, and B. Lehner. 2003. A global hydrological model for deriving water availability indicators: Model tuning and validation. *Journal of Hydrology* 270: 105–134.

TECHNICAL NOTES

The water stress indicator calculation is based on a global water balance model, coupled with estimates of water use by sector (agriculture, domestic, and industrial). We derived these data from the WaterGAP model developed by the University of Kassel in Germany (Alcamo et al. 2003; Döll et al. 2003). The WaterGAP model combined precipitation, temperature, the location of reservoirs and lakes, and a water-routing network to produce the estimates of runoff by grid cell at a 0.5-degree resolution. In this model, water use statistics by country and sector were combined with satellite-derived land use data, irrigated area, as well as population density to estimate water use by grid cell. To estimate the water stress index, we aggregated runoff and water use by ecoregion and calculated the ratio of water use to availability. The index does not account for the use of water from alternate sources such as groundwater, desalination, or reuse of wastewater. It also does not provide any information on the water needs of the ecosystem and does not take into account water resources that are deemed unusable or degraded due to pollution. The model assumes all water available as runoff in an ecoregion can be available for human use. Water stress indices provide a sense of where pressure on water resources is high, but they are not substitutes for local data.

GROUNDWATER MAP DATA SOURCE

Struckmeir, W., and A. Richts. 2007. UPDATE of Struckmeir, W., A. Richts, et al. 2006. *Groundwater Resources of the World*. Hannover, Germany: BGR; Paris: UNESCO. Digital media.

TECHNICAL NOTES

We derived the dominant groundwater features from the Groundwater Resources of the World data set, a product of the World-wide Hydrogeological Mapping and Assessment Programme (WHYMAP) (Struckmeir and Richts 2007). The WHYMAP Groundwater feature containing the largest surface area within an ecoregion was deemed the dominant feature. Groundwater classes are equivalent to classes stated in the WHYMAP data set.

REFERENCES

Department of Water Affairs, Republic of South Africa. 1998. South Africa's National Water Act (Act No. 36). Available at www-dwaf.pwv.gov.za/Documents/Legislature/nw_act/NWA.doc.

European Space Agency. 2006. Earth from Space: A shrinking sea and a gateway to space. Available at www.esa.int/esaEO/SEM22IBUQPE_index_2.html.

Micklin, P. P. 1988. Desiccation of the Aral Sea: A water management disaster in the Soviet Union. *Science* 241: 1170–1176.

Postel, S. 1999. *Pillar of Sand: Can the Irrigation Miracle Last?* Washington, DC: Worldwatch Institute.

Revenga, C., J. Brunner, N. Henninger, K. Kassem, and R. Payne. 2000. *Pilot Analysis of Global Ecosystems: Freshwater Systems*. Washington, DC: World Resources Institute.

State of California Department of Fish and
Game. 2004. *September 2002 Klamath River
Fish Kill: Final Analysis of Contributing Factors
and Impacts.* Available at www.pcffa.org/
KlamFishKillFactorsDFGReport.pdf.

World Bank. 2009. "The Sea Is Coming Back"
and "Syr Darya Control and Northern
Aral Sea Project" project profiles. Available
at http://web.worldbank.org/WBSITE/
EXTERNAL/NEWS/0,,contentMDK:217787
43-menuPK:141310-pagePK:34370-piPK:3442
4-theSitePK:4607,00.html.

Overfishing

FISHERIES STATUS MAP DATA SOURCE

Food and Agriculture Organization of the
United Nations (FAO). 2005. Review of the
state of world marine fishery resources. FAO
Fisheries Technical Paper 457. Rome: Author.
Available at www.fao.org/docrep/009/y5852e/
Y5852E02.htm#ch1.2.

TECHNICAL NOTES

We used data from figure A2.2 of FAO's
Fisheries Technical Paper 457 (FAO 2005) to
depict the state of the fish stocks by FAO fishing
area in 2004. These data represent the percentage of stocks exploited beyond maximum sustainable yield (MSY) levels (i.e., stocks that are
overfished, depleted, or recovering), at MSY levels (i.e., fully fished), and below MSY levels (underexploited and moderately exploited) in 2004.
The pie charts in the map represent the status of
441 stocks, for which sufficient data were available. According to the FAO report (2005), in
twelve out of seventeen fishing regions, at least
70 percent of the stocks are already fully fished
or overfished, pointing to the need for increased
control of fishing capacity. The report also notes
that the Western Central Atlantic and Western
Indian Ocean are the two FAO statistical areas
with the highest percentage of stocks for which
no information on state is available and that
the results for the Southern Ocean are heavily
influenced by the underexploitation of its krill
stocks. The FAO terminology defines an *underexploited stock* as an underdeveloped or new
fishery believed to have a significant potential
for expansion in total production. *Moderately
exploited stocks* include those that are exploited
with a low level of fishing effort and therefore
are believed to have some limited potential for
expansion in total production. *Fully exploited
stocks* are those that are operating at or close to
an optimal yield level, with no expected room
for further expansion. *Overexploited or overfished
stocks* include those being exploited at or above

a level believed to be sustainable in the long
term, with no potential room for further expansion and a higher risk of stock depletion or collapse. *Depleted stocks* are those where catches are
well below historical levels, irrespective of the
amount of fishing effort exerted. And *recovering stocks* are those in which catches are again
increasing after having been depleted or after a
collapse from a previous high. For further information on fisheries and aquaculture, please see
www.fao.org/fishery/en.

REFERENCES

Food and Agriculture Organization of the
United Nations (FAO). 2007. *The State of the
World Fisheries and Aquaculture 2006.* Rome:
FAO Fisheries Department.

Kura, Y., C. Revenga, E. Hoshino, and
G. Mock. 2004. *Fishing for Answers: Making
Sense of the Global Fish Crisis.* G. Mock and
C. Revenga, eds. Washington, DC: World
Resources Institute.

Marine Stewardship Council. 2008. Certified
Fisheries page. Available at www.msc.org/
html/content_484.htm.

Monterey Bay Aquarium Seafood Watch
Program. 2008. Available at www.mbayaq
.org/cr/seafoodwatch.asp008.

Pauly, D., V. Christensen, J. Dalsgaard,
R. Froese, and F. Torres Jr. 1998. Fishing down
marine food webs. *Science* 279: 860–863.

Wildlife Trade

ILLEGAL TRADE MAP DATA SOURCE

The Nature Conservancy (TNC). 2008. Map
of sample trade routes for different wildlife
and wildlife parts and products. Unpublished.
The Nature Conservancy, Arlington, Virginia,
USA.

TECHNICAL NOTES

We present examples of illegal wildlife trade
routes in the map that were derived from multiple documented sources listed here. These
sources carried out studies or verify instances
of trade for each species or product. We drew
examples of trade routes from known source
and destination countries. Lines depicting
these routes do not necessarily or accurately
describe the actual route taken in transit. This
map shows only a selection of the sources and
destinations of illegal trade in these species and
products, and it does not include the much
larger number of other species and products
traded legally and illegally around the world.
We compiled trade route information for the
map from the following sources:

Birdlife International. 2008. CITES and the
wild bird trade. Available at www.birdlife.org/
action/change/cites/index.html.

Camperio Ciani, A., L. Palentini, M. Arahou,
L. Martinoli, C. Capiluppi, and M. Mouna.
2005. Population decline of *Macaca sylvanus*
in the Middle Atlas of Morocco. *Biological
Conservation* 121: 635–641.

Herrera Hurtado, M., and B. Hennesey. 2007.
Quantifying the illegal parrot trade in Santa
Cruz de la Sierra, Bolivia, with emphasis
on threatened species. *Bird Conservation
International* 17: 295–300.

International Fund for Animal Welfare. 2007.
Bidding for extinction: A snapshot survey of
illegal trade in elephant ivory on eBay sites in
Australia, Canada, China, France, Germany,
Netherlands, UK, USA. IFAW self-published
report. Yarmouth Port, MA: Author.

Ng, J., and Nemora. 2007. Tiger trade revisited in Sumatra, Indonesia. Petaling Jaya,
Malaysia: TRAFFIC Southeast Asia.

Petrossian, A. 2006. International Caviar
Importer Association. Caviar: A Trader's
Perspective. Page 99 in *Proceedings of the
International Sturgeon Enforcement Workshop
to Combat Illegal Trade in Caviar*, ed. A.
Knapp, C. Kitschke, and S. von Meibom.
Workshop, 27–29 June 2006, Brussels,
Belgium. Prepared by TRAFFIC Europe for
the European Commission.

Theile, S. 2003. *Fading Footsteps: The Killing
and Trade of Snow Leopards.* The Hague:
TRAFFIC International.

TRAFFIC. 2007a. Alarming upsurge in rhino
poaching. Available at www.traffic.org/
home/2007/6/6/alarming-upsurge-in-rhino
-poaching.html.

TRAFFIC. 2007b. Shahtoosh smuggler
fined in Thai first. Bangkok, Thailand, 27
August 2007. Available at www.traffic.org/
home/2007/8/27/shahtoosh-smuggler-fined
-in-thai-first.html.

———. 2008. 23 tonnes of pangolins seized in
a week. Available at www.traffic.org/home/
month/march-2008.

REFERENCES

ASEAN-WEN. 2005. Web site. Available at
www.asean-wen.org.

INTERPOL. 2008. INTERPOL Wildlife
Crime Unite Web site. Available at www
.interpol.int/Public/EnvironmentalCrime/
Wildlife/Default.asp.

International Union for Conservation of Nature
(IUCN), Conservation International, Arizona

State University, Texas A&M University, University of Rome, University of Virginia, Zoological Society London. 2008. An analysis of mammals on the 2008 IUCN Red List. Available at www.iucnredlist.org/mammals.

Karesh, W. B., R. A. Cook, E. L. Bennett, and J. Newcomb. 2005. Wildlife trade and global disease emergence. *Emerging Infectious Diseases.* Available at www.cdc.gov/ncidod/EID/vol11no07/05-0194.htm.

Knights, P. 1994. Doom in the marketplace: Asia's appetite for animal body parts may spell extinction for some of the world's noblest creatures. *Defenders.*

Ling, C. M. 2008. Effect of the Bangkok bust. *New Straits Time Online.* Available at www.nst.com.my/Current_News/NST/Sunday/Focus/20080406095953/Article/index_html.

Reuters. 2007. New UN database to help combat wildlife crime. Available at www.reuters.com/article/environmentNews/idUSL0476594320070604.

Tourism Authority of Thailand. 2007. Thai customs stop 1,400 endangered animals on their way to illegal pet markets. Available at www.tatnews.org/special_interest/Wildlife/3313.asp.

TRAFFIC. 2008. *Wildlife Trade: What Is It?* Available at www.traffic.org/trade/.

United Nations Environment Programme. At a Glance: Biological diversity. Available at www.unep.org/OurPlanet/imgversn/105/glance.html.

WildAid. 2008. *Endangered and Trafficked Species Guide.* Available at www.wildaid.org/endangeredspecies/.

World Bank. 2005. *Going, Going, Gone: The Illegal Trade in Wildlife in East and Southeast Asia.* Washington, DC: Environment and Social Development, East Asia and Pacific Region, World Bank. Available at http://siteresources.worldbank.org/INTEAPREGTOPENVIRONMENT/Resources/going-going-gone.pdf.

Essay: Alder and Pauly

REFERENCES

Cascorbi, A. 2003. Southern bluefin tuna (*Thunnus maccoyii*). *Seafood Watch Seafood Report: Tunas* 18: 18.

Cheung, W. W. L., V. W. Y. Lam, J. L. Sarmiento, K. Kearney R. Watson, and D. Pauly. 2009. Projecting global marine biodiversity impacts under climate change scenarios. *Fish and Fisheries* (doi: 10.1111/j.1467-2979.00315x).

Fischlin, A., G. F. Midgley, et al. 2007. Ecosystems, their properties, goods and services. Pages 211–272 in *Climate Change 2007: Impacts, Adaptation and Vulnerability. Contribution of Working Group II to the Fourth Assessment Report of the Inergovernmental Panel on Climate Change,* ed. M. L. Parry, O. F. Canziani, J. P. Palutikof, P. J. van der Linden, and C. E. Hanson. Cambridge: Cambridge University Press.

Food and Agriculture Organization of the United Nations (FAO). 2007. *FishStat Plus.* Rome: FAO Fisheries Department.

Harley, C. D. G., A. Randall Hughes, et al. 2006. The impacts of climate change in coastal marine systems. *Ecology Letters* 9: 228–241.

Hilborn, R., J. M. Orensanz, et al. 2005. Institutions, incentives and the future of fisheries. *Philosophical Transactions of the Royal Society* 360: 47–57.

International Convention on the Conservation of Atlantic Tuna (ICCAT). (2006). Supplemental Recommendation by ICCAT Concerning the Western Atlantic Bluefin Tuna Rebuilding Program, Madrid, Spain, ICCAT: 3.

Jacquet, J., and D. Pauly. 2008. Trade secrets: Renaming and mislabeling of seafood. *Marine Policy* 32: 309–318.

Morato, T., R. A. Watson, et al. 2006. Fishing down the deep. *Fish and Fisheries* 7: 24–34.

Pauly, D., J. Alder, et al. 2005. Marine fisheries systems. Pages 477–512 in *Millennium Ecosystem Assessment, 2005: Current State and Trends: Findings of the Condition and Trends Working Group, Volume 1: Ecosystems and Human Well-being,* ed. R. Hassan, R. Scholes, and N. Ash. Washington, DC, Island Press.

Sumaila, U. R., A. D. Marsden, et al. 2007. A global ex-vessel fish price database: Construction and applications. *Journal of Bioeconmics* 9: 36–51.

United Nations Environment Programme. 2007. *Global Environment Outlook 4.* Nairobi: Author.

Fire

FIRE CONDITION MAP DATA SOURCE

Shlisky, A., J. Waugh, P. Gonzalez, M. Gonzalez, M. Manta, H. Santoso, E. Alvarado, et al. 2007. *Fire, Ecosystems and People: Threats and Strategies for Global Biodiversity Conservation.* GFI Technical Report 2007-2. Arlington, VA: The Nature Conservancy.

TECHNICAL NOTES

Spatial data on the status and trends of fire regimes were developed under the Global Fire Partnership, a collaboration of nongovernment and academic institutions and summarized in Shlisky et al. (2007). The fire regime and its status and trends were established through a formal expert workshop process. Workshops were held around the world from 2004 to 2006.

FIRE REGIME FIGURES DATA SOURCE

Shlisky, A., J. Waugh, P. Gonzalez, M. Gonzalez, M. Manta, H. Santoso, E. Alvarado, et al. 2007. *Fire, Ecosystems and People: Threats and Strategies for Global Biodiversity Conservation.* GFI Technical Report 2007-2. Arlington, VA: The Nature Conservancy.

REFERENCE

Goens, D. W., and P. L. Andrews. 1998. Weather and fire behavior factors related to the 1990 Dude fire near Payson, AZ: Case study report. Wildland Fire Lessons Learned Center, Tucson, Arizona, USA. Available at www.wildfirelessons.net/CaseStudies.aspx.

Dams and Reservoirs

FLOW DISRUPTION MAP DATA SOURCE

Nilsson, C., C. A. Reidy, M. Dynesius, and C. Revenga. 2005. Fragmentation and flow regulation of the world's large river systems. *Science* 308, no. 5720: 405–408.

TECHNICAL NOTES

The degree to which natural river flows have been disrupted by dams and their reservoirs was calculated by Nilsson et al. (2005) based on the number of dams in each river basin assessed; the location of the dams, on the main stem or the tributaries; the length of river segments between dams; and the amount of annual river flow held in reservoirs. In total, 292 large river systems covering 54 percent of the world's land area were assessed. Large river systems include those basins that have one or more river channel sections with a virgin mean annual discharge of at least 350 cubic meters per second. The analysis was done using river basins rather than individual freshwater ecoregions, as flow calculations can only be measured using hydrological drainage units.

PLANNED DAMS MAP DATA SOURCE

The Nature Conservancy (TNC). 2009. Planned dams and dams under construction data set. Unpublished. The Nature Conservancy, Arlington, Virginia, USA.

TECHNICAL NOTES

We created the map of planned dams by compiling information from multiple sources, including the International Journal of Hydropower and Dams, the World Resources Institute, contacts at national ministries, Google Earth, and Web and literature searches. Because information on the location of dams was confidential in many countries, data were not available for many regions of the world. Some countries—like Argentina, Brazil, Canada, and the United States—had publicly available information on planned dams, or data were available on request from government agencies and international institutions. For other countries, data were hard to come by. This map, therefore, presents information on large dams that were planned or under construction for those countries for which information was available. All dams included were going to be more than fifteen meters in height, and most are planned for hydropower use. A planned dam is defined as a dam currently undergoing the process to be built (including feasibility studies, approvals, planning, etc.) or one that is under construction already. Dams that are either complete or merely potential sites for construction were not included in this map.

REFERENCES

Environment News Service. 2008. Water rushes down Grand Canyon in high flow experiment. Available at www.ens-newswire.com/ens/mar2008/2008-03-07-01.asp.

Hvistendahl, M. 2008. China's Three Gorges Dam: An environmental catastrophe? *Scientific American* online. Available at www.sciam.com/article.cfm?id=chinas-three-gorges-dam-disaster.

Nilsson, C., C. A. Reidy, M. Dynesius, and C. Revenga. 2005. Fragmentation and flow regulation of the world's large river systems. *Science* 308, no. 5720: 405–408.

O'Connor, J., J. Major, and G. Grant. 2008. Down with the dams: Unchaining U.S. rivers. *Geotimes* 53: 22–27. Available at www.geotimes.org/mar08/article.html?id=feature_dams.html.

Postel, S., and B. Richter. 2003. *Rivers for Life: Managing Water for People and Nature*. Washington, DC: Island.

Sun, J. 2006. *Report on Unsafe Reservoir Reinforcement of the Yangtze Water Resources Commission (in Chinese)*. Beijing: Ministry of Water Resources.

Turvey, S. T., R. L. Pitman, B. L. Taylor, J. Barlow, T. Akamatsu, L. A. Barrett, X. Zhao, et al. 2007. First human-caused extinction of a cetacean species? *Biology Letters* 3: 537–540.

Xie, P. 2003. Three-Gorges Dam: Risk to ancient fish. *Science* 302, no. 5648: 1149–1151.

Zoological Society of London. 2007. EDGE of Existence Web site. Available at www.edgeofexistence.org.

Sediment Flow

SEDIMENT FLOW MAP DATA SOURCE

Syvitski, J. P. M., C. J. Vörösmarty, A. J. Kettner, and P. Green. 2005. Impact of humans on the flux of terrestrial sediment to the global coastal ocean. *Science* 308, no. 5720: 376–380.

TECHNICAL NOTES

We calculated the change between preindustrial and modern sediment flow to marine ecoregions, based on estimates of sediment delivery for the world's rivers by Syvitski et al. (2005). Syvitski et al. (2005) modeled preindustrial sediment loads using the Area Relief Temperature sediment delivery model (ART) version of the INSTAAR-DBFM model, which was tested on basins where current or past data were available for sediment loads before humans dominated their landscapes. Modern sediment was similarly modeled by Syvitski et al. (2005) with a discharge relief temperature sediment delivery model (QRT) that accounts for human-induced changes to runoff, including sediment trapped in reservoirs.

REFERENCES

Australian Government and Queensland Wetlands Programme. 2007. *Final Report: GBR Coastal Wetlands Protection Programme, 2005–2007 Pilot Programme*. Available at www.environment.gov.au/coasts/publications/gbr-programme/pubs/final-report.pdf.

Britsch, L. D., and J. B. Dunbar. 1993. Land-loss rates, Louisiana Coastal Plain. *Journal of Coastal Research* 9: 324–338.

Bryant, D., L. B. Burke, J. M. McManus, and M. D. Spalding. 1998. *Reefs at Risk*. Washington, DC: World Resources Institute, ICLARM, UNEP World Conservation Monitoring Centre, and United Nations Environment Programme.

Cowardin, L. M., V. Carter, F. C. Golet, and E. T. LaRoe. 1979. Classification of wetlands and deepwater habitats of the United States 79/31; and 2000 Thematic Mapper data. Available at www.esri.com/mapmuseum/mapbook_gallery/volume19/mining3.html.

Food and Agriculture Organization of the United Nations. 1995. *Effects of Riverine Inputs on Coastal Ecosystems and Fisheries Resources*. FAO Fisheries Technical Paper No. 349. Rome: Author.

Neil, D. T., A. R. Orpin, P. V. Ridd, and B. Yu. 2002. Sediment yield and impacts from river catchments to the Great Barrier Reef lagoon: A review. *Marine and Freshwater Research* 53, no. 4: 733–752.

Syvitski, J. P. M., C. J. Vörösmarty, A. J. Kettner, and P. Green. 2005. Impact of humans on the flux of terrestrial sediment to the global coastal ocean. *Science* 308, no. 5720: 376–380.

Melting Ice and Rising Seas

SEA-LEVEL RISE MAP SOURCES

Thieler, E. R., and E. S. Hammar-Klose. 1999. National assessment of coastal vulnerability to sea-level rise: Preliminary results for the U.S. Atlantic coast. U.S. Geological Survey Open-File Report 99-593, 1 map sheet. Available at http://pubs.usgs.gov/of/of99-593/.

———. 2000a. National assessment of coastal vulnerability to sea-level rise: Preliminary results for the U.S. Gulf of Mexico Coast. U.S. Geological Survey Open-File Report 00-179, 1 map sheet. Available at http://pubs.usgs.gov/of/of00-179/.

———. 2000b. National assessment of coastal vulnerability to sea-level rise: Preliminary results for the U.S. Pacific Coast. U.S. Geological Survey Open-File Report 00-178, 1 map sheet. Available at http://pubs.usgs.gov/of/of00-178/.

U.S. Geological Survey, based on data from Thieler and Hammar-Klose (1999, 2000a, 2000b). Available at http://woodshole.er.usgs.gov/project-pages/cvi/.

REFERENCES

Blanchon, P., A. Eisenhauer, J. Fietzke, and V. Liebetrau. 2009. Rapid sea-level rise and reef back-stepping at the close of the last interglacial highstand. *Nature* 458: 881–884.

Cahoon, D. R., P. F. Hensel, T. Spencer, D. J. Reed, K. McKee, and N. Saintilan. 2006. Coastal wetland vulnerability to relative sea-level rise: wetland elevation trends and process controls. Pages 271–292 in *Wetlands and Natural Resource Management*, ed. J. T. A. Verhoeven, B. Beltman, R. Bobbink, and D. F. Whigham. Berlin: Springer.

Gilman, E. L., J. Ellison, N. C. Duke, and C. Field. 2008. Threats to mangroves from climate change and adaptation options: a review. *Aquatic Botany* 89: 237–250.

Intergovernmental Panel on Climate Change (IPCC). 2007. *Climate Change 2007: Synthesis Report.* Contribution of Working Groups I, II, and III to the Fourth Assessment Report of the Intergovernmental Panel on Climate Change. Geneva: Author.

McGranahan, G., D. Balk, and B. Anderson. 2007. The rising tide: Assessing the risks of climate change and human settlements in low elevation coastal zones. *Environment and Urbanization* 19: 17–37.

Pfeffer, W. T., J. T. Harper, and S. O'Neal. 2008. Kinematic Constraints on Glacier Contributions to 21st Century Sea-level Rise. *Science* 321:1340-1343.

Disappearing Glaciers

SNOWMELT TIMING MAP DATA SOURCES

Adam, J. C., A. F. Hamlet, and D. P. Lettenmaier. 2008. Implications of global climate change for snowmelt hydrology in the twenty-first century. *Hydrological Processes* (doi: 10.1002. hyp.7201).

Chang, A. 1995. Nimbus-7 SMMR global monthly snow cover and snow depth. National Snow and Ice Data Center, Boulder, Colorado, USA. Digital media.

TECHNICAL NOTES

To calculate the change in snowmelt peak timing by ecoregion, we summarized weekly averages of snowmelt for each 0.5-degree cell. Weekly snowmelt averages were derived using the Variable Infiltration Capacity (VIC) macroscale hydrologic model, which simulates spatially distributed total runoff and snowmelt over all global land areas for two time periods (past period covers 1961–1990; future period, 2025–2054). These modeled data were provided by the Department of Civil and Environmental Engineering at the University of Washington in Seattle and Washington State University in Pullman (Adam et al. 2008). We calculated the change in snowmelt peak as the number of weeks' difference between past peak week and future peak week for each 0.5-degree cell and then averaged these values across each ecoregion. We excluded areas where past snow cover was consistently absent over a ten-year period by using a snow cover mask we derived from the 0.5-degree Nimbus-7 SMMR satellite data (Chang 1995). We also excluded areas where peak snowmelt varied little throughout the averaged year by using a mask of cells greater than one standard deviation of the past peak snowmelt range. The Upper Amur (Shilka)

has very high results largely due to extreme decadal shifts in precipitation. Local peak time shifts within ecoregions can be longer than this summarized map relates.

ASIAN GLACIERS MAP DATA SOURCES

Armstrong, R., B. Raup, S. J. S. Khalsa, R. Barry, J. Kargel, C. Helm, and H. Kieffer. 2007. GLIMS glacier database. National Snow and Ice Data Center, Boulder, Colorado, USA. Digital media.

National Snow and Ice Data Center (NSIDC). 2007. World glacier inventory. World Glacier Monitoring Service and National Snow and Ice Data Center/World Data Center for Glaciology, Boulder, Colorado, USA. Digital media.

REFERENCES

Barnett, T. P., J. C. Adam, and D. P. Lettenmaier. 2005. Potential impacts of a warming climate on water availability in snow-dominated regions. *Nature* 438, no. 17: 303–309.

Hall, M. H. P., and D. B. Fagre. 2003. Modeled climate-induced glacier change in Glacier National Park, 1850–2100. *BioScience* 53, no. 2: 131–140.

Rieman, D. E., D. Isaak, S. Adams, D. Horan, D. Nagel, C. Luce, and D. Myers. 2007. Anticipated climate warming effects on bull trout habitats and populations across the interior Columbia River Basin. *Transactions of the American Fisheries Society* 136: 1552–1556.

Essay: Hoekstra

REFERENCES

Ashford, G. and J. Castleden. 2001. *Inuit Observations on Climate Change.* Final Report. International Institute for Sustainable Development. Available at www.iisd.org/casl/PROJECTS/inuitobs.htm.

Emanuel, K. 2005. Increasing destructiveness of tropical cyclones over the past 30 years. *Nature* 436 (doi: 10.1038/nature03906).

Friedman, L. 2009. Coming soon: Mass migrations spurred by climate change. *New York Times*, March 2.

Gates, B. 2009. Bill Gates' 2009 annual letter to the Bill & Melinda Gates Foundation. Available at www.gatesfoundation.org/annual-letter/Pages/2009-annual-letter-introduction.aspx.

Intergovernmental Panel on Climate Change. 2007a. *Climate Change 2007: Mitigation of Climate Change.* Geneva: World Meteorological Organization and United Nations Environment Programme.

———. 2007b. *Climate Change 2007: The Physical Science Basis.* Geneva: World Meteorological Organization and United Nations Environment Programme.

McKinsey and Company. 2009. *Pathways to a Low-Carbon Economy.* Available at www.mckinsey.com/globalGHGcostcurve.

McMichael, A. J., D. H. Campbell-Lendrum, C. F. Corvalán, A. K. Githeko, J. D. Scheraga, and A. Woodward, eds. 2003. *Climate Change and Human Health: Risks and Responses.* Geneva: World Health Organization.

Menzel, A., T. H. Sparks, N. Estrella, E. Koch, A. Aasa, R. Ahas, K. Alm-Kübler, et al. 2006. European phenological response to climate change matches the warming pattern. *Global Change Biology* 12.

Vedeld, P., A. Angelsen, E. Sjaastad, and G. Kobugabe Berg. 2004. *Counting on the Environment: Forest Incomes and the Rural Poor.* Environment Economics Series Paper no. 98. Washington, DC: World Bank.

Westerling, A. L., H. G. Hidalgo, D. R. Cayan, and T. W. Swetnam. 2006. Warming and earlier spring increase western U.S. forest wildfire activity. *Science* 313, no. 5789 (August 18): 940 (doi: 10.1126/science.1128834).

World Resources Institute. 2009. Climate Analysis Indicators Tool. Available at http://cait.wri.org.

Terrestrial Invaders

TERRESTRIAL INVADERS MAP DATA SOURCE

Long, J. L. 2003. *Introduced Mammals of the World: Their History, Distribution and Influence.* Collingwood, Australia: CSIRO.

TECHNICAL NOTES

The numbers of introduced and established or probably established mammals were based on Long (2003). These data for many countries and oceanic islands were presented in a table in the book's introduction and included translocations and reintroductions. Some regions included in the table covered broader geographies than countries (e.g., North America, South America, Russian Federation and associated independent states). To be able to show these data at country level, we compiled the data for these regions from the text descriptions of species in the book.

REFERENCES

BBC News. 2005. Experiment ends in wild rat chase. Available at http://news.bbc.co.uk/2/hi/asia-pacific/4366480.stm.

Forseth, I., and A. Innis. 2004. Kudzu (Pueraria montana): History, physiology, and ecology combine to make a major ecosystem threat. *Critical Reviews in Plant Sciences* 23, no. 5: 401–413.

Global Invasive Species Database. 2009. *Oryctolagus cuniculus.* Available at www.issg.org/database/species/ecology.asp?si =19&fr=1&sts=sss.

Long, J. L. 2003. *Introduced Mammals of the World: Their History, Distribution and Influence.* Collingwood, Australia: CSIRO.

Towns, D. R., and K. G. Broome. 2003. From small Maria to massive Campbell: Forty years of rat eradications from New Zealand islands. *New Zealand Journal of Zoology* 30: 377–398.

Wiles, G. J., J. Bart, R. E. Beck, Jr., and C. F. Aguon. 2003. Impacts of the brown tree snake: Patterns of decline and species persistence in Guam's avifauna. *Conservation Biology* 17, no. 5: 1350–1360.

Freshwater Invaders

FRESHWATER INVADERS MAP DATA SOURCE

The Nature Conservancy (TNC). 2009. Global database of freshwater invasive species. Unpublished. The Nature Conservancy, Arlington, Virginia, USA.

TECHNICAL NOTES

We collected data according to the methods of Molnar et al. (2008). The occurrence, ecological impact, and pathways of introduction for freshwater invasive species were compiled in a geographically referenced database. Information about 550 species was systematically collected from a wide variety of global, regional, national, and subnational data sources. Non-native distributions were documented by freshwater ecoregion. The threat of each species to native biodiversity was scored using the following categories: 4, disrupts entire ecosystem processes with wider abiotic influences; 3, disrupts multiple species, some wider ecosystem function, and/or keystone species or species of high conservation value (e.g., threatened species); 2, disrupts single species with little or no wider ecosystem impact; 1, little or no disruption. Species in the top two categories (scores of 3 or 4) are considered "harmful invasive species" in this atlas (n=367), and the number of these are displayed in the map by ecoregion.

The following work was used:

Molnar, J. L., R. Gamboa, C. Revenga, and M. Spalding. 2008. Assessing the global threat of invasive species to marine biodiversity:

Framing the big picture. *Frontiers in Ecology and the Environment* 6, no. 9: 485–492.

REFERENCES

Pimentel, D., L. Lach, R. Zuniga, and D. Morrison. 2000. Environmental and economic costs of nonindigenous species in the United States. *BioScience* 50, no. 1: 53–65.

Pringle, R. M. 2005. The origins of the Nile perch in Lake Victoria. *BioScience* 55, no. 9: 780–787.

Yellowfish Working Group. 2008. *Technical Report on the State of Yellowfishes in South Africa 2007.* Ed. N. D. Impson, I. R. Bills, and L. Wolhuter. Report to the Water Research Commission, WRC Report No. KV 212/08. Available at www.wrc.org.za/downloads/ report percent20lists/web. percent20rpts/ devco/KV212-web-conservation.pdf#page=105.

Marine Invaders

MARINE INVADERS MAP DATA SOURCE

Molnar, J. L., R. Gamboa, C. Revenga, and M. Spalding. 2008. Assessing the global threat of invasive species to marine biodiversity: Framing the big picture. *Frontiers in Ecology and the Environment* 6, no. 9: 485–492.

TECHNICAL NOTES

The occurrence, ecological impact, and pathways of introduction for marine invasive species were compiled in a geographically referenced database by Molnar et al. (2008). Information about 329 species was systematically collected from a wide variety of global, regional, national, and subnational data sources. Non-native distributions were documented by marine ecoregion. The threat of each species to native biodiversity was scored using the following categories: 4, disrupts entire ecosystem processes with wider abiotic influences; 3, disrupts multiple species, some wider ecosystem function, and/or keystone species or species of high conservation value (e.g., threatened species); 2, disrupts single species with little or no wider ecosystem impact; 1, little or no disruption. Species in the top two categories (scores of 3 or 4) are considered "harmful invasive species" in this atlas (n=187), and the number of these are displayed in the map by ecoregion.

SHIPPING LANES MAP DATA SOURCE

National Oceanic and Atmospheric Administration. 2005. SEAS BBXX database of the Global Ocean Observing System Center, Atlantic Oceanographic and Meteorological Laboratory, NOAA. Available at www.aoml.noaa.gov/phod/trinanes/BBXX.

TECHNICAL NOTES

Each data point represents the location where a ship voluntarily dropped an expendable bathythermograph (XBT) for oceanographic data sampling (temperature at depth). The data are freely available at www.aoml.noaa.gov/phod/trinanes/ BBXX/ through NOAA Coast Watch Caribbean and Gulf of Mexico Node. These data were collected by the National Meteorological Service's (NMS) World Meteorological Organization (WMO) Voluntary Observing Ships (VOS) scheme (www.vos.noaa.gov). Ships from many countries participate voluntarily to collect meteorological data throughout the global oceans. We are displaying a subset that represents one year's worth of data (October 14, 2004–October 15, 2005) consisting of 2,583,216 data points, or 4,504 ships. This year represented the most detailed available, with better protocols and better data collection, and it contained the most representative set of ship locations. Points have been developed in a 0.1-degree grid. Contributing vessels are almost entirely large commercial vessels.

INVASION PATHWAYS FIGURE DATA SOURCE

Molnar, J. L., R. Gamboa, C. Revenga, and M. Spalding. 2008. Assessing the global threat of invasive species to marine biodiversity: Framing the big picture. *Frontiers in Ecology and the Environment* 6, no. 9: 485–492.

TECHNICAL NOTES

Known and likely introduction pathways for harmful marine invaders (n=187) each species were recorded by Molnar et al. (2008). The most common pathways were determined by counting the number of species associated with each pathway, with most species potentially being transported over more than one pathway.

REFERENCES

Anderson, L. W. J. 2005. California's reaction to *Caulerpa taxifolia*: A model for invasive species rapid response. *Biological Invasions* 7: 1003–1016.

Carlton, J. T. 1999. The scale and ecological consequences of biological invasions in the world's oceans. Pages 195–212 in *Invasive Species and Biodiversity Management*, ed. O. Sandlund, P. Schei, and A. Viken. Dordrecht, The Netherlands: Kluwer.

Meinesz, A., T. Belsher, T. Thibaut, B. Antolic, K. Ben Mustapha, C.-F. Boudouresque, D. Chiaverini, et al. 2001. The introduced green alga *Caulerpa taxifolia* continues to spread in the Mediterranean. *Biological Invasions* 3, no. 2: 201–210.

Molnar, J.L., R. Gamboa, C. Revenga, and M. Spalding. 2008. Assessing the global threat of invasive species to marine biodiversity: Framing the big picture. *Frontiers in Ecology and the Environment* 6, no. 9: 485–492.

Terrestrial Animals at Risk

THREATENED ANIMALS MAP DATA SOURCES

World Wildlife Fund (WWF). 2006. WildFinder: Database of species distributions, ver. Jan-06. Available at www.gis.wwf.org/WildFinder.

International Union for Conservation of Nature (IUCN). 2008. IUCN Red List of Threatened Species summary statistics. Available at www.redlist.org.

TECHNICAL NOTES

We compiled a vertebrate species list for each ecoregion from WWF's WildFinder database (WWF 2006). This list was then compared against the IUCN Red List of Threatened Species (2008) to determine the number of species per ecoregion that are threatened. *Threatened species* are those listed by IUCN Red List as Vulnerable, Endangered, or Critically Endangered (www.redlist.org).

IMMINENT EXTINCTION MAP DATA SOURCE

Alliance for Zero Extinction (AZE). 2007. AZE Site and Species Database, GIS data. Available at www.zeroextinction.org.

ANIMALS AT RISK FIGURE DATA SOURCE

International Union for Conservation of Nature (IUCN). 2008. IUCN Red List of Threatened Species summary statistics. Available at www.redlist.org.

REFERENCE

International Union for Conservation of Nature (IUCN). 2008. IUCN Red List of Threatened Species summary statistics. Available at www.redlist.org.

Freshwater Animals at Risk

THREATENED MAMMAL, BIRD, AND CROCODILE MAP DATA SOURCE

The Nature Conservancy (TNC). 2009. Data on threatened freshwater mammal, bird, and crocodile species compiled from multiple sources. Unpublished. The Nature Conservancy, Arlington, Virginia, USA.

TECHNICAL NOTES

We generated the map of number of freshwater mammals, birds, and crocodilian species per ecoregion that are threatened with extinction from multiple sources, including species range maps, as well as geographic range descriptions from literature and online sources (our primary sources are listed below). *Threatened species* refer to those listed by IUCN Red List as Vulnerable, Endangered, or Critically Endangered (www.redlist.org). We added together the numbers of threatened species for each of the taxonomic groups by ecoregion. When species range maps were used and a range overlapped several ecoregions, species were counted as present in all those ecoregions that had part of the range. Some ecoregions with long and narrow shape may have an overestimation of species given the way the range polygons were drawn. This is particularly true of the Amazonas High Andes ecoregion (312), where the mountain range has been used as a range boundary for hundreds of species.

We determined threatened freshwater birds by first selecting freshwater obligates—those birds that need freshwater habitats to breed (e.g., swamps) or feed (e.g., fish, aquatic invertebrates). (See technical notes for "Birds" for more details.) We then compared this list of freshwater species to the list of threatened bird species and range maps from the *Threatened Birds of the World 2004* by BirdLife International. Information on threatened crocodilian species is from the IUCN-SSC Crocodile Specialist Group. Presence/absence in ecoregions was assessed visually from online range maps. Threatened freshwater mammals include aquatic or semiaquatic species that spend a considerable amount of time in freshwater to feed and that usually live in the riparian vegetation close to rivers, lakes, marshes, swamps, and so forth. (See the "Mammals" technical notes for more details.) Threatened status was from the IUCN Red List. Both range species maps and visual assessment of locations were used to assign mammals to ecoregions. Distribution data on threatened fish and freshwater turtles were not available at the global level at the time of publication.

The following were our primary data sources:
BirdLife International. 2000. *Threatened Birds of the World*. Barcelona: Lynx; and Cambridge: BirdLife International.

———. 2004 *Threatened Birds of the World* [CD]. Cambridge: BirdLife International.

International Union for Conservation of Nature (IUCN). 2008. IUCN Red List of Threatened Species. Available at www.redlist.org.

IUCN–Species Survival Commission (SSC) Crocodile Specialist Group. 2008. Web site. Available at http://iucncsg.org/ph1/modules/Home/.

THREATENED AMPHIBIAN MAP DATA SOURCE

International Union for Conservation of Nature (IUCN), Conservation International, and NatureServe. 2006. Global Amphibian Assessment. Available at www.iucnredlist.org/amphibians. Digital media.

TECHNICAL NOTES

We generated the map of the number of freshwater amphibian species per ecoregion that are threatened with extinction using data from the Global Amphibian Assessment (GAA) (IUCN et al. 2006). The GAA assessed the conservation status of 5,918 amphibian species, and we analyzed the subset of 4,035 that depend on freshwater during some stage of their life cycle. Strictly arboreal species that do not require freshwater for their larval stage, species that develop directly from eggs without a larval stage, as well as few live-bearing species were excluded from this analysis. As of 2006, 1,356 freshwater amphibians were considered threatened. It is important to note, however, that for 1,427 amphibian species, there were insufficient data to assess their conservation status—these are classified by the GAA as "data deficient." Therefore, these estimates for threat are conservative.

REFERENCES

Baille, J.E.M., C. Hilton-Taylor, and S.N. Stuart, eds. 2004. *2004 Red List of Threatened Species: A Global Species Assessment*. Gland, Switzerland: IUCN.

Darwall, W., K. Smith, T. Lowe, and J.-C. Vié. 2005. *The Status and Distribution of Freshwater Biodiversity in Eastern Africa*. IUCN–Species Survival Commission (SSC) Freshwater Biodiversity Assessment Programme. Gland, Switzerland: IUCN.

International Union for Conservation of Nature (IUCN). 2008. IUCN Red List of Threatened Species. Available at www.redlist.org.

IUCN–SSC Crocodile Specialist Group. 2008. Web site. Available at http://iucncsg.org/ph1/modules/Home/.

Kottelat, M., and J. Freyhof. 2007. *Handbook of European Freshwater Fishes*. Cornol, Switzerland: Kottelat; and Berlin: Freyhof.

Webb, G., chair, Crocodile Specialist Group Steering Committee, personal communication, January 10, 2008.

Marine Animals at Risk

THREATENED SEABIRD AND MARINE MAMMAL MAPS DATA SOURCE

International Union for Conservation of Nature (IUCN). 2008. IUCN Red List of Threatened Species. Available at www.redlist.org.

TECHNICAL NOTES

Using the online IUCN resource, the threatened species for each ecoregion were filtered for marine species only. *Threatened species* refer to those listed by IUCN Red List as Vulnerable, Endangered, or Critically Endangered (www.redlist.org). We downloaded the digital GIS data and summarized it by marine ecoregion to result in the number of threatened species per marine ecoregion.

REFERENCES

Dulvy, N. K., Y. Sadovy, and J. D. Reynolds. 2003. Extinction vulnerability in marine populations. *Fish and Fisheries* 4: 25–64.

International Union for Conservation of Nature (IUCN). 2008. IUCN Red List of Threatened Species. Available at www.redlist.org.

McClenachan, L., J. B. Jackson, and M. J. Newman. 2006. Conservation implications of historic sea turtle nesting beach loss. *Frontiers in Ecology and the Environment* 4: 290–296.

CHAPTER 5

Taking Action Introduction

REFERENCES

Chape, S., M. Spalding, and M. Jenkins, eds. 2008. *The World's Protected Areas: Status, Values, and Prospects in the Twenty-first Century.* Berkeley: University of California Press.

Leopold, A. 1949. *A Sand County Almanac.* Oxford: Oxford University Press.

Millennium Ecosystem Assessment. 2005. *Ecosystems and Human Well-being: Synthesis.* Washington, DC: Island.

Protected Areas on Land

PROTECTED AREA MAP DATA SOURCES

Collaborative Australian Protected Area Database (CAPAD). 2006. Available on request from the Australian Government, Department of Environment, Water, Heritage and the Arts at www.deh.gov.au/parks/nrs/capad. Digital media.

Conservation Biology Institute (CBI). 2006. Protected Areas Database (PAD), version 4. Conservation Biology Institute, Corvallis, Oregon, USA. Available at www.consbio.org/cbi/projects/PAD. Digital media.

UN Environment Programme (UNEP)/International Union for Conservation of Nature (IUCN). 2007. Protected areas extracted from the 2007 World Database on Protected Areas (WDPA). The WDPA is a joint product of UNEP and the IUCN, prepared by UNEP-WCMC and the IUCN WCPA working with Governments, the Secretariats of MEAs, and collaborating NGOs. For further information, contact protectedareas@unep-wcmc.org or go to www.WDPA.org.

TECHNICAL NOTES

We derived estimates of protected area coverage from the World Database of Protected Areas (WDPA, UNEP/IUCN 2007) with supplements for the United States (CBI 2006) and Australia (CAPAD 2006). The WDPA is the most comprehensive global catalog of protected areas and includes data about their sizes, locations, and IUCN classifications of management designation. The WDPA was assembled by a broad alliance of organizations that aimed to maintain a freely available, accurate, and current database that is accepted as a global standard by all stakeholders.

The distribution of all protected areas was mapped in a Geographic Information System and then summarized to calculate the total area of all protected areas in each ecoregion and biome, respectively. We included all categories of protected areas in our estimates, except those that lacked location data or that had nonpermanent status. Protected areas with only point location and area data were mapped as circles with appropriate radii. Portions of any protected areas that extended into the marine environment were clipped out. Overlapping protected areas were combined to avoid double-counting errors. The time series of cumulative protected area coverage was derived from the WDPA based on the reported year of designation. The number and total area of different categories of protected areas were calculated based on the IUCN classification assigned to each protected area. These categories indicate the intended management objectives for each protected area, but they do not necessarily predict whether that management is occurring or is effective. Protected areas for which no IUCN category was assigned were not included in these tallies.

A note about Antarctica designation of "not applicable": Antarctica is often regarded as a special case; not owned by a nation, its management falls under the jurisdiction of the twenty-seven nations that are signatories to the Antarctica Treaty System. There are provisions for designation of protected areas under this system, although only small areas have so far been established. At the same time, the general environmental regulations pertaining to the continent and, to some degree, to the surrounding waters are regarded by many as equivalent to, or perhaps stricter than, those applied to many protected areas elsewhere in the world.

RISE IN PROTECTION FIGURE DATA SOURCE

UN Environment Programme (UNEP)/International Union for Conservation of Nature (IUCN). 2007. Protected areas extracted from the 2007 World Database on Protected Areas (WDPA). The WDPA is a joint product of UNEP and the IUCN, prepared by UNEP-WCMC and the IUCN WCPA working with Governments, the Secretariats of MEAs, and collaborating NGOs. For further information, contact protectedareas@unep-wcmc.org or go to www.WDPA.org.

TECHNICAL NOTES

We calculated the total cumulative protected area by summarizing the World Database of Protected Areas (WDPA) over five-year increments based on the recorded year of protected area establishment. Protected areas for which an establishment date was not recorded were omitted from this analysis.

PROTECTION BY BIOME MAP DATA SOURCE

Hoekstra, J. M., T. Boucher, T. H. Ricketts, and C. Roberts. 2005. Confronting a biome crisis: Global disparities of habitat loss and protection. *Ecology Letters* 8: 23–29.

REFERENCES

Biodiversity Action Plan of Mongolia. 1996. Ministry of Nature and Environment of Mongolia, UNPD/GEF Project on Biodiversity of Eastern Mongolian Steppe, Ulaanbaatar, Mongolia.

Chape, S., M. Spalding, and M. Jenkins, eds. 2008. *The World's Protected Areas. Status, Values, and Prospects in the Twenty-first Century.* Berkeley: University of California Press.

Hoekstra, J. M., T. Boucher, T. H. Ricketts, and C. Roberts. 2005. Confronting a biome crisis: Global disparities of habitat loss and protection. *Ecology Letters* 8: 23–29.

UNESCO World Heritage Centre. 2008. World Heritage Site list: Mongolia factsheet. Available at http://whc.unesco.org/en/tentativelists/936/.

Protecting Rivers, Lakes, and Wetlands

PROTECTED WETLANDS MAP DATA SOURCE

UN Environment Programme (UNEP)/International Union for Conservation of Nature (IUCN). 2007. Protected areas extracted from the 2007 World Database on

Protected Areas (WDPA). The WDPA is a joint product of UNEP and the IUCN, prepared by UNEP-WCMC and the IUCN WCPA working with Governments, the Secretariats of MEAs, and collaborating NGOs. For further information, contact protectedareas@unep-wcmc.org or go to www.WDPA.org.

TECHNICAL NOTES

We derived the area of wetlands of international importance protected under the Ramsar Convention in each freshwater ecoregion from a subset of areas included in the World Database on Protected Areas (WDPA) compiled by the UNEP World Conservation Monitoring Centre (UNEP/IUCN 2007). All Ramsar sites in the database were included, except those known to be purely marine in extent, as indicated by the Marine Classes noted as subtidal in the WDPA. Intertidal marine Ramsar sites, however, are included in the analysis because the sites may include both brackish and fresh-waters. Area attributes for those Ramsar sites within the WDPA that were only available as point data were aggregated for each ecoregion, and each point was counted in only one ecoregion. In a very few cases where in reality Ramsar boundaries cross ecoregion boundaries, we assigned the entire area of the site to the single ecoregion in which the WDPA point was located.

U.S. WILD AND SCENIC RIVERS MAP DATA SOURCE

National Atlas of the United States. 2005. Parkways and scenic rivers. Reston, VA: Author. Available at http://nationalatlas.gov/atlasftp.html.

REFERENCES

Abell, R., J. D. Allan, and B. Lehner. 2007. Unlocking the potential of protected areas for freshwaters. *Biological Conservation* 134: 48–63.

Bureau of Land Management, National Park Service, U.S. Fish and Wildlife Service, U.S. Forest Service, and the Hanford Reach National Monument (U.S. Fish and Wildlife Service, U.S. Department of the Interior). 2008. Information on river mileage classifications for components of the National Wild and Scenic Rivers system. Available at www.rivers.gov/publications/rivers-table.pdf.

Ramsar Convention on Wetlands. 2009. Information on the Convention. Available at www.ramsar.org.

Skukuza Freshwater Group. 2006. *The Skukuza Statement: Keeping Our Rivers, Lakes and Freshwater Wetlands Alive: A Call for Action.* South African National Parks (SANParks), the Council for Scientific and Industrial Research (CSIR), The Nature Conservancy (TNC), and Worldwide Fund for Nature (WWF).

Swarts, F. A., ed. 2000. *The Pantanal of Brazil, Bolivia and Paraguay: Selected Discourses on the World's Largest Remaining Wetland System.* Gouldsboro, PA: Hudson MacArthur; and Jardim, Brazil: Waterland Research Institute.

Marine Protected Areas

PROTECTED AREA MAP DATA SOURCE

Spalding, M., L. Fish, and L. Wood. 2008. Towards representative protection of the world's coasts and oceans: Progress, gaps and opportunities. *Conservation Letters* 1, no. 5: 217–226.

TECHNICAL NOTES

A global listing of 5,045 marine protected areas was developed by Spalding et al. (2008) using the World Database on Protected Areas (UNEP/IUCN 2008) and data from the related work undertaken at the University of British Columbia (Wood et al. 2008). These data were overlain on the map of marine ecoregions (shelf areas only) to derive total area coverage statistics. It is not currently possible to assess the effectiveness of MPAs at a global scale, so the map shows an optimistic assessment of area protected. Looking beyond shelf areas, Spalding et al. (2008) point out that only 1.91 percent of waters within exclusive economic zone areas, and 0.717 percent of the entire world ocean surface lie within protected areas. Data sources for Spalding et al. (2008) included the following:

UN Environment Programme (UNEP)/ International Union for Conservation of Nature (IUCN). 2008. Protected areas extracted from the 2008 World Database on Protected Areas (WDPA). The WDPA is a joint product of UNEP and the IUCN, prepared by UNEP-WCMC and the IUCN WCPA working with Governments, the Secretariats of MEAs, and collaborating NGOs. For further information, contact protectedareas@unep-wcmc.org or go to www.WDPA.org.

Wood, L. J., L. Fish, J. Laughren, and D. Pauly. 2008. Assessing progress towards global marine protection targets: Shortfalls in information and action. *Oryx* 42: 340–351.

REFERENCES

Halpern, B. 2003. The impact of marine reserves: Do reserves work and does reserve size matter? *Ecological Applications* 13: S117–S137.

Norse, E. A., and L. B. Crowder, eds. 2005. *Marine Conservation Biology: The Science of Maintaining the Sea's Biodiversity.* Washington, DC: Island.

Roberts, C. M., L. Mason, and J. P. Hawkins. 2006. *Roadmap to Recovery: A Global Network of Marine Reserves.* Amsterdam: Greenpeace International.

Protecting Nature's Services

ECOSYSTEM SERVICES FIGURE DATA SOURCE

Millennium Ecosystem Assessment. 2005. *Ecosystems and Human Well-being: Synthesis.* Washington, DC: Island.

REFERENCES

Costanza, R., R. D'Arge, R. DeGroot, S. Farber, M. Grasso, B. Hannon, K. Limburg, et al. 1997. The value of the world's ecosystem services and natural capital. *Nature* 387: 253–260.

Egan, T. 2007. *The Worst Hard Time.* Boston: Houghton Mifflin/Harcourt.

Food and Agriculture Organization of the United Nations (FAO), Fisheries Department. 2004. *The State of the World's Fisheries and Aquaculture 2004, Part 1.* Available at www.fao.org/docrep/007/y5600e/y5600e04.htm#p_1.

Intergovernmental Panel on Climate Change (IPCC). 2007. *Climate Change 2007: Synthesis Report Summary for Policy Makers.* Geneva: World Meteorological Organization and United Nations Environment Programme.

Millennium Ecosystem Assessment. 2005. *Ecosystems and Human Well-being: Synthesis.* Washington, DC: Island.

New Carbon Finance. 2009. Carbon market up 84 percent in 2008 at $118 bn. Press release, January 8.

Vedeld, P., A. Angelsen, E. Sjaastad, and G. Kobugabe Berg. 2004: *Counting on the Environment: Forest Incomes and the Rural Poor.* Environment Economics Series Paper no. 98. Washington, DC: World Bank.

International Cooperation

TRANSBOUNDARY PROTECTION MAP DATA SOURCE

UN Environment Programme (UNEP)/ International Union for Conservation of Nature (IUCN). 2008 Protected areas extracted from the 2008 World Database on

Protected Areas (WDPA). The WDPA is a joint product of UNEP and the IUCN, prepared by UNEP-WCMC and the IUCN WCPA working with Governments, the Secretariats of MEAs, and collaborating NGOs. For further information, contact protectedareas@unep-wcmc.org or go to www.WDPA.org.

REFERENCE

Millennium Ecosystem Assessment, ed. 2005. *Ecosystems and Human Well-being: Policy Responses. Findings of the Responses Working Group.* Washington, DC: Island.

Greening the Marketplace

CERTIFIED FISHERIES MAP DATA SOURCE

Marine Stewardship Council (MSC). 2009. Certified fisheries information. Available at www.msc.org/track-a-fishery/certified.

TECHNICAL NOTES

We obtained information on marine fisheries certified as sustainable and well managed by the Marine Stewardship Council (MSC, www.msc.org) from the MSC Web site's certified fisheries profiles. Individual fishery profiles described geographic fishing areas where each fishery operates. These areas tend to correspond to national fishing area designations. Using these designations and mapped information on the MSC Web site, we assigned certified fisheries manually and approximated as much as possible to marine ecoregional boundaries.

REFERENCES

Forest Stewardship Council. 2009. Web site. Available at www.fscus.org.
Marine Stewardship Council. 2009. Information on MSC products and activities. Available at www.msc.org/about-us.
Smithsonian National Zoological Park. 2009. Migratory Bird Center: Support bird-friendly coffee. Available at http://nationalzoo.si.edu/ConservationAndScience/MigratoryBirds/Coffee/.[AP2]Collaborative Solutions.

Collaborative Solutions

REFERENCES

Community Markets for Conservation (COMACO). 2008. Web site. Available at www.itswild.org/home.
Jacobs-Small, B. 1999. St. Lucia: Managing seas and coasts for preservation, pleasure and profit. Island Beat: The Panos Institute of the Caribbean. Available at www.panosinst.org/productions/island/ib18e.php.

National Invasive Species Council. 2008. Web site. Available at www.invasivespeciesinfo.gov/council/main.shtml.
United Nations. 1992. Earth Summit Agenda 21. Available at www.un.org/esa/sustdev/documents/agenda21/index.htm.
———. 1987. *Report of the World Commission on Environment and Development: Our Common Future.* Document A/42/427. Available at www.un-documents.net/wced-ocf.htm.
Walsh, B. 2008. Eco-bargain: Save animals, reduce poverty. *Time,* February 1. Available at www.time.com/time/health/article/0,8599,1709186,00.html.

Essay: Daily et al.

REFERENCES

Brick, P., D. Snow, and S. B. Van de Wetering. 2000. *Across the Great Divide: Explorations in Collaborative Conservation and the American West.* Washington, DC: Island.
Daily, G. C., and K. Ellison. 2002. *The New Economy of Nature: The Quest to Make Conservation Profitable,* Island Press, Washington, DC.
Kareiva, P., and M. Marvier. 2007. Conservation for the people. *Scientific American* 297: 50–57.
Leopold, A. ca. 1934. Conservation economics. *Journal of Forestry.* Reprinted: Pages 193–202 in *The River of Mother God and Other Essays by Aldo Leopold,* ed. Susan Flader and J. Baird Callicot. Madison: University of Wisconsin Press, 1991.
Pejchar, L., P. Morgan, M. Caldwell, C. Palmer, and G. C. Daily. 2007. Evaluating the potential for conservation development: Biophysical, economic, and institutional perspectives. *Conservation Biology* 21: 69–78.
Rosenzweig, M. L. 2003. *Win-Win Ecology: How the Earth's Species Can Survive in the Midst of Human Enterprise.* Oxford: Oxford University Press.
Stanton, R. 2002. *Environmental Stewardship for the 21st Century: Opportunities and Actions for Improving Cultural Diversity in Conservation Organizations and Programs.* A report prepared for the Natural Resources Council of America. Available at www.naturalresourcescouncil.org/ewebeditpro/items/O89F3675.pdf.

Rule of Law

REFERENCES

Alaska Department of Fish and Game. 2003. Alaska's salmon management: Story of success factsheet. Available at www.adfg.state.ak.us/special/salmonmngmnt.pdf. Alaska Department of Fish and Game, Juneau, Alaska, USA.
Andreen, W. L. 2004. Water quality today: Has the Clean Water Act been a success? *Alabama Law Review* 55: 537–593. Available at SSRN: http://ssrn.com/abstract=554803.
Daily, G. C., and K. Ellison. 2003. *The New Economy of Nature: The Quest to Make Conservation Profitable.* Washington, DC: Island.
Dowie, M. 2005. In law we trust: Can environmental legislation still protect the commons? *Orion Magazine,* July/August 2005. Abridged Web version available at www.orionmagazine.org/index.php/articles/article/122/.
U.S. Environmental Protection Agency. 2007. *National Water Quality Inventory: Report to Congress—2002 Reporting Cycle.* Washington, DC: U.S. EPA Office of Water. Available at www.epa.gov/305b.
U.S. Fish and Wildlife Service. 2008. Calculated based on data from the 2005–2006 Species Recovery Report to Congress. U.S. Fish and Wildlife Service, Arlington, VA, USA.
U.S. Fish and Wildlife Service. 2009. Environmental Conservation Online System: Summary of Listed Species. Available at http://ecos.fws.gov/tess_public/TESSBoxscore.

Individual Action

REFERENCES

Alliance of Religions and Conservation. 2008. Web site. Available at www.arcworld.org.
Buckman, G. 2008. *Tasmania's Wilderness Battles: A History.* Sydney: Allen & Unwin.
Goldman Prize. Web site. Available at www.goldmanprize.org.
Desmond, K. 2008. *Planet Savers: 301 Extraordinary Environmentalists.* Sheffield, UK: Greenleaf.
National Trust. 2008. Web site. Available at www.nationaltrust.org.uk.
The Nature Conservancy. 2008. Web site. Available at http://nature.org.

Restoring Nature

REFERENCES

Beschta, R. L., and W. J. Ripple. 2006. River channel dynamics following extirpation of wolves in northwestern Yellowstone National Park, USA. *Earth Surface Processes and Landforms* 31: 1525–1539.

———. 2007. Increased willow heights along northern Yellowstone's Blacktail Deer Creek following wolf reintroduction. *American Naturalist* 67: 613–617.

Halofsky, J. S., and W. J. Ripple. 2008. Fine-scale predation risk on elk after wolf reintroduction in Yellowstone National Park, USA. *Oecologia* 155: 869–877.

Ripple, W. J., and R. L. Beschta. 2003. Wolf reintroduction, predation risk, and cottonwood recovery in Yellowstone National Park. *Forest Ecology and Management* 184: 299–313.

———. 2004. Wolves and the ecology of fear: Can predation risk structure ecosystems? *BioScience* 54: 755–766.

———. 2005. Linking wolves and plants: Aldo Leopold on trophic cascades. *BioScience* 55: 613–621.

———. 2006. Linking wolves to willows via risk-sensitive foraging by ungulates in the northern Yellowstone ecosystem. *Forest Ecology and Management* 230: 96–106.

———. 2007. Restoring Yellowstone's aspen with wolves. *Biological Conservation* 138: 514–519.

Ripple, W. J., E. J. Larsen, R. A. Renkin, and D. W. Smith. 2001. Trophic cascades among wolves, elk and aspen on Yellowstone National Park's northern range. *Biological Conservation* 102: 227–234.

Society for Ecological Restoration International. 2008. Global Restoration Network database. Available at www.globalrestorationnetwork .org.

Tolson, J., M. L. Magdich, T. Seidel, G. A. Haase, and B. Fazio. 1999. Return of a Native. *Endangered Species Bulletin* 24, no. 3: 14–15.

Index

About the Authors

Jonathan M. Hoekstra is an ecologist and conservation scientist with expertise in evolutionary ecology, global conservation priorities, and endangered species protection and policy. He currently provides strategic and scientific leadership for Nature Conservancy efforts that help people and nature confront the threats of climate change.

Jennifer L. Molnar is a Nature Conservancy senior scientist who led global analyses of habitat conditions and threats, with a focus on marine and freshwater systems. She has experience in estuarine ecosystems, invasive species, hydrology, and environmental remediation and currently works on a team that studies the services that nature provides to people.

Michael Jennings led The Nature Conservancy's global evaluation of terrestrial habitats. He has developed river management plans for the National Park Service and conservation assessments for the U.S. Fish and Wildlife Service. He currently works on conservation biology, community ecology, biogeography of climate change, and habitat classification at the University of Idaho.

Carmen Revenga is a senior scientist who led The Nature Conservancy's global assessments on freshwater ecosystems and biodiversity. She has more than 15 years of experience and has published widely on the conditions of freshwater ecosystems, water resources policy, and marine and inland fisheries. She currently leads The Nature Conservancy's global fisheries strategy.

Mark D. Spalding is a senior marine scientist who led The Nature Conservancy's global marine assessment. He has two decades of experience in global reviews, and has authored books that include the *World Atlas of Coral Reefs, The World's Protected Areas,* and the forthcoming *World Mangrove Atlas.*

Timothy M. Boucher is a senior conservation geographer at The Nature Conservancy, where he led spatial assessments of global habitat conditions, protections and threats. He has worked in international conservation science and geographic information systems for 15 years, traveling extensively to conduct field assessments on six continents.

James C. Robertson is a Geographic Information Systems manager for The Nature Conservancy who led spatial analyses for the freshwater and marine global habitat assessments. Before joining the Conservancy, he instructed conservation mapping workshops in the United States and China and applied expertise to international species conservation at the Smithsonian National Zoological Park.

Thomas J. Heibel contributed analysis to The Nature Conservancy's global freshwater and marine assessments. He is currently a renewable energy analyst with BCS Incorporated, consulting for federal and state governments, and has previous research experience in conservation biology, with expertise in marine, freshwater and coastal ecosystems.

Katherine Ellison is a Pulitzer Prize-winning journalist and author of four books, including *The New Economy of Nature: The Quest to Make Conservation Profitable,* co-authored with biologist Gretchen Daily. As a former foreign correspondent, she reported from seven continents, winning such prizes as the Overseas Press Club's award for human rights reporting.